# FREAKS AND GEEKS®

## The Complete Scripts
## Volume 1
## Episodes 1-9

**Introduction by Paul Feig**

NEWMARKET PRESS • NEW YORK

Freaks and Geeks Created by Paul Feig

Executive Produced by Judd Apatow

Pilot Episode Directed by Jake Kasdan

Book Edited by Andrew Jay Cohen, Paul Feig, and Judd Apatow

Episodes Written by Judd Apatow, Steve Bannos, Paul Feig, Jeff Judah, Jon Kasdan, Rebecca Kirshner, Patty Lin, Bob Nickman, Gabe Sachs, J. Elvis Weinstein, and Mike White

Scrapbook Design by Andrew Jay Cohen

Photography by Saeed Adyani, Mike Ansell, Byron Cohen, Paul Drinkwater, Chris Haston, Ethan Hill, Kurt Iswarienko, Gabe Sachs, and Sam Urdank

Scripts Prepared by Jeff Warrington

Book Production by Paul Sugarman

Project Assistance by Keith Hollaman, Shannon Berning, and Kristy Cox

Special thanks to Esther Margolis, Publisher of Newmarket Press



www.freaksandgeeks.com

Cover design by Timothy Shaner

This book is published in the United States of America.

First Edition

10 9 8 7 6 5 4 3 2 1

Library of Congress Cataloging-in-Publication Data available upon request.

ISBN 1-55704-645-X

QUANTITY PURCHASES

Companies, professional groups, clubs, and other organizations may qualify for special terms when ordering quantities of this title. For information, write Special Sales Department, Newmarket Press, 18 East 48th Street, New York, NY 10017; call (212) 832-3575; fax (212) 832-3629; or e-mail mailbox@newmarketpress.com.

www.newmarketpress.com

Manufactured in the United States of America.

# CONTENTS

# INTRODUCTION

## WELCOME TO THIS BOOK!

This is embarrassing. I really think this book is sort of overkill. I mean, we only made 18 episodes of this show. That's it. That's not even a full season. A full season is 22 episodes, although in the old days of television, they used to do something like 39 episodes of a show per season. Thirty-nine! Can you imagine? I almost died doing *18* episodes of this show. Well, not literally "died," but it was really, really hard work, writing nonstop and being on the set and working in the editing room and being at the sound mixes and stressing that we wouldn't get everything done that we had to do and, even if we did, wondering if it was all going to be good enough. By the time we were canceled, I was almost relieved. Until I got completely depressed that all we had worked so hard for was over, and we'd never get to write for these characters again. But the reason I was so tired when it was over was that Judd and I really faced this show as if each week's episode was its own little independent film. And so all of us in the writers room worked our tails off trying to do just that. Not that other TV shows *don't* work as hard. All shows pretty much do. But I like to feel like we worked at least as hard as some of the better shows on TV, and a little harder than some of the worst ones.

I mean, hey, it's all about making yourself feel important, you know?

Especially when you've been canceled.

Oh, my poor self-esteem.

Look, here's the thing. TV can be as good or as bad as you want to make it. But you can never forget that you're usually dealing with a powerful television network that wants certain specific things out of a show…

Well, *one* specific thing, mainly:

Ratings.

They want the largest number of people in this country who have televisions in their houses to tune those televisions to their network so that their ratings will be high, and they can then charge top dollar to advertisers to run ads during their shows. And in order to get the home audience to watch their shows so that they can charge all that money, the networks have to figure out which shows will:

A) make people tune in,

B) make them keep watching once they tune in,

C) make them tune in the next week and, most importantly,

D) make them keep tuning in week after week and month after month and then year after year until the show ends its run and gets a massive send-off by millions and millions of loyal fans who are then so distraught that their favorite show is now gone that they'll buy the DVDs and watch the show in syndication and become loyal viewers of all the spin-off shows that the actors who aren't sick of their characters decide to do for millions of dollars per episode and hopefully watch those shows until those series end and spawn a whole new host of spin-offs that then continue to draw in those original fans and a whole generation of new fans and on and on until the network can rest their entire schedule on this one idea that a show creator came up with years earlier and everyone can retire as billionaires.

That's the goal of network TV.

And we sure as hell didn't make that happen.

But, what we did do was make 18 episodes of a show that we think was pretty good and that seemed to find a small (by network standards) but very cool following of smart, cool people who discovered something to relate to in our show's earnest but awkward characters whose lives we all got to be a part of for a few brief months during the 1999/2000 television season.

So what's up with this book?

Well, these are the actual scripts from which the first nine shows were shot. Scripts are interesting in that they show you the roadmap that was used during production. Sometimes you'll see that a scripted scene is exactly the same as it was in the finished show, and other times you'll see that we changed something on the set or in the editing room, and so the scene is actually quite a bit different. Either Judd or myself or both of us and the writer whose script we were shooting were always on the set to watch each scene rehearsed before it was filmed, and so we were able to see if a scene and its dialogue were working or not. Sometimes, a scene would come off exactly the way we thought it would when we were all in the writers room; other times what seemed funny and real on the page played as forced and unnatural when it was actually coming out of the mouths of our amazing cast of actors. And so, in those cases, we would try to figure out on the set how to change it to make it better, consulting with the actors who knew their characters even better than we did. And out of all this would come a much better and funnier or more real and emotional scene. And then, when we get into the editing room, the script in essence no longer even exists, and the editors build the show out of the pieces of film that were shot by our directors. Then Judd and/or myself would go in and work the episode to make sure that it moved at a good pace and that the music interacted effectively with the action on the screen and that the whole thing felt like an hour of television that would be as good as it could be.

And so, that's why what hits your TV screen is often times quite different from what was originally in the written script.

So, this book is a way to compare the two and, hopefully, learn a little bit about scriptwriting in general. That is, if you want to get into scriptwriting. If you don't, and you're just a fan of the show, then take a look and see what the show looked like before it was filmed. It'll sort of be like looking at the blueprints to your house before it was built. Only the blueprints to your house probably aren't that funny, whereas we think that our scripts were actually pretty entertaining. But that's just us writers talking. I'm sure your architect probably thinks his blueprints are entertaining as hell. But he'll just have to deal with his own self-esteem issues.

Anyway, thanks for buying this book and on behalf of all the writers and producers who worked on *Freaks and Geeks,* we'd like to say, "Please enjoy our work."

Read on!

Paul Feig
Creator/co-executive producer of *Freaks and Geeks*

**NOTE TO ASPIRING TELEVISION SCRIPT WRITERS:**
Because of layout constraints, the pagination of the scripts in this book do not accurately convey the original page count of these screenplays when they were used for production. Simply put, the scripts as presented here all seem to go well over 60 pages, which would get you thrown out of the writers room on an actual one-hour TV show. One-hour scripts should all strive to be around 50 to 55 pages long. Any longer and the executive producer will usually make you cut it down. Just wanted you to know so that if you turn in a script that's 65 pages and the show runner yells at you, you don't say, "But Paul and Judd said scripts can be this long." Hey, we're not taking the fall for your long-windedness, you big tattletale.

# **FREAKS AND GEEKS**

"PILOT"

Episode #1

Written by Paul Feig

Directed by Jake Kasdan

They told me I had to write an introduction to the pilot, so here it is:

"Hello, Captain. My name is Paul and I'll be assisting you on this flight."

Wow, it's hard to believe our show made it 18 episodes with jokes like that.

Actually, the story of how this pilot came about is rather unique for the world of television development. You see, normally, to get a show off the ground, you have to go to a network and "pitch" them the idea, which they then approve of or they throw you out of the office. If they approve, you go and write up a story and bring it to them and they give their notes and thoughts and you rewrite it and if they approve it after that (it usually takes a couple of tries), then they let you go and write the script. And then you bring them the script and they give you notes and you rewrite and the process repeats and repeats until they're happy with everything. And then from that, they decide if they want to shoot the pilot or not.

Whew. It's a pretty exhausting process.

With *Freaks and Geeks*, however, I wrote the pilot as what's called a "spec script," which means I wrote it on my own not knowing if anybody would want it or not. Then, when I showed it to Judd Apatow, he sold it to DreamWorks (where he had a deal at the time), and they in turn sold it to NBC, who wanted to film it as a pilot, which was really out of the ordinary. And so we shot the pilot and then we were picked up and put on the fall schedule.

We'll just end our backstory on that happy note.

But here's the thing. My spec script was a lot different from the script that we finally shot. In the time that I was waiting for DreamWorks to negotiate my contract, Judd told me that I should write a second episode for the show. I did, and when we got the greenlight from NBC to make the pilot, Judd and director Jake Kasdan wanted to do a lot of work on the pilot script. I showed them the second episode I had written, which introduced the character of Kim Kelly and had Lindsay going deeper into how the death of her grandmother made her decide to change her life, and Judd and Jake both thought that we should fuse the two scripts into one. And so, after a few weeks of tearing up the two scripts and coming up with different ways to tell the story, I rewrote the pilot and something very close to what we ended up shooting appeared on the page.

However, when we did our first official read-through with the cast, Judd, Jake and I could tell there was something wrong. The script originally already had Lindsay being one of the freaks. But we realized we were missing the natural drama and tension that would result from Lindsay meeting the freaks for the first time (not to mention that it was a cleaner way to introduce the audience to all the characters). And so I stayed up all night and changed the script to accommodate this final element. And that's the script we shot and that you have in this book and are about to read (I mean, unless you've got something *better* to do).

But before I let you go, I'd like to address one thing that's slightly off topic. Over the course of our show and in the subsequent years, critics and fans have sometimes said that they found the characters of Sam and Lindsay's parents, the Weirs, to be a bit cartoony and unrealistic. If that's true, then that means my actual parents were cartoony and unrealistic (and they sort of were, I guess). My father was a great guy but he was a bit blustery and always had some scary tale ready to convince you not to do something that he didn't want you to do. And my mother was such an eternal optimist that she had a hard time dealing with anything that wasn't happy and uplifting. In truth, when I first wrote the script, I made Harold Weir a bit of a milquetoast, a nondescript guy who was just trying to be nice to his kids. But it was Judd who told me that I needed to give Harold more of an attitude, and so I sat down and remembered my father telling me stories about kids who always seemed to die doing exactly whatever it was I happened to be contemplating doing at that moment. And so, Harold *"You Know What Happened To Her? She Died!"* Weir was born.

Having had both my parents pass away in the past few years, I would like to dedicate this script and this book to them. Because without them, there would have been no *Freaks and Geeks.*

And on that slightly depressing but sincere note…

On with the show!

—Paul Feig

FREAKS AND GEEKS

"PILOT"

**CAST LIST**

NICK ANDOPOLIS
SAM WEIR
JEAN WEIR
HAROLD WEIR
DANIEL DESARIO
KEN MILLER
LINDSAY
MILLIE KENTNER
DON
ELI
GIRL #1
ALAN
KEVIN
TOM
CINDY
KIM KELLY
MR. FREDRICKS
NEAL SCHWEIBER
MOUSY GIRL #1
MOUSY GIRL #2
HARRIS
BILL HAVERCHUCK
MR. KOWCHEVSKI
MR. ROSSO
FOOTBALL PLAYER
SEIDELMAN
MARK
MS. COLLINS
KAREN
SEAN
POPULAR GIRL #1
COLIN

FREAKS AND GEEKS

"PILOT"

**SET LIST**

**INTERIORS:**

WEIR HOUSE
/DINING ROOM
MCKINLEY HIGH SCHOOL
/LOCKER ROOM
/HIGH SCHOOL CAFETERIA
/GEEK TABLE
/TRASH AREA
/HALLWAY
/MR. ROSSO'S OFFICE
/GYM
/CLASSROOM
/ANOTHER CLASSROOM
LINDSAY'S BEDROOM

**EXTERIORS:**

MCKINLEY HIGH SCHOOL
/BACK OF SCHOOL
/FOOTBALL FIELD
/BLEACHERS
/SMOKING PATIO
NOME DRIVE DEAD END
NICK'S HOUSE
NEIGHBORHOOD STREET

1

TEASER

EXT. HIGH SCHOOL FOOTBALL FIELD - DAY

CHYRON UP: "WILLIAM MCKINLEY HIGH SCHOOL: MICHIGAN."

MUSIC UP: NATALIE IMBRUGLIA "TORN"

We are on the football field of a medium-sized high school in a semi-rural part of Michigan. Flatlands. Roads stretch into subdivisions one way and green fields the other. The football team is practicing. GRUNTING. The coach, MR. FREDRICKS, HOLLERING.

MR. FREDRICKS
All right, you ladies. Let's see some hustle out there!

We MOVE UP AND OVER the football field to find a FOOTBALL PLAYER and a CHEERLEADER in the bleachers. As we get CLOSER, we can see that they're very good looking teenagers.

CHEERLEADER
(serious; sincere)
You seem so distant these days, Brett. Is there something I did? 'Cause if there is, I want you to tell me ...

FOOTBALL PLAYER
Ashley, it's just ...

CHEERLEADER
I'm ready to work through whatever it is we need to work through, but we need to communicate. I need you to talk to me.

FOOTBALL PLAYER
(sighs)
It's just ... I love you <u>so much</u> ... it scares me.

They kiss passionately. The MUSIC SWELLS -- "Nothing's right! I'm torn!/I'm all out of faith!" Then, we MOVE DOWN away from them and the music transitions into:

MUSIC UP: VAN HALEN'S "YOU REALLY GOT ME"

CHYRON UP: "1980"

--CONTINUE DOWN UNDER THE BLEACHERS to find a group of burn-outs -- The Freaks. They wear army jackets or old plaid hunting jackets and worn jeans. Cigarette butts surround them. The music blares from a portable cassette player.

(CONTINUED)

CONTINUED:

A wild-haired freak, MARK, is heading under the bleachers toward DANIEL, a friendly but slightly dangerous freak, NICK, a tall freak who's playing air drums, and KEN, a thick freak.

DANIEL
... You know that Molly Hatchett shirt I was wearing the other day?
(beat)
You know, the one with the executioner guy holding the bloody axe? And under his foot he's got the severed head?

KEN
Yeah. It's my shirt.

DANIEL
Yeah. So, my mom makes us go to church every week and we have to dress up. So, when we get there, the stupid priest won't let me in.

KEN
What the hell was his problem?

DANIEL
It was the shirt. I was wearing your shirt. He couldn't deal with the fact that it had a bloody head on it.

MARK
You can't wear stuff like that to church, man.

DANIEL
Why not? It's church. They're supposed to forgive people there. Okay, you hate my shirt, so forgive me. Let me in.

NICK
I believe in God.
(the guys all look at him)
I have felt his power. He plays drums for Led Zepplin and his name is John Bonham! Woooo!!!

MOVE off them to FIND -- LINDSAY WEIR, a cute fifteen year old with unwashed hair and wearing burn-out clothes. She watches the freaks. We can see she wants to go over but doesn't.

We PAN AWAY over to -- another group congregated outside the school auditorium, which is next to the bleachers -- The Geeks.

(CONTINUED)

MUSIC CHANGE: KENNY LOGGINS "I'M ALL RIGHT"

The geeks aren't really nerds per se, as much as they're rather immature, under-developed guys. They dress in either pullover shirts or tucked-in plaids and wear jeans in different colors. We DRIFT OVER to them. They're all acting like BILL MURRAY in "CADDYSHACK."

BILL
"... Final hole at Augusta. This Cinderella story."

NEAL
(pretends to swing club)
"Oh, he got all of that one. It looks like a mirac-- *It's in the hole!*

We MOVE IN on SAM WEIR, 14. He's the very definition of awkward. But he's very animated and is obviously the leader of this group.

SAM
(doing Bill Murray)
"Mr. Gopher, it's Mr. Squirrel here. I'm not a plastic explosive or anything."

This really cracks up the group. Sam looks pleased. LOUD OFF-SCREEN LAUGHTER. The geeks look over to see ALAN WHITE, a wiry kid, and his TWO SHORT BUDDIES approaching.

ALAN
Hey, Sam Weir, you really like Bill Murray, don't you?

SAM
Yeah. He's great.

ALAN
(coming right up to Sam)
Bill Murray sucks.

SAM
No, he doesn't. He's cool.

ALAN
Yeah? What is he -- your boyfriend, Sam Queer?

Alan shoves Sam back hard. The geeks go silent as Alan's buddies LAUGH.

(CONTINUED)

CONTINUED: (3)

ALAN (cont'd)
It's fighting time, Weird. I hope your folks took out some insurance on you.

Sam nervously looks to his fellow geeks but they all look away, happy not to be in the line of fire.

SAM
Leave me alone, Alan.

ALAN
What? I'm sorry. I don't speak geek.

Alan pushes Sam back hard. Sam stumbles and falls. The bullies all LAUGH.

ALAN (cont'd)
I always wanted to know what it'd be like to fight a girl.

Alan heads over to Sam and is about to jump on him when a voice intervenes--

LINDSAY (O.S.)
I'm a girl. You wanna see what it'd be like to fight me?

They all look over to see Lindsay standing there, arms crossed. The geeks look surprised.

ALAN
(surprised, then recovers)
Ooo, Weird's sister has to protect him.

LINDSAY
I'm not protecting him. I'm just trying to figure out why it is that you've gotta pick fights with guys who weigh less than a hundred pounds.

Alan stares at her, not sure what to do. She takes a step closer, like she might actually fight him. Alan steps back. One of his buddies steps up next to him.

BULLY #2
Watch out, Alan. I think she's high.

LINDSAY
Yeah, I might just go psycho on you. Wanna try me?

Alan's completely thrown by the situation. Finally, he starts to back away. Points at Sam.

(CONTINUED)

CONTINUED: (4)

ALAN
You're dead, Weird. You hear me? When your crazy freak sister isn't around, I'm gonna cream you.

Alan takes off, his buddies in tow. Lindsay watches after them with disgust. She turns back to the geeks. Sam's embarrassed.

SAM
You didn't need to do that. I coulda handled it.

LINDSAY
Yeah, I know.

He walks over and they start to leave together.

SAM
By the way, I weigh a hundred and three pounds.

LINDSAY
Sorry.

ON THEIR BACKS as they walk away, together.

LINDSAY (cont'd)
Man, I hate high school.

CUT TO:

<u>OPENING CREDIT SEQUENCE</u>

<u>ACT ONE</u>

INT. WEIR FAMILY DINING ROOM - EVENING

The WEIRS are gathered around the dinner table, having supper. Sam and Lindsay eat in silence, while their fifty-something parents, HAROLD and JEAN, stare at Lindsay.

JEAN
You know, I ran into Mrs. Patton at Farmer Jack today. She said she saw you smoking.

LINDSAY
Well, she's crazy.
(off Jean's look)
Mom, I can't believe you. Do you seriously think I would start smoking?

(CONTINUED)

6

CONTINUED:

HAROLD
(not looking up from his food)
I had a friend who used to smoke. You know what he's doing today? Dead. You think smoking makes you look cool? Let's go dig him up now and see how cool he looks.

LINDSAY
Daddy, if I started smoking, I would tell you.

DAD
Uh-huh.

JEAN
Oh, Lindsay, the TJ Maxx at the mall just got the cutest new skirts in. You want to go clothes shopping tomorrow afternoon?

LINDSAY
(acting disappointed)
I would but I have plans with Kate.

JEAN
Oh, what are you doing?

LINDSAY
(embarrassed)
Going to the mall.

JEAN
Do you need a ride?

Jean tries to hide her hurt and goes back to her food. Sam looks up from his plate.

SAM
Hey, dad, guess what? They're gonna show "Monty Python and the Holy Grail" at Parkway Saturday night. Neal, Bill and I are gonna watch it twice in a row.

HAROLD
Great.

JEAN
Sam, isn't the Homecoming dance Saturday night?

SAM
(confused)
Yeah.

(CONTINUED)

7

CONTINUED: (2)

JEAN
Aren't you going?

SAM
No, why would I do that?

JEAN
Well, your sister's going.

LINDSAY
No I'm not!

JEAN
Honey, high school's for learning but it's also where you should be learning to socialize. That's what school dances are all about.

LINDSAY
No, they're not. They're just a chance for all the popular kids to experiment with sex in their cars.

JEAN
Lindsay!

HAROLD
Hey!

LINDSAY
I mean, if that's what you want me to do, I'd be happy to go.

HAROLD
There was a girl in our school who had pre-marital sex. Do you know what she did on graduation day? Died. Of an overdose. Heroin.

SAM
Dad, are any of your friends alive?

HAROLD
The smart ones.

JEAN
Well, I'm sure there's plenty of kids who are just dying for someone to ask them.

LINDSAY
Mom, that's the stupidest thing I've ever heard.

(CONTINUED)

CONTINUED: (3)

JEAN
Honey, it's stupid until you consider how happy it'll make someone who really wants to go.

LINDSAY
Nobody I know wants to go. Dad.

HAROLD
Great. That works out perfect. I'm having a midnight madness deer hunting sale that night. You can come wait on all those nice hunters.
(with a smug smile)
The choice is yours.

Lindsay just SIGHS, defeated.

SAM
Hey, dad, I was thinking of asking your friend to the dance but I just heard she died of a heroin overdose.

Sam LAUGHS.

HAROLD
Keep joking, Sam. The poor house is filled with comedians.

CUT TO:

INT. HIGH SCHOOL CAFETERIA - DAY

CU-- A plate full of an unidentifiable meat and beans dish is set down on a tray. PULL BACK to reveal NEAL, a sexy-as-they-come, animated geek -- the type that when he enters a room, the sexual energy is palpable.* Neal takes his tray and heads into --

The seating area of the cafeteria. The great melting pot. All the students are sitting at the numerous round tables, each with their own group. We see the popular kids LAUGHING and being LOUD. The jocks are eating tons of food. FOLLOW Neal into the room. He passes and we STAY ON--

ELI, a retarded student, who is walking by a group of jocks. One of the jocks, KEVIN, calls out to Eli.

KEVIN
(pointing to a huge jock)
Hey, Eli, Tom needs a hug.

Eli gets a happy look. This is obviously some key phrase to Eli. He throws open his arms and hugs TOM.

* This description was added in the final draft in order to make Samm Levine feel better about himself. Oh hell, who are we kidding? The description is true. Watch out ladies! —P.F.

CONTINUED:

ELI
My buddy!

And just as quickly, Eli lets go of him and heads merrily off.

TOM
You're such a jerk, Handelman.

The jocks CRACK UP, and and we MOVE AWAY, catching up with Neal. He scans the room, then spots his friends, and we WHIP with his gaze to-- Sam and BILL HAVERCHUCK, a tall, slow-witted geek. Neal walks up to them.

NEAL
(doing William Shatner)
Excuse me, Bones, may I join you here in the Enterprise mess hall?

BILL
I don't get it. Who's that?

NEAL
John Wayne.

Neal sits down as Sam opens his lunch and pulls a note out of his lunch bag.

CU-- The note-- "ANY GIRL WOULD BE LUCKY TO GO TO THE DANCE WITH YOU, LOVE MOM." Sam grimaces.

SAM
Why does my mom always put a note in my lunch? It's so embarrassing.

BILL
At least your mom doesn't write the note on the bag.

He holds up a brown paper bag which has written in large red letters: "I LOVE YOU, LITTLE MAN -- MOM."

SAM
Are you guys going to the Homecoming dance?

NEAL
No.

BILL
I really don't see that happening.

(CONTINUED)

10

CONTINUED: (2)

SAM
I didn't think so.

Just then, an attractive PREGNANT FREAK GIRL walks by. The geeks all stop eating and watch her walk by, in awe.

BILL
Isn't that Patty's sister?

SAM
Yeah, they said she was out of school because she was sick.

NEAL
Yeah, sick with morning sickness.

BILL
(whispers)
So, she's pregnant?

NEAL
(sarcastic)
No, she's stealing a basketball from the gym.

SAM
So, that means she had sex.

Sam and Bill make horrified faces as they consider this. Sam stares after the pregnant girl again. His face is filled with both wonder and fear.

SAM (cont'd)
She's in twelfth grade?

NEAL
Yeah.

SAM
So, she had sex in eleventh grade.

NEAL
Uh-huh.

SAM
How many months pregnant is she?

NEAL
Seven.

SAM
So that means she had sex in February.

(CONTINUED)

CONTINUED: (3)

NEAL
It's a cold month.

We can see from Sam's face that the whole idea of sex is overwhelming. Suddenly, SMASH! A hand comes down on Sam's unopened packet of Twinkies, smashing them flat.

ALAN
Oh, I'm sorry. Did I crush your Twinkies?

Sam looks up to see it's Alan White, the bully. Sam's scared but looks at Alan, upset.

SAM
What's you do that for?!

ALAN
What are you gonna do? Go cryin' to your sister, Sam Rear?

SAM
No. No, I'm not.

Sam turns around and yells over to MR. KOWCHEVSKI, a tough looking teacher who's a cafeteria monitor.

SAM (cont'd)
Mr. Kowchevski, Alan smashed my Twinkies.

Mr. Kowchevski heads over. Alan's in shock.

ALAN
(quietly; to Sam)
Oh my God. You are such a woman.

MR. KOWCHEVSKI
Alan, don't you have anything better to do than to crush Mr. Weir's dessert?

ALAN
Yes, sir. I was just bending over to talk to him and I accidently leaned on them.

MR. KOWCHEVSKI
Well, then, why don't you do the nice thing and go buy him some new ones?

ALAN
Yes, sir.

Alan glares down at Sam, then heads off to the snack bar.

(CONTINUED)

CONTINUED: (4)

SAM
Thanks, Mr. Kowchevski.

MR. KOWCHEVSKI
The world hates stool pigeons and Nancy boys, Sam. Remember that.
(<u>ALTERNATE LINE:</u>)
Sam, don't be such a wussy.

Mr. Kowchevski walks away. Sam looks after him, confused.

NEAL
You shouldn't let Alan do that to you.

SAM
I don't see you doing anything.

NEAL
My dad tells me to stay out of fights that don't affect me directly.

SAM
Well, it'd sure be nice if you guys backed me up once in a while. My sister does and she's a <u>girl</u>.

NEAL
But if we back you up, then Alan's gonna terrorize us, too.

Neal and Bill stare at Sam as this sinks in. Sam tries to respond but knows Neal's right. SIGHS. Just then, MILLIE, the school brain, approaches, on a mission.

MILLIE
Where's your sister?

SAM
(indignant)
I don't know.

She walks away, scanning the room and we FOLLOW her, as she heads to the back of the cafeteria. LINGER ON-- A table full of popular girls, eating lunch and having a great time.

POPULAR GIRL #1
(talking a mile a minute)
So, then, Steve goes, "Why are you following me?" and I go, "I'm not following you," and he goes, "Then why are you behind me?" and I go, "Cause you're in front of me!"

(CONTINUED)

CONTINUED: (5)

The girls all SCREAM WITH LAUGHTER. KLANK! Eli's lunch box hits the table as he plops down in one of their seats.

ELI
Hi! Do you like meatballs?

The girls all freeze, then force friendly smiles.

POPULAR GIRL #1
Uh ... yeah.

ELI
Me too. Let's all go to the homecoming dance together.

Eli smiles, opens the lid, pulls out a sandwich and starts eating merrily as the girls sit in silence, not sure what to do. LINDSAY ENTERS FRAME. We MOVE WITH her as she walks over to Daniel, who's pounding down a soda by the garbage can.

LINDSAY
Hi, Daniel.

DANIEL
Hey, Lindsay, what's up? Where you been?

LINDSAY
You know ... around.

DANIEL
Hey, c'mon. Let's hit the patio.

LINDSAY
The <u>smoking</u> patio?
(nervously)
Okay.

DANIEL
It's alright. They don't bite.

CUT TO:

EXT. SMOKING PATIO - DAY

There are about twenty five kids milling about the outdoor area. Cigarette butts are everywhere. We see Ken hit a girl freak, KAREN, on the ass with a piece of Bunsen burner hose.

KAREN
Ow! Get away from me, you scuzz!

(CONTINUED)

14

CONTINUED:

KEN
I'm sorry. Your butt was calling to me.
(ALTERNATE LINE:)
I'm sorry. Except I'm not.

All the guys LAUGH. We PAN OVER to patio door. Daniel pushes it open. Lindsay stands behind him, looking a little nervous. Daniel sees his friends.

DANIEL
(yelling)
Hey, Nicholas, did you get those M-80s?

NICK
No.
(nods "Yes")

Daniel takes off into the center of the patio. Lindsay steps out the door onto the smoking patio as if she were stepping onto the moon. She walks into the crowd, trying to look cool. She's not. Her eyes dart from side to side, taking in the freaks.

Up ahead, Daniel is talking to Nick and Ken. He waves Lindsay over. She takes a nervous breath and heads over.

DANIEL
Do you guys know Lindsay?

KEN
Haven't had the pleasure.

NICK
Hey, you were in my English class last year. You're that chick who got an A.

LINDSAY
Yeah, well ... what are you gonna do?

She forces a little LAUGH. The guys just nod politely. An uncomfortable moment passes. Then ...

LINDSAY (cont'd)
Are you guys going to the homecoming dance?

KEN
Pardon?

DANIEL
That's a good one, Linds. You're joking, right?

(CONTINUED)

CONTINUED: (2)

LINDSAY
Uh, my dad's kinda making me go.

NICK
Your dad's making you go to a dance? What's that all about?

KEN
Who's your dad? Hitler?

The guys LAUGH. Lindsay looks like she wished she didn't say anything.

LINDSAY
I just thought maybe you guys were gonna go. You know, to make fun of people. I mean, that could be kinda funny, right?

DANIEL
You know what? Why don't you go and we'll meet you there.

KEN
I would go but I have a prior engagement. My cousin just sent me a bunch of mushrooms and I'm going to eat them.

NICK
Yeah. Besides, you know they're going to play disco. Disco sucks.
(he mockingly acts out drumming a disco beat)
Wooo-hooo! I'd rather make out with Principal Farber.

DANIEL
Again?

NICK
Shut up.

Nick punches Daniel on the arm really hard. Daniel grabs Nick's chest and gives him a purple nurple. Nick counters with a SMACK to Daniel's forehead. Daniel fakes a punch to Nick's arm, but then punches him on the outer thigh super hard. It really hurts.

NICK (cont'd)
Oh my God, I can't wait 'til your not paying attention.

Daniel LAUGHS then notices-- Millie standing nearby, too uncomfortable to actually approach this group.

(CONTINUED)

CONTINUED: (3)

DANIEL
What's she want?

They all turn to look at her. Lindsay sees Millie and looks mortified. Millie gets more uncomfortable. She gestures to Lindsay to come over.

KEN
Friend of yours, Linds?

LINDSAY
I'll be right back.

Lindsay heads over to Millie, looking back at the freaks over her shoulder.

ANGLE ON: Millie as Lindsay walks up. Lindsay talks quietly.

LINDSAY (cont'd)
Millie! What are you doing out here?

MILLIE
What are you doing out here? This place is for freaks.

LINDSAY
Millie, go away.

MILLIE
Lindsay, today's the deadline to enter the Academic Decathlon. Mr. Rosso said you didn't turn in your application.

LINDSAY
What? Millie, I'm not entering.

MILLIE
But ... you're our best Math-lete.

LINDSAY
Can we not talk about this now?

MILLIE
Lindsay, what's wrong with you?

LINDSAY
There's nothing wrong with me. I just don't want to be in the Decathlon. Now please leave me alone.

Lindsay starts to leave. Millie calls after her.

(CONTINUED)

CONTINUED: (4)

MILLIE
Well, are you at least gonna help us sell refreshments at the homecoming dance? We're trying to raise money to buy the school a computer.

Lindsay turns, makes a "be quiet" gesture and heads back to the freaks. Millie just stares after Lindsay, completely confused.

CUT TO:

INT. CAFETERIA/GEEK TABLE - CONTINUOUS

CU-- BAM! A fist comes down hard on the table with a new packet of Twinkies pinched between the thumb and first finger. It's Alan. Neal looks down at his lunch, avoiding eye contact.

ALAN
Here's your new dessert, Weird.

Alan lets go of the Twinkies, revealing that he's smashed the end of one of the Twinkies between his fingers. Alan looks over at Mr. Kowchevski and gives an "everything's fine" smile.

Mr. Kowchevski nods his approval and turns away. Alan immediately socks Sam sharply in the ribs.

ALAN (cont'd)
That's for telling on me. And all I can say is you'd better watch your ass in gym today.
(to Bill, seeing his lunch bag)
You too, little man.

Alan kicks the leg of Sam's chair hard, gives Bill a menacing look and leaves. Bill looks horrified.

BILL
Oh, my God. He just marked me. I'm a dead man.

NEAL
You made a key mistake. Never make eye contact when you're an innocent bystander.

BILL
Why didn't you tell me that before he came over?

NEAL
I thought you knew the rule.

(CONTINUED)

CONTINUED:

SAM
You guys have got to help me or he's never gonna leave me alone.

CUT TO:

INT. CAFETERIA/TRASH AREA - MOMENTS LATER

Bill is dumping the remains of his lunch into a large trash can, as Sam and Neal stand nearby, waiting. The conversation doesn't skip a beat.

NEAL
Here's my advice. You should handle Alan the same way Han Solo dealt with Jabba the Hut. Avoid him.

SAM
Just avoid him, forever?

NEAL
No. Only four years.

Bill approaches--

BILL
Hey, Sam, there's Cindy Sanders.

The guys all look up and stare. Sam turns and sees that they're all staring at CINDY SANDERS, the ultimate pretty girl-next-door. Sam's eyes light up.

NEAL
Dream on, Sam.

Cindy's looking around, then looks over at Sam and sees him staring. His eyes go wide and he looks away quickly.

SAM
... oh, man.

BILL
(looking at Cindy)
Uh-oh. Incoming.

Sam looks at Bill. Bill points secretly back at Cindy. Sam looks over and sees Cindy walking toward him, staring right at him. Sam looks like he's going to have a heart attack.

CINDY
Hey, Sam, I've been looking all over for you.

The geeks eyes go wide. She takes a jacket out of her backpack.

(CONTINUED)

CONTINUED:

CINDY (cont'd)
Is this your jacket?

She produces a white windbreaker, shows it to wide-eyed Sam.

SAM
... yeah ...

CINDY
You left it in science. I didn't want it to get all dirty.

SAM
(too friendly)
Oh, thanks, Cindy! That was really nice of you.

CINDY
I'll see you later.

She smiles kindly and leaves. Sam watches after her, still holding his breath. The other geeks look at him in awe.

BILL
Sam ... you are so in.

SAM
What?

BILL
She brought you your jacket. That means she saw it, remembered it was yours, picked it up and carried it through the halls.

NEAL
People probably saw her with it and everything.

BILL
Cindy Sanders is in love with you, man.

A shocked Sam considers this.

SAM
I wonder if she has a date for the dance?

He smells the jacket as he watches Cindy walk away. PUSH IN ON-- Sam staring after Cindy.

BILL
Can I smell it?

END OF ACT ONE

ACT TWO

INT. HALLWAY - DAY

Sam, Neal and Bill are heading to their classes.

SAM
You really think Cindy likes me?

BILL
(doing "Kung Fu" voice)
The stars point to "yes," Grasshopper.

NEAL
No way. We're not her species.

SAM
Hey, you guys, do me a favor and ask around to see if Cindy has a date for the Homecoming dance?

BILL
Who would I ask?

NEAL
Are you crazy? The dance is tomorrow and she's a cheerleader. Do the math.

SAM
I know, but my dad always tells me that pretty girls never get asked out because guys are too afraid to talk to them.

BILL
(serious)
Really? Maybe I should ask out Farrah Fawcett Majors.

NEAL
If you do, Lee Majors will kick your butt.

BILL
(hadn't thought of that)
And he's bionic. Good call. I owe you.

SAM
Just ask around, okay?

Neal nods "okay." Bill and Sam head off for class. Neal stands and watches them go. He turns and runs into Ken.

(CONTINUED)

CONTINUED:

KEN
Get outta the way.

Neal runs away.

BILL EXITS FRAME and we BACK TO-- Lindsay and the freaks, as they come around the corner. Lindsay looks a little more comfortable. Ken slips Daniel a piece of paper.

KEN (cont'd)
Here's the chemistry exam you ordered.

DANIEL
Alright! Nice going.
(looks at the paper)
Where's the answers?

KEN
You just said to steal the test.

DANIEL
Great. Now I gotta read. Thanks a lot.

KIM KELLY, a tough, attractive freak girl, comes up to them.

KIM
I'm cuttin'. Gimme a smoke.
(ALTERNATE)
I'm cuttin'. Who's got gum?

Ken pulls the cigarette from behind his ear and holds it out to Kim. She looks at it, disgusted.

--ALTERNATE ACTION-- Ken reaches into the depths of his pocket and pulls out a terrible looking stick of gum in a wore wrapper.

KIM (cont'd)
Yeah, great. Why don't you just blow your nose in some bread and make me a sandwich too.
(ALTERNATE)
Yeah, great. You wanna chew it first too?

KEN
It's the only one I got.
(ALTERNATE LINE:)
Why's everyone crawling up my butt today?

LINDSAY
I've got one, Kim.

Lindsay reaches into her bag. Kim ignores Lindsay.

(CONTINUED)

CONTINUED: (2)

KIM
(to Daniel)
What's she doing here?

DANIEL
Uh ... she's our friend.

KIM
(to Daniel)
What, are you doin' her so she'll help you with your math homework?

DANIEL
Shut the hell up.

LINDSAY
Hey, Kim --

KIM
I wasn't talking to you, brain. Don't you have a test to take or something?

NICK
Hey, will you be cool ... please?

LINDSAY
Did I do something to you?

KIM
You're here.

Lindsay's completely thrown by Kim's anger. She tries to regroup. Tries to be friendly.

LINDSAY
I've got just as much right to be here as you do.

Kim stares at her a beat, then bursts out into mean LAUGHTER.

KIM
Hey, brain, I shoplift from your daddy's store. You're just some rich kid who's trying to piss off her parents. You think you can hang with these guys? You think that's gonna make you cool?

LINDSAY
(stares a beat; scared)
Kim, I don't know what to tell you.

Kim seems to soften. She looks at Lindsay strangely.

(CONTINUED)

CONTINUED: (3)

KIM
You know what? I'm sorry. Let's be friends.

In one quick move, Kim reaches down, grabs Lindsay's bag out of her hand, holds it by the bottom and flings its contents all over the hall.

KIM (cont'd)
There. Now we're friends. See you at the mall.

Kim throws Lindsay's bag back at her. Lindsay looks shell-shocked. She looks at the contents of her bag all over the floor. Slowly, without making eye contact with Kim, Lindsay walks over and starts picking up her stuff.

DANIEL
(angry; to Kim)
Hey, what are you, on your period?!

KIM
Hey, if you want to stand around with your little poser girlfriend and pretend with her, then that's your waste of time. Just keep her the hell away from me.

Kim storms away. Nick, Ken and Daniel watch her go, completely confused. The school bell RINGS. The hallway starts to clear.

KEN
That is exactly why I don't carry a purse.

Ken takes off for class. Nick and Daniel look at Lindsay picking up her stuff. Nick makes an apologetic face.

NICK
I gotta get to shop class. It's the only one I can pass.

Nick takes off. Daniel walks over, stoops down and helps a shaken Lindsay pick up her stuff.

LINDSAY
Don't you have to get to class too?

DANIEL
I'll survive.

CUT TO:

INT. LOCKER ROOM - DAY

Sam, Neal and Bill are in the locker room, about to change into their gym clothes.

BILL
Hey, how come your sister dresses so weird now?

NEAL
Yeah, she's always wearing your dad's old army jacket.

SAM
I don't know. She's been doing a lot of weird stuff ever since our grandma died.

Just then, Alan walks by in his gym shorts. BOOM! He hits Sam's metal locker hard with his fist. Neal saunters away.

ALAN
You're dead, Rear.

Alan points at Sam menacingly. Bill musters his courage.

BILL
Hey, Alan --

ALAN
What?!

BILL
(swallows; then)
What's the point of all this?

ALAN
What's the point? The point is ... you're dead too.

Alan gives them both a menacing look, then stalks off to the gym. They watch him go. After a beat ...

BILL
I kinda wish I didn't come to school today.

Sam keeps staring after Alan, depressed. Bill SIGHS.

CUT TO:

INT. HALLWAY - DAY

Eli is walking happily down the hallway. He walks up to TWO GIRLS. Lindsay is nearby at her locker, looking upset.

ELI
Will you go to the homecoming dance with me?

GIRL #1
I would but I have a date.

ELI
(to the other girl)
Will you go to the homecoming dance with me?

The girl stares at Eli with an "as if" look. A senior named DON overhears and walks over to Eli.

DON
Hey, Eli. There's a bee on your books.

ELI
Really? Where?

DON
I've got it.

Don smacks Eli's books out from under his arm, sending them flying down the hallway. Lindsay looks mad and heads over.

DON (cont'd)
I saved your life, Eli.

ELI
Thank you.

LINDSAY
(to Don)
What's the matter with you, you jerk?!

DON
Oh, I'm sorry. I didn't mean to upset your husband.

The girls LAUGH. Lindsay glares at him.

LINDSAY
What if he was my husband? Would that be some kind of joke to you?

(CONTINUED)

CONTINUED:

DON
Wouldn't be a joke to me. I think you two make a perfect couple.

The girls LAUGH again. Lindsay stares them all down.

LINDSAY
Yeah, maybe we do. Eli, do you want to go to the homecoming dance with me?

ELI
(eyes light up)
Yes!!!

Don and the girls go silent. Eli starts dancing.

ELI (cont'd)
Hooray! Eli's going to the homecoming dance. Eli's got a wife.

Lindsay takes Eli's arm and they walk down the hall away from the stunned group.

CUT TO:

INT. LOCKER ROOM - DAY

Sam, Neal and Bill are heading toward the gym door along with other students, all wearing gym shorts.

BILL
I don't think these shorts are very flattering.

SAM
No, you look good.

BILL
Thanks.

MR. FREDRICKS, the gym teacher, stops the class. He points at TWO JOCKS who are trying to sock each other in the crotch.

MR. FREDRICKS
Hey, Heckle and Jeckle, you wanna play grabtail, you do it on your own time.
(to the class)
All right, guys, I just wanted to let you know that since it's Friday and in honor of the Homecoming game tomorrow, I thought I'd give you all a day off.

The class REACTS positively. Sam looks absolutely relieved.

(CONTINUED)

CONTINUED:

NEAL
(raising hand)
Can we go home?

MR. FREDRICKS
C'mon, Schweiber, don't be an idiot. I mean we're gonna do something fun. I'm gonna let you guys play Dodgeball.

The jocks CHEER. The geeks and freaks put their heads in their hands. Dodgeball is their Kryptonite. Sam peeks over at Alan. Alan's staring at Sam with an evil smile on his face. Sam looks sick.

CUT TO:

INT. GYM - DAY - MINUTES LATER

Pandemonium! Red rubber playground balls of all sizes are flying back and forth like cannon fire. It's pretty much bullies, jocks, and huge, mean "farmers" on one side, and geeks and freaks on the other side.

The balls coming from the bully side are whizzing in like bullets. BOOM! They make a huge sound as they hit the retractable wooden bleachers that make up the gym wall. BOOM! BOOM! The balls from the geek side arc lazily in and drop short of the enemy.

Sam, Neal and Bill are huddled against one end of the wall as their fellow students run back and forth in front of them in a panic, occasionally getting hit and HOWLING IN PAIN. Balls continue to hit the wall around them. It's war.

NEAL
Somebody please tell me what's supposed to be fun about this.

BILL
If we just let ourselves get hit, then we can sit out.

<u>BOOOOOMMMM!!!</u> A cantalope-sized ball rockets into the wall like a bullet, just missing Sam. They all jump.

SAM
Uh ... let's just pretend we were hit. Nobody'd know.

NEAL
I don't think we can.

(CONTINUED)

CONTINUED:

Neal points over at Mr. Fredricks. He's staring right at them.

MR. FREDRICKS
Hey, c'mon, you ladies! Put down your mascara, get in there and play!

BOOM! Another ball rockets in, this time scattering the guys. Sam falls down. Bill starts to freak.

BILL
I can't take it, man. I gotta get outta here!

Bill takes a deep breath, lets out a loud and long YELL like Rambo running into battle and sprints across the gym. A huge farmer kid, SEIDELMAN, sees Bill.

SEIDELMAN
Look, "Little Man's" making a run for it!

BILL
Only my mom's allowed to call me that!

BOOM! A ball hits Bill full force in the head, ricochetting straight up in the air. Bill goes down hard. The bully side CRACKS UP.

ALAN
(looking at Sam)
All right, now it's time to smear Weir.

The group of bullies and farmers all grab balls and zero in on Sam. Neal, who's standing with Sam, sees this.

NEAL
Oh, no. Sam, get away from me!

Neal tries to run but it's too late. BOOM! Neal takes one in the groin. He doubles over.

NEAL (cont'd)
Oh, my God!

Neal's down on his hands and knees, red-faced with pain. The bully side LAUGHS.

SEIDELMAN
Hey, kid, now you can sing soprano in choir!

Mr. Fredricks LAUGHS. Neal's still on his hands and knees, beet red. He's trying not to cry.

(CONTINUED)

CONTINUED: (2)

MR. FREDRICKS
All right, Schweiber. Walk it off.

Neal gets up, holding his groin with one hand and his stomach with the other. His eyes are red as he staggers off to the side when WHAP! Another ball hits him full force in the side of the face. He's dazed.

MR. FREDRICKS (cont'd)
Hey, Seidelman, that's illegal. You're outta there.

Neal stands stunned, holding his face for a second, then runs to the locker room to cry. Seidelman shrugs and walks to the sideline. When he gets there, Mr. Fredricks gives him a playful punch on the arm, shakes his head and LAUGHS.

MR. FREDRICKS (cont'd)
Sit down, knucklehead.

Alan looks at Sam, who is standing by himself in an empty area. Alan starts to stalk him. Sam runs over to a crowd of freaks. Mark is there.

MARK
Hey, kid, get away from us. That psycho's after you.

Alan hurls his ball at them. BOOM! It hits the wall as they all duck. Mark picks up the ball, winds up and throws it back at Alan with all his might, losing his balance and falling onto the floor. Alan catches the ball easily.

MARK (cont'd)
(looking up)
He caught my ball. I'm out! Woo hoo!

Mark celebrates and runs to the side. BOOM! BOOM! BOOM! A volley of balls comes in, hitting all three freaks surrounding Sam. They fall over in pain, leaving Sam a sitting duck. Sam looks around. He's the only one left on his side. The bully side has about eight huge guys and Alan left.

ALAN
Nowhere to hide, Weird.

BOOM! BOOM! BOOM! BOOM! A barrage of balls comes in as Sam takes off running. The balls just miss him, flying in as Sam runs back and forth, arms and legs flying.

(CONTINUED)

CONTINUED: (3)

BILL
Go, Sam, go!

Suddenly, the barrage stops. Sam stops and looks over, panting. He sees the big guys lined up, all holding balls, staring at him. They smile evilly.

ALAN
I told you you were dead, Rear.

Alan's holding the smallest, deadliest ball of the lot. He winds up to take the hardest throw of his life. Sam freezes in terror.

In SLOW MOTION, Alan unwinds and throws a comet straight at Sam. Sam puts his hands out to protect himself and closes his eyes.

BOOM! Back to real speed. We hear the ball hit Sam. Sam flies back into the wall. Then Alan's eyes go wide. Sam is stunned. He looks down and sees that he's caught the ball between his arms and chest. The geeks all CHEER. Alan stares in absolute shock.

SEIDELMAN
(laughing uproariously)
Ah ha ha! The girl got you out!

MR. FREDRICKS
All right, White. Take a seat.

A humiliated Alan storms off to the side as Sam looks over at Neal and Bill, who give him a thumbs up.

BILL
Throw it back!

Sam looks at the seven remaining guys, including Tom (the jock who Eli hugged). They're all huge. We see Sam get an idea. He smiles, then lobs the ball high in the air. Everyone watches it go up.

SAM
(to himself)
Catch it. C'mon, catch it.

The ball descends. The huge guys watch it come down. Tom holds his hands out to catch it. Sam smiles, breathes a SIGH of relief.

(CONTINUED)

CONTINUED: (4)

Suddenly, the jock puts his arms behind his back and steps back, letting the ball hit the ground, bouncing away. They smile at Sam, menacingly.

SAM
(to huge guys)
I give up, guys. Okay? Let's just start another game. You win.

The guys all stop.

TOM
Really? You give up? Okay, we win.

The guys all voice agreement and turn to leave. Sam smiles, relieved. Then ... BOOOOOOOOOMMMMMM!!!!! The huge guys all turn back and blast Sam with seven balls at once as Alan CHEERS from the sidelines and all the farmers, bullies and jocks LAUGH and celebrate.

ANGLE ON BILL AND OTHER GEEKS - On the sidelines.

BILL
(to geeks)
Dodgeball's kind of a stupid game, isn't it?

ANGLE ON SAM - he's groggy, laying on the ground. He looks up and sees Alan standing over him.

ALAN
You just signed your death warrant.

CUT TO:

EXT. BLEACHERS - DAY

A girls gym class is sitting in the bleachers waiting to play field hockey. Lindsay, in her gym clothes, sits away from the other girls. Two MOUSY GIRLS are talking and pointing at Lindsay.

MOUSY GIRL #1
She asked Eli to the homecoming dance.

MOUSY GIRL #2
She was probably high. I heard freak girls smoke their armpit hair.

The girls LAUGH as Lindsay gives them a glare, then notices Eli and two guys at the far end of the bleachers.

ANGLE ON: Two students, SEAN and Kevin, are goofing on ELI.

(CONTINUED)

CONTINUED:

SEAN
So, Eli, that Jimmy Carter is some President. He's really doing a hell of a job, don't you think?

ELI
Yup, yup. Hell of a job.

SEAN
But I'm a little concerned about his handling of the economy, aren't you?

ELI
Yes. A little concerned.

Sean and Kevin LAUGH. So does Eli, who seems to love this.

SEAN
Oh, come on, Eli, give the guy a break! Look what he's done in the Middle East.

ELI
Yeah, yeah. The Middle East.

Kevin LAUGHS again, which makes Eli LAUGH more.

SEAN
You know what? I bet you'd make a good President, Eli.

ELI
President Eli! Yeaaa!

Lindsay approaches, shaking her head.

LINDSAY
Guys, cut it out. Leave him alone.

SEAN
What? We're having a political discussion here.

LINDSAY
Eli, you don't have to talk to them. They're just being mean.

ELI
They're my buddies.

SEAN
<u>See</u>, we're his buddies, aren't we, Mr. President?

(CONTINUED)

CONTINUED: (2)

The guys start singing "Hail to the Chief" and salute him. Eli salutes back. The guys stifle their laughter.

LINDSAY
No, they're not your buddies.

ELI
I'm making them laugh.

LINDSAY
Yeah, but it's a bad kind of laughing.

ELI
I like making them laugh.

LINDSAY
Not this way. There's a good kind of laughing and a bad kind of laughing. This is bad. They're only laughing because you're retarded.

Eli stares at Lindsay. His whole face changes.

ELI
(intensely)
I'm not retarded. I'm special.

LINDSAY
You're right. I'm sorry. You're special.

ELI
I'm not retarded, I'm special!

LINDSAY
Eli, I'm sorry. Take it easy. Calm down!

ELI
YOU'RE RETARDED! I don't want to go to the dance with you!

Eli runs to the other side of the bleachers, then when he tries to go down to ground level he looses his footing and FALLS hard. A CRACK is heard. Eli has broken his arm. He SCREAMS in pain. A woman gym teacher rushes up to calm him as the students look on. Eli flails, out of control, crying.

(CONTINUED)

CONTINUED: (3)

Lindsay just stares at the scene helplessly, in shock, unable to move.

SEAN
I'm the mean one? How does that work?

END OF ACT TWO

ACT THREE

EXT. SCHOOL - DAY

Sam, Neal and Bill stand before HARRIS and COLIN, two odd, slightly older geeks who are their mentors. They have come to Harris and Colin to seek guidance.

HARRIS
Ah, yes, interesting problem. Freshman bullies. He's clearly acting out his insecurity in a new environment. If you can disconnect emotionally, it's really quite sad.

COLIN
Not that you should feel sorry for him. His kind should be destroyed.

SAM
So what do we do?

HARRIS
I recommend the "Cressman Conundrum."

BILL
What's that?

HARRIS
Tom Cressman. He was my freshman tormentor. The idea is -- if you fight your bully, afterwards, whether you win or lose, they'll usually leave you alone.

BILL
That makes sense.

HARRIS
He broke my tailbone but the results were effective.

SAM
What happened?

(CONTINUED)

CONTINUED:

COLIN
He got expelled.

HARRIS
It's a good plan.

NEAL
It's a terrible plan. I'm not fighting Alan. He's not <u>my</u> tormentor. I know every route he takes to each class and I avoid those halls. It's that simple. You want to get through this? Start leaving school out the janitor's door like I do.

Neal turns to go. BAM! He runs right into Alan, knocking Alan's notebook out of his hand. It THUNKS to the floor. Alan looks down at it, then glares at Neal. A long beat passes--

ALAN
Nice work, dork. You just got your name added to the death list.

Alan picks up his notebook and heads off. Neal looks at Harris.

NEAL
All right. Let's hear about this stupid Cressman Conundrum.

CUT TO:

INT. MR. ROSSO'S OFFICE - DAY

A defeated and angry Lindsay sits across from Mr. Rosso.

MR. ROSSO
So, what's going on here?

LINDSAY
I tried to do something nice in this stupid school where nothing nice ever happens. And now Eli hates me and he has a broken arm. What's the point? I'm not even going to try anymore.

MR. ROSSO
No ... why aren't you taking part in the Academic Decathlon?

LINDSAY
... What?

(CONTINUED)

36

CONTINUED:

MR. ROSSO
We need you. You're our best Math-lete.

LINDSAY
Oh God, please don't say that word.

MR. ROSSO
Are you having some problems at home?

LINDSAY
No, I'm not.

MR. ROSSO
Is it a boy?

LINDSAY
No.

MR. ROSSO
Hey, you can tell me. I know it seems "square" to actually talk to your guidance counselor, but I was a kid once too. And not that long ago.

LINDSAY
Mr. Rosso, there's nothing to tell. Trust me.

MR. ROSSO
Okay, I see the problem here. Let's just rap as people. No pressure. From now on I'm not Mr. Rosso, guidance counselor. I'm just Jeff, your friend who cares.

LINDSAY
Jeff.

MR. ROSSO
Exactly. And you're not Ms. Weir, high school student. You're Lindsay, a girl who seems like she needs a friend. So come on, Linds, talk to your buddy Jeff.

She just stares at him. There's no way he'll understand.

LINDSAY
Jeff ... I've never felt better in my life.

MR. ROSSO
Well, then someone should tell your face.

(CONTINUED)

CONTINUED: (2)

He laughs. She just stares at him.

CUT TO:

INT. HALLWAY - DAY

The geeks are standing by a water fountain in another part of the hallway.

SAM
Harris said if Alan's standing, we don't have a chance. Our first goal is to get him on the ground.

NEAL
How are we supposed to do that? Saw off his legs?

BILL
Should I wear a cup for this?

NEAL
That's between you and your God.

Sam turns and sees Cindy down the hall, and stares. She sees Sam and gives a friendly smile. Sam eyes go wide. He forces a smile back. Kim is standing near Cindy and mistakenly thinks Sam is staring at her. Kim and her two hot, scary friends, Sue and Karen, start walking toward Sam.

KIM
Hey, geek, you got a problem?

SAM
Uh ... no. I was just looking at a friend of mine.

KIM
Are you telling me I look like a friend of yours?

KAREN
Hey, Kim, I think he likes you.

Karen and Sue LAUGH. Kim looks at them, then back at Sam. Moves her face close to his.

KIM
Is that true? Do you like me? Do you love me?

(CONTINUED)

CONTINUED:

Even though she's mocking him, there's something hard to read in her face. Could she be serious? The fact that she's so close has Sam dizzy and off-guard.

SAM
I ... like you like a friend.

KIM
(moving closer; softly)
I don't think so. I think you like me like me. I think you want to kiss me. Do you want to kiss me?

She's very close now. We can feel the chills shooting down Sam's spine. Neal and Bill are paralyzed.

SAM
I ... uh ... I don't know.

KIM
C'mon. Give me a kiss. I'll be your girlfriend.

She moves in to kiss Sam. His eyes are wide in terror and anticipation. Suddenly, she PUSHES Sam against his locker, making the metal doors BANG with a metallic rattle.

KIM (cont'd)
In your dreams, geek.

Karen and Sue LAUGH UPROARIOUSLY. Kim bursts out LAUGHING too. They walk away.

NEAL
Maybe we could get her to beat up Alan.

CUT TO:

MUSIC over the next series of mini-scenes --

INT. CLASSROOM - DAY

A chemistry class. We HEAR Mr. Kowchevski lecture as we see Bill and Neal at their desks. Neal confers with another kid.

MR. KOWCHEVSKI (V.O.)
When certain volatile elements are mixed together, the reactions can be both explosive and deadly ...

(CONTINUED)

39

CONTINUED:

NEAL
Apparently Cindy was supposed to go to the dance with Craig Goblatt but he tried to go to second base with her and she got mad.

BILL
First base is kissing but what's second again?

NEAL
I'll tell you when I get there.

BILL
Harold Spenser told me that Cindy lives in a tent.
(off Neal stares)
What, you think it's not true?

CUT TO:

INT. ANOTHER CLASSROOM - DAY

CU -- Sam's writing "Mrs. Cindy Weir" over and over in his notebook. PULL BACK TO SEE: Sam is sitting in class as the teacher, MS. COLLINS, lectures. Millie is across the aisle from Sam. Millie leans over to him.

MILLIE
(whispering)
Why's your sister throwing her life away?

SAM
(surprised)
Is she?

MILLIE
Yes. Everybody's worried.

MS. COLLINS
Ms. Kentner, is there something you'd like to share with the class?

MILLIE
(mortified)
No, Ms. Collins. I'm so sorry.

Ms. Collins goes back to lecturing as Millie sits back in her chair, her hand on her face as if it's the end of the world.

MILLIE (cont'd)
Oh, my God. I can't believe I just got in trouble.

(CONTINUED)

CONTINUED:

SAM
(leaning over)
Hey, does Cindy have a date for the dance tomorrow?

MILLIE
(a quick, panicky whisper)
Shut up, shut up, shut up.

CUT TO:

INT. CLASSROOM - DAY

In a darkened room, Lindsay watches a 16mm film with her class. SLOW PUSH IN TO CU: Lindsay stares at the screen blankly. She looks very depressed. Slightly damaged.

ANGLE ON NICK: Nick looks over and sees her. He looks concerned. Leans over to her.

NICK
(whispering to Lindsay)
You okay?

LINDSAY
Is it just me or does the whole world suck?

NICK
C'mon, it can't be that bad.

LINDSAY
Eli won't go to the dance with me.

NICK
See, even Eli's too cool to go to the dance.

Nick laughs. Lindsay just looks at him. She's really down.

NICK (cont'd)
(studies her a beat)
Hey, after class, you and me are cutting outta here.

LINDSAY
Cutting?

NICK
Yeah, I've got something to show you that's gonna make you feel better.

CUT TO:

EXT. SCHOOL - DAY

The door opens and Nick comes out. He looks back and signals for Lindsay to come. Lindsay steps outside nervously, looking back into the school. Suddenly, she bolts off as if she were making a jail break. Nick LAUGHS and takes off after her.

MUSIC ENDS.

CUT TO:

EXT. NICK'S HOUSE - DAY

Lindsay and Nick stand before Nick's garage in a lower middle class neighborhood.

NICK
Alright, Lindsay, prepare to have your mind blown.

Nick hits his garage door opener. The door slowly opens to reveal the world's largest, crappiest looking drum set.

NICK (cont'd)
Check it out. Fourteen racked toms, six floor toms, ten cowbells, four rides, five snares, a roto-tom rack and it's all mounted on my infamous quadruple kick drum system. Six more pieces and I've got a bigger kit than Neal Peart from Rush.

LINDSAY
(confused)
That's great, Nick.

NICK
Yeah. All these teachers tell you to work. I'll work. But I'm gonna work on what I want to work on. My drum kit. This is my passion. This is the essence of who I am now. Before I had this, I was lost.

Lindsay nods, empathetic.

NICK (cont'd)
You see what I'm saying, right? You gotta find your reason for living. You need to find your gigantic drum kit. You know?

(CONTINUED)

CONTINUED:

LINDSAY
(trying to joke)
Maybe I'll buy a clarinet.

NICK
(stares a beat)
I know I sound like an idiot. And before Kiss took off, Peter Criss was just an idiot with a big, gigantic drum kit and some goofy make-up. So, what, I should give up and go into the Army like my brothers did just because everybody else has written me off? Forget that, cause I know what I'm going to do with my life.

LINDSAY
Oh, no, I'm sorry, Nick. That's not what I meant. It seems like everything I say today is wrong. I appreciate your advice. I'm sure you're gonna make it. Bigger than Peter Criss.

Nick lights the tip of a GONG MALLET.

NICK
Count on it.

Nick swings the flaming mallet and hits the gong. It RINGS OUT loudly. Lindsay laughs as Nick gives her a huge smile. He has made his point.

CUT TO:

EXT. NEIGHBORHOOD STREET - DAY

Lindsay and Nick are walking down the sidewalk.

NICK
If you're not going to the dance, why don't you come to my house? A bunch of guys who play guitar are gonna come over and we're gonna try to play "Dark Side of the Moon" or something. Just tell your dad you went.

LINDSAY
I can't do that.

NICK
Really? Okay. Hey, I got it, then. You tell your dad you got a date. I'll put on a suit, whatever, and come pick you up.
(MORE)

(CONTINUED)

43

CONTINUED:

NICK (cont'd)
Talk nice to your dad, then we'll go to the school, walk up to the door of the dance, look inside and then take off. This way, you can tell your dad you went to the dance. You wouldn't be lying.

LINDSAY
You'd really do that?

NICK
Absolutely.

Mr. Rosso drives up in his CAR, a DODGE DUSTER.

MR. ROSSO
Hello there.

LINDSAY
Hello, Jeff.

MR. ROSSO
Guess who's in trouble?

CUT TO:

EXT. NEIGHBORHOOD STREET - MOMENTS LATER

Lindsay and Mr. Rosso stand next to his car. Nick is sitting on the curb in the background.

MR. ROSSO
Here's the deal. If you take part in the Academic Decathlon, I'll forget this ever happened.

LINDSAY
You're forcing me to be a Math-lete? That is so not fair.

MR. ROSSO
The world is not black and white, it's gray. And I really think it'd be good for you.

LINDSAY
(glancing back at Nick; softly)
Jeff ... there's no way I can do that.

Mr. Rosso studies her face. She looks desperate. Mr. Rosso suddenly becomes cold and business-like.

MR. ROSSO
Fine, Miss Weir. Then maybe it's time for some tough love.
(MORE)

(CONTINUED)

CONTINUED:

MR. ROSSO (cont'd)
How 'bout I call your parents and let them know their daughter's turning into a burn-out who skips class.

LINDSAY
But--

MR. ROSSO
And you know what? I can't make you be a Math-lete but I can make you work the refreshment table at the homecoming dance. I'll see you tomorrow night at seven.

Off Lindsay's reaction.

CUT TO:

<u>END OF ACT 3</u>

<u>ACT FOUR</u>

INT. WEIR FAMILY DINING ROOM - EVENING

Sam and Lindsay are at the dinner table with their parents. The mood is tense. They are halfway through their meals. Mr. Weir is staring at Lindsay, who keeps her head down.

HAROLD
You know who used to cut class? Jimi Hendrix. You know what happened to him? He died. Choking on his own vomit.

LINDSAY
Dad, I skipped Latin.

HAROLD
Yeah, I can see why you wouldn't want to learn about that. It's only the building blocks of our language.

JEAN
Well ... at least you're going to the dance now. We can go look for a dress ... at the mall.

More silence.

HAROLD
You can't cut corners in this life. You know who cut corners? Kennedy. Kennedy cut corners when he was running the Bay of Pigs.
(MORE)

(CONTINUED)

CONTINUED:

HAROLD (cont'd)
Many good men lost their lives because of it. You know who else cut corners? Janis Joplin.

Lindsay jumps up.

LINDSAY
(exploding)
Dad, what are you talking about?!! You don't make any sense! I just cut class. And guess what? Everybody's still alive! Just leave me alone! Leave me alone!!!

And she bolts out of the dining room. Stunned silence.

HAROLD
You understand what I'm saying, don't you, Sam?

SAM
(beat)
Yeah.

HAROLD
Good boy. Pass the rolls.

Jean just glares at Harold as they go back to eating.

CUT TO:

INT. LINDSAY'S BEDROOM - EVENING

Lindsay is sitting on her bed, eyes red. A light KNOCKING. Sam sticks his head in.

SAM
Um ... can I come in?

Lindsay doesn't say no, so Sam comes in and closes the door behind him. He looks uncomfortable. Lindsay stares "yes?"

SAM (cont'd)
Do you think that me, Neal and Bill could beat Alan up?

LINDSAY
Just Alan? Yeah. Alan and his buddies? No to maybe.

SAM
Yeah. That's what I thought.
(a deep breath; then ...)
Why are you throwing your life away?

(CONTINUED)

CONTINUED:

LINDSAY
Did dad tell you to ask me that?

SAM
Uh ... no. Millie did.

LINDSAY
I figured. Forget it. Tell her to mind her own business.

Sam looks down. Thinks. Then ...

SAM
Just because Millie asked me to ask you, it doesn't mean I was gonna tell her what you said.

Lindsay looks at Sam. His face shows true concern. She thinks a beat, then ...

LINDSAY
Did mom and dad ever tell you that I was the only one with grandma when she died?

SAM
(surprised)
No.

Lindsay stares at the picture in her hand. It's a picture of an old woman, kind and happy looking. After a beat ...

LINDSAY
They went down to the cafeteria for coffee. All of a sudden, Grandma looked so terrified. I called for the nurse but there wasn't any time. Grandma grabbed my hand and said "I don't want to go." She was so scared. I said "Can you see Heaven or God or a light or anything ...?"

SAM
What'd she say?

LINDSAY
"No. There's nothing."
(beat)
She was a good person all her life. And that's what she got.

(CONTINUED)

CONTINUED: (2)

Lindsay stares at Sam, troubled. Sam looks dumbfounded. This is far more than he can process. Finally ...

SAM
So ... you <u>do</u> think we could beat up Alan?

Lindsay can't help but smile.

LINDSAY
Yeah. He's a goner.

Sam gives her a worried nod and exits. Lindsay SIGHS, then smiles to herself, feeling just a tiny bit better.

CUT TO:

EXT. FOOTBALL FIELD - DAY

Very TIGHT ON-- A grimacing, growling FOOTBALL PLAYER'S face, through the face guard on his green helmet.

FOOTBALL PLAYER (OS)
Thirty two, sixty eight, ninety four...

Very TIGHT ON-- His OPPONENT's face, through a red helmet.

FOOTBALL PLAYER (OS, cont'd)
...hut, hut, hike!

ANGLE DOWN THE AISLE created by the defensive line and the offensive line, as they all SLAM into each other, and FALL to the ground.

CUT TO:

INT. HALLWAY - SAME

Sam walks swiftly down the hall, in a hurry. Millie calls out to him.

MILLIE
Sam!

SAM
(not stopping)
Can't talk. The Cressman Conundrum is in motion.

Millie watches him go, confused.

CUT TO:

EXT. SCHOOL - DAY

Lindsay exits the school. Ken is leaning against the wall. Lindsay sees Eli walking with a cast. She runs to him.

LINDSAY
Hey, Eli, are you okay?

ELI
I'm fine.

LINDSAY
Can I sign your cast?

ELI
No.

Eli runs off.

LINDSAY
Eli!

KEN
(To Lindsay)
Ouch.

CUT TO:

EXT. NOME DRIVE DEAD END - DAY

Neal and Bill walk up to a scary looking dead end street. Look around nervously.

BILL
Where's Sam? It's almost three o'clock. Alan's gonna be here.

NEAL
I'll bet he forgot his math book. I'm sure he'll be here.

Suddenly, Harris appears out of nowhere. Neal and Bill jump.

NEAL (cont'd)
Harris! You came to help us?

HARRIS
(shrugs)
I just came to watch. This should be exciting.

(CONTINUED)

CONTINUED:

BILL
Oh, man, where's Sam?

NEAL
Don't worry. Sam's gonna be here.

EXT. BACK OF SCHOOL - DAY

Sam pushes open the back door of the school. We HEAR the homecoming game in the distance. Sam starts to run when ...

CINDY (O.C.)
Hi, Sam.

Sam stops dead in his tracks. He turns to see Cindy in full cheerleader uniform, heading out of the girls' locker room, looking beautiful. He's immediately taken.

SAM
Hi, Cindy!

CINDY
What are you doing?

SAM
Just going home. How 'bout you?

CINDY
(indicates her cheerleading outfit)
Cheering at the game.

SAM
Well ... you're dressed for it.

They laugh together. Sam looks nervously at his watch. He's gonna be late.

CUT TO:

EXT. NOME DRIVE DEAD END - DAY

A newspaper blows down the street ominously as Neal, Bill and Harris wait for Sam and Alan.

NEAL
Where's Sam? It's three o'clock.

HARRIS
Don't let Alan hit one of your pressure points. If he does, you won't feel it right away but you'll drop dead three days later.

(CONTINUED)

CONTINUED:

BILL
My stomach hurts.

NEAL
You'll be fine.

BILL
No, it really hurts. I think I should go home. This is how Houdini died.

HARRIS
You should also guard your face. If the other guy hits you in the nose, it could drive the nose bone into your brain, then you'll crap your pants and die.

BILL
Shut up, would you!

NEAL
He's right. There are a lot of ways to die in a fight. Maybe we should put this off.

BILL
There's Sam. Hey, Sam!!! Over here!!

Bill starts waving. In the distance, a small figure on a bike appears.

NEAL
You moron, that's not Sam. It's Alan!

CUT TO:

EXT. SCHOOL - CONTINUOUS

Sam is still speaking with Cindy.

CINDY
Can you believe Mr. Samek gave us a pop quiz?

SAM
(nervously laughs)
That guy. He was a prisoner of war in Korea, so he always thinks he has to toughen us up.

CINDY
I didn't know that. Do you talk to him a lot?

SAM
(caught; trying to be cool)
Uh ... no. No way. Teachers suck.

(CONTINUED)

CONTINUED: 51

He looks at his watch. He's gonna be really late.

CUT TO:

EXT. NOME DRIVE DEAD END - CONTINUOUS

Alan pulls up. He's not sure what's going on. The geeks are trapped. Harris watches dispassionately, arms folded.

ALAN
What are you losers doing on my street?

NEAL
Nothing.

BILL
We're here to beat you up.

NEAL
Bill!

BILL
Well, we <u>are</u>.

ALAN
Oh, are you?

NEAL
He's just kidding.

Alan pushes Neal.

ALAN
I wasn't talking to you, dork.

Harris smiles and chuckles to himself. Alan turns to him.

ALAN (cont'd)
What's your problem, freaky?

HARRIS
I'm just watching.

ALAN
Yeah, well watch this.

Alan pushes Harris into Neal. They stumble back. The geeks all look at each other. Suddenly, Bill SCREAMS and jumps on Alan's back.

ALAN (cont'd)
You are so dead.

(CONTINUED)

CONTINUED:

He throws Bill off his back, but then Neal pushes Alan backwards over the fallen Bill, sending Alan to the ground.

Harris gets up, sees Alan down and goes to gingerly kick Alan in the stomach, but Alan catches his foot and throws him to the ground.

CUT TO:

EXT. SCHOOL - CONTINUOUS

Sam and Cindy are still talking.

CINDY
Well, I gotta get to the game. I'll see ya.

SAM
Yeah. See ya.

She turns to leave. Before he can think, Sam blurts out.

SAM (cont'd)
Hey, Cindy?

She turns back.

CINDY
Yeah?

SAM
Um ... do ... uh ...

CUT TO:

EXT. NOME DRIVE DEAD END - CONTINUOUS

It's a really ridiculous fight with a lot of grappling and very few punches landing effectively.

EXT. SCHOOL - CONTINUOUS

Sam takes a deep breath.

SAM
Do you want to go to the Homecoming dance with me?

CINDY
I'm already going with Dan Lewis. He asked me two weeks ago.

(CONTINUED)

CONTINUED:

SAM
Oh, okay. I just thought I'd ask in case you didn't have anyone to go with. Not that you wouldn't. It's just that my dad says the prettiest girl in the school usually doesn't have a date. Uh, you know, because most guys are afraid to ask them.

Cindy smiles, caught off guard.

CINDY
Sam, do you really think I'm the prettiest girl in school?

SAM
You were voted prettiest girl three years in a row.

CINDY
You're sweet, Sam.
(a warm smile)
Well, I'd better get back. Hey, if you're there tonight, I'll save a dance for you.

SAM
Oh, okay. That could be good. See ya.

She waves and runs back onto the field. Sam watches her go. He has a huge smile on his face. He seems both happy and relieved. He turns and runs off.

CUT TO:

EXT. NOME DRIVE DEAD END - CONTINUOUS

Finally Alan pushes a flailing Bill and Neal away. Harris is on the ground.

ALAN
Hey, knock it off! Get away from me, you psychos! You tore my shirt. You're going to buy me a new shirt.

Alan gets back on his bike.

ALAN (cont'd)
You guys are dead! Really dead!

He pedals off. Neal touches his slightly bloody nose.

(CONTINUED)

CONTINUED:

NEAL
I got punched in the nose but I'm still alive. I guess the nose bone must have missed my brain.

BILL
My stomach doesn't hurt anymore.

HARRIS
(shrugging)
Cressman Conundrum. 'Nuff said.

Sam catches up to them. He notices a few scrapes and bruises. Neal has a torn short. Bill has a bloody nose.

SAM
Did you guys fight Alan?

NEAL
No, we're into punk rock now.

SAM
I am so sorry. I was talking to Cindy.

NEAL
It's all right. You should see how he looks.

BILL
We tore his shirt.

NEAL
So, what did she say?

SAM
She's got a date. But she's saving a dance for me.

BILL
So, you're going?

SAM
Heck, yeah.

NEAL
(smiling)
You gotta go slow dance.

SAM
Definitely slow dance.
(beat)
Thanks. I'll be there for the next fight.

(CONTINUED)

CONTINUED: (2)

BILL
God, I hope there's not a next fight.

They all smile, relieved, as Neal shows off his cut arm.

NEAL
(bad English accent)
"Tis merely a flesh wound."

BILL
(bad English accent)
"You silly bastard, I cut your arm off."

NEAL
"Did not."

SAM
"You're a loony. What you gonna do, bleed on me?"

CUT TO:

INT. GYM - NIGHT

MUSIC UP: STYX "COME SAIL AWAY"

The dance is in full swing. The gym has been decorated by somebody with paper and balloons. A banner reads: "GO BIG GREENS -- WE'LL GET 'EM NEXT YEAR!" Couples dance, wallflowers congregate. Everybody's a little "dressed up," pretty awkward. Many hold slickers and rain coats.

ANGLE ON LINDSAY: Lindsay stands behind the punch bowl and the stacked cups, looking out at the crowd. She watches the scene tentatively. PULL BACK to see Millie is standing next to her, happily bopping to the music.

MILLIE
I'm really glad you got in trouble and had to be here, Lindsay.

Lindsay gives her a look. Millie shrugs.

MILLIE (cont'd)
I'm sorry but I am.

CONTINUE PULLING BACK to reveal Kim Kelly standing on the other side of Lindsay, looking beyond bored and upset.

KIM
(to Lindsay)
Man, this is lame.

(CONTINUED)

CONTINUED:

Lindsay looks surprised that Kim has acknowledged her.

LINDSAY
Yeah.

TING TING TING! Kim, Lindsay and Millie look over as we CONTINUE TO PULL BACK to reveal Nick standing next to Millie, playing the lip of the glass punch bowl with two butter knives. He feels their stares and looks at them.

NICK
What? What's up?

Kim rolls her eyes and goes back to looking bored as Lindsay gives Nick a pained smile.

ANGLE ON: Sam is winding his way through the non-dancers on the sidelines. Looking around. He sees something.

SAM'S POV: Cindy Sanders is standing around with some other girls, people-watching and talking.

ANGLE ON SAM: Sam takes a deep breath and wades into the crowd toward Cindy.

ANGLE ON LINDSAY: Lindsay is watching people dance. Mr. Rosso comes up next to her, looking guilty.

MR. ROSSO
Look, I know you're not happy about this but don't make me the bad guy here. If the worst thing in your life is somebody makes you go to a dance, then I'd say you have a pretty good life.

Lindsay looks like she wants to dismiss what Mr. Rosso said, but she can't. She thinks, then looks at the dance floor.

LINDSAY'S POV: She watches all the faces. Good-looking kids, not-so-good looking kids, kids having fun, kids not having fun.

Lindsay looks at the scene, studying the diverse crowd. She doesn't know what to think.

ANGLE ON SAM: Sam comes up to Cindy. The music is still the slow part of the Styx song.

SAM
Hey, Cindy.

CINDY
Hey, Sam.

(CONTINUED)

CONTINUED: (2)

Sam forces a nervous smile. Cindy gives him a friendly smile back. We can almost hear his heart pounding. Musters his courage.

SAM (cont'd)
Uh ... you said you'd save a dance for me and I was wondering ... uh ... can I have it now ... if you're not busy?

CINDY
I'm not busy.

She smiles and offers her hand. He takes it uncomfortably and they make their way onto the floor, through the couples entwined in the "slow dance." Sam's eyes betray the degree to which he has no clue what to do next.

Sam just keeps walking. Cindy wonders where he's headed as they reach the opposite side of the floor. They stop and turn to each other. Sam tries to figure out where his hands go.

SUDDENLY ... the song's pace abruptly changes into the FAST PACED ROCK SECTION OF "COME SAIL AWAY." Cindy smiles and starts fast dancing. Sam panics. He's spent his whole life trying to avoid the dreaded fast dance. He looks at Cindy, gorgeous and unself-conscious.

CINDY
Come on, Sam!

And though it's very clumsy, Sam starts to dance.

ANGLE ON LINDSAY: She is watching Sam. She smiles. Looks around and sees something.

LINDSAY'S POV: Eli is standing on the side, wearing an ill-fitting tuxedo and bopping his head too fast for the music, obviously with some fast song in his head. His sleeve is rolled up, exposing his cast.

ANGLE ON LINDSAY: Lindsay stares. Millie looks at her.

MILLIE
What are you thinking about, Lindsay?

LINDSAY
I think I'm gonna dance with Eli.

Lindsay starts to walk past Mr. Rosso.

LINDSAY
I'll be right back, Jeff.

(CONTINUED)

CONTINUED: (3)

MR. ROSSO (cont'd)
Uh ... Lindsay?
(she looks at him)
Maybe you should start calling me "Mr. Rosso" again.

She smiles and heads off.

Lindsay walks over to Eli. She smiles at him. He scowls at her.

Not backing down, she simply takes Eli's hand and walks him onto the dance floor. The other dancers watch them. Some point. A few laugh. Lindsay just ignores them. She stops in the center of the dance floor.

Eli won't dance. Lindsay starts dancing. Slowly, Eli smiles and begins to dance. Tentative at first, then he starts to get into it. A lot of students are watching now.

ANGLE ON: Mr Rosso sees Lindsay and Eli. He watches, suprised.

ANGLE ON KIM: She watches Lindsay and Eli, unsure. Sean is standing by her. He points and LAUGHS at Eli.

SEAN
Oh my God. Check out Eli. Oh, I wish I had a camera.

Kim punches him hard on the arm, surprising him.

SEAN (cont'd)
Ouch.

KIM
Shut up.

SEAN
What did <u>I</u> do?

Kim continues watching Lindsay and Eli, oddly touched.

ANGLE ON LINDSAY AND ELI: Eli is really into his dancing now, spinning and laughing. Lindsay watches him, her face filled with joy. She laughs and her body becomes looser, all her tensions releasing. It's the first time we've seen Lindsay look truly happy.

PAN TO-- Sam and Cindy, still dancing. Sam is starting to get the hang of this ... kinda.

(CONTINUED)

CONTINUED: (4)

Lindsay smiles at her brother. She has tears in her eyes. Happy tears. Sam smiles back, having fun, but still kind of embarrassed.

PULL AWAY and CRANE UP, looking down on the dance. And from this vantage, it seems to be one of those rare moments in high school, when everybody is having a great time.

ANGLE ON: Mr. Rosso watching the scene proudly.

MR. ROSSO
(smiling)
Some days, I've got the best job in the world.

THE END

# FREAKS AND GEEKS

"BEERS AND WEIRS"

Episode #2

Written by J. Elvis Weinstein & Judd Apatow

Directed by Jake Kasdan

I was flattered when Judd told me he wanted to use one of the ideas I pitched at a writer's audition for the first episode. When he said he and I would be writing it together, I was relieved. I knew from experience that the first episode of a new show can turn into a quagmire with everyone from the network and studio, as well as the show, trying to recapture the "magic" of the pilot that got the show picked up in the first place. Often, all of the above have different theories on what that magic is, and creative chaos can ensue. With Judd's name there beneath the title along with mine, none of it would be considered my fault. Phew! Oh yeah, and I'd never actually written an hour-long drama in my life, so entrusting the first episode solely to me would have been downright reckless.

As it turned out, there wasn't any of the aforementioned turmoil, just a bunch of people who were really excited to do something good (in television, that tends to make you feel like you're getting away with something).

Judd and I wrote the first draft of this episode fairly quickly by splitting up the writing of individual scenes (post-discussion) and then integrating them together. The first thing I wrote was the student assembly scene—beyond that, in the words of so many a government witness, I don't recall.

My initial idea about the keg of fake beer was a much more cynical thing about outing phonies who acted drunk just to be cool (based on a real-life experience). It was Judd's much sweeter notion to use it as a vehicle for Sam to save his sister. I just wanted it on the record that Judd Apatow actually injected sweetness into a situation once.

Once we began filming, since it was the first episode, this was really Jake, Paul, and Judd's baby. I was merely a nanny. As a result, I did something I rarely if ever do—I shut up, watched, and learned. I learned a ton that week...not about shutting up, I still haven't mastered that, but it was a great experience.

—J. Elvis Weinstein

FREAKS AND GEEKS

"BEERS AND WEIRS"

**CAST LIST**

LINDSAY WEIR
SAM WEIR
HAROLD WEIR
JEAN WEIR
DANIEL DESARIO
NICK ANDOPOLIS
BILL HAVERCHUCK
NEAL SCHWEIBER
KEN MILLER
KIM KELLY
MILLIE KENTNER
CINDY SANDERS
MR. ROSSO
MR. KOWCHEVSKI
MARK
HARRIS
SEAN
SARA
JOCK
GREASY LOOKING GUY
CARL
CALVIN
SHIRTLESS FREAK
BETH
POLICE OFFICE

FREAKS AND GEEKS

"BEERS AND WEIRS"

**SET LIST**

**INTERIORS:**

MCKINLEY HIGH SCHOOL
/HALLWAY
/AUDITORIUM
/CLASSROOM
/CAFETERIA
WEIR HOUSE
/DINING ROOM
/DOOR
/LIVING ROOM
/KITCHEN
/HALLWAY
/SAM'S ROOM
/PARENTS' BEDROOM
/LINDSAY'S BEDROOM
LOCAL LIQUOR/GROCERY STORE
SQUAD CAR

**EXTERIORS:**

MCKINLEY HIGH SCHOOL
/SMOKING PATIO
/NEAR THE SMOKING PATIO
/HALLWAY
/BASEBALL FIELD
RESIDENTIAL STREET
WEIR HOUSE
/FRONT YARD

TEASER

FADE IN:

INT. WEIR KITCHEN - MORNING

CLOSEUP on SKY BLUE FABRIC - We slowly pan out to see the outline of buttocks and pan out further to reveal it's HAROLD WEIR'S boxer shorts. He stands wearing them, an undershirt, and black socks while pouring himself some coffee. JEAN scrambles some eggs at the stove, SAM and LINDSAY sit at the table.

JEAN
Lindsay, how'd you like to go buy some new clothes at the mall? Those old jeans of yours are looking pretty ragged.

LINDSAY
No, thanks. I like my jeans.

SAM
Dad's the one who could use some pants.

HAROLD
(sitting down)
Who am I trying to impress? When it's your house, you can wear a tuxedo to breakfast.

Jean walks over with the pan of eggs and starts serving them to everyone.

JEAN
Oh, I called Mrs. Amendella and she's going to stay with you kids while your father and I are in Chicago.

Sam looks to Lindsay.

LINDSAY
Mom, no. We don't need a baby-sitter anymore. I can take care of Sam.

SAM
I can take care of myself.

(CONTINUED)

CONTINUED:

HAROLD
Oh, yeah, that's a great idea. I can just see you guys eating candy for breakfast and drawing pictures on the walls.

LINDSAY
How old do you think we are, Dad? I've been baby-sitting for the Kellers for two years already.

HAROLD
Yeah, but that's for <u>their</u> kids.

JEAN
I don't know. Maybe you are a little old to have a baby-sitter.
(to Harold)
Maybe they are ready.

Jean looks at Harold.

HAROLD
Fine. Mrs. Amendella makes the house smell like an old lady anyway.

JEAN
I hear Peter Lemengello is playing the closing night gala.

HAROLD
No, it's Paul Anka.

SAM
(joking)
Paul Anka. Can I come?

HAROLD
There's not a thing in the world wrong with Paul Anka. I guess you'd prefer we listened to some of that punk rock I've been reading about. You know those Sex Pistols? They spit on their audience.

JEAN
That's terrible.

(CONTINUED)

CONTINUED: (2)

HAROLD
Yeah, that's what I want to do, spend my hard earned money to be spit on. Now that's entertainment.

LINDSAY
Dad, every generation is scared of the music that comes from the next. I'm sure your parents hated Elvis.

HAROLD
Elvis didn't expectorate on his fans.

SAM
No, but he died on the toilet.

HAROLD
Well, that's paradise compared to where those Sex Pistols are gonna end up.

CUT TO:

MAIN TITLES

ACT ONE

FADE IN:

INT. HALLWAY - MORNING

Students are entering the school. It's a typical school morning. Lindsay enters. She stops and takes in the scene.

She sighs and heads in. MILLIE and a couple of SMART NERDY GIRLS are talking by the trophy case. They look over at Lindsay.

MILLIE
Hi, Lindsay.

LINDSAY
Hey.

Lindsay keeps walking. Behind her, we see the girls watching her and talking about her, concerned.

Lindsay feels their eyes on her, but doesn't turn. NICK comes out of a hallway, sees her and walks next to her.

(CONTINUED)

CONTINUED:

NICK
(depressed)
Hey, Lindsay.

LINDSAY
Hey, Nick.
(sees his demeanor)
What's the matter?

NICK
John Bonham died.

LINDSAY
Last week.

NICK
Lindsay, he's dead. There's no more Led Zeppelin.

LINDSAY
Why don't they just get a new drummer?

Nick just stares at her. She'll never understand.

NICK
Look, let's just forget it.

They head out to the smoking patio.

CUT TO:

EXT. SMOKING PATIO - CONTINUOUS

Lindsay and Nick join KIM, DANIEL and KEN.

KIM
What you do is you look for something in the store that's expensive but looks really cheap. Then you switch price tags with something really cheap. Then you put the original price tag back on and return it for credit. That's how I got this jacket. Ten bucks this thing costs me.

KEN
(mocking her jacket)
It's beautiful. Clearly worth all the effort.

(CONTINUED)

CONTINUED:

LINDSAY
My dad caught a shoplifter once. He had to lock him in the store until the cops came. He says that shoplifters cost him a fortune.

KIM
I guess poor Lindsay won't get a new car for her sixteenth birthday. However will she live?

LINDSAY
People like my dad work hard.

KIM
You think shoplifting is easy?

DANIEL
If I had a store and I caught some kid stealing, I'd just take him out back and deal with it myself.

KIM
(mocking)
Oh would you, Mr. tough man?

DANIEL
Yeah, I would, tough woman.

KIM
(mocking harder)
Oh, like the time John Ergner kicked your ass?

DANIEL
Hey, you mind flapping your lips somewhere else?

NICK
Did you guys break up or something?

Lindsay's ears perk up.

KIM
No, we didn't break up... I dumped his loser ass.

DANIEL
Is that what happened? Okay, whatever. If that makes you feel better.

(CONTINUED)

CONTINUED: (2)

NICK
(trying to change the subject)
Hey, does anyone want to see "The Wall" with me Saturday night? I'm going to try an experiment and see it straight once.

KEN
Don't do it. You'll regret it. Trust me.

LINDSAY
I can't, my parents are going out of town and I have to watch my brother.

Long pause.

DANIEL
Maybe we could all hang out at your house.

KEN/NICK
(through fake cough)
Kegger... kegger.

LINDSAY
You mean a party?

KIM
Yeah, right. Lindsay's too lame to ever let anyone enter her precious little house.

Beat.

LINDSAY
Sure. Why not? I like parties.

DANIEL
Cool.
(to Kim)
Who's the only lame one?

KIM
Up yours.

Kim storms off.

(CONTINUED)

CONTINUED: (3)

DANIEL
All right I'm gonna need ten bucks from everyone for the keg. Give it up.

Lindsay grimaces, then hesitantly looks in her purse for money.

NICK
Please, Lindsay. The house drinks free.

Nick laughs.

LINDSAY
(in too deep)
Thanks.

CUT TO:

EXT. NEAR THE SMOKING PATIO/INT. SCHOOL HALLWAY - CONT.

NEAL and BILL look at Lindsay through a window.

NEAL
Why does she hang out with those guys?

BILL
I don't know. Why don't you go over there and ask her?

NEAL
(to himself)
They're going to ruin her life. If you don't care about high school, then you won't get into a good college, then you'll have no future, and you'll wind up dead or in jail.

BILL
Really?

NEAL
Were you asleep during "Scared Straight"?

Neal looks at Lindsay, forlorn. Bill studies him.

BILL
You're in love with Lindsay.

(CONTINUED)

CONTINUED:

NEAL
No, I'm not. What are you talking about?!

BILL
Why are you getting so mad?

NEAL
I'm not!
(beat)
Why would you say that?

BILL
Because you have your book in front of your pants.

NEAL
Shut up-- jerk. I don't love her, I care about her because she's my good friend's sister.

Neal walks away.

NEAL (CONT'D)
(turns back-covering)
Maybe you should ask yourself why you don't care..

CUT TO:

INT. HALLWAY - DAY

Sam stands at his locker. Lindsay calls to him from twenty yards away.

LINDSAY
Sam.

Sam looks at Lindsay, then points to himself, not sure if she was calling to him. It is unusual for her to acknowledge his existence during school hours. Sam walks over to Lindsay.

LINDSAY (CONT'D)
Sam, I'm having a keg party tomorrow night.

SAM
You are?

LINDSAY
Yeah, so you can't tell Mom and Dad.

(CONTINUED)

CONTINUED:

SAM
What if your friends wreck our house?

LINDSAY
They're not going to wreck our house. I'll have plenty of time to clean up before Mom and Dad get back.

SAM
What if Dad finds out.

LISA
Don't worry. That's my problem.

SAM
No, it's not, 'cause he'll yell at me for not telling on you.

LINDSAY
So, are you gonna tell on me?

SAM
(long beat)
I guess not.

LINDSAY
Thanks, Sam. See you later.

She walks away.

CUT TO:

INT. SCHOOL AUDITORIUM - LATER

The seats are filled with students. On stage, HARRIS and Millie are in the middle of performing a scene. Millie holds a prop liquor bottle with three X's on it.

HARRIS
Give me your keys, man. You're drunk.

MILLIE
(acting drunk)
I'm not drunk. Get out of my way!
I'm fine!

HARRIS
No, you're not, and I'm not going to drive with you.

(CONTINUED)

CONTINUED:

MILLIE
I don't care.

HARRIS
If you try to drive now, I'm going to call the police.

MILLIE
I thought you were my friend!

CINDY SANDERS enters the scene.

CINDY
He is your friend, Daisy.

MILLIE
Who are you?

CINDY
I'm the designated driver. I made a pledge not to drink at this party so I could help people get home safe.

MILLIE
Wow, that's cool. I should have done that.

ANGLE ON: Lindsay, sitting with Daniel and Ken. Ken is fast asleep.

DANIEL
(to Lindsay, making fun)
That designated driver is pretty hot. I'd like to get her drunk.

Lindsay slaps his arm playfully. They laugh.

ONSTAGE:

CINDY
If you drive right now, you're not only a danger to yourself, you're a danger to everyone else on the road.

HARRIS
You're like a loaded gun.

(CONTINUED)

CONTINUED: (2)

MILLIE
(pretending to start to cry)
I didn't want to hurt anyone.

CINDY
We know that.

HARRIS
So what do you say? Can I have your keys?

Millie hands Harris her keys. MR. ROSSO steps in.

ROSSO
And freeze!

The actors freeze.

ROSSO (CONT'D)
Let's hear it for the "Sober Students Improv Players!"

There is an unenthusiastic smattering of applause. The actors relax.

ROSSO (CONT'D)
That was a good example of how to prevent a tragedy. But there's an even better way to save lives... and that's not to drink or do drugs in the first place.

ANGLE ON: Neal nodding to himself at this valuable information.

ROSSO (CONT'D)
Now I know what you're thinking: "Mr. Rosso, you don't understand. If I don't drink, I won't be cool!" Well, you know what I say to that? Maybe if you don't drink, you <u>will</u> be cool.

ANGLE ON: LINDSAY AND DANIEL

DANIEL
Ken's got the right idea.

Daniel puts his head down on Lindsay's shoulder.

(CONTINUED)

CONTINUED: (3)

DANIEL (CONT'D)
Wake me up when he's done talking.

He pretends to sleep. Lindsay smiles. She's digging Daniel big time.

ANGLE ON: Nick and a FREAK, who are sitting in another part of the auditorium. Nick sees Lindsay and Daniel. He looks troubled.

ON STAGE:

ROSSO
And right now our thespians, Millie, Harris and Cindy, will show you how you can stay sober and still be cool.

Millie and Harris ready themselves.

ROSSO (CONT'D)
OK, what I need from you people is a kind of party where drinking might occur.

The audience is silent for a beat, then:

JOCK
A sex party!

The audience bursts out laughing. The group of jocks surrounding him go nuts.

ANGLE ON: Sam, Bill, and Neil laughing.

ROSSO
All right, I think I heard someone say "birthday party."

Harris and Millie huddle up.

ROSSO (CONT'D)
OK, you're at a birthday party, and... go.

MILLIE
Hi, Bob, Happy Birthday! Here's your present.

She mimes handing him a box which he mimes taking.

(CONTINUED)

CONTINUED: (4)

HARRIS
Thanks, Mary. Would you like a beer? Everybody's having one.

MILLIE
No, thank you. I prefer to get high on life.

HARRIS
Wow, that's cool. I think I'm not going to drink either.

MILLIE
I knew you'd make the right choice.

HARRIS
This is the best birthday ever.

MILLIE
Come on, let's get a glass of pop.

HARRIS
I hope they have orange.

MILLIE
Hey, it's a party, isn't it?

They both laugh.

ANGLE ON: LINDSAY AND DANIEL

DANIEL
I can't take any more of this. You wanna get out of here?

LINDSAY
Sure.

DANIEL
I'll go first. You count to ten, then come.

Daniel gets up and walks out. Lindsay turns to watch for a second then fixes her hair.

ON STAGE:

ROSSO
And freeze. As you can see, nothing is more contagious than good judgement. Jimmy, lights. But if you still think drinking is cool...

(CONTINUED)

CONTINUED: (5)

The LIGHTS GO DOWN. Lindsay leaves. The image of a pretty girl comes up on a screen.

ROSSO (CONT'D)
Why not ask Jenny Powell if drinking is cool. Oh, that's right, you can't ask her... because she crashed into a phone pole this winter driving drunk after a New Years party.

CLOSE-UP on Sam who is very spooked by this.

Another FACE comes on screen.

ROSSO (CONT'D)
And you can't ask John Yablonsky either. He died from alcohol poisoning at a fraternity party.

CLOSE-UP on Neal who is very spooked by this. PAN OVER to Bill who is reading a comic book, smiling.

Another FACE

ROSSO (CONT'D)
Or Kenny Blake who overdosed...

Sam is terrified. He and Neal exchange concerned looks.

CUT TO:

INT. HALLWAY - DAY

Lindsay and Daniel walk through the deserted hallway as WE HEAR the assembly echoing in the auditorium. Lindsay's clearly nervous but a little excited.

LINDSAY
Pretty lame assembly, huh?

DANIEL
Yeah, I love being told not to drink by a pothead guidance counselor.

LINDSAY
There's probably a bar in the teacher's lounge.

(CONTINUED)

CONTINUED:

DANIEL
Probably. Hey, I hope you don't mind, I invited my cousin and a couple of his friends to the party.

LINDSAY
That's cool. What grade are they in?

DANIEL
No grade. They're older.

LINDSAY
(suddenly scared)
Oh. Okay.

CUT TO:

INT. HALLWAY - LATER

Sam, Neal and Bill are standing at their lockers, deep in conversation.

NEAL
(very serious)
We gotta do something about your sister's party.

BILL
What's the big deal? It's just beer.

NEAL
Yeah, beer at a freak party. My cousin's friend was at a freak party, and someone put angel-dust in her drink.

SAM
(haunted)
Oh, man.

NEAL
We can't stop the party. But if we go, we can try to contain it.

BILL
I can't come, "Dallas" is on.

(CONTINUED)

CONTINUED: (2)

NEAL
What? "Dallas" sucks.

BILL
Hey, you suck! "Dallas" rules!

SAM
So, you're just going to let Lindsay end up like one of those pictures?

Sam and Neal walk away. Bill calls after them.

BILL
Fine I'll go... but I'm watching "Dallas" there.

Two girls walk by. They stifle a laugh.

BILL (CONT'D)
I'm just kidding with 'em.

Bill follows after.

FADE OUT.

END OF ACT ONE

ACT TWO

FADE IN:

INT. PARENTS' BEDROOM/WEIR HALLWAY/FRONT DOOR - DAY

Harold is scurrying around, rushing to leave. Sam follows, trying to look responsible. As Harold picks up his bags, we follow him through the hallway to the front door.

HAROLD
Now if the hot water heater makes that noise, call the gas company. I don't want to come home to a couple of dead kids. There's fifty bucks on the dining room table. That should be enough. Lindsay's in charge of it. And it's not for "Star Wars" cards or those... goofy packs.

SAM
"Wacky Packs."

(CONTINUED)

CONTINUED:

HAROLD
Whatever. Don't blow it.

Lindsay is listening in the living room. When Jean calls to her, we follow her into the kitchen.

INT. WEIR KITCHEN - CONTINUOUS

Jean is showing Lindsay a stack of frozen tupperware dishes.

JEAN
Lindsay, come here. This is dinner for Friday, this is lunch and dinner for Saturday. If you need anything else, Dad left fifty dollars on the dining room table.

ANGLE ON: HAROLD AND SAM

Sam looks at Lindsay, then at his parents. He looks like he wants to spill the beans.

HAROLD
All right. Let's go.

Jean and Lindsay walk to the front door.

HAROLD (CONT'D)
I want to get there before the welcome mixer.

SAM
Wait!

HAROLD
What is it?

Sam considers telling on Lindsay. She glares at him.

SAM
Uh... have a good trip.

HAROLD
Thanks. We'll be back Sunday night. Don't do anything stupid.
(he turns to the door, then back)
And turn off the lights when you go out. I'm not made of money.

(CONTINUED)

CONTINUED:

JEAN
Bye-bye kids, I love you.

They exit. When the door shuts, Lindsay runs into the living room, excited. She immediately turns on the stereo.

80's rock sound alike STARTS TO PLAY. Lindsay bops around in a good mood. Sam follows behind her like a puppy dog.

SAM
At assembly today, they did these improvisations about drinking and driving. It was pretty funny.

LINDSAY
I saw, that's why I left.

SAM
At assembly today, they showed these pictures of these kids who died in drunk driving accidents. Did you know those kids?

LINDSAY
No.

SAM
Their mom talked. She was pretty sad. It kind of freaked everybody out.
(long beat)
Oh, at assembly today, they said that if you drink too much in one night you can die from alcohol poisoning. It happened to this guy.

LINDSAY
Sam, you sound like Dad.

She sits down and turns on the TV. Sam stands in front of her.

SAM
I just don't know why you have to have beer at your party. You've never had beers at any of your other parties and they were fun.

LINDSAY
Those were birthday parties, Sam. We went bowling.

(CONTINUED)

CONTINUED: (2)

SAM
Remember that party where you had the magician? That was fun. Why can't you have a magician?

LINDSAY
Why am I talking to you? I'm in charge... leave me alone.

She gets up and walks away.

SAM
Leave me alone.

CUT TO:

INT. CLASSROOM - THE NEXT DAY

Lindsay is sitting in Trigonometry class looking preoccupied. She is listening to MR. KOWCHEVSKI, who is lecturing at the blackboard.

KOWCHEVSKI
Come on, people, do I need a jackhammer to get this into your brains? We covered this on Monday. Let's do it -- again...

As Mr. Kowchevski writes on the board, Lindsay senses someone looking at her. She looks a couple rows over.

ANGLE ON: TWO UNSAVORY LOOKING FREAKS smiling at her. They give her a thumbs up and mouth the words "PAR-TAY." Lindsay forces a smile, then looks away, concerned.

KOWCHEVSKI (CONT'D)
Y equals the cosine of X. Now let's graph it.

There's a knock at the door. Kowchevski looks bugged and goes to the door. A student, SARA, stands there with a note from the principal's office.

SARA
There's an emergency phone call for Lindsay Weir. It's her mom.

Lindsay hears this. She pales. The class looks at her.

KOWCHEVSKI
(concerned; kind)
Oh, sure, okay. Lindsay, go ahead.

(CONTINUED)

CONTINUED:

A very worried-looking Lindsay gathers up her stuff and exits the class.

CUT TO:

INT. HALLWAY - CONTINUOUS

Lindsay comes out of class. Sara's heading down the hall.

LINDSAY
(quite concerned)
Do you know what's wrong?

Sara motions her to come with her. Lindsay follows, almost running. She looks very scared about the phone call.

Sara and Lindsay round a corner. Nick is standing there. Lindsay looks more than surprised to see him.

NICK
Hey, Lindsay, what's up?

LINDSAY
I've gotta get to the office. There's some emergency with my parents.

Nick cracks a smile.

NICK
Yeah, I know. They want you to come with them to buy a keg.

LINDSAY
What?

Sara and Nick smile. Lindsay's confused.

NICK
Hey, thanks, Sara.

SARA
I'll see ya' at the party tonight.

Sara exits.

NICK
We're cutting. Daniel's paying his older brother twenty bucks to buy us a keg. Everyone's waiting at the car.

(CONTINUED)

CONTINUED:

LINDSAY
(completely thrown)
Oh, uh... yeah. All right.

NICK
You okay?

LINDSAY
(no)
Yeah. It's just that whole emergency phone call thing... I'm fine.
(forcing enthusiasm)
Let's go get us some beer.

Nick laughs. They head off down the hall.

CUT TO:

INT. CAFETERIA - DAY

Sam, Neal and Bill are eating lunch. Mr. Kowchevski roams the cafeteria.

BILL
Maybe you could call your parents and tell them you fell and hit your head and have them come home before the party.

SAM
Then what happens when they come home and see my head is fine.

BILL
Well... we'd have to hit your head and give you a bump.

NEAL
Like in that Dirty Harry movie where the bad guy yells at this black guy so he'll beat him up, then he blames it on Clint.
(doing impression)
"It was Callahan!"

SAM
I'm not going to let you guys hit me.

They sit in silence for a long time, contemplating their options.

(CONTINUED)

CONTINUED:

BILL
Hey, guys. Whenever my uncle visits my mom gives him non-alcoholic beer so he won't get all drunk and yell at everyone.

SAM
What's non-alcoholic beer?

BILL
It's like beer, but it doesn't have that ingredient that makes you drunk.

NEAL
Alcohol?

BILL
Yeah, that's it.

SAM
That's a great idea!
(realizing)
Oh, but we'd have to buy a whole keg of it.

NEAL
That's going to be expensive.

SAM
I don't have any money.

NEAL
I don't either.

BILL
Yes, you do.

NEAL
No, no way.

SAM
Why not?

NEAL
That's my Bar Mitzvah money.

SAM
Come on, this is important.

(CONTINUED)

CONTINUED: (2)

NEAL
Every time you guys have a problem you want to dip into my Bar Mitzvah money. It's not like I get to have another one.

Sam looks at him with a pleading stare.

BILL
(mocking Neal)
Come on, for Lindsay?

NEAL
(long beat; then)
Fine.

BILL
Mazel Tov.

NEAL
Oh, shut up.

INT. LOCAL LIQUOR/GROCERY STORE - DAY

Sam, Neal and Bill enter. They look at the vast wall of different booze bottles behind the counter.

SAM
What if somebody robs this place while we're in here? People are always getting shot in liquor stores.

BILL
Do ya think they sell Yoohoo here? I'm thirsty.

NEAL
Yeah, ask the guy. Maybe he can change your diaper too.

BILL
That was unnecessary.

They walk to the counter. There is a GREASY LOOKING GUY behind the counter.

SAM
Hi.

GREASY LOOKING GUY
We're outta Pop Rocks.

(CONTINUED)

CONTINUED:

SAM
Um, a keg of beer please.

GREASY LOOKING GUY
(sarcastic)
I don't see that happening, little fella.

NEAL
(cocky)
We'd like non-alcoholic beer.

GREASY LOOKING GUY
I can't give you that.

BILL
Why not? There's not any alcohol in it.

GREASY LOOKING GUY
I don't know, somehow I'll get in trouble.

SAM
Please. We really need it.

GREASY LOOKING GUY
What for?

BILL
We're gonna switch the keg at his sister's party.

The guy soaks this in, then bursts out LAUGHING.

GREASY LOOKING GUY
That's awesome.

CUT TO:

EXT. RESIDENTIAL STREET - DAY

Sam, Neal and Bill are pulling the keg home in a child's red wagon.

SAM
Bill, put your jacket over it so if someone drives by they can't see it.

Bill takes off his jacket and covers the keg.

(CONTINUED)

CONTINUED:

NEAL
I hope this thing doesn't explode. Isn't there a less bumpy road?

SAM
Why would it explode?

NEAL
'Cause it's filled with compressed air. If we hit a pot hole, we're dead men.

They all stop, look at each other terrified, then start to push the wagon really, really slowly, as if transporting a bomb.

BILL
Sam, is your sister really worth all this?

FADE OUT.

END OF ACT TWO

ACT THREE

FADE IN:

INT. WEIR LIVING ROOM - DAY

MUSIC UP: FOGHAT'S "SLOW RIDE"

The KEG is sitting in the corner of the living room. Lindsay sets a bunch of bags that read "THE ROCK SHOP" on the coffee table. A bunch of rolled-up posters stick out of one of the bags. Lindsay pulls one out and unrolls it.

It's a blacklight poster of a rock and roll-style unicorn. Trippy looking but really lame. Lindsay puts it flat on the ground, steps back and stares at it. She wrinkles her nose, unsure.

ANGLE ON: The geeks are peeking around the corner from the hallway as Lindsay turns and goes into the kitchen.

SAM
How are we gonna get the real keg into my room without Lindsay knowing?

(CONTINUED)

CONTINUED:

NEAL
I'll distract her while you and Bill switch the kegs.

BILL
I'm tired of moving this stupid keg. Let me distract her.

NEAL
(intensely)
I'm distracting her.

SAM
C'mon, hurry up.

NEAL
I'm goin' in.

Neal quickly checks his breath with a cupped-hand-sniff test and heads to the kitchen. Sam and Bill scamper to the keg.

CUT TO:

INT. WEIR KITCHEN - CONTINUOUS

Lindsay is pouring bags of chips into bowls. Neal enters.

NEAL
Hi, Lindsay.

LINDSAY
What are you doing here?

NEAL
Sam, Bill and I are just hanging out.
(grabs the bag of chips)
Oh, please. Allow me.

He opens the bag of chips with a smile.

CUT TO:

INT. WEIR LIVING ROOM - CONTINUOUS

Sam and Bill are having a hard time moving the keg. It is standing face up. They try to roll it on its bottom edge but it keeps pulling to the right.

SAM
C'mon. Push.

(CONTINUED)

CONTINUED:

BILL
I am pushing. It's heavy.

SAM
Careful! Watch my foot.

BILL
Hey, it's your foot. You can watch it too, you know.
(beat)
Ow, ow, ow! Hey, that's my foot!

CUT TO:

INT. WEIR KITCHEN - DAY

NEAL
So, what kind of music are you gonna play tonight? You should play some Chicago. They have a really hot horn section.

LINDSAY
I don't know. I think I'm gonna play some Zeppelin, Foghat, maybe some Sabbath.

NEAL
(joking)
Friday Night, always a good night for some Sabbath.
(no response from Lindsay)
'Cause Friday night... is the Sabbath-- for Jews.

Neal makes the universal symbol for "ta da." Lindsay just rolls her eyes and heads to the fridge.

NEAL (CONT'D)
(loosens his collar)
So, what else do you have to eat?

CUT TO:

INT. WEIR HALLWAY - DAY

The boys are struggling to carry the real keg down the hall.

SAM
You think Neal's okay?

(CONTINUED)

CONTINUED:

BILL
Oh, he's having a great time.

SAM
Why?

BILL
'Cause he's in love with your sister.

SAM
What?!

Sam drops his end. THUD!!!

CUT TO:

INT. WEIR KITCHEN - CONTINUOUS

Lindsay is cutting cheese. She hears the noise. Neal panics. He COUGHS loudly to cover the thud.

LINDSAY
(calling out)
Sam! What was that?

CUT TO:

INT. WEIR HALLWAY - CONTINUOUS

SAM
(calling back)
Uh, nothing. Bill fell.

CUT TO:

INT. WEIR KITCHEN - CONTINUOUS

LINDSAY
Figures.

NEAL
Yeah, I hear you. He certainly is a Clumsy Claude, that Bill.

LINDSAY
Don't you want to go play with those guys?

NEAL
No, I like talking to you.

(CONTINUED)

CONTINUED:

Neal gives her a trying too-hard smile. She stifles a laugh and goes back to cutting cheese. Neal gives himself a little celebratory fist pump. He's in.

CUT TO:

INT. WEIR LIVING ROOM - DAY

Sam and Bill are really struggling as they move the nonalcoholic keg back into the living room.

BILL
Hey, if Neal marries your sister, he'll be your brother-in-law. And if you have kids, Neal would be their Uncle Neal. And I bet Lindsay's kids will look like Neal.

SAM
Bill, shut up! He doesn't love Lindsay.

BILL
That's not what he told me.

THUD! They drop the non-alcoholic keg where the other keg used to be.

CUT TO:

INT. WEIR KITCHEN - DAY

Lindsay looks up, bugged.

NEAL
I think Bill's got an ear infection. It's messing with his equilibrium.

Neal peeks into the living room and sees the guys are still working, pushing the keg into position. He turns back to see Lindsay heading toward him to go to the living room.

NEAL
Uh, I think you need more M&M's!

LINDSAY
I don't have any more.

NEAL
No, I saw some over here. Look.

(CONTINUED)

CONTINUED:

Neal ushers her back to the other side of the kitchen. She looks ready to kill him.

CUT TO:

INT. WEIR LIVING ROOM - DAY

Sam and Bill give the final push to get the new keg in place. Bill's hand slips and hits the spigot, causing beer to spray out onto the front of his pants.

BILL
Oh, no.

LINDSAY (O.C.)
I told you we were out of M&Ms. Now get out of my way.

Lindsay comes into the living room. Sam and Bill jump and face her. Bill has a huge wet beer stain down the front of his pants.

LINDSAY (CONT'D)
What are you guys d--?

Lindsay sees Bill's wet stain. This makes Sam and Neal look at it too. Bill gets self-conscious.

BILL
Uh... it's...

LINDSAY
You don't have to explain. Neil told me.
(points to her ear)
Well, help him. Give him something to wear.

The Geeks exit quickly.

BILL
What did you tell her?

Lindsay watches them go, completely grossed out. She shakes her head and gets back to work.

DISSOLVE TO:

INT. WEIR LIVING ROOM - NIGHT

MUSIC UP: TED NUGENT'S "FREE FOR ALL" BLARES

(CONTINUED)

CONTINUED:

ANGLE ON: The front door. DING DONG! Lindsay walks up to the front door and opens it, revealing Daniel, Nick and Ken. They are the first to arrive. They walk into the living room.

FREAKS' POV: Lindsay stands there looking very excited. Behind her, the Weir living room looks like a head shop. Black light "rock and roll" posters (not really bands but goofy rock images) hang everywhere. A lava lamp sits on the coffee table.

LINDSAY
Hi! What do you think?

The freaks walk in and look around.

KEN
What do you think we are? Hippies?

NICK
Shut up, man.
(to Lindsay)
I think it looks great.

DANIEL
(smiles)
Yeah, it's... pretty cool.
(looks at a poster)
I like that Unicorn.

Lindsay looks a little embarrassed.

LINDSAY
It's just that our house is so boring looking. I thought I'd try to make it a little more party-like.

Ken turns down the stereo volume a bit.

KEN
I'll tell you how to make it more party-like. Point me to the keg.

LINDSAY
Oh. It's in the corner.

KEN
Then I am in the corner.

Ken and Nick head over.

(CONTINUED)

CONTINUED: (2)

DANIEL
(to Lindsay)
Don't be nervous. This party's gonna rock.

LINDSAY
Thanks.

DANIEL
Is this the main room?

LINDSAY
Yeah, why?

DANIEL
It's probably big enough. Word's getting around.

He walks off. Lindsay looks nervous.

CUT TO:

INT. SAM'S ROOM - NIGHT

Bill is watching TV. The real keg is in the closet. Neal is covering it with clothes just in case anyone looks in the closet. Sam enters.

SAM
People are here.

NEAL
All right. It's going down.

BILL
You're standing in front of the TV.

Neal moves. As Sam speaks, Bill's eyes never leave the TV.

NEAL
What do you think is gonna happen?

SAM
Hopefully, everybody's gonna drink a bunch of fake beer, have to pee a lot and then go home 'cause they're bored.

NEAL
This is genius.

(CONTINUED)

CONTINUED:

BILL
(to himself)
It was my idea. I'm the genius.

SAM
Here's the plan. Bill, you guard the keg. Neal and I will patrol the party.

NEAL
I'll keep an eye on Lindsay.

Sam rolls his eyes, then Sam and Neal exit. Bill gets up and turns up the volume. We hear the theme to "The Dukes of Hazard." Bill, the genius, smiles.

CUT TO:

INT. WEIR LIVING ROOM - NIGHT

MUSIC UP: FOGHAT'S "SHE'S MY BABY"

More freaks are entering the party. Others are in the living room, some laying around, others talking and laughing. They're all drinking the fake beer. Neal walks by MARK and SEAN who are sipping their beers.

MARK
This beer sucks.
(to the other freak)
Does this beer taste weird to you?

NEAL
It's imported. Nothing's too good for our friends.

Neal exits.

SEAN
Daniel probably bought cheap beer and kept the extra cash.

MARK
Definitely.

ANGLE ON: SAM is walking nervously through the freaks. A group of freaks is standing by the wall, holding a family portrait of the Weirs and laughing.

(CONTINUED)

CONTINUED:

SEAN
Look at that old guy! He must be wasted. His eyes look like ping pong balls.

Sam comes up to them and takes the frame.

SAM
Hey, shut up! That's my dad.

The freaks look at Sam, confused.

CUT TO:

INT. WEIR LIVING ROOM - CONTINUOUS

Millie walks in. She looks uncomfortable. Lindsay sees her and walks over to her.

LINDSAY
Millie. Hi.

MILLIE
I saw all the cars in front of your house.

LINDSAY
Yeah, we're kind of just hanging out.

MILLIE
You missed a pop quiz in chemistry today.

LINDSAY
I did? Really?

MILLIE
Yeah, were you skipping out with your new friends? Or should I call them "drinking buddies."

LINDSAY
Millie.

MILLIE
(re: party)
Why are you doing this Lindsay? You're asking for trouble.

Sean comes up to Millie with a beer.

(CONTINUED)

CONTINUED:

SEAN
Hey, do you want a beer?

MILLIE
No, thank you. I prefer to get high on life.

SEAN
Whoa! You're that chick from that thing yesterday. Would you give me a ride home?

MILLIE
Yes, I would.

SEAN
(imitating her)
"Yes I would !"

He laughs and rushes away.

MILLIE
Why is that so funny?

LINDSAY
Millie, I gotta get back to the party. Do you want to stay?

SFX: DOORBELL

Lindsay walks to the front door.

CUT TO:

EXT. WEIR HOUSE - NIGHT

A FREAK enters the house as a car SCREECHES to a halt at the end of the driveway. Lindsay steps outside onto the porch (Millie follows), just in time to spot--

Four OLDER FREAKS coming up the driveway, three: DEZ, JIMMY, and TODD are in their mid twenties, CARL is forty. Lindsay's never seen them before.

LINDSAY
(confused)
Uh, Hi. Can I help you?

JIMMY
(looking Lindsay up and down)
No doubt.

(CONTINUED)

CONTINUED: (2)

CARL
We're friends of Daniel's.

Then Kim approaches from behind them, just arriving.

KIM
Hey, Jimmy.

JIMMY
Hey, sweet cheeks. Where's your boy?

KIM
Hopefully under a truck. I dumped his ass.

CARL
That means you're available.

The forty year old freak, CARL, grabs Kim and throws her over his shoulder.

JIMMY
No way, old man. She's mine!

He slaps her ass as he carries her into the party.

CARL
Come on, boys. Let's move. I've got to use the can.

Kim shrieks with laughter. The older freaks follow, making a lot of noise.

Millie looks at Lindsay in horror. Lindsay is full of dread.

MILLIE
Who are those guys?

LINDSAY
They're... my guests.

A freak carrying two beers walks by. Lindsay grabs one of the beers and chugs it down.

FADE OUT.

END OF ACT THREE

ACT FOUR

FADE IN:

INT. WEIR KITCHEN - LATER

MUSIC UP:

CONTINUOUS STEADY CAM SHOT - "GOODFELLAS" STYLE

We are looking at a full cup of beer being held on a kitchen table full of empty beer cups. The cup is lifted up.

VOICES (O.C.)
GO, GO, GO, GO...

PULL BACK to reveal Lindsay raising the cup and downing it. CONTINUE PULLING BACK to reveal she is having a drinking contest with Ken. They're surrounded by cheering freaks.

Lindsay finishes hers and slams it down. She BELCHES loudly. She's a bit of a mess. Ken slams his down and grabs for another full cup. Lindsay stands up, "drunk."

LINDSAY
Oh, man, I gotta pee.

KEN
I'll consider that a forfeit. Who dares to be the next challenger?

Lindsay gets up and stumbles out of the kitchen. We FOLLOW her toward the living room. She walks past Nick and CALVIN, a black freak. Calvin is downing a beer.

CALVIN
(finishing proudly)
I've had five beers already and I'm not even buzzed.

NICK
You are the MAN!

MILLIE
(coming up to them)
I haven't had any and I'm sailin'. I'm having way more fun than any of you.

Lindsay winces to herself at Millie. The freaks get weirded out and move away as Millie smiles proudly.

(CONTINUED)

CONTINUED:

We CONTINUE with Lindsay as she walks past Harris, who is about to attempt to shot-gun a beer. Mark walks up to Harris.

MARK
I thought you were a sober student.

HARRIS
I just do that cause it looks good on my transcript for college.

He starts to shot-gun the beer, but can't do it, and winds up spitting up all the beer and choking.

Lindsay walks on through the living room. The party is in full swing. There are about twenty five people in the living room, all with near-beers in their hands, in various stages of "drunk."

She walks past an older, SHIRTLESS FREAK who is holding a beer and dancing around drunkenly with his shirt off, making his stomach do waves like a hula dancer as his friends watch and laugh.

SHIRTLESS FREAK
WOOOOOOOOO!!!

Lindsay recoils from the "wooo" in her ear. She walks past Sam and Neal. We stay on Sam and Neal. Sam looks astonished.

SAM
Are you sure we put out the right keg?

NEAL
It worked even better than we wanted. They really think they're drunk.

SAM
You think so?

NEAL
Look at them. They're wasted. That's the placebo effect working for you my friend. Check out that Ken guy.

They look at an apparently drunken Ken, who is attempting to eat one of Jean's frozen dinners. He chops at the frozen meal with a fork.

SAM
What if they trash the house 'cause they think they're drunk?

(CONTINUED)

CONTINUED: (2)

NEAL
They won't.
(beat)
I don't think.

SAM
This could be bad.

They watch in amazement.

CUT TO:

INT. SAM'S ROOM - NIGHT

MUSIC UP: THEME TO "DUKES OF HAZARD"

BILL is sitting next to the keg, totally engrossed in television. We hear banjo music and hooting and hollering. "Yee-haaa!!"

Bill looks at the keg, then back at the T.V.

Bill picks up the pump and very hesitantly licks it with the tip of his tongue. He looks like a child tasting a new type of vegetable.

CUT TO:

INT. WEIR LIVING ROOM - NIGHT

Sam is taking a bunch of nick nacks off of a shelf. He takes the items and walks into his parents' room.

CUT TO:

INT. PARENTS' BEDROOM - NIGHT

Sam walks in the room with the nick nacks. We see the room is filled with the many objects that Sam is worried will get broken.

CUT TO:

INT. LINDSAY'S BEDROOM - NIGHT

Through Lindsay's bedroom doorway, we SEE her walking back from the bathroom. She stops when she notices something in her room.

PULL BACK TO REVEAL Daniel is standing in her room, looking at her loaded trophy shelf. Lindsay comes in.

(CONTINUED)

CONTINUED:

LINDSAY
Hey, Daniel. What're you doing?

DANIEL
Just looking at all this stuff. How old are you here?

He shows her a photograph.

LINDSAY
I was twelve. I was so geeky.

DANIEL
You win a lot, don't you?

LINDSAY
(embarrassed)
I guess... I've been meaning to put those in the basement.

DANIEL
(reading one of the trophies)
"First Place - Algebra Division." Oh that's right, you're one of those...

LINDSAY
Mathletes. I know, it's pretty stupid. I don't do it anymore.

DANIEL
What's so stupid about it?
(pointing to a picture of her)
You look pretty happy here.

Daniel gives Lindsay a big smile. Lindsay blushes. There's a nice moment of connection between them.

DANIEL (CONT'D)
Hey, if I won a blue ribbon I'd be pretty pumped. I wouldn't wear it around or anything, but...

Lindsay laughs, and the two smile at each other.

CUT TO:

INT. SAM'S ROOM - NIGHT

Bill is drinking beer directly from the tap. He looks around and sees a little plastic baseball helmet with some change in it. He dumps out the change.

Bill puts the plastic helmet up to the tap and squirts a beer into it. Bill drinks, then takes a breath. He has a beer mustache.

CUT TO:

INT. WEIR LIVING ROOM - NIGHT

The freaks are all hanging out having a mellow, fun time. Millie walks into the room. She sits down at the piano and begins to play.

NICK
Who's that?

KIM
Oh, no. That's the chick from the assembly.

DANIEL AND LINDSAY take a seat.

DANIEL
Check it out.

Lindsay turns and sees Millie. She looks embarrassed.

Kim is talking with an older freak. She looks over and sees Daniel with Lindsay. She doesn't look pleased.

ON MILLIE

WE begin to recognize the song. It is the DOOBIE BROTHER'S SONG "JESUS IS JUST ALRIGHT."

MILLIE
(sings)
Jesus is just alright with me.
Jesus is just alright, oh yeah.
Jesus is just alright with me.
Jesus is just alright.

Lindsay covers her eyes in embarrassment. Millie begins to really get into it.

(CONTINUED)

CONTINUED:

MILLIE (CONT'D)
I don't care what they may say. I don't care what they may do. I don't care what they may say. Jesus is just alright.

The freaks don't know what to make of it. Nick thinks it's cool. When she starts the next verse he walks to the piano and starts singing with her and drumming on the piano.

NICK/MILLIE
Jesus is just alright with me.
Jesus is just alright, oh yeah.
Jesus is just alright with me.
Jesus is just alright.

Everyone laughs and has a good time. On the next verse, Nick just scats the "do-do-do-doos" of the melody as Millie plays piano. Everyone claps and cheers.

ANGLE ON: SAM AND KEN

Ken looks like he is about to pass out. Sam takes this moment to ask him a few questions.

SAM
Hey, Ken.

KEN
Hey.

SAM
Have you ever killed a guy?

KEN
No.

SAM
Ever commit a felony?

KEN
Several.

SAM
Do you guys like my sister?

KEN
Sure.

SAM
Will you make sure she doesn't get in too much trouble?

(CONTINUED)

CONTINUED: (2)

KEN
Okay.

SAM
Thanks.

KEN
(after a beat)
Who's your sister? She's not that chick who's singing, is she?

SAM
No.

KEN
Good.

CUT TO:

INT. SAM'S ROOM - NIGHT

Bill is now drunk. He is drinking from a full helmet now. He laughs as he watches T.V.

FEMALE VOICE ON T.V. (V.O.)
I can't live like this anymore, J.R.! I can't go on with this lie!

BILL
(slurring)
You better be careful, J.R., or you're gonna get shot again.

SFX: THE PHONE RINGS.

Bill looks for a phone, but there isn't one in the room.

CUT TO:

INT. HALLWAY - CONT.

Bill walks down the hall looking for a phone.

CUT TO:

INT. PARENTS BEDROOM - NIGHT

Bill walks in the room, sits on the bed, then answers the phone.

(CONTINUED)

CONTINUED:

BILL
(into the phone)
J.R. Ewing.
(beat)
No, I'm just joking, Mrs. Weir. It's Bill! I'm sleeping over. How are you?
(beat)
I'm having a truly wonderful... Thank you for asking.
(beat)
Sam? He's around here somewhere. May I tell you something? You guys are doing a great job raising him.
(beat)
I only say it 'cause I mean it. I love that kid. I really love him. Really.
(beat)
Hold on, I'll get him.

CUT TO:

INT. LIVING ROOM - NIGHT

One of the Older Freaks, CARL, accidentally spills beer on Ken.

KEN
(stands up)
Hey!

Ken, who is wet with near beer is squared off with Carl. Lindsay is looking on in horror.

KEN (CONT'D)
Come on! Let's go!

CARL
You feel froggy then leap, Junior!

KEN
(moving in)
I'll frog all over your butt, old man.

Carl shoves Ken backwards. He stumbles and is about to fall on the Glass coffee table. Daniel swoops in and catches Ken. Lindsay's terror turns to relief. Ken starts to lunge towards Carl. Daniel changes his grip on Ken and subdues him with a sleeper hold (arms around his head).

(CONTINUED)

CONTINUED:

DANIEL
(with authority)
Not here man! Be cool.

Ken tries to squirm free, Daniel tightens the hold.

DANIEL (CONT'D)
Be cool!

Ken calms down.

KEN
All right, I'm cool, let go of my head.

Daniel cautiously lets go. There is a moment of tension.

DANIEL
OK, are we cool?

KEN
Yeah.

CARL
Whatever.

DANIEL
Let's see it.

Ken and the Carl hug each other, each slapping each other on the back as they do. Lindsay walks over to Daniel.

LINDSAY
Thanks, Daniel.

DANIEL
What, am I gonna let them trash your house? Then we couldn't party here tomorrow night.

He laughs.

LINDSAY
(in love)
What... what's the deal with you?

DANIEL
The deal? I don't know. I'm just a dirtbag.

(CONTINUED)

CONTINUED: (2)

ANGLE ON: SAM

Bill walks over to Sam.

BILL
Wcw, this party sure is rockin'.

SAM
I wonder what time everyone will leave.

There is a long silence.

SAM (CONT'D)
Aren't you supposed to be guarding the keg?

BILL
Oh, yeah. Your mom is on the phone.

SAM
What? Why didn't you tell me?

BILL
I just... spaced.

Sam runs off. Bill stares at a woman as she-walks-by.

BILL (CONT'D)
(to the woman)
Hello there, sexy lady.

She just walks by.

ANGLE ON: LINDSAY AND DANIEL TALKING

Sam walks over.

SAM
Lindsay.

LINDSAY
Leave me alone.

SAM
Mom is on the phone.

LINDSAY
(to Daniel)
I'm sorry. I'll be right back.

(CONTINUED)

CONTINUED: (3)

DANIEL
(smiles)
I'm not going anywhere.

Lindsay smiles, then exits.

CUT TO:

INT. WEIR KITCHEN - NIGHT

Neal is speaking with Calvin.

NEAL
What are you talking about? You're one of the most popular kids in school!

CALVIN
That's why it's reverse discrimination. I'm like a novelty to every one.

NEAL
I could live with that.

CALVIN
You don't want to trade places with me, believe me.

NEAL
Well, I'm Jewish. That's no cake walk either. I was elected school treasurer last year and I didn't even run.

CALVIN
We were kidnapped from our homeland and brought here to be slaves.

NEAL
We were slaves, too. My people built the pyramids.

CALVIN
But that was like three thousand years ago.

NEAL
That don't make the bricks any lighter.

(CONTINUED)

CONTINUED:

CALVIN
That's true, it doesn't.

Calvin cracks up. Neal joins him.

CUT TO:

INT. PARENTS' BEDROOM- NIGHT

Lindsay talks to her parents.

LINDSAY
(into the phone)
No, we're just hanging out.
(beat)
I'm just tired. No, he's in the other room watching T.V. with his friends.
(beat)
I know, but I didn't want to bother you, and he begged me to let them sleep over.
(beat)
Okay, well have fun.

CUT TO:

INT. WEIR LIVING ROOM - NIGHT

Sam walks up to Sean, who is sitting on the glass coffee table.

SAM
Uh, could you not sit on there please? It's glass.

SEAN
(getting up)
Sorry, man.

There is a KNOCK at the door. Sam goes to answer it. As soon as he leaves, the freak sits back down on the table.

ANGLE ON: FRONT DOOR

Sam opens the door. It's CINDY SANDERS and her older, pretty, large-breasted cousin BETH.

CINDY
Hi, Sam.

(CONTINUED)

CONTINUED:

SAM
(surprised)
Hi, Cindy. I didn't know you were coming.

CINDY
Neal invited me. This is my cousin Beth. She's visiting from Boca Raton.

SAM
(nervous)
Oh, hi.

They enter.

BETH
Where's the beer?

SAM
(pointing to the corner)
It's over there.

CINDY
(peppy)
Don't worry, I'm the designated driver.

Cindy and her friend head off.

KEN
(seeing Beth)
Good god, two more kegs have arrived.

Sam checks himself over to make sure he looks all right. Bill stumbles up to him.

SAM
Why did Neal invite her? Now she's gonna see all the dumb stuff in my house.

BILL
Neal's plan is to distract you so he can hit on your sister.

SAM
He's so dead. What am I going to say to Cindy?

(CONTINUED)

CONTINUED: (2)

BILL
Don't say anything. I mean, you gotta be dominant. It's all about dominance. I saw this show about monkeys on PBS. If you talk to her first, that's a sign of weakness and she won't pick you as her mate.

SAM
(sniffing)
Are you drunk?

BILL
Yeah... I think so.

SAM
Oh, man. Go back to my room, lock the door, and don't drink anymore!

BILL
That's good. Very dominant.

Bill staggers off.

CUT TO:

INT. WEIR LIVING ROOM

LINDSAY walks to where she was hanging with Daniel, but he is not there. She walks around the party looking for him.

LINDSAY
Have you seen Daniel?

A freak shrugs "no."

CUT TO:

INT. WEIR HALLWAY - MOMENTS LATER

Lindsay walks down the hall. She sees Harris. They jockey for position. Finally, she walks by.

HARRIS
Thanks for the dance.

Lindsay opens up her bedroom door. She hears something. Through the shadows she sees a couple kissing on her bed. She can't figure out who it is.

(CONTINUED)

CONTINUED:

KIM
Ow! Watch it Romeo, you're leaning on my hair.

We reveal that it is Kim and Daniel. Lindsay is crestfallen.

DANIEL
Hey, we're busy.
(sees Lindsay)
Oh, hey, Linds.

LINDSAY
Oh, sorry.

Kim smiles.

KIM
Don't worry. We threw your teddy bears on the floor.

Lindsay closes the door and walks to the front door. We track with her as she walks away, dazed.

CUT TO:

EXT. WEIR FRONT YARD - NIGHT

Nick is standing outside. Lindsay, in shock, walks out to the front yard.

LINDSAY
Daniel and Kim are making out in my room.

NICK
Oh.

LINDSAY
I thought they broke up.

NICK
(laughs)
Yeah, they break up like every week.
(beat)
You don't look like you're having any fun.

LINDSAY
I'm not.

(CONTINUED)

52.

CONTINUED:

He gives her a hug. She hugs him hard. She needs a friend right now.

NICK
Hey, just relax. It's a party. When it's over I'll stay and help you clean up. It'll be fine.

LINDSAY
I'm so glad you're here.

NICK
Me, too.

Lindsay feels something.

LINDSAY
What are you doing?

We reveal that Nick is trying to open up her bra strap.

NICK
Nothing.

LINDSAY
Stop it.

She pulls away.

LINDSAY (CONT'D)
What are you doing!?

NICK
I'm sorry. I'm sorry. I'm really wasted.

She walks away.

NICK (CONT'D)
(calling after)
John Bonham died.

Lindsay runs into the house.

CUT TO:

INT. LIVING ROOM - CONTINUOUS

Lindsay runs to her parents bedroom. Neal sees this, then follows. He hesitates at the door, then knocks.

CUT TO:

INT. PARENTS' BEDROOM - CONTINUOUS

Neal enters the bedroom to find Lindsay sprawled face down on the bed.

NEAL
Lindsay? Are you OK?

LINDSAY
I'm fine. I'll be out in a minute.

Neal doesn't leave the room. He takes a beat, then speaks in his most understanding voice.

NEAL
Sometimes it helps to talk to someone.

LINDSAY
I'm too drunk to talk.

NEAL
That's OK, I speak "drunk."

She looks at Neal. He gives her a goofy smile. This makes Lindsay more depressed. She falls over and puts her head on the bed.

LINDSAY
I'm wasted and I hate my life.

NEAL
You shouldn't hate your life.

LINDSAY
Why not? It sucks.

Neal starts to move slowly toward the bed. He stares at Lindsay.

NEAL
No, it doesn't. You're a beautiful young girl. The world is your oyster.

LINDSAY
Oh, please leave me alone.

NEAL
No.

(CONTINUED)

CONTINUED:

LINDSAY
Why?

NEAL
Because I... I... because you're Sam's sister. I'm not going to leave you in this condition.

Neal sits on the bed. Lindsay looks at him for a beat, then starts sobbing. She cries on Neal's shoulder.

LINDSAY
(crying and hugging)
I'm so wasted, I wish I didn't throw this party.

NEAL
That's right. Tell it to Neal. Let it all out.

Neal is in heaven from the contact.

CUT TO:

INT. WEIR KITCHEN - NIGHT

Cindy is still talking to the group of people. Sam is now standing near her, looking around everywhere but at her. It's not working. He moves in closer. Just then Nick comes up to him.

NICK
Have you seen your sister around?

SAM
No, not recently.

NICK
Oh, well if you see her, tell her I'm sorry.

SAM
For what? Did you break something?

NICK
No. Forget it.

Nick walks off.

CUT TO:

INT. WEIR LIVING ROOM - NIGHT

A bunch of freaks, led by Ken, are gathered around the coffee table. They pound their fists on the table loudly.

FREAKS
Go, go, go, go, go!

In unison, they all drink, then cheer.

CUT TO:

INT. PARENTS' BEDROOM - NIGHT

Neal is sitting on the bed beside a prone Lindsay. They are startled by the cheer of the crowd.

LINDSAY
What's going on out there? I didn't even want to have this party. I did it for Daniel, next thing I know he's making out with Kim on my bed.

Lindsay starts to cry a little harder. Neal starts stroking her hair a little.

NEAL
Typical.

He subtly sniffs her hair and drinks in the heavenly scent.

LINDSAY
All my new friends think I'm some goody two-shoes and all my old friends think I'm trying to throw my life away. What the hell am I supposed to do?

NEAL
May I speak freely? That Daniel guy. You can do much better. And hey, at least people showed up to your party. When I was in sixth grade my mom threw me a surprise party. You know what the surprise was? Nobody showed up, except Bill and Sam.

Lindsay laughs.

SFX: There is a KNOCK at the bedroom door.

(CONTINUED)

CONTINUED:

LINDSAY
(to door)
Yeah?

CARL (O.C.)
Whoever's in there, we need five bucks from everyone. We're going to get another keg.

Lindsay and Neal look at each other in horror.

LINDSAY
Oh, my God.

CARL (O.C.)
Hey, cancel that. They just found fifty bucks on the piano.

NEAL
You've got to do something.

LINDSAY
If I go out there and kick everyone out, I am going to look so lame.

She collapses on the bed in a heap.

NEAL
Why don't you just call the cops? That's what my dad always does. Pretend to be an angry neighbor.

LINDSAY
So they can come in and find the keg?

NEAL
Not without a warrant.

LINDSAY
No, I can't. I can't handle any of this.

NEAL
Of course you can. You're Lindsay Weir. You can do anything. You're smart and pretty. You never take any crap. You're the perfect girl and... I've been in love with you since I was five years old.

Lindsay starts crying hysterically.

(CONTINUED)

CONTINUED: (2)

NEAL (CONT'D)
Maybe I should just call the cops.

Neal picks up the phone.

LINDSAY
Would you?

Neal holds out his hand, then clears his throat.

NEAL
Let me handle it.
(on phone, speaking like his dad)
Yes, hello? Police? I'm trying to sleep and there's a very loud party going on next door. It's been going on forever. I need my rest! I'm old and I've got to work tomorrow. It's 13 Nome Drive. Thank you. Hurry up, I'm so tired.

He hangs up the phone.

NEAL (CONT'D)
Done. I'd say this party has a life expectancy of five minutes.

Lindsay looks at Neal. We don't know what she'll do. She kisses and hugs him.

LINDSAY
I don't know what to say.

OPTIONAL LINE:

LINDSAY (CONT'D)
What do I say?

NEAL
You want me to do it?

LINDSAY
Wouldn't you?

Neal holds out his hand. Lindsay hands him the phone and finishes dialing. Neal clears his throat.

NEAL
(on phone, speaking in an old lady voice)
Yes, hello? Police?
(MORE)

(CONTINUED)

58.

CONTINUED: (3)

NEAL (CONT'D)
I'm trying to sleep and there's a very loud party going on next door. It's been going on all night, I need a rest!

Lindsay stifles laughter.

NEAL (CONT'D)
It's 5478 Nome Drive. Please hurry, I'm old. Thank you.

He hangs up the phone.

NEAL (CONT'D)
Done. I'd say this party has a life expectancy of five minutes.

Lindsay kisses Neal on the cheek, then hugs him.

LINDSAY
Thank you, Neal.

Neal is in heaven.

CUT TO:

INT. WEIR LIVING ROOM - MOMENTS LATER

Cindy and Beth are now sitting on the couch talking to Calvin. Sam sits on the other side of the couch with Calvin in between them. He sits there quietly for a moment, then.

SAM
(to Calvin)
Hey, how's it going?

CALVIN
What, man? I promise, I'm not going to break anything! OK?

Calvin gets up and walks away. Sam has no cover. Cindy looks over and notices him.

CINDY
Hi, Sam.

SAM
Oh, hi Cindy, I didn't see you there. How's it going?

CINDY
Pretty good.

(CONTINUED)

CONTINUED:

BETH
Where are all the cute guys?

SAM
Oh, the bus hasn't arrived yet?

They all laugh.

CINDY
There is one cute guy here.

She points to Sam. He blushes. Cindy and Beth crack up.

CINDY (CONT'D)
Sam, you're so red. You look like a tomato.

For a moment life is perfect. Just then, police cars pull up in front of the house. Lindsay and Neal rush into the room.

NEAL
Oh my God, the police are here.

LINDSAY
The neighbors must have called them.

Cindy rushes off. Sam can't believe it. All of the freaks rush out the back door.

LINDSAY (CONT'D)
(to Sam)
You were right. I should have gotten a magician.

SAM
I don't know. This wasn't so bad.

The oldest freak runs the fastest.

CARL
Oh no, I'm on parole.

In a corner, near the fireplace Ken rises, alarmed--

KEN
What happened to the chick from Boca Raton? I want to party with her.

Sam overhears, despondent.

(CONTINUED)

CONTINUED: (2)

SAM
She left with Cindy Sanders.

Ken joins in with a group of THREE FLEEING EXTRAS.

NICK
I'll see ya', Lindsay. I'm sorry.

He exits. Daniel walks over to Lindsay.

DANIEL
Great party, Linds. We had a good time.

Lindsay can tell that he didn't mean anything bad by his actions -- he's just Daniel.

LINDSAY
I'm glad you had a good time.

DANIEL
I knew you had it in you.

Lindsay smiles a little. Kim approaches.

KIM
Let's get out of here.
(to Lindsay)
You're a wonderful hostess.

She hands Lindsay a stuffed animal.

KIM (CONT'D)
Have us back soon.

They exit. There is a knock at the door. Lindsay answers it.

POLICE OFFICER
We got a call about some noise.

NEAL
You can't come in here without a warrant.

They walk in.

LINDSAY
It's only us. We're just hanging out.

They look around and see a few geeks and a keg of beer.

(CONTINUED)

CONTINUED: (3)

POLICE OFFICER
(referring to the keg)
What's that?

LINDSAY
Oh...that. It's...

He walks to the keg.

POLICE OFFICER
Where are your parents?

LINDSAY
They're out of town.

POLICE OFFICER
I'm going to need their phone number.

SAM
Wait. It's not what you think.

He walks to the keg and leans it over revealing a stamp on the bottom which says "NON-ALCOHOLIC BEER. "

SAM (CONT'D)
It's non-alcoholic beer.

The police officer sighs, trying to figure out what to do.

NEAL
It's a project for school... Sober Students.

There is a very long pause.

POLICE OFFICER
Have a good night.

He walks out the door. Lindsay looks at Sam in shock.

LINDSAY
I can't believe you.

SAM
I was trying to save your life.

She turns and looks at Neal.

NEAL
Hey, at least you're not going to get a hangover.

(CONTINUED)

CONTINUED: (4)

LINDSAY
I'm going to bed.

She turns and walks toward her room. Bill's legs are hanging out the bathroom door.

LINDSAY (CONT'D)
Give it up, Bill. It's fake beer.

She walks into her room. We hear Bill throw up.

SFX: BILL THROWING UP.

BILL
Good night, Lindsay.

OPTIONAL VERSION WITHOUT LINDSAY'S LINE.

She simply steps over Bill. He pukes after she enters her room.

CUT TO:

INT. SQUAD CAR - NIGHT

The police officer speaks into his CB radio. Walkie talkie.

POLICE OFFICER
It was nothing. Just a couple of geeks drinking fake beer.

OPTIONAL LINE:

POLICE OFFICER (CONT'D)
...Pretty sad.

FADE OUT.

THE END

# **FREAKS AND GEEKS**

"TRICKS AND TREATS"

Episode #3

Written by Paul Feig

Directed by Bryan Gordon

Oh, we had such grand plans when *Freaks and Geeks* first began. I envisioned us being a hugely popular show that people built their evenings around, looking forward to that one night a week when they could spend some quality time with their friends from McKinley High School and the fictional Michigan town of Chippewa. I imagined that tens of millions of homes would sit down around the electronic fireplace that is TV and thrill to the misadventures of the freaks and the geeks as they made their way through the year, celebrating holidays with them as if they were members of the family. And so, during the first two weeks when we assembled the writing staff and tried to figure out what our first batch of stories would be, I immediately volunteered to write the Halloween episode. And it promptly became the first and last holiday episode we ever did.

The reason for this was that we were literally biting our nails up until the night this episode aired, wondering if NBC was going to show it the night before Halloween instead of postponing it because of a possible game seven of the World Series. If they did postpone it, they would end up running the episode sometime in November, when Halloween would only be a distant memory and a few extra pounds on the butts of the kids who ate all the candy in their Halloween sacks. And so we quickly decided that because of the erratic schedule NBC had us on—pulling us off and on the air like an embarrassing relative you don't want your friends to see—it simply wasn't worth the angst of trying to produce Thanksgiving and Christmas and President's Day shows that could end up airing sometime in the summer.

But when I put pen to paper on this episode, the world was still our oyster.

I had always had such mixed feelings about Halloween as a kid that I couldn't wait to put them all on display in this script. And so what you have here is Halloween as I knew it growing up in the Midwest. Back then, it was all about kids soaping windows (or *waxing* them, if they were really delinquents), destroying mailboxes, blowing up things with firecrackers, kicking in carved pumpkins, and engaging in other modes of destruction that made the evening less a celebration of ghosts and goblins and more a cause for increasing one's homeowner's insurance. And I'm not even talking about Devil's Night, the night-before-Halloween mayhem that regularly saw vacant homes in downtown Detroit set ablaze. And then add to this the persistent rumors of candy laced with razor blades, rat hair, straight pins, and LSD, and you had a night of mind-bending terror that never seemed to sync up with the fun-filled myth of Halloween as an opportunity to wear festive costumes and get to know your friendly neighbors who would give you free goodies—you know, the way Halloween was usually represented on television.

Before I let you go, I have to give a nod to Judd Apatow, who talked me out of having Bill dress as a "country hobo," a costume I devised just so that when the geeks are confronted by Alan White and Bill tells Alan he's a country hobo, Alan could reply, "You're a country *homo?*" Ah, what could have been.

Enjoy and leave a couple rolls of Smarties for me.

—Paul Feig

FREAKS AND GEEKS

"TRICKS AND TREATS"

**CAST LIST**

LINDSAY WEIR
SAM WEIR
HAROLD WEIR
JEAN WEIR
DANIEL DESARIO
NICK ANDOPOLIS
BILL HAVERCHUCK
NEAL SCHWEIBER
KEN MILLER
KIM KELLY
MILLIE KENTNER
MR. ROSSO
HARRIS
ALAN WHITE
MRS. WHITMAN
POPULAR GIRL #1
POPULAR GIRL #2
CHAIN SMOKING WOMAN
ANGRY MOTHER
LITTLE KIDS
MRS. KENT
JILL

FREAKS AND GEEKS

"TRICKS AND TREATS"

**SET LIST**

**INTERIORS:**

MCKINLEY HIGH SCHOOL
/HALLWAY
/ENGLISH CLASS
/CAFETERIA
WEIR HOUSE
/LINDSAY'S BEDROOM
/KITCHEN
/DINING ROOM
/LIVING ROOM
/SAM'S BEDROOM
/HALLWAY
DANIEL'S TRANS AM
DANIEL'S UNCLE'S CADILLAC *

**EXTERIORS:**

BUS STOP
MCKINLEY HIGH SCHOOL
/SMOKING PATIO
/UNDER THE BLEACHERS
WEIR HOUSE
NEIGHBORHOOD STREET
DANIEL'S TRANS AM
SMOKER'S HOUSE
FANCY HOUSE
/FRONT DOOR
RUN-DOWN HOUSE
/FRONT DOOR
DANIEL'S UNCLE'S CADILLAC *

TEASER

INT. WEIR KITCHEN - DAY

Sam, Neal and Bill are at the kitchen counter. Tons of spice bottles, oil bottles, vinegar, condiments, baking supplies and other kitchen food items cover the counter. A blender half filled with water sits in front of them.

BILL
Okay, here's the bet. For ten bucks, I will drink this much of anything.

Bill indicates two inches of liquid with his fingers.

SAM
Anything?

BILL
Anything. I mean, as long as it's something you can eat.

SAM
Let's put in toothpaste.

NEAL
Yeah, and mouthwash.

BILL
No, wait, mouthwash has alcohol in it. I can't get drunk again. My mom'll kill me.

SAM
You can't get drunk off mouthwash.

BILL
Look, no toothpaste or mouthwash, okay? It has to be stuff from the kitchen. It can't be anything from the bathroom or the garage.

NEAL
Okay, fine.

BILL
And it has to be food. Nothing from under the sink. No cleansers, no detergent, no furniture polish and no cut up bits of sponge. Got it?

(CONTINUED)

CONTINUED:

SAM
Okay.

BILL
I mean, I'm just trying to win ten
bucks here. I don't want to die.

Sam and Neal exchange a look, then nod in agreement.

SAM
Okay. Deal.

BILL
Deal.

They shake hands.

SAM
Okay, now you've gotta step into
the soundproof booth.

Sam picks up a huge pair of shooting range headphone ear protectors and hands them to Bill.

BILL
I hope these don't mess up my hair.

Bill puts on the headphones.

SAM
And close your eyes.

BILL
What?

Sam pulls one of the headphones off Bill's ear.

SAM
You can't watch what we put in.

Sam and Neal pull a knit winter cap over Bill's head and eyes.

BILL
Okay. But I'm trusting you.

Bill readjusts his headphones and closes his eyes. Sam and Neal start grabbing bottles of spice and oil. They begin mixing them into the glass of water.

(CONTINUED)

CONTINUED:

NEAL
Put in mustard. It's an Ipecac. It'll make him barf.

SAM
Don't make him barf. My mom cooks dinner in here.

NEAL
If we're not trying to make him barf, then why are we doing this?

BILL
I can hear everything you're saying.

SAM
Hey, c'mon, Bill. Quit listening.

BILL
I can't help it.

NEAL
Then hum so you can't hear us.

Bill starts humming some nameless tune. Sam thinks a beat, then squeezes in a bunch of mustard.

NEAL (CONT'D)
(showing Sam a bottle)
Sam ... cheyenne pepper.

SAM
Ooo, good one. Hand me the pickle juice.

Neal reaches off-screen and grabs a jar of pickles. Sam takes it and pours it in. As they talk, they dump in vinegar, sea salt, chocolate chips, garlic powder, capers, cumin, bay leaves, hot dogs, etc.

NEAL
(as they pour stuff in)
My cousin drank a jar of pickle juice once and he had to sit on the toilet for ten hours. He read a whole book while he was in there.

SAM
Okay, I think we've got enough stuff. Mix it up.

(CONTINUED)

CONTINUED:

Neal turns on the blender and mixes the hideous swill. Sam and Neal exchange pleased looks. Bill continues humming. He's really into whatever song's in his head.

NEAL
(tapping Bill)
All right. It's showtime.

Bill eyeballs the glass of sludge. He looks skeptical.

BILL
Let me see the money first.

Sam and Neal each pull out five dollar bills.

BILL (CONT'D)
How come you guys have all this money? I never have any.

NEAL
(looking at the glass)
Gee, no kidding.

SAM
C'mon, drink it already.

BILL
Okay, okay, don't rush me.

Bill picks up the glass and holds it up to the light. Inspects it.

BILL (CONT'D)
There better not be any soft soap in here.

Bill gives them a suspicious look, then sniffs the liquid. He makes a small face, sniffs it again, shrugs and downs half the glass.

SAM/NEAL
Eww!

Sam and Neal stare expectantly, ready for anything. Bill just sits there and smacks his lips. Then he looks at them calmly.

BILL
Okay. Pay up.

Sam and Neal continue to study him, waiting for him to blow. Bill looks completely unaffected. The geeks exchange looks.

(CONTINUED)

CONTINUED:

NEAL
(not buying it)
Give me that. I bet it doesn't even taste bad.

Neal grabs the glass and takes a sip. He gags.

NEAL (CONT'D)
Oh, my god...

Neal and Sam look at Bill in awe. Bill cockily takes the glass back and picks up his money.

BILL
Pleasure doing business with you.
(to himself)
I wonder if I could make a living doing this?

Bill takes another drink as Sam and Neal shake their heads and walk away, grossed out.

ALTERNATE:

Neal grabs the glass and takes a sip. He looks at Bill and Sam surprised.

NEAL
Oh, my God. It's good.

Sam gives him a weird look, then grabs the glass and takes a sip.

SAM
We should sell this.

BILL
Does this mean I don't get my ten bucks?

CUT TO:

<u>MAIN TITLES</u>

ALTERNATE OPENING

FADE IN:

INT. LINDSAY'S ROOM - MORNING

MUSIC UP: KISS' "BETH"

An album spins on a turntable. LINDSAY is getting ready for school. She's buttoning up her shirt. She looks up and sees herself in her mirror.

She studies herself for a beat. Looking at her face, her hair. She moves a strand of hair out of her face. Does she thinks she's pretty?

She turns her shoulders slightly, as if posing. She adjusts her shoulders. Checking herself out.

She unbuttons the top button on her shirt. Wrinkles her nose, unsure. She poses again. "Beth" hits a particularly sappy section.

Lindsay unbuttons the next button. Really studying herself. Trying to figure out if she's sexy or not. Suddenly...

JEAN (O.C.)
(from downstairs)
Lindsay, hurry up! I poured the milk on your Count Chocula and it's getting all soggy!

Buzzkill. Lindsay SIGHS, buttons up her shirt, throws on her army jacket, makes a face at herself in the mirror and leaves.

CUT TO:

MAIN TITLES

FADE IN:

INT. WEIR KITCHEN - MORNING

Lindsay and SAM are at the kitchen table, eating cereal. HAROLD is tying his tie, getting ready for work. JEAN enters from outside with a large pumpkin.

JEAN
(excited)
Hey, look. L and H Realty gave everyone in the neighborhood free pumpkins. Wasn't that nice?

(CONTINUED)

CONTINUED:

HAROLD
There's nothing nice about it. It's a cheap way to get customers. They give you a twenty cent pumpkin and you give them ten grand to sell your house.

JEAN
Well, I just think it was nice.

Lindsay pours herself some more cereal. A plastic whistle wrapped in plastic drops into her bowl from the box.

SAM
Hey, can I have the prize?

LINDSAY
(picking it up)
My bowl. My prize.

Sam holds out his hand and makes a brotherly "c'mon, you don't want it" face. Lindsay smiles and hands him the prize. Sam unwraps the whistle.

JEAN
Aw, I love when you two get along.

TWEEEEEEEEEEEEEET!!! Sam blows the whistle and it emits an ear-splitting shriek. The whole family jumps.

HAROLD
Sam! What are you trying to do, kill me?

SAM
Uh... sorry.

JEAN
What are you going out as for Halloween, Sam?

SAM
I'm not going out. Bill and I are going to see "The Nude Bomb" at Parkway.

HAROLD
Hey, that's a dirty movie.

SAM
Dad, it's the Get Smart movie.

(CONTINUED)

8.

CONTINUED:

JEAN
(genuinely surprised)
You're not going trick or treating?

SAM
Mom, I'm in ninth grade.

JEAN
But you went out last year.

SAM
Last year I was in junior high.

JEAN
But--

HAROLD
Honey, the boy's fourteen years old. He can miss a night of walking around the neighborhood begging like a tramp. Halloween's for little kids anyway.

Jean looks a little hurt by this. She turns to Lindsay.

JEAN
Lindsay, you're still going to hand out candy with me, aren't you? Remember how much fun we had last year looking at all the kids' costumes?

LINDSAY
I told you I was going to do it, mom.

JEAN
Good. Because we're really going to have a fun time- I promise.

LINDSAY
What'll you give me if we don't?

Lindsay laughs. Jean gives her a "that's not funny" look, then sits down at the table with her cup of coffee. She throws a disappointed look toward Sam.

CUT TO:

EXT. BUS STOP - MORNING

The daily bus stop routine. Kids are waiting for the bus at the end of Sam's street.

(CONTINUED)

CONTINUED:

A couple of kids stand next to the street sign pole. One sits on a large rock. Another is tossing pebbles into the ditch. No one speaks. Everyone seems tired. It's a typical morning.

NEAL and BILL are standing in silence. Sam and Lindsay walk up. Neal is wearing a baseball cap. Neal sees Lindsay and nods coolly.

NEAL
Lindsay. Long time no see.

LINDSAY
I saw you out here yesterday.

NEAL
That's a long time in my book.

Neal gives her a smile. Lindsay rolls her eyes.

SAM
(looking at Neal) )
Why you wearing a hat?

NEAL
'Cause it's the day before Halloween.

BILL
Is that your costume? 'Cause it kinda sucks.

NEAL
No. It's "Devil's Day." Every year, the seniors bring in cans of hair removal foam and spray it on freshmen's heads. Then all your hair falls out.

SAM
(worried)
Really?

LINDSAY
No. That stupid rumor's been around for years.

NEAL
Yeah, I know. I was just goofing on them.

BILL
No, you weren't.

NEAL
Yes, I was.

(CONTINUED)

CONTINUED:

Neal makes a "Bill's crazy" gesture to Lindsay. Just then, MILLIE walks up behind Lindsay.

MILLIE
Hey, Lindsay. What are you doing tomorrow night? My church is having a dance. You wanna come?

LINDSAY
Oh, well, I would go but I've gotta hand out candy with my mom.

MILLIE
(shrugging)
Oh...okay.

Millie pulls a pack of Lik-em-Aid out of her pocket. Holds it up to Lindsay.

MILLIE (CONT'D)
You want some Lik-em-Aid? My mom's giving them out tomorrow night, so I took a bunch for school.

Millie tears open the package and takes out the Lik-em-Aid candy dipping stick.

LINDSAY
You're gonna eat candy now? It's 7:30 in the morning.

MILLIE
It's just Lik-em-Aid. It makes my spit taste like fruit juice.

Millie digs out a mound of green powder and eats it. Lindsay looks grossed out. A RUMBLE is heard. Lindsay and Millie look over.

ANGLE ON: Daniel's yellow Trans Am pulls up to the bus stop. DANIEL leans out the window. KIM's in the passenger seat.

DANIEL
(calling out) )
Hey, Lindsay, what's up?

All the kids at the bus stop look over at Lindsay. Lindsay heads over to his car, giving little "yeah, I'm cool" looks to the other kids. Millie walks behind her.

(CONTINUED)

CONTINUED:

LINDSAY

Hey, Daniel.
(bending to see inside the car)
Hey, Kim.

KIM

(flatly)
Hello, brain.

DANIEL

This your bus stop?

LINDSAY

Yeah.

Millie walks up next to Lindsay, bends down and peers into the car as she eats Lik-em-Aid. Lindsay looks at her, annoyed and embarrassed.

MILLIE

We've had the same bus stop since Kindergarten. How fast does your car go?

DANIEL

(amused)
One fifty, if I hook up the nitrous tank.

MILLIE

Your car's really loud. My dad says you need a muffler. Once he even threw a rock at you when you drove by but I guess you didn't hear it.

Daniel and Kim laugh. Lindsay is dying of embarrassment.

KIM

Hey, kid, what the hell are you eating? Laundry soap?

MILLIE

No, it's Lik-em-Aid. Want some?

Millie sticks the packet into the car.

LINDSAY

Millie...

KIM

Uh... I'll pass.

(CONTINUED)

12.

CONTINUED:

DANIEL
(to Lindsay)
We gotta get going. I'd give you a ride but I've got an engine block in the back seat.

Daniel licks his finger and sticks it in the Lik-em-Aid. He pulls out his powder-covered finger and sticks it in his mouth. He makes a "that tastes pretty good" face. Millie laughs.

DANIEL(CONT'D)
(to Millie)
Thanks for the candy, skinny.

VROOM VROOM! Daniel revs his car.

KIM
(yelling over engine noise)
Hey, Lindsay. You've got some really cool friends there.

Daniel tries not to laugh as Kim makes a mocking sincere face at Lindsay. Daniel's car PEELS OUT. Millie puts her fingers in her ears as the car disappears.

MILLIE
See, my dad's right. He needs a muffler.
(then)
Hey, do you really think Kim thinks I'm cool?

Lindsay just looks at Millie as Millie takes another mouthful of Lik-em-Aid.

CUT TO:

INT. MCKINLEY HIGH SCHOOL - DAY

The halls of McKinley. Students are coming in. Lindsay enters, looking a bit depressed at having to be there. As she walks, she looks around.

LINDSAY'S POV: Jocks and cheerleaders walk with their arms around each other. Popular kids holding court with their friends.

Lindsay takes it all in. A couple of POPULAR GIRLS approach.

(CONTINUED)

CONTINUED:

POPULAR GIRL #1
Are you going to Sara's party tomorrow night?

POPULAR GIRL #2
Yeah, but I'm going to Jim's party first.

POPULAR GIRL #1
Oh, cool, let's drive together.

They both see Lindsay. The girls look at her army jacket, then make a face to each other. Lindsay gives them a dirty look. Just then, MR. ROSSO calls to her. He's standing in the front office doorway holding an attendance report.

MR. ROSSO
Hey, if it isn't the Amelia Earhart of McKinley high.

LINDSAY
What does that mean?

MR. ROSSO
Well, you head to class but you never seem to get there.

A bunch of kids look over and try not to laugh. Lindsay looks pained. She walks over to Rosso to quiet him down.

LINDSAY
Mr. Rosso, could you not humiliate me in front of the whole school?

MR. ROSSO
Hey, c'mon, Lindsay. Don't turn me into The Man here. I'm just trying to help you.
(serious)
And if, when you graduate, it turns out I did help you but you hate me, I'm okay with that.

Lindsay sees the popular girls are standing at their locker, listening. Lindsay just wants to get out of there.

LINDSAY (SARCASTIC)
I'm gonna be late for class.

(CONTINUED)

CONTINUED:

MR. ROSSO
(snaps fingers; points at her)
See, it's working already.

LINDSAY
That's right. I hate you.

Rosso laughs, and then gets a sad "was she joking?" look as she walks away.

Mr. Rosso watches her go, concerned. Millie walks up behind him, sucking on the Lik-em-Aid stick and holding an open packet of powder.

MILLIE
Hey, Mr. Rosso, look. I ate all the cherry and now my tongue's red.

Millie sticks out her tongue. It indeed is really red.

MR. ROSSO
(walking away, preoccupied)
That's great, Millie.

Millie shrugs and digs her candy stick into the powder, scooping a huge pile into her mouth.

MILLIE
Man, I love this stuff.

SMASH CUT TO:

INT. ENGLISH CLASS - DAY

Millie is sitting at her desk which is off to the side. A "TEACHER'S AIDE" sign sits in front of her. She's a twitching, finger-tapping mess, clearly tripping from too much Lik-em-Aid. She's sucking on the Lik-em-Aid stick.

MRS. WHITMAN, the very humorless and intimidating old English teacher, picks up a stack of graded essays off Millie's desk.

MRS. WHITMAN
Millie, are you okay?

MILLIE
(talking much too fast)
Yes, Mrs. Whitman, I am. I feel really great.
(MORE)

(CONTINUED)

15.

CONTINUED:

MILLIE (CONT'D)
Would you like me to hand those essays back to the students?

MRS. WHITMAN
Uh, why don't you just sit there and lay off the candy for a while?

Millie nods spastically. Mrs. Whitman gives her a look and walks up to the front of the class. She holds up the stack of essays. Sam, Neal and Bill are at their desks.

MRS. WHITMAN (CONT'D)
Embarrassing. That's the only word I can think of to describe these essays about your favorite books.

Mrs. Whitman starts flipping through the essays.

MRS. WHITMAN (CONT'D)
(reading)
"Charlie and the Chocolate Factory."
(looking at Sam)
The novelization of "Star Wars."
(looking right at Neal)
"Cavat on Cavat?"

Neal looks around as if to say "who's favorite book is that?"

MRS. WHITMAN (CONT'D)
I'd like to remind you all of one small fact-- you're high school students. And today each of you is going to start reading like one.

Mrs. Whitman picks up a copy of "Crime and Punishment" off her desk and holds it up for the class to see. Sam looks worried.

MRS. WHITMAN (CONT'D)
"Crime and Punishment" is a good example of the kind of book you should be reading now.

Mrs. Whitman picks up a stack of paperbacks and starts dropping them on students' desks as she drones monotonously.

MRS. WHITMAN (CONT'D)
It is the story of Raskolnikov, a disillusioned young man on the fringes of society, the bleak slums of St. Petersburg.
(MORE)

(CONTINUED)

CONTINUED:

MRS. WHITMAN (CONT'D)
In it, Fyodor Dostoevsky was seeking to create what some would call an existential enigma -- a protagonist who is both a nihilist and a moralist.

The entire class looks at her as if she was speaking French, except for Millie who nods knowingly (albeit spastically). Sam looks quite distraught as Mrs. Whitman drops a book in front of him. Sam looks at the cover.

SAM'S POV: On the cover is a dark, sober looking painting of a man standing in a doorway. The cover couldn't look more depressing and intimidating. Sam flips through the pages. Hundreds of pages of tiny print.

MRS. WHITMAN (CONT'D)
I know this all sounds confusing to you but soon you'll all know what I'm talking about... because I expect you to have the first-half of this book read by Monday.

The whole class MOANS.

MRS. WHITMAN (CONT'D)
It's time to grow up, people.

Sam looks upset and completely freaked out.

CUT TO:

EXT. SMOKING PATIO - DAY

The smoking patio is filled with freaks. Daniel and Kim are grabbing at each other and wrestling playfully, while NICK and KEN are kicked back on the bleachers. Daniel grabs Kim from behind and licks her ear.

DANIEL
You like that, huh? That get you hot?

KIM
(screaming playfully)
Cut it out, you jerk.

Daniel spins her around and acts like he's trying to bite her nose. The sexual overtones are strong.

KEN
Knock it off. You're making me sick.

(CONTINUED)

CONTINUED:

DANIEL
(to Ken)
Hey, why don't you make out with
Nick and we'll call it a foursome.

KEN
Why don't you make out with my butt
and we'll call it love.

Kim and Nick laugh. Daniel gives Ken a "good one" smile.
Lindsay walks up. Kim gives her an icy look.

KIM
Uh oh, be cool. The narc's here.

LINDSAY
(trying to joke)
Yeah, watch out or I'll "bust" you.

Lindsay laughs nervously. Kim turns and starts stalking in on
Lindsay. Kim's suddenly very serious.

KIM
Hey, I ain't joking. I just heard
what you did to Brian Stoker. Saw
him smoking a J outside the Quik-
Fill and told some cops inside.
Brian's in prison now, man, and his
brother's looking for you.

Kim's right in Lindsay's face. Lindsay's completely thrown.
It's a tense moment.

LINDSAY
What? I didn't do that.

KIM
(after a beat)
Yeah, I know. I'm just messin' with
you.

Kim immediately goes back to hanging all over Daniel. He and
Kim laugh as Lindsay forces a chuckle and tries to recover.

NICK
She got me, too. That was pretty
funny.

LINDSAY
Hilarious.

(CONTINUED)

CONTINUED:

DANIEL
(to Kim)
Who made you so funny...looking?

Kim starts punching him playfully and this, once again, degenerates into a sexually-charged wrestling session. Ken looks pained.

KEN
(getting up)
I'm gonna go poke my eyes out.

And he's gone. Nick and Lindsay stand in an uncomfortable silence except for the sounds of Daniel and Kim laughing and grabbing. Finally, Nick turns to Lindsay.

NICK
You wanna skip?

LINDSAY
I can't. Rosso's got it out for me today.

NICK
Oh, man, I'm so sick of that guy.
(impersonating Rosso)
Hey, Lindsay, I think we need to "rap" again. I'm a hundred year old hippie.

NICK (CONT'D)
What are you doing for Halloween?

LINDSAY
Oh, I'm gonna help my mom hand out candy.

They all stop and stare at Lindsay. She feels dumb.

LINDSAY (CONT'D)
I know. It's kinda dorky but... she's really into it.

KIM
(laughing)
No, it doesn't sound dorky at all.

NICK
Hey, at least she's being nice. Just because you hate your mother doesn't mean everybody else does.

(CONTINUED)

CONTINUED:

DANIEL
No, everybody hates her mother.

Kim cracks up. Daniel smiles, pleased with his joke.

LINDSAY
Why, what are you guys doing?

DANIEL
Me, Kim and Nick are going out. We're borrowing my uncle's big ass Caddie. We thought maybe you'd want to come with us.

Kim shoots Daniel a look.

LINDSAY
You mean like a double date?

KIM
Hey, if that's what you want to call it in your diary, princess.

Lindsay desperately wants to say yes. She thinks a beat.

LINDSAY
I can't.

KIM
Your loss.

The bell RINGS. The freaks start to disperse.

NICK
Hey, I think it's nice that you're helping your mom out. I'll see you later.

LINDSAY
Yeah, I'll see you.

Nick takes off. Lindsay just sighs, upset at her missed opportunity.

CUT TO:

INT. CAFETERIA - DAY

The geeks are at their usual table. Bill and Neal are eating. Sam has his copy of "Crime and Punishment" in front of him. He's staring at the cover.

(CONTINUED)

CONTINUED:

SAM
This is gonna take like a trillion years to read. I don't even know what it's about.

NEAL
Whitman said it's about an ax murderer.

BILL
That's kinda cool.

SAM
I guarantee you, it's not going to be cool. Look at how small the printing is.

NEAL
Perhaps you've never heard of a little thing called "Cliffs Notes."

BILL
Yeah, but you still have to read them.

SAM
(frustrated)
Whitman's such a jerk. She's always saying we have to be "young adults." We're not adults. We're kids until we turn eighteen, you know.

NEAL
Maybe you are but when I hit thirteen, I became a man.

BILL
Only in your temple. Not in the real world.

Sam studies the painting of the man on the cover of the book. The book couldn't look more intimidating. Sam gets an idea.

SAM
We should go trick or treating tomorrow night.

NEAL
What? We're too old.

(CONTINUED)

CONTINUED:

SAM
No, we're not. We went out last year. C'mon, let's go out tomorrow night.

NEAL
I can't. I'm going to the Jaycees haunted house. The Hot Dog On A Stick girls from the mall are working it.

BILL
Ooo, the tall ones? They're hot.

SAM
Then why don't we just go trick or treating first?

NEAL
Then why don't we don't just <u>buy</u> the candy?

SAM
(sarcastic)
Yeah, that's really fun.
(then)
C'mon, I'm telling you, we'd have a blast. It's better than sitting home reading some stupid Russian book.

Neal and Bill consider this. Bill stammers a half-hearted response.

BILL
Uh... sure, I... uh... I guess. I mean... uh, I don't, care.

Sam smiles, then he and Bill look at Neal.

NEAL
(very skeptical)
I don't know.

SAM
We might meet some girls.

NEAL
Yeah, eight year olds dressed like Princess Leia.

Sam gives Neal a "c'mon" look.

(CONTINUED)

CONTINUED:

SAM
So, what does this mean? You're never gonna dress like Groucho again?

NEAL
(thinks a beat; as Groucho)
"Well, that would be the most ridiculous thing I ever heard."

Neal seems happy with his decision. Sam laughs and they all go back to their lunches. Sam looks happy.

FADE OUT.

END OF ACT ONE

ACT TWO

FADE IN:

EXT. MCKINLEY HIGH SCHOOL - DAY

Lindsay is heading out a door to the side parking lot. She sees a DORKY GUY in his late teens leaning against a huge old Olds Cutlass (a grandma car).

MILLIE (O.C.)
Tommy!

Lindsay looks over to see Millie come sprinting around from the front of the school, her arms thrown open wide. She runs up to the dorky guy and they embrace.

Lindsay's face is filled with confusion, then her eyes go wide.

ANGLE ON: Millie and the dorky guy kiss! It's a tame-looking, closed-mouth kiss but it seems to go on forever. Just lips pressed flat together, no tongues, no head movement, no nothing.

Lindsay can't believe it. She walks slowly forward, trying to figure it all out. Finally, Millie and the dorky guy end the kiss. Millie looks over and sees Lindsay. Her face goes blank.

MILLIE (CONT'D)
(caught in the act)
Lindsay...!

(CONTINUED)

CONTINUED:

Millie makes a face to the dorky guy to "be cool," then runs over to Lindsay.

MILLIE (CONT'D)
(trying to be cool)
Hey, Lindsay, what's up?

LINDSAY
Millie, who is that?

MILLIE
Who?

LINDSAY
Millie!

MILLIE
(cracking)
Oh, man, you weren't supposed to see. That's Tommy, my secret love. We met this summer at church camp.

LINDSAY
Millie... you have a boyfriend? Why didn't you tell me?

MILLIE
(after a beat)
I didn't want to make you feel bad. Since you don't have a boyfriend and all.

LINDSAY
What does that have to do with anything?

MILLIE
(suddenly worried)
Lindsay, you've gotta keep this a secret. I mean, Tommy and I don't even French kiss yet. Tommy says if you do before you've been dating for six months, you'll go to Hell.

Lindsay just stares at Millie for a beat. Then she turns and heads toward the football field. Millie calls after her.

MILLIE (CONT'D)
Lindsay, promise me you won't tell my dad you saw me doing this.

(CONTINUED)

CONTINUED:

LINDSAY
(stops, turns back to Millie)
Millie, I'm not going to tell anybody I saw you doing this. Trust me.

Millie makes a "whew" face as Lindsay heads off, on a mission.

CUT TO:

EXT. UNDER THE BLEACHERS - DAY

A very laid back Daniel and Nick are hanging out under the bleachers. Other freaks hang in different parts of the freak hideout.

NICK
So, wait a minute. They're called Santana but that's not Santana who's singing?

DANIEL
No, man, Santana is the guitar player.

NICK
Then how'd he get them to name the band after him?

DANIEL
I don't know, man. Maybe he's just a bad ass.

Lindsay walks up. Strong and direct.

LINDSAY
I'm gonna go out with you guys tomorrow night.

NICK
Really? That's great!

DANIEL
(friendly mocking)
Hey, what about your mom? How's she gonna hand out candy all by herself?

(CONTINUED)

25.

CONTINUED:

LINDSAY
(to the guys) )
Oh... she'll survive.

Daniel and Nick laugh. Lindsay looks happy about her decision as Nick gives her a very pleased smile.

CUT TO:

INT. WEIR DINING ROOM - EVENING

The Weirs are having dinner. Lindsay no longer looks happy but guilty, her eyes shifting from Jean to Harold, then to Jean again. Jean is humming "The Monster Mash" happily. Harold glances up at her as if she's nuts.

Jean sees Lindsay looking at her. Jean leans over to Lindsay, playful.

JEAN
(singing in a bad Boris Karloff voice; to Lindsay)
"They did the mash/They did the Monster Mash/They did the mash/It was a graveyard smash..."

Jean giggles. Lindsay forces a smile and goes back to her meal. No idea how to break the news to mom.

SAM
Hey, mom, Neal, Bill and I decided to go trick or treating tomorrow night.

JEAN
Oh, Sam, really?! That's great. We have to get you a costume.

SAM
I'm gonna make my own. I'm going out as Gort. He's the robot from "The Day the Earth Stood Still."

JEAN
Ooo, "Gort." How exciting.

HAROLD
Sam, what are you doing? You're too old to go trick or treating.

(CONTINUED)

CONTINUED:

JEAN
Oh, Harold.

HAROLD
Well, it's true. There was this kid in my neighborhood when I was growing up. Scott Byron. He kept on trick or treating well into his twenties. You know where he's living now? At home. With his ninety year old mother. He's the laughing stock of the community. Never took a wife, either.

JEAN
What's wrong with getting to act like a kid every once in a while?
(to Lindsay)
I know we're gonna have a great time tomorrow night, aren't we, sweetie?

Lindsay looks at her mom. Jean smiles at her. Lindsay looks pained.

LINDSAY
(forcing a smile)
We sure are, mom.

Jean giggles and goes back to her food, happily humming "Monster Mash" where she left off. Lindsay stabs her meatloaf, completely in turmoil.

CUT TO:

INT. MCKINLEY HIGH SCHOOL - HALLWAY - DAY

The geeks are walking through the halls. Sam's excited.

SAM
And bring pillow cases this year. No grocery bags. If your bag rips, you're on your own.

BILL
I'm gonna bring my plastic pumpkin.

NEAL
Don't bring that. It gets full after one street.

(CONTINUED)

CONTINUED:

BILL
Not if you eat the candy as you go.

NEAL
Last time you did that you puked before we got past our bus stop.

HARRIS joins them as they walk.

HARRIS
Hey, I heard you guys are going out for tricks or treats.

SAM
How'd you hear about that?

HARRIS
Word gets out. People talk.

The geeks exchange an embarrassed look.

HARRIS (CONT'D)
You'd better be careful. I heard that Halloween candy is going to be especially dangerous this year.

BILL
They say that every year.

HARRIS
Yeah, but this year there's a bunch of evil hippies who don't want Reagan to be president, so they're planning on injecting candy with heroin to turn kids into drug addicts.

SAM
That's not true. You just have to watch out for pins and razor blades.

BILL
And rat hair. That's a big one.

HARRIS
You'll be wishing for rat hair. Word on the street is that hippies are also putting their poo in fun-sized chocolate bar wrappers and handing them out.

(CONTINUED)

CONTINUED:

BILL
(upset)
Oh, man, I love the fun-sized ones.

NEAL
That's stupid. Like nobody'd be able to tell what it really was.

HARRIS
Yeah, but they dip them in chocolate so you can't tell until it's too late.

The geeks look at each other, worried.

HARRIS (CONT'D)
Hey, can I go with you guys tonight? It sounds like it might be fun.

The geeks give Harris a "you've gotta be kidding" look.

CUT TO:

INT. WEIR LIVING ROOM - DAY

Lindsay comes into the house. It's completely decorated with orange and black streamers and ghost and goblin cutouts. She looks around at it with dread.

LINDSAY
Mom?

JEAN (O.C.)
I'm in the kitchen.

Lindsay tries to muster some resolve. She heads into the kitchen.

CUT TO:

INT. WEIR KITCHEN - CONTINUOUS

Lindsay walks in and her face falls.

Jean is dressed like a cowgirl. She's taking a tray of cookies out of the oven. The kitchen is filled with Halloween cookies, decorated with black and orange frosting and bowls of punch. Jean is a flurry of activity.

(CONTINUED)

CONTINUED:

JEAN
Where've you been? You're gonna miss the first trick or treaters. The cutest ones always come early.

LINDSAY
I was hanging with my friends.

JEAN
Lindsay, look what I'm going to hand out this year. Halloween cookies!

LINDSAY
That's great, mom.

Sam comes into the kitchen.

SAM
What's up with all the cookies?

JEAN
Sam, I laid out your robot costume on your bed.

SAM
You didn't rip it, did you?

JEAN
No, but I wrote "My son's the cutest boy in the world" on the front of it.

Jean giggles at her joke as Sam rolls his eyes and gives Lindsay a look. Lindsay's in total turmoil.

JEAN (CONT'D)
(picking up a plate of cookies)
Lindsay, I got you a costume. Go put it on. I'll put the cookies by the front door.

Jean walks past Lindsay and gives her a kiss on the cheek.

JEAN (CONT'D)
We're gonna have so much fun!

And she's gone. Lindsay and Sam exchange a look.

(CONTINUED)

CONTINUED:

SAM
I kinda hate when mom gets goofy like that.

Sam shakes his head and starts eating cookies. Lindsay, completely unsure of what to do, sighs and heads for her room.

CUT TO:

INT. SAM'S BEDROOM - DAY

MUSIC UP: THE OPENING BASS LINE OF CHEAP TRICK'S "GONNA RAISE HELL"

Sam's pulling on the silver cardboard legs of his homemade robot costume. He looks happy. He stops when he sees his copy of "Crime and Punishment" sitting on his night stand.

He picks it up, looks at it, then opens the night stand drawer, throws the book inside and closes the drawer. He gives a satisfied nod that seems to say "screw you, Whitman." THE MUSIC KEEPS PLAYING as we...

CUT TO:

INT. NEAL'S BATHROOM - DAY

Neal is in front of the bathroom mirror wearing his Groucho costume. He has no make-up on yet. He studies his face in the mirror.

He looks at his eyebrows, then frowns. He picks up a pair of tweezers and starts pulling hairs out from between his eyebrows. After a couple of pulls, he stops. Studies his face. Frowns again.

JUMP CUT TO:

Neal now has a small strip of shaving cream between his eyebrows and is shaving the small patch with a disposable razor.

He finishes, towels off the excess shave cream, runs his fingers over the now hairless patch and smiles, pleased.

He picks up some black make-up and puts some on his finger. He puts the black make-up right under his nose, making a Charlie Chaplin mustache. He smiles and wiggles the mustache like the Little Tramp.

(CONTINUED)

31.

CONTINUED:

NEAL
Hi, I'm Charlie Chaplin.
(studies himself; frowns)
Oh man, I'm Adolph Hitler.

Neal gets more make-up on his finger and continues his mustache out. It looks more like Groucho.

NEAL (CONT'D)
(as Groucho)
"I once shot an elephant in my pajamas. How he got in my pajamas, I'll never know."

Neal smiles, then picks up a plastic cigar and wiggles it like Groucho. He's pleased.

Then he keeps looking at himself. He puts more make-up on his finger and extends his mustache out into a mustache that hangs down around the corners of his mouth.

NEAL
"Howdy, partner."

Neal then extends the mustache down even further to the bottom of his face, making it a full Fu Manchu.

NEAL (CONT'D)
(as Charlie Chan)
"Ah, honorable number one son."

He looks and sees how goofy he's made his mustache.

NEAL
What am I doing?

He grabs a piece of Kleenex and starts rubbing off the excess mustache.

(In addition to this, Samm Levine will be entertaining us all with his other Groucho-esque hijinx when we tell him to ad-lib some dialogue and actions -- Enjoy!)

CUT TO:

INT. BILL'S MOM'S BEDROOM - DAY

Bill is standing in front of his mother's mirror dressed in a woman's pantsuit. He puts on a broach, then a bobbly necklace.

(CONTINUED)

32.

CONTINUED:

He picks up some lipstick and puts it on. Then he picks up a folded piece of paper and bites it to remove excess lipstick. He smiles at himself.

Then he picks up an eyebrow pencil and starts to draw on eyebrows, very carefully.

He rubs a bit of rouge on his cheeks. Looks at himself. Frowns, then picks up a Kleenex and wipes some of it off.

Happy with his make-up, Bill poses for a beat, then picks up a blond wig and puts it on. He straightens it, then primps his new hair.

Once he's happy with his hair, he becomes Jamie Summers.

BILL
(in a weird feminine voice; talking to person in mirror)
Hi, I'm Jamie Summers. You know, the Bionic Woman.
(to another person in mirror)
No, I'm sorry, Steve Austin, but I can't marry you. I'm mad at you. Well, you're just going to have to get over it.
I've got a thing going with Superman. Oh, wait, I'll get it.
(picks up phone)
Hello, Jamie Summers here. Hello? What? I'm sorry, I can't hear you. Let me put the phone on my bionic ear.
(switches ears)
That's better. Hey, don't talk so loud. I've got bionic hearing, for Pete's sake. Oh yes, hello, Oscar Goldman. No, I had to take Max the Bionic Dog to the pound. He kept leaving bionic poops on my carpet.
(laughs; puts down phone; talks to person in mirror)
What? Excuse me?
(he grabs his boobs)
Oh, no, <u>these</u> aren't bionic. They're all real, mister.
(starts to leave, then turns back to mirror a la Taxi Driver)
(MORE)

(CONTINUED)

33.

CONTINUED:

BILL (CONT'D)
I'm sorry, did you have something else to say to me? Huh? I guess you think you're pretty funny, huh? Hey, I heard that crack, pal. Oh, it wasn't you? Huh? Okay, fine. I guess I'll just go...

Bill turns away, then turns back and does the slow motion bionic punch complete with DO-DO-DO-DO sound effect. He smiles, pleased at his bionic powers.

BILL (CONT'D)
(as himself)
I'm so glad I didn't dress up as a hobo again this year. I am so hot.

Bill smiles, then quickly picks up the phone again, complete with bionic arm sounds.

BILL (CONT'D)
(into phone; high energy)
Oscar Goldman, it's me, Jamie Summers! Steve Austin's trapped in the core of the nuclear reac-- Oh, go ahead and use the phone, Mom. I'm sorry.

Bill quickly puts the phone back down, looking caught and embarrassed.

CUT TO:

INT. LINDSAY'S ROOM - DAY

Lindsay's sitting on her bed. She's staring at a hanging bag that says NORM'S COSTUMES AND BALLOONS on it. We can't tell what the costume is.

Lindsay gets up and touches the bag. She starts to lift the bag to see what the costume is, then decides against it.

She looks at some photos taped to the frame of the mirror over her desk.

ANGLE ON: A photo of Lindsay and Jean from last Halloween. Jean and Lindsay are both dressed like cats in black leotards and ears, with black noses and whiskers painted on. They look very happy.

Lindsay stares at the photo sadly. Confused.

(CONTINUED)

CONTINUED:

MUSIC OUT.

CUT TO:

INT. WEIR LIVING ROOM - DUSK

DING DONG! The doorbell rings. Jean excitedly runs to the front door.

JEAN
(opening door)
Lindsay! Hurry up! Our first little visitor is here -- YEEEEAAAAAGGGGHHHH!!!

Jean SCREAMS in terror.

JEAN'S'POV: Standing there is Harris, dressed in his usual clothes but with a large knife sticking through his head. The wound around it looks bloody, fresh and completely real. He stares at Jean blankly.

Jean tries to pull herself together.

JEAN (CONT'D)
My goodness, what an interesting... costume. Here you go.

Jean hands Harris a cookie. He takes a big bite. He doesn't move, standing there chewing and staring at Jean.

JEAN (CONT'D)
(after a beat)
Um... did you want another cookie?

HARRIS
Okay.
(beat)
I'm here to go out for tricks or treats with Sam.

JEAN
Oh! You're one of Sam's friends. I'm sorry. Come on in.

Harris steps in, still chewing his cookie, staring at Jean's cowgirl outfit.

HARRIS
I like your costume. You look like Richard Benjamin in "Westworld."

(CONTINUED)

CONTINUED:

Just then, Harold comes in the front door, home from work. He sees Jean in her cowgirl outfit. He's immediately intrigued.

HAROLD
Sa-ay, don't you look nice?

Harold looks her up and down, then at Harris standing next to him. Harold flinches when he sees the ax in Harris' head.

HAROLD (CONT'D)
What the hell are you supposed to be?

HARRIS
A guy with a knife through his head.

HAROLD
Oh. Well... mission accomplished.

Lindsay enters the living room. She looks resolved.

LINDSAY
Mom, I need to talk to you--

DING DONG.

JEAN
Lindsay, put your costume on. The trick or treaters are arriving.

LINDSAY
But, mom--

Jean opens the door, revealing Neal and Bill. Neal is in a full-on Groucho Marx costume, while Bill is dressed like a woman, complete with wig and make-up.

NEAL & BILL
(in unison)
Trick or treat, smell our feet, give us something good to eat.

JEAN
(laughing)
Oh, my, don't you both look great!

BILL
(re: ax)
Hey, Harris, that looks really real.

(CONTINUED)

CONTINUED:

HARRIS
How do you know it's not?

Neal grabs Jean and hugs her tight.

NEAL
(as Groucho)
"If I held you any tighter, I'd be behind you. "

HAROLD
Hey! Cut that out.

JEAN
My goodness, Bill. Aren't you...lovely?

BILL
I'm Jamie Summers, the Bionic Woman.

Bill shows her his wrist. It has a bionic circuit board crudely drawn on it. Jean looks confused but covers.

JEAN
Of course you are.

Everybody starts talking and checking out each other's costumes. Lindsay can't figure what to do.

HONK HONK. Lindsay hears the car horn outside.

JEAN (CONT'D)
What's that?

Lindsay looks at the geeks and Harold, who are busy talking. Jean and Lindsay lock eyes, then Lindsay heads for the door in all the confusion.

LINDSAY
Mom... I'm gonna go hang with my friends for a little bit. I'll be back.

JEAN
What? Lindsay, wait--

LINDSAY
I'll be right back.

JEAN
But...

(CONTINUED)

CONTINUED:

And she's gone. A confused Jean goes to the door and looks out.

EXT. WEIR HOUSE - SIMULTANEOUSLY

JEAN'S POV

Lindsay runs out to Daniel's uncle's gigantic Cadillac. Nick is holding the door open and the back seat up. Lindsay jumps in the back, Nick gets in the back with her, Kim shuts the door and the car heads off down the street.

INT. WEIR LIVING ROOM - CONTINUOUS

ANGLE ON: JEAN

She watches the car head off down the road. She looks completely crestfallen as Harold, Neal and Bill continue to chatter inside the house. Harris comes up next to Jean.

HARRIS
You don't have any fake blood around, do you? I want to freshen up my wound before we go out.

Jean just gives Harris a look, as we...

FADE OUT.

END OF ACT TWO

ACT THREE

FADE IN:

INT. WEIR LIVING ROOM - DUSK

Harold and Jean are in the living room. Harold is staring at her as she primps the house, trying to cover her disappointment.

HAROLD
She did _what_?

JEAN
She said it was only going to be for a little while. She'll be back. I know she's been looking forward to this.

Jean goes to the hall closet.

(CONTINUED)

CONTINUED:

HAROLD
Uh, yeah. Well, she'd better be back, that's all I can say. That daughter of yours is on thin ice.

Jean pulls out a Dracula costume hanging on a hanger.

JEAN
Until she comes back, would you put this on and help me pass out candy?

HAROLD
What? But--

Jean gives him a very sad, pleading look. Harold gives in, begrudgingly. Jean hands him the costume and heads to the kitchen. Harold does not look pleased.

CUT TO:

INT. DANIEL'S CADILLAC - DUSK

MUSIC UP: APRIL WINE'S "SHE'S A ROLLER"

Kim's upper body is sticking out of Daniel's passenger window.

KIM
WOOOOOOOOOOOOOOOOO!!!

INT. DANIEL'S CADILLAC - CONTINUOUS

Daniel is driving. He cracks up at Kim. In the backseat, Nick and Lindsay are sitting close together.

PAN OVER TO REVEAL Ken is sitting next to Lindsay. He is staring straight ahead, in his own world. Lindsay looks over at him, confused at his presence. He slowly turns and looks at her. He holds up a small kid's mask up to his face.

KEN
Boo.

Lindsay smiles uncomfortably. Then she looks at Nick.

NICK
(quietly; re: Ken)
His plans fell through.

Lindsay nods and gives Nick a "that's cool" smile. Ken goes back to staring straight ahead.

(CONTINUED)

CONTINUED:

Kim pulls her head back in the car, turns the radio up really loud and starts singing to the music.

KIM (CONT'D)
"She's a roller/A high roller, baby..."

DANIEL
(turning music down)
Knock it off, blondie. You're gonna blow my speakers.

KIM
Oh, I'm sorry, grandpa. I'll try not to blow anything of yours from now on.

LINDSAY
(excited)
Hey, what are we gonna do? You guys wanna go to the haunted house? It's supposed to be really scary.

Kim throws a look back at Lindsay that says "are you insane?" Nick sees this and quickly covers for Lindsay.

NICK
That could be kinda fun.

KIM
For who? Losers?

CUT TO:

DANIEL
Hey, shut up. I like haunted houses.

KIM
I rest my case.

Kim and Nick laugh. Daniel smiles. Lindsay looks at them all, wide-eyed at being part of the group.

DANIEL
(to Lindsay)
We're just gonna drive around and see where the night takes us. That cool with you?

LINDSAY
Yeah, sure. I'm up for anything.

(CONTINUED)

CONTINUED:

Daniel gives Lindsay a smile and nods. Kim rolls her eyes, turns the radio back up and starts dancing around in the front seat. Daniel looks at Kim dancing and laughs. Kim smiles at him and keeps rocking out.

Nick gives Lindsay a sincere smile.

NICK
(yelling over music) )
I'm really glad you decided to come.

Lindsay gives him a surprised smile.

LINDSAY
Really?
(off Nick's nod)
Thanks. So am I.

Lindsay and Nick have a nice moment. Then, Ken looks back over at them.

KEN
You two are adorable.

Lindsay gives Nick a look. Nick laughs and starts bopping his head and drumming on the back of Daniel's seat to the music. Lindsay laughs and starts bopping her head too. She looks like she's going to have fun.

CUT TO:

EXT. NEIGHBORHOOD STREET - DUSK

Sam, in his elaborate but crappy looking homemade robot costume, is walking along with Neal, Bill and Harris. They're in a good mood. LITTLE KIDS in costumes and their parents pass the geeks. Most turn, stare and laugh.

BILL
Why's everybody staring at me? You'd think they'd never seen the Bionic Woman before.

NEAL
They just probably didn't know she was so hot in real life.

BILL
You are joking, right?

(CONTINUED)

41.

CONTINUED:

HARRIS
I met the real Jamie Summers at the Auto Show last year.
(pointing at Bill's chest)
Her boobs weren't that big.

SAM
Hey, we should go right to the rich neighborhood. They hand out the best candy.

HARRIS
That's not true. Rich people traditionally give out the cheapest candy. That's how they stay rich.

BILL
I just hope people are handing out stuff I can eat. I'm allergic to peanuts, licorice and nougat.

NEAL
How can you possibly be allergic to nougat?

BILL
I don't know. My doctor says I've got more allergies than anybody he's ever seen.

SAM
Then I've got dibs on your malt balls.

BILL
You can have them. I just want the Pixie Stix. Pixie Stix rule.

SAM
Sorry, friend. Chunkys are the best.

HARRIS
I must admit, I'm a wax lips man myself.

SAM
I'll trade you all my wax lips for all your malt balls.

HARRIS
You're on.

(CONTINUED)

CONTINUED:

The guys head off down the street, knocking into each other and having a good time. They look happy.

EXT. WEIR HOUSE - DUSK

Little kids in costumes are standing at the front door.

LITTLE KIDS
Trick or treat!

Jean opens the door. Her face lights up as she sees the kids' costumes.

JEAN
Oh, aren't you all the cutest things? Harold, come look.

Harold pushes past Jean in his Dracula outfit.

HAROLD
(raising his arms like a bat)
I vant to suck your blood!

The kids SCREAM and run away.

HAROLD (CONT'D)
Wait! No! Look, I was just kidding. I'm not really a vampire. I own a sporting goods store!

An ANGRY MOTHER storms up to Harold and Jean.

ANGRY MOTHER
Hey, what's the big idea scaring my kids?

HAROLD
I didn't mean to... I just...

JEAN
I'm so sorry about that. I made him put on the costume.
(hands woman some cookies)
Here, give these to your children. They're homemade.

ANGRY MOTHER
Are you crazy? I've been lecturing my kids for weeks not to take any unwrapped candy.
(MORE)

(CONTINUED)

CONTINUED:

ANGRY MOTHER (CONT'D)
Those cookies could have pins and razor blades in them.

JEAN
I would never do that.

But the woman has stormed away. Jean looks shocked and hurt. Harold watches the woman go, then sees Jean's sad face. He looks her cowgirl outfit up and down.

HAROLD
(trying to be sexy)
Hey, c'mon, cowgirl. Enough of this kids' stuff. Let's head to the barn and I'll give you a good roll in the hay.

JEAN
Oh, Harold, please. Not now.

She pushes past him back into the house. He looks upset.

CUT TO:

INT. DANIEL'S CADILLAC - DUSK

Cheap Trick's "GONNA RAISE HELL" is blaring. Kim is dancing in the front seat. Nick is playing drums on the back of the seat. Lindsay's leaning forward, listening to Daniel.

DANIEL
I mean, think about it. All the people in this town are really religious, you know, but just because it's Halloween, they'll hang pictures of devils and witches and ghosts all over their houses. It's a joke.

LINDSAY
Yeah, I know. It's total hypocrisy.

NICK
Yeah, Lindsay. Exactly.

KIM
You wanna know what I think about it?

Kim lets out a HUGE LONG BURP like a truck driver. Daniel and Nick crack up. Lindsay is taken aback at first, then can't help but laugh when she sees how pleased Kim looks with herself.

(CONTINUED)

CONTINUED:

KEN
Lovely. Your years in charm school have really paid off.

KIM
I'm glad you approve. How are things at ass school?

Daniel laughs. Lindsay leans forward.

LINDSAY
Ooo, you know what? We should go to a movie. There's a new "Friday the 13th" playing.

KIM
Hey, brain, why are you so hung up on doing something? What, are we too boring for you?

NICK
No, man, she's right. We shouldn't just drive around.

DANIEL
Hey, man, we ain't gonna just drive around. It's Halloween night. And I know what it's time for us to do. We are...

Daniel turns up the stereo just in time for Cheap Trick to sing their chorus.

SONG
"...Gonna raise hell!"

Kim holds out her hand to Daniel. Daniel "gives her five" as Nick laughs. Lindsay looks nervous but tries to cover with a forced look of excitement. Kim throws a skeptical smirk at Lindsay that says "you're out of your league."

CUT TO:

EXT. SMOKER'S HOUSE - DUSK

The front door of a house. The geeks come up to it, look at each other with excited smiles, then call out loudly.

THE GEEKS
Trick or treat!

(CONTINUED)

CONTINUED:

They give each other another smile that says "that felt good." A CHAIN SMOKING WOMAN opens the door and immediately eyes the geeks suspiciously.

CHAIN SMOKING WOMAN
What do you want?

BILL
Uh... trick or treat?

She eyes them as the geeks open their pillowcases to receive candy.

CHAIN SMOKING WOMAN
Aren't you guys a little old for this?

The geeks all look at each other, thrown.

SAM
We're only freshmen in high school.

CHAIN SMOKING WOMAN
High school? That's too old.

The geeks just stare at her. They don't know what to do. The woman sighs, grabs some old looking Circus Peanuts (those orange spongy things) from a tupperware bowl and reluctantly drops one into Sam's bag.

CHAIN SMOKING WOMAN
(to Sam)
What the hell are you supposed to be, anyway? The tin man?

SAM
I'm Gort the robot from "The Day the Earth Stood Still."

CHAIN SMOKING WOMAN
Well, you look like the freakin' tin man.

She shakes her head disapprovingly as she drops candy into Bill, Neal and Harris' bags. Sam looks over at Neal, who is glaring at him. Sam just looks away.

BILL
(pulling out a circus peanut)
(MORE)

(CONTINUED)

CONTINUED:

BILL (CONT'D)
Ma'am, are there any peanuts in these peanuts? I hope not, 'cause I could die.

CUT TO:

EXT. NEIGHBORHOOD STREET - DUSK

Daniel's car is parked on a suburban street. The freaks are leaning against Daniel's car looking at a modest house with a large pumpkin on the porch. The pumpkin has a goofy, elaborately-carved face.

KIM
I say we make Lindsay do it.

DANIEL
No, I'm going in.

NICK
No, no, man. Let me do it.

Nick gives Lindsay a wink and heads up the walk to the house, looking around as he goes. Lindsay watches, looking very nervous. Daniel looks at her and laughs.

DANIEL
Hey, relax, it's Halloween. We're supposed to do this stuff.

Lindsay tries to look cool. Kim just looks at her and rolls her eyes. TWO KIDS dressed like cops are about to walk up the house's walkway. Ken holds out his hand.

KEN
Hey, Starsky and Hutch, keep it moving. Nothing to see here.

The kids look scared and move on.

ANGLE ON: Nick gets up to the porch. Looks around, then he kicks in the face of the pumpkin with his hiking boot. Daniel and Kim crack up. Nick bolts back to the car as they all jump in.

NICK
Oh, man, I think he's home!

Daniel drops the car into gear and PEELS OUT just as the front door opens.

Mr. Rosso comes out and sees the smashed pumpkin. Hears the car racing off.

(CONTINUED)

CONTINUED:

MR. ROSSO
(staring down at pumpkin sadly)
Oh, man... that is so uncool.

INT. DANIEL'S CADILLAC - CONTINUOUS

Daniel, Nick and Kim are laughing. Lindsay looks a little dazed in the backseat, looking at the freaks wide-eyed.

LINDSAY
I can't believe we did that.

KEN
Yes, congratulations to us all. I'm so glad I'm not at the Ted Nugent concert.

NICK
(to Lindsay)
Hey, Rosso's always buggin' you, right?

LINDSAY
You did that for me?

NICK
Yeah.

Lindsay gives Nick a big smile. Daniel sees this and does a goofy imitation of Lindsay, complete with girl's voice and pulling his shirt out to make fake boobs.

DANIEL
(doing a goofy girl voice)
Gee, Nicky, it's so charming the way you kicked in that pumpkin for me.

Kim, Ken and Lindsay laugh as Daniel makes an "ain't I funny" face to them. Nick blushes. We can see Lindsay's really having a good time now.

CUT TO:

MONTAGE

MUSIC UP: CHEAP TRICK'S "GONNA RAISE HELL"

EXT. FANCY HOUSE/FRONT DOOR - DUSK

LINDSAY

walks nervously up to the front door of a fancy house. There's a poorly carved pumpkin sitting there.

(CONTINUED)

CONTINUED:

Lindsay looks around, very nervous, then back at Daniel's car. The freaks all make "go ahead" gestures to her.

Lindsay looks around again, then daintily kicks in the face of the pumpkin. It gets stuck on her foot. She tries to dislodge it and goes into a panicky dance when it won't come off.

The freaks are cracking up as Lindsay finally kicks off the pumpkin and bolts back to the car. When she gets there, Nick gives her five. Kim gives her a look that shows she's a little impressed-- but only a little. Lindsay's pleased.

EXT. RUN-DOWN HOUSE/FRONT DOOR - DUSK

THE GEEKS

are at the front door of a run-down house. A HIPPIE-TYPE GUY is giving them candy. The geeks look very scared. Bill looks into his bag.

BILL'S POV: A "fun-sized" chocolate bar sits on top of the other candy.

Bill just looks back at the hippie, who gives him a smile that suddenly looks a little weird. Bill looks like he's going to faint.

EXT. DANIEL'S CADILLAC - DUSK

THE FREAKS

Lindsay and Kim are sticking out the windows of Daniel's car. They are dancing around and waving to all the trick or treaters.

EXT. NEIGHBORHOOD STREET - DUSK

THE GEEKS

are walking along. They don't look like they're having much fun. Suddenly, they hear a HONK. They look over.

GEEKS POV: A car goes by with the Hot Dog on a Stick girls inside. They're wearing their brightly-colored uniforms. They point and laugh at the geeks.

Neal turns and glares daggers at Sam as Bill waves to the girls. Neal slaps his hand down and stalks away.

EXT. DANIEL'S CADILLAC - DUSK

LINDSAY

is hanging out the window of Daniel's car, holding a baseball bat. Daniel drives down the shoulder of the road. Lindsay has the bat cocked back, getting ready to hit something. She looks a little awkward but she's concentrating.

ANGLE ON: A mailbox painted like an American flag approaching with the words "F. Kowchevski" painted on the side.

Lindsay winds up the bat and as Daniel drives past the mailbox, Lindsay swings the bat and BASH! She knocks the mailbox off its post and into the ditch. Lindsay raises her arms in victory and screams triumphantly. (Shoot an option of this with Nick hitting mailbox and Lindsay hugging him.)

INT. DANIEL'S CADILLAC - DUSK

INSIDE THE CAR

Lindsay pops back in as Daniel, Ken and Kim laugh uproariously and applaud for Lindsay. Nick grabs Lindsay and gives her an excited hug. Lindsay looks like she's having the time of her life.

MUSIC OUT.

CUT TO:

INT. WEIR LIVING ROOM - DUSK

Jean is at the door with MRS. KENT, an overly friendly neighborhood mother who is there with her little girl, JILL.

MRS. KENT
(holding a cookie)
Oh, these are so cute. But, Jean, you know, they train the kids not to take unwrapped foodstuffs. You should see. All the parents are dumping the cookies on your lawn.

JILL
They're all covered with ants.

JEAN
What?

MRS. KENT
Well, Happy Halloween.

(CONTINUED)

CONTINUED:

They leave as Jean slowly closes the door and sighs sadly. Harold's sitting on the couch, watching TV in his vampire outfit.

JEAN
I can't take this anymore. Harold, run up to Farmer Jack and get some candy.

HAROLD
Dressed like this? But I--

Harold sees Jean's sad face. He GROANS and gets off the couch.

HAROLD (CONT'D)
Okay, I'll be right back. Just turn off the porch light and don't answer the door until I get back.
(mumbling)
Stupid kids' holiday.

He begrudgingly heads into the kitchen as Jean sits heavily on the couch, trying not to cry.

CUT TO:

EXT. NEIGHBORHOOD STREET - DUSK

The geeks are trudging along, looking a little worse for wear.

NEAL
I can't believe this! I can't believe the Hot Dog On A Stick girls saw us! That's months of ground work down the drain.

SAM
Like they'd ever go out with you.

NEAL
Hey, shut up! They like me. They always give me free lemonade refills.

ALAN (O.C.)
Well, well, well. If it isn't the geek patrol.

The geeks turn and look as ALAN and three of his large buddies appear out of the bushes.

(CONTINUED)

CONTINUED:

NEAL
Oh, no, NO, <u>NO</u>.

The geeks freeze as Alan and crew stalk toward them.

CUT TO:

INT. DANIEL'S CADILLAC - DUSK

Ted Nugent's "Motor City Madhouse" BLARES. Daniel is driving fast. He and Kim are headbanging to the music. Nick is playing the drums on the back of the front seat. Lindsay is leaning up between Daniel and Kim like the family dog.

LINDSAY
I've got it, I've got it! Let's go soap the school's windows!

DANIEL
Nah, I say we get down to some serious damage. Kenneth?

Ken pulls out a carton of eggs from under the front seat and shows them to Kim, Nick and Lindsay.

KEN
Breakfast anyone?

They all laugh and grab for the eggs.

CUT TO:

EXT. NEIGHBORHOOD STREET - DAY

Alan and his large buddies continue their walk toward the geeks, staring at Bill in disbelief.

ALAN
Oh--my--God.

SAM
(nervously)
Hey, Alan. Uh... what's up?

ALAN
(to his buddies)
I knew they were homos but I didn't know they were such huge homos.
(ALTERNATE LINE)
I don't know who's ass I want to kick first.

(CONTINUED)

CONTINUED:

NEAL
You better back off, Alan. We kicked your ass once and we'll kick it again.

ALAN
I don't think so. That was three against one. Now we've got us a fair fight. It's time to settle the score.

SAM
We don't want to fight, Alan.

ALAN
Fine. You don't have to. Just give us all your candy and you're free to go.

HARRIS
Okay, here.

Harris tosses his pillowcase of candy to the bullies. The geeks give Harris a look.

BILL
Forget it. We went through a lot for this candy.

ALAN
You'd better shut your mouth, little girl.

BILL
Hey, I'm not a little girl. I'm the bionic woman.

ALAN
Yeah? Prove it.

And with that, Alan and his buddies rush at the geeks. Sam is immediately pushed over. RIIIPPPPP!!! The cardboard pants of his robot outfit split, as does one of the arms.

Two of Alan's buddies jump on Neal as his other buddy pushes Harris down. Bill's wig is ripped off.

NEAL
(being roughed up)
No, cut it out! Just take the candy. This is my grandpa's coat.

(CONTINUED)

CONTINUED:

HARRIS
Ow! I fell on my knife!

Alan and his buddies grab the geeks' pillowcases and run off, LAUGHING. Neal jumps up, furious.

NEAL
That's it! That is it!
(pointing at Sam)
This is all your fault! I never should have let you talk me into this!

SAM
I didn't talk you into anything!

NEAL
Well, it sure as hell wasn't my idea!

SAM
Oh, yeah, I guess you're too cool getting free lemonade refills.

BILL
(putting his wig back on)
C'mon, guys, let's stick with the plan. Is this on straight?

CUT TO:

INT. DANIEL'S CADILLAC - CONTINUOUS

Daniel is driving slowly as the freaks are scanning out their windows for potential victims. Kim sees something and leans forward.

KIM
Jackpot!

LINDSAY
Where?

LINDSAY (CONT'D)
Up ahead. Throw when I tell you to.

The freaks all get into throwing position. Lindsay looks at Kim. Kim gives her an approving look. Lindsay brightens.

CUT TO:

EXT. NEIGHBORHOOD STREET - CONTINUOUS

The geeks are in a huge argument. Sam and Neal are really going at it.

NEAL
You're the one who's such a baby that he's gotta have a little baby's evening!

SAM
Oh, yeah, and going to some stupid haunted house is that much better?!

As they argue on the sidewalk, Daniel's Cadillac is coming up the road toward them.

INT. DANIEL'S CADILLAC - CONTINUOUS

Lindsay has her arm cocked back, ready to throw her egg.

KIM
Now!

Kim, Nick and Lindsay launch their eggs and laugh.

CUT TO:

EXT. NEIGHBORHOOD STREET - CONTINUOUS

Bill hears the car and turns, just in time to see the eggs flying out the car window.

BILL
(dropping to the ground)
Incoming!

Sam turns and looks. SMACK! An egg hits Sam in the forehead.

SAM
Oh, man!

NEAL
Harris, hit the deck!

Neal and Harris drop on top of Bill. SMACK! SMACK! Two more eggs hit Sam on the arm and in the chest.

BILL
Hey, get off my dress.

Lindsay pops up out of the T-top and yells at them.

(CONTINUED)

CONTINUED:

LINDSAY
HAPPY HALLOWEEN!!!!!

Sam stands staring at the egg running down his costume in shock. Egg drips from his forehead onto his face. Bill stands up and stares after the car.

BILL
Hey, Sam... I think that was Lindsay.

SAM
What?

Sam looks after the car. His jaw drops.

SAM'S POV: Lindsay sticking out the top of Daniel's car. She sees that she has indeed just egged her brother. Her joy immediately turns to horror.

LINDSAY'S POV: Sam's egg-covered face is staring back at her. Sam looks stunned. His mouth just hangs open in shock.

INT. DANIEL'S CADILLAC - CONTINUOUS

Lindsay drops back down into the car as the freaks continue to laugh.

LINDSAY
Oh my God... we just egged my little brother.

Lindsay looks stunned as the freaks all turn and look at her.

END OF ACT THREE

ACT FOUR

FADE IN:

EXT. NEIGHBORHOOD STREET - DUSK

The geeks stand staring at the egg-covered Sam. Neal looks down at his egg-sprayed Groucho costume.

NEAL
(after several beats)
I'm going home.

(CONTINUED)

CONTINUED:

And with this, Neal turns and silently walks away. Bill and Harris watch Neal go, then turn and look at the still-stunned Sam. They have no idea what to say.

CUT TO:

INT. DANIEL'S CADILLAC - DUSK

The freaks are all staring at Lindsay.

LINDSAY
Oh, my God. Stop the car.

DANIEL
It's just eggs, Lindsay. He'll be fine.

The freaks try to look concerned. They all exchange looks, then suddenly burst out laughing. Lindsay looks at them, upset.

LINDSAY
I said stop the car!

Daniel makes a face to himself and pulls the car over. Nick sees that this is deadly serious to Lindsay. He immediately feels bad.

LINDSAY
Let me out.

DANIEL
Ah, c'mon, Lindsay. Take it easy.

NICK
He'll be okay, I swear.

LINDSAY
No, I've gotta go get him.
(pushing on the seat)
C'mon, let me out!

KIM
What the hell, man?

NICK
All right, c'mon, Kim. Let her out.

DANIEL
(sighing)
Don't get out. We'll get him.

(CONTINUED)

CONTINUED:

Daniel throws the car in reverse and backs up toward Sam. Nick looks like he wants to console Lindsay but she's freaked. Kim just stares at her.

CUT TO:

EXT. NEIGHBORHOOD STREET - CONTINUOUS

Bill and Harris see the car backing up toward them.

BILL
Uh, oh. They're coming back to finish us off. Run for it!

HARRIS
Cut through a backyard. It's our only chance.

Bill and Harris take off running. Sam just stands and stares at the car as it approaches. He looks very mad. The car pulls up next to him. Lindsay is leaning out the back window. Kim stares at him from the front seat.

LINDSAY
Sam, I'm sorry. Get in the car.

Sam just glares at her.

LINDSAY
C'mon, Sam, I'm really sorry. Let us give you a ride home.

KIM
C'mon, geek, get in the car!

That's it. Sam turns and starts storming off down the road. Lindsay throws a "thanks for nothing" look at Kim. Daniel throws a look to Nick, then keeps backing up, keeping pace with Sam. Sam won't look at them as he walks.

DANIEL
Hey, kid, it wasn't your sister's fault. She didn't know it was you.

NICK
Yeah, man, she's really upset. Swear to God.

LINDSAY
It's true, Sam.

(CONTINUED)

CONTINUED:

Sam throws a deadly look at Lindsay, then takes off running toward the backyard of the house he's in front of. Lindsay watches him go.

LINDSAY'S POV: The legs of Sam's costume rip and fall off as he runs. Sam disappears into the backyard.

Lindsay just sighs, completely depressed and defeated.

KEN
Is it just me or does he seem upset?

LINDSAY
Oh, man. I'm in so much trouble. Just take me home.

NICK
Hey, Lindsay--

KIM
Ah, take her home. I told you she'd be a drag.

Lindsay just sits back heavily, numb. Daniel looks at her, feels bad when he sees her upset face. He puts the car in gear and pulls a U-turn. Kim throws him a "told you" look.

CUT TO:

EXT. NEIGHBORHOOD STREET - DUSK

MUSIC UP: THE MOODY GUITAR SOLO FROM CHEAP TRICKS' "GONNA RAISE HELL"

Sam is walking home by himself, ripped and covered with egg. He looks very angry.

Slowly, his eyes start to turn red and tear up.Sam angrily wipes his eyes, trying desperately not to cry. THE MUSIC KEEPS PLAYING as we...

CUT TO:

INT. WEIR LIVING ROOM - DUSK

Jean is sitting in the living room drinking coffee and eating a cookie. The huge pile of Halloween cookies is on the coffee table in front of her. Jean looks beyond depressed. DING DONG.

(CONTINUED)

CONTINUED:

KIDS (O.C.)
Trick or treat!

Jean looks at the door, then at the new bag of candy next to her. She doesn't get up. She simply SIGHS, takes another cookie off the pile and starts eating it.

MUSIC OUT.

Sam enters from the kitchen, egged, costume tattered, spirit broken. Jean looks over and sees him. She GASPS.

JEAN
Oh, my God! Sam! What happened?

SAM
I got egged.

Harold runs in from the other room, having heard Jean's yell.

HAROLD
What's the matter? What's going on?

JEAN
Sam was attacked.
(rushing over to Sam)
Oh, my poor baby, are you all right? Did you get egg in your eyes?

SAM
(suddenly embarrassed)
I'm fine.

Just then, Lindsay comes in the front door. She stops when she sees Sam, certain she's in trouble. Sam just glares at her. Jean and Harold see Lindsay.

HAROLD
Well, well, well. Look who's here. So happy you could grace us all with your presence.

Jean's more concerned with Sam at the moment.

JEAN
(upset; doting)
What kind of terrible people would throw eggs at my little boy? And after you worked so hard on your costume, too.

(CONTINUED)

CONTINUED:

HAROLD
Who the hell did this to you, Sam?

Sam looks at his parents, then at Lindsay. Lindsay gives Sam a pleading look.

SAM
(after a beat)
Some freaks.

JEAN
"Freaks?" Like circus freaks?

HAROLD
Jean, I don't think there's bearded ladies going around throwing eggs at kids. He means hippies.
(to Sam)
Do you know who these "freaks" were?

SAM
(pointedly at Lindsay)
It was just a bunch of dirtbags.

JEAN
Oh, honey...

Jean hugs Sam and starts trying to clean him off, trying to wipe dried egg off his face. Sam throws another angry look at Lindsay. He's embarrassed by the whole situation.

JEAN (CONT'D)
(fawning over Sam)
My poor little baby.

SAM
I'm not a baby!

And with this, Sam bolts off to his room. Jean and Harold are surprised. SLAM! Sam shuts himself in his bedroom.

HAROLD
Well, I'm certainly glad we all decided to celebrate Halloween. Last time I had this much fun I was pinned down in a fox hole by the North Koreans.

Harold sees Jean's sad face. It's like kicking a dog when she's down. He sighs, feeling bad for her.

(CONTINUED)

CONTINUED:

HAROLD (CONT'D)
I'm sorry, honey. You did a nice job.

Harold gives her a supportive smile, then turns to Lindsay.

HAROLD (CONT'D)
And you are on thin ice, missy.

Harold gives Lindsay the ultimate "I'm very, disappointed in you" look and exits. Jean looks at Lindsay.

JEAN
I didn't expect to see you back so soon.

LINDSAY
(covering; feeling guilty)
Mom, I told you I was only going out for a little bit.

JEAN
Who were those people you went off with?

LINDSAY
Just some friends from school.

JEAN
Anyone I know?

LINDSAY
Not really.

JEAN
If you didn't want to hand out candy with me, you could have just told me.

LINDSAY
No, I couldn't. I didn't want to make you feel bad.

Lindsay stops, realizing the irony of her statement. Jean just gives her a look, then sadly starts taking down Halloween decorations.

JEAN
(sighing; defeated)
I don't know, Lindsay.
(MORE)

(CONTINUED)

CONTINUED:

JEAN (CONT'D)
The world's such a different place than the one I grew up in. Everybody just seems so much... meaner these days.

LINDSAY
Mom... your friends never threw eggs when you were a kid?

JEAN
(after a beat, defeated)
I don't know. I guess so. I just know that I never did.

Jean sits back down on the couch and grabs another cookie. She looks at it. A happy pumpkin face is drawn on it in frosting. Jean looks like she might cry.

Lindsay watches her mom for a beat. Lindsay has no idea what to say. She turns and heads off to her room as Jean puts the cookie back on the pile and sighs.

INT. SAM'S BEDROOM - EVENING

Sam is sitting on his bed. His ruined robot costume is in a heap in the corner. Sam stares at it, depressed.

Lindsay knocks on his door as she pokes her head in. Sam sees it's her and freezes her out.

LINDSAY
(trying to joke)
Nothing like getting yelled at by dad when he's dressed like a vampire, huh?

Sam ignores her, looking down.

LINDSAY (CONT'D)
Thanks for not turning me in.

Silence.

LINDSAY (CONT'D)
I'm really sorry. You know that, don't you?

Sam just keeps looking down. Lindsay stares at him another beat, then sighs and turns to leave. As she's almost out the door...

(CONTINUED)

CONTINUED:

SAM
Nobody thinks you're cool, you know.

Lindsay stops in the doorway.

LINDSAY
(without looking back at him)
Trust me... I know.

She leaves. Sam looks after her, upset and confused.

DISSOLVE TO:

INT. WEIR LIVING ROOM - EVENING

Jean is sitting on the couch, too depressed to even eat cookies. DING DONG!

KIDS (O.C.)
Trick or treat!

Jean looks like she's not going to answer the door again, then thinks a second. Her face shows a bit of resolve as she picks up the bag of candy and heads to the door.

LINDSAY (O.C.)
Mom?

Jean looks over.

ANGLE ON: Lindsay is standing there, looking pretty, dressed as... Prince Charming! Lindsay looks confused.

JEAN
Oh, it's the wrong costume. You were supposed to be my little princess.

LINDSAY
Well, I guess I'll just have to be your little prince instead.

Jean stares at the costume and starts to giggle. This makes Lindsay crack a smile. DING DONG DING DONG!

KIDS (O.C.)
Trick or treat!

LINDSAY
I'll get it.

(CONTINUED)

CONTINUED:

Lindsay goes to the door and opens it. There's a bunch of little kids in costumes. Jean looks at them, suddenly happier than a clam.

JEAN
Oh, my gracious! Aren't you all the cutest things! Aren't they cute, Lindsay?

Lindsay smiles at the kids, then looks at her mom having fun fawning over the kids.

LINDSAY
Yeah. They are.

Lindsay watches her mom hand out candy to the kids, then joins in, looking happy for the moment.

DISSOLVE TO:

EXT. WEIR HALLWAY - LATER THAT NIGHT

Harold is heading down the dark hall, looking tired. He passes Sam's room and sees light coming from under the closed door. He stops and goes back to it.

Harold listens at the door, then knocks lightly on it.

HAROLD
Sam, can I come in?

SAM (O.C.)
(after a beat)
Yeah.

INT. SAM'S BEDROOM - CONTINUOUS

Harold peeks his head into Sam's room.

HAROLD'S POV: Sam is sitting up in bed, reading "Crime and Punishment." He looks at his dad.

Harold gives him a concerned fatherly smile.

HAROLD
You okay, Sam?

SAM
Yeah. I'm just reading a book for school.

(CONTINUED)

CONTINUED:

Sam stares at his dad. Sam looks neither depressed nor happy. Just resigned. Harold nods, staring at his son.

HAROLD
Is it any good?

SAM
I don't know yet. Everyone's name is really weird and long.

HAROLD
Well... don't stay up too late.

SAM
I won't, dad.

Harold gives Sam another supportive smile. Sam gives his dad a small smile back and goes back to his book as Harold closes the door.

FADE OUT.

END OF SHOW

# FREAKS AND GEEKS

"KIM KELLY IS MY FRIEND"

Episode #4

Written by Mike White

Directed by Lesli Glatter

Busy Philipps was one of the primary reasons I wanted to write on *Freaks and Geeks*. When I saw the scene in the pilot in which Kim Kelly sexually humiliates Sam Weir (the scene was later cut), I knew this was the show I'd been waiting for. I loved Busy's big lips and the psychotic look in her eyes. I liked that she was kind of pretty and definitely scary. She reminded me of my older cousin Tami who ditched school to drink beer in parking lots and used baby-sitting me as an alibi to sneak out to Tom Petty concerts. I worshiped Tami.

When Judd was looking for a staff member to write an episode for the Kim Kelly character, I sprung. A story for Kim would be easy—my cousin had provided me over the years with so much true-life comical material. What happens to Lindsay when she visits the Kellys pretty much happened to me one day over at my Aunt Sharon's house—even the mother-daughter cat fight and the mad dash to the car. I was proud of the script. I thought it was funny.

However, when I saw the first assembly, I got nervous. Like a lot of things I'd written over the years, something amusing on the page had turned dark and disturbing when enacted on film. Busy and Linda were great and the story tracked, but was it funny? Judd said it was and pooh-poohed my anxieties. I could tell, though, that Paul didn't like it. His distressed reaction was the first of many people who felt the episode was too acidic for a Saturday night tweener show. Attempted hit-and-runs, domestic violence, talk of drug overdoses, and hints of incest. Eight o'clock is the family hour.

The show never aired on NBC—at least in the first run. I was chagrined, but also a little proud. My episode was too edgy. I was keeping it real. I fought the law and the law won. I was also kind of relieved that my cousin Tami would never see how I'd exploited her life for my art. I realized later that there wasn't much chance of that happening—even if it had aired.

Tami isn't the rebel blonde she used to be. She's a single mom, raising two kids, working as a receptionist at a plastic surgeon's office. She still listens to Tom Petty and still parties on occasion. At my Aunt Sharon's for Christmas dinner, I eagerly asked her what she thought of *Freaks and Geeks*. I assumed she'd be a fan since the show takes place in the late seventies, the very years she was tormenting her parents and cutting class to smoke out. Tami sipped her Chardonnay and shrugged. "*Freaks and Geeks*? I avoided those people in high school. Why would I want to watch a show about them now?"

—Mike White

FREAKS AND GEEKS

"KIM KELLY IS MY FRIEND"

**CAST LIST**

LINDSAY WEIR
SAM WEIR
HAROLD WEIR
JEAN WEIR
DANIEL DESARIO
NICK ANDOPOLIS
BILL HAVERCHUCK
NEAL SCHWEIBER
KIM KELLY
MILLIE KENTNER
MR. KOWCHEVSKI
KAREN SCARFOLLI
COOKIE KELLY
ARLO
CHIP KELLY
FEMALE TEACHER
PERKY BLONDE
GOOD-LOOKING GUY

FREAKS AND GEEKS

"KIM KELLY IS MY FRIEND"

**SET LIST**

**INTERIORS:**

MCKINLEY HIGH SCHOOL
/HALLWAY
/CAFETERIA
/CLASSROOM
WEIR HOUSE
/KITCHEN
/SAM'S BEDROOM
/DINING ROOM
/LIVING ROOM
/HALLWAY
KIM'S GREMLIN
KIM KELLY'S HOUSE

**EXTERIORS:**

MCKINLEY HIGH SCHOOL
/SMOKING PATIO
WEIR HOUSE
/STREET
KIM KELLY'S HOUSE
KIM'S GREMLIN
BASKETBALL COURT

TEASER

FADE IN:

INT. MCKINLEY HIGH SCHOOL - MORNING

The halls of McKinley are teeming with STUDENTS congregating before first period.

We SCAN the crowd - kids gossip, flirt, argue - before resting on MILLIE, walking purposefully through the throng. She carries an open box of colorful donuts. She passes by DANIEL and NICK. Daniel casually grabs a rainbow sprinkle from her box. She spins around.

MILLIE
Hey. That's for my French class.

DANIEL
Aww, but I love sprinkles.

MILLIE
(after a huff of irritation)
Fine. Just eat it.

NICK
(puppy-dog adorable)
Hey. Could I have one, too? I've got this thing... it's called, the munchies.

Millie considers his request. She relents, holding the box out to Nick.

MILLIE
Just take one of the plains, okay?

But before Nick can grab a donut, KIM and her friend, KAREN SCARFOLLI approach, engrossed in conversation. Not looking where she's going, Karen inadvertently knocks the box over, the donuts all fall to the ground.

DANIEL
Whoa.

KAREN
(unapologetic; to MILLIE)
People are walking here, okay?

Millie looks at her dead, dirty donuts and becomes distraught. She stares the Freaks down a la Mia Farrow facing the coven of witches in the finale of Rosemary's Baby.

(CONTINUED)

CONTINUED:

MILLIE
You're all maniacs!

She takes off down the hall. The Freaks can't help but giggle. Nick and Daniel grab a few donuts from the floor and commence to chow. Nick, mouth full, looks at Karen.

NICK
What's your problem?

KAREN
(storming away)
My problem is your face, dirtbag.

Daniel and Nick look to Kim. Kim grabs a chunk of donut sticking out of Daniel's mouth and sticks it in her own.

KIM
Ricky dumped her this morning. She's on the warpath.

DANIEL
Well, if she's looking for new customers, tell her I'd be up for a test-drive.

Daniel grins, suggestively.

KIM
Shut up, Daniel.

Kim shoves Daniel's donut into his face, then wanders off after Karen. We FOLLOW her.

KIM (CONT'D)
Karen. Wait up.

Kim pushes past a GOOD-LOOKING GUY and a PERKY BLONDE. We STAY on them as they walk up the hall.

PERKY BLONDE
Jeez, Perry. You're looking huge.

GOOD-LOOKING GUY
Yeah, I've been working out after school.

He retracts his arm to flex his bicep for her, just as SAM, NEAL and BILL turn the corner. The Guy accidentally hits Sam in the chest with a HARD THUD. The Perky Blonde SHRIEKS, startled.

(CONTINUED)

CONTINUED: (2)

GOOD-LOOKING GUY (CONT'D)
Sorry, little guy. I didn't see you. Did I hurt you, sport?

Sam shakes his head. The Good-Looking Guy and the Perky Blonde take off. Sam has the wind knocked out of him. He clutches his chest.

SAM
I... can't... breathe.

Neal and Bill watch with interest as Sam slowly gets his breath back.

NEAL
You okay?

Sam nods.

BILL
That guy hit you in the solar plexus.

They all approach Sam's locker.

NEAL
Fellas - my brother sent me this amazing chem set.

Neal surveys the scene, making sure there are no eavesdroppers. Then, in a whisper...

NEAL (CONT'D)
I propose - after school - we make acid, pour it on the sidewalk and watch it kill the bugs.

Bill is giddy at the thought. Sam is having trouble opening his locker. Suddenly, Karen Scarfolli is tapping him on the shoulder. She's pissed. Kim stands behind her, watching.

KAREN
What are you doing?! That's my locker.

Sam realizes he's standing in front of the wrong locker.

SAM
Oh, I'm sorry. You're right.
(points to adjacent locker)
This is my locker.
(MORE)

(CONTINUED)

CONTINUED: (3)

SAM (CONT'D)
I just got hit in the solar plexus - I'm a little out of it.

KAREN
I don't want to hear your life story. I want you to move your ass.

KIM
Was this guy trying to break into your locker?

SAM
I was confused. I thought it was my locker.

KAREN
Yeah, you're very confused, Peewee. Are you sure you're even in the right school? You look like you should be in fifth grade. How old are you?

SAM
Fourteen.

The SCHOOL BELL RINGS.

KAREN
You can't be fourteen, Midget. You haven't even hit puberty.

Karen grabs his shirt and yanks it upward. Sam's naked torso is exposed. Karen inspects his armpits.

KAREN (CONT'D)
I knew it. You don't even have hair in your pits.

Kim can't help but laugh.

KIM
Come on, Karen. Let's go.

KAREN
You swear you're fourteen?
(he nods; then, with a sneer)
Then you're a geek. Which one's your locker?

Sam feebly points to his locker. Karen takes a LIPSTICK out of her shirt pocket and writes "GEEK" down Sam's locker.

(CONTINUED)

KAREN (CONT'D)
Now you'll always know which one's yours and which one's mine. Okay, Geek?

Sam stumbles away from his locker.

As he walks down the hall, he sneaks a look down his shirt at one of his armpits. Disgusted with what he sees, he shakes his head and we...

CUT TO:

MAIN TITLES

ACT ONE

FADE IN:

INT. CAFETERIA - DAY

Swarming with students. LINDSAY walks away from the food register with her tray, nearly colliding with a GIGGLING GIRL who is being playfully chased by a MALE JOCK. Lindsay scans the room for a place to sit. She spots...

Kim, Daniel and Nick eating at a nearby table.

AT THE TABLE

DANIEL
So why'd Ricky dump Karen? Is she like a prude? Does she not, you know, go the distance?

Daniel smirks at Nick, who laughs.

NICK
Go the distance.

Lindsay sits down at their table. Nick smiles at her, but Daniel and Kim hardly notice.

KIM
No, she's not a prude. She's a slut. Obviously.

DANIEL
Yeah, obviously, if she's a friend of yours.

Kim leans in, conspiratorially.

(CONTINUED)

CONTINUED:

KIM
Last week, she started getting it on with Ricky's older brother.

DANIEL
Cool.

KIM
Yesterday, he walked in on them.

Kim uses a hand gesture to indicate something sexual. Nick and Daniel shake their heads, in disbelief.

LINDSAY
Who walked in on who?

KIM
(mimicking)
Who walked in on who?
(shaking her head)
People are so gossipy at this school, It's like... get a life.

Kim sticks her finger in Lindsay's pudding, then licks it. Lindsay, revolted, grabs her tray and jumps to her feet. The Freaks watch as Lindsay sits down at another table.

KIM (CONT'D)
What's with her?

AT LINDSAY'S NEW TABLE

Lindsay sits with a group of left-overs: a GIRL with head-gear, an overweight boy (GORDON CRISP) and an IMPISH BOY who whispers to himself. Lindsay smiles at them all.

LINDSAY
Hi.

GORDON CRISP
That's Gary Moss's seat. But he's sick today. He's got impetigo.

Lindsay reacts. After a moment, Nick comes over and sits across from her.

NICK
You're gonna sit over here now?

LINDSAY
I just don't feel like getting abused today.

(CONTINUED)

CONTINUED: (2)

Lindsay, worked up, gesticulates with her hands for emphasis.

LINDSAY (CONT'D)
I mean, I give up. I go out of my way to be nice, but it's like... no matter what I do, you know?

She accidentally gets her jacket sleeve caught in the headgear of the girl sitting next to her. The Girl YELPS in pain.

LINDSAY (CONT'D)
Oh my god. I'm so sorry.

The Girl says nothing, disentangling her head gear, then scooting away.

NICK
I'm gonna talk to Kim. Right now.

LINDSAY
No, don't.

NICK
(indignant)
Yeah. I am! It's cool when you hang out and she shouldn't ruin everything for everyone just 'cause she's always on her period.

LINDSAY (MORTIFIED)
No, Nick. No! It's okay.

NICK
It's not okay. That's the thing.

LINDSAY
Just please don't. Don't say anything to her. Promise me you won't.

NICK
Okay. Whatever you want.

Lindsay gives him an appreciative smile.

CUT TO:

INT. HALLWAY - DAY

Sam is frantically wiping the lipstick "GEEK" off his locker. Neal and Bill stand behind him, observing.

(CONTINUED)

CONTINUED:

NEAL
(doing his best Rod Serling)
A defaced locker, a humiliated Freshman and a busty succubus from Hell. Perhaps we have left McKinley High and entered the chilling corridors of the Twilight Zone.

SAM
You're not funny.

NEAL
I can't believe she smelled your pits.

BILL
I thought she was gonna make love to you.

Sam rolls his eyes.

BILL
Your locker's right next to hers. What if she starts ripping your clothes off every day?

SAM
Well, what am I supposed to do? Fight her? She's a girl. My dad has a rule. You don't fight girls.

NEAL
My dad has a rule. You don't piss your pants in school.

SAM
I didn't piss my pants.

Suddenly, Sam's face drops when he sees... Karen Scarfolli stomping towards them. Sam turns to leave, but too lae.

KAREN
Hey! What happened to my artwork?!
(banging on his locker)
I spent a long time on that.

SAM
I... I washed it off.

(CONTINUED)

CONTINUED: (2)

KAREN
How are you gonna remember which one's your locker?!

SAM
I'll remember.

KAREN
No, you won't. You're an idiot.

SAM
(almost inaudibly)
Hey. I don't want to have to fight you.

Bill lets out an involuntary "OOOH". Karen glares at Neal.

KAREN
What was that, Bilbo Baggins?

NEAL
(pointing to BILL)
I didn't say anything. It was him.

KAREN
Are you guys deformed or something? I mean, what's the deal?

As she approaches, Neal and Bill back up, frightened by her.

KAREN (CONT'D)
I'm just gonna have to mark this locker again - this time with something permanent - like geek blood.

All three bolt, scattering in different directions. Karen watches them flee, disgusted.

CUT TO:

INT. ANOTHER PART OF HALLWAY - CONTINUOUS

Lindsay approaches Daniel, who is loitering in the hall.

LINDSAY
What are you doing?

DANIEL
Kim wants me to wait for her. She's on the phone with her mom.

(CONTINUED)

CONTINUED:

He points across the hall. Kim is on the pay phone.

KIM
I said, I don't know! Are you deaf?! I'll try, okay?! Would you stop yelling at me, you psychopath?

Watching Kim rant, Daniel shakes his head.

DANIEL
Sometimes relationships can be a drag.

LINDSAY
Especially if you're going out with her.
(instantly regretting)
Sorry.

DANIEL
No, I know. Kim can be cool, though. You just gotta get to know her.

KIM
(on the phone)
Mother, you have really lost it this time. You need help! God!

Kim slams down the pay phone and approaches them.

KIM
As usual, my mom's being a total shrew.

The BELL RINGS. Daniel grimaces.

DANIEL
Oh, great. Biology. I think I have a test or something. See ya guys later.

Daniel wanders off, leaving Lindsay and Kim alone together.

KIM
So... how's it going?

LINDSAY
(a bit suspicious)
What?

Even though she's trying to be nice, Kim is a bit annoyed.

(CONTINUED)

CONTINUED: (2)

KIM
I said, how's it going?

LINDSAY
Fine. I guess.

KIM
What are you doing after school?
(off Lindsay's shrug)
Meet me after school, okay? We can hang.

LINDSAY
Okay.

Kim takes off. Lindsay is in shock, watching Kim go. Millie approaches, also watching Kim.

MILLIE
I heard about what she does in the yearbook dark room.

LINDSAY
What she does?

MILLIE
You know.

Millie contorts her face, conspiratorially.

LINDSAY
What? I don't know what you're talking about.

MILLIE
She does it.

LINDSAY
What do you mean, 'it'?

MILLIE
She fornicates it, okay?!

LINDSAY
I doubt it. And so what if she does?

MILLIE
I just think it's sad.

(CONTINUED)

CONTINUED: (3)

LINDSAY
We can't all be girl scouts,
Millie.

MILLIE
Oh, so you don't even care that she
fornicates it in the yearbook dark
room?

LINDSAY
At least she doesn't spend her
whole life worrying about what
other people think of her.

Millie puckers her mouth, her eyes full of judgment.

LINDSAY (CONT'D)
(defiant)
What?

MILLIE
(prissy)
Nothing.

LINDSAY
I gotta get to class.  See ya.

CUT TO:

INT. CLASSROOM - DAY

The BELL RINGS in Western Civ class. As the students head for the door, the TEACHER shouts out...

FEMALE TEACHER (O.S.)
And I expect legible handwriting. I
can't spend my time trying to
decipher your chicken scrawl.
That's not my job.

Sam exits into the hall. He is intercepted by a troubled Bill.

BILL
You gotta come see this.

SAM
What is it?

BILL
Hurry, man.

(CONTINUED)

CONTINUED:

Bill leads Sam across the hall. Sam stops dead in his tracks when he sees...

A few feet away - HIS LOCKER - on it, written in big black lettering, the word, "PYGMY GEEK". It is already a conversation piece. A few students have gathered around the locker, commenting.

SAM
(horrified)
What's a pygmy?

BILL
It's a dwarf. From Australia. That's a nickname. If you don't get rid of that, you're gonna be called "Pygmy Geek" for the next four years.

Sam quickly opens his bookbag and takes out a handful of pens. He settles on a big black marker. Wielding his marker, he pushes his way through the crowd.

He frantically begins blacking out the words. He is almost done when MR. KOWCHEVSKI appears behind him.

MR. KOWCHEVSKI
Weir!

Sam spins around. Kowchevski is incensed.

MR. KOWCHEVSKI (CONT'D)
What the hell are you doing?!

A group of students "ooh" in unison.

MR. KOWCHEVSKI (CONT'D)
Oh, grow up.

SAM
I'm... somebody wrote on my locker.

MR. KOWCHEVSKI
So, that's your locker?

SAM
Yes.

MR. KOWCHEVSKI
No, it isn't. It's the school's locker. That's gonna have to be re-painted, bub.

(CONTINUED)

CONTINUED: (2)

SAM
But it wasn't me.

Mr. Kowchevski grabs the pen from Sam's hand.

MR. KOWCHEVSKI
This wasn't you?

SAM
Yeah, but, ummm...

As Kowchevski talks, he inadvertently touches his face with Sam's pen, getting an ink stain on his cheek.

MR. KOWCHEVSKI
You kids don't respect school property. You just don't get it.
(has an idea)
Okay. You're gonna write an essay - by tomorrow - five hundred words.
(searching)
Why vandalism... why the property of the school should be respected and why we should respect it. And if you don't have the essay by tomorrow, you're gonna be on trash detail for a week. Got me?

Sam nods. Mr. Kowchevski, unaware that his face has ink on it, seems satisfied and walks away.

CUT TO:

EXT. UNDER THE BLEACHERS - DAY

STUDENTS are leaving for the day. Among them is Lindsay.

KIM (O.S.)
Lindsay!

Lindsay turns. Kim and Daniel are sitting on the patio together. Nick is also here, asleep. Kim gets up and approaches Lindsay.

KIM (CONT'D)
Where you going?

LINDSAY
I don't know. Home.

KIM
What are you doing for dinner?

(CONTINUED)

CONTINUED:

Lindsay shrugs.

KIM (CONT'D)
You wanna come over to my house?

LINDSAY
(confused)
Look, did Nick say something to you?

KIM
What?

LINDSAY
Did he tell you to be nice to me?

KIM
Oh, yeah. I just figured since we see each other all the time, we might as well try to get along. So you wanna have dinner at my house or not?

LINDSAY
(suspicious)
I don't know.

KIM
(annoyed)
Fine. Forget it. I tried.

Kim starts walking away. Lindsay calls out.

LINDSAY
Kim. Yeah.

KIM
Yeah, what?

LINDSAY
Yeah, I'll have dinner at your house.

KIM
(pleased)
All right. My parents are jerks. They love to kill my buzz. But after dinner, we'll ditch 'em and catch a movie or something.

LINDSAY
That sounds cool.

(CONTINUED)

CONTINUED: (2)

KIM
I'll pick you up at your house. Five-thirty.

LINDSAY
Okay.

Kim smiles. Lindsay smiles back, a bit astonished.

LINDSAY (CONT'D)
(happy)
Well, see ya at five-thirty.

KIM
Later.

Lindsay walks away. After a few strides, she turns back. Kim sits on Daniel's lap. Daniel gives Kim a kiss. Lindsay smiles to herself as she walks away and we...

FADE OUT.

END OF ACT ONE

ACT TWO

FADE IN:

INT. WEIR KITCHEN - DAY

JEAN prepares dinner. Sam stands before the refrigerator.

JEAN
How was school, sweetheart?

SAM
(snapping)
I don't want to talk about it.

JEAN
Oh. Okay, then.

Sam takes out a tupperware container of left-over pasta salad, grabs a fork and begins to eat heaping forkfuls.

JEAN (CONT'D)
Samuel, you're going to ruin your dinner.

SAM
I'm loading up on carbs.

(CONTINUED)

CONTINUED:

JEAN
(holding up a potato)
But we're having carbs for dinner.

SAM
(jumping on her)
You want me to stay a midget? Is that what you want?

JEAN
You're not a midget.

SAM
Yes, I am. And it's because there's no food in this house. I'm malnourished.

Sam shoves his face full of pasta. Jean is defensive, opening the pantry.

JEAN
No food. Well, what's all this? Beef jerky, fruit roll-ups. You're just finicky.

Lindsay enters the kitchen.

LINDSAY
Mom, is it okay if I skip out on dinner?

JEAN
(frustrated)
What? Why?

LINDSAY
I was invited over to Kim Kelly's house.

Sam's mouth drops open.

JEAN
Who's Kim Kelly?

LINDSAY
She's a friend.

JEAN
(pleased)
Oh, yeah? A new friend? What's she like?

(CONTINUED)

CONTINUED: (2)

LINDSAY
I don't know. She's just this girl.

SAM
Kim Kelly's a psycho.

Lindsay and Jean both turn to Sam. He shovels pasta into his mouth.

SAM (CONT'D)
She and Karen Scarfolli. They're violent. They run around the school, being evil.

JEAN
That doesn't sound very nice. Why do you want to be friends with a girl like that?

LINDSAY
She's not evil, Mom.

Lindsay shoots a look at Sam.

LINDSAY (CONT'D)
She's just different. She doesn't wear frilly dresses or prance around like a cheerleader. Just because a girl is strong-willed and speaks her mind doesn't mean she's a psycho.

JEAN
Well, you should have told me yesterday. I'm making veal piccata. Maybe another night.

LINDSAY
Mom, she's coming to pick me up in fifteen minutes!

JEAN
Eat with your friend.

Lindsay is a bit guilt-stricken.

CUT TO:

EXT. WEIR HOUSE - DAY

Lindsay is waiting on the lawn for Kim to arrive. Sam exits the house, taking out the trash. He approaches Lindsay.

SAM
I can't believe you're friends with Kim Kelly.

LINDSAY
Don't talk to me, okay?

SAM
Kim Kelly's my enemy.

LINDSAY
Look, if you're gonna start being a tattle-tale and trying to get me into trouble, then maybe you better go to a different high school. I don't need some spy reporting on my every move.

SAM
Why are you hanging out with her?

LINDSAY
Why not?

SAM
She and her friends are mean to me. They wrote "geek" on my locker.

LINDSAY
Well, maybe you are a geek.

Just as the words leave her mouth, Lindsay regrets them. Sam's face falls.

LINDSAY (CONT'D)
I'm just kidding.

But Sam says nothing. He hefts up the trash bag and walks toward the street curb, where the trash cans are waiting to be unloaded. Lindsay calls out after him.

LINDSAY (CONT'D)
Sam - I didn't mean it.

(CONTINUED)

20.

CONTINUED:

Suddenly, a GREMLIN appears, speeding down the street. The car approaches and comes to a SCREECHING halt in front of the Weir house, inches away from colliding with a startled Sam. Of course, it's Kim Kelly. She yells out the window...

KIM
Hey! Move it or lose it!

Sam, almost in tears, promptly drops the trash bag and runs into the house. Lindsay watches him, feeling sympathetic.

Kim HONKS her horn, waving to Lindsay.

INT. KIM'S GREMLIN - MOMENTS LATER

Lindsay hops into the passenger seat. Kim is scowling, clutching her stomach.

KIM
I got the worst cramps. I just about died on the way over here.

LINDSAY
Hey, Kim.

KIM
What?

LINDSAY
Can you do me a favor? Can you quit picking on my brother?

KIM
(pointing to the house)
Oh, yeah. I keep forgetting that's your brother. He looks like all those other geeks.

Kim turns up the RADIO. She likes the song that's playing. She grins, rocking along to the music. Lindsay smiles, too. And the car PEELS OUT.

CUT TO:

INT. WEIR KITCHEN - MOMENTS LATER

Sam comes tearing into the kitchen, startling Jean.

SAM
I hate Lindsay and her stupid friends.

JEAN
You don't hate your sister.

(CONTINUED)

CONTINUED:

SAM
Yes, I do. She sucks!

Sam grabs a banana from the counter, quickly peels it and stuffs it in his mouth. Jean watches him, astonished.

EXT. KIM KELLY'S HOUSE - DAY

Kim's neighborhood is noticeably less affluent than Lindsay's. She lives in a run-down tract home. The yard grass is dead and there's a stripped car in the driveway. Kim's Gremlin pulls up and parks.

INT. KIM'S GREMLIN - CONTINUOUS

Kim prepares to see her parents. As they sit in the car, she drops Visine in her eyes, chews gum and checks herself out.

KIM
All right, I'm warning you right now, my parents are seriously whacko.

LINDSAY
Yeah. Mine, too. Don't worry about it.

KIM
No. They're mental, okay?!

LINDSAY
Oh. Okay.

KIM
They're looking for a reason to sell my Gremlin.

LINDSAY
They are?

KIM
They're such cheap bastards! But my Aunt Cathy gave me that car and it's mine!

LINDSAY
(a bit confused)
Right.

KIM
My Aunt Cathy was so rad. She lived in LA - she was in "Kojak." She doinked Ryan O'Neal at a party once.

(CONTINUED)

CONTINUED:

LINDSAY
Wow. She sounds... awesome.

KIM
Oh, well, she's dead. She O.D.'d on coke.

Lindsay is stunned.

KIM (CONT'D)
(desperate)
So you see - there's a lot riding on this dinner. I can't lose my car. You get it?

LINDSAY
I'm not sure if I do.

Kim rolls her eyes, frustrated.

KIM
My parents hate everybody. They hate Daniel. They hate Karen. The only person they like is you.

LINDSAY
But... I've never even met them.

Kim opens her car door and they both pile out.

EXT. KIM KELLY'S HOUSE - CONTINUOUS

Kim and Lindsay walk toward the house. COOKIE KELLY comes out to the porch, waiting for them. She is pretty, but rather hard-looking.

KIM
Well, I've told them all about you. How you're like this golden girl and everything and how you get good grades. My mother's gonna be pressing you for information. Just follow my lead.
(under her breath)
And remember - I spend the night at your house every Friday. Oh, and last weekend we drove to your vacation house in Benton Harbor and went water-skiing.

LINDSAY
Wait, what?

(CONTINUED)

CONTINUED:

But Kim's mother is now within earshot.

COOKIE
(smiling)
Hi, there. You must be Lindsay.

LINDSAY
Yeah. Nice to meet you.

COOKIE
Kim, did you pick up any soda?

KIM
I forgot.

COOKIE
(annoyed)
Yeah? Well, I forgot to make you dinner. How do you like that?

CUT TO:

INT. KIM KELLY'S HOUSE - MOMENTS LATER

Kim and Lindsay are at the dinner table with Cookie and Kim's step-father, ARLO. Arlo is the burly, silent-type. Cookie spends most of her energy suppressing an explosive temperament. The cramped house is cluttered and in disrepair. Take-out fried chicken is what's for dinner.

Cookie stares at Lindsay for an extended moment, while sucking on a chicken bone.

COOKIE
Kim says you're a genius.

LINDSAY
(embarrassed)
No. I'm not. At all.

UNDER THE TABLE - Kim gives Lindsay's leg a firm kick.

Lindsay's face registers pain and shock. She locks eyes with a grimacing Kim.

LINDSAY (CONT'D)
I get good grades, I guess.

COOKIE
Well, why don't you help out Kim? She's hanging on for dear life.

(CONTINUED)

CONTINUED:

KIM
B.S. I get good grades.

COOKIE
I don't want to blow your mind, sister, but D's are not good. D's are bad.

KIM
I got one D, okay? I told you - my History teacher was a pervert. I wasn't gonna go to his house after school to get tutored!

Cookie suddenly erupts, her face turning beat red.

COOKIE
CAN IT, KIM! You're gonna wake up Chip.

Lindsay notices Kim's older brother, CHIP, asleep on the couch, his mouth agape. Kim bites her lip, then acidly...

KIM
At least I know how to read.

ARLO
(defensive)
What was that?

KIM
Nothing.

COOKIE
So, I hear you girls had a fun weekend.

Lindsay glances over at a bug-eyed Kim.

LINDSAY
(weakly)
Yeah, it was great. We went water-skiing. I love to water ski.

COOKIE
And you have a vacation house up there in Benton Harbor? That must be nice. Your family must be very wealthy.

LINDSAY
Hardly.

(CONTINUED)

CONTINUED: (2)

UNDER THE TABLE - Kim gives Lindsay another swift kick in the shin. Lindsay YELPS in pain, then composes herself.

COOKIE
Kim told us you're affluent.

LINDSAY
Well, we do all right. I'm not really supposed to talk about that. My father always says, a farmer never reveals how many cows he's got.

ARLO
Your father's a farmer?

LINDSAY
No. He owns A-1 sporting goods.

ARLO
Yeah? Can you get us a discount?

COOKIE
Well, we don't live in a mansion, as you can see. We don't have a swimming pool and a tennis court like you do.

Lindsay reacts to this.

ARLO
(annoyed with COOKIE)
Hey. We may not be rich. But we get by.

COOKIE
(barking)
Yeah. Just barely.

LINDSAY
I think you have a very nice house.

A deranged sneer appears on Cookie's face.

COOKIE
Why thank you, Princess. Aren't you the sweetst thing?

Lindsay withers under Cookie's strange gaze.

CUT TO:

INT. SAM'S BEDROOM - DAY

Sam is trying to write his essay. Bill and Neal are distracting him, playing on the floor with Neal's chem set. Bill smells a vial of sulphur.

BILL
This smells like a fart.

NEAL
Bill, hold this test tube.

BILL
Yeah, right. I'm not gonna get my fingers melted off just so you can get your kicks.
(displaying his fingers)
I need these fingers.

NEAL
Why? So you can pick your rumpus all day? Just hold the test tube.

BILL
I read there's this chemical that eats away your flesh. And this kid got just a tiny, little bit on him and now he's going to Disneyland for a last hurrah.

NEAL
What was the name of the chemical?

BILL
I think it was chromium or something.

NEAL
Chromium?! I've got some of that...

Neal holds a test tube, full of liquid. He lets the contents fly... right into Bill's face.

NEAL (CONT'D)
...right here!

Bill SCREAMS, clawing at his own face. Neal laughs.

BILL
You better be joking! What was in that?

(CONTINUED)

CONTINUED:

NEAL
It was water, spaz. Relax.

SAM
(spinning around)
You guys, I'm trying to write an essay, all right? Could you please shut up?

Neal and Bill are a bit taken aback by Sam's bark.

BILL
How many words you got?

Sam counts his words.

SAM
Thirty-three. It's not fair. If I have to write an essay, Karen Scarfolli should have to write a big, fat book.

BILL
She's weird, man. I think she's a sex fiend. You should change lockers. What if she comes to school really horny one day?

NEAL
If it were me, I'd go over to Karen Scarfolli's house and make her write it.

SAM
(rolling his eyes)
I'm sure you would.

NEAL
I would. You can't let chicks humiliate you in public like that.

SAM
She didn't humiliate me.

NEAL
She kind of did.

SAM
(offended)
Yeah, well when she started picking on you, you just ran away. Bilbo Baggins.

(CONTINUED)

CONTINUED: (2)

Bill stifles a laugh. Neal is embarrassed.

NEAL
Yeah? Well, at least I'm not a pygmy.

Bill's eyes widen. There is a deafening silence in the room as Neal and Sam have a stare-down.

CUT TO:

INT. KIM KELLY'S HOUSE - MOMENTS LATER

Cookie continues to grill Lindsay.

COOKIE
So, Lindsay - how long has your family had that house in Benton Harbor?

LINDSAY
Oh, a few years.

COOKIE
You know, I did waitress up there one summer. I know the area pretty good. Where's your house at?

LINDSAY
Oh, uh... it's right by the water.

COOKIE
Yeah? What neighborhood?

LINDSAY
Well, it's near... it's over by...

Lindsay trails off. Cookie furrows her brow.

KIM
Mom, Lindsay invited me back up this week-end to go fishing. Can I go?

COOKIE
What street's it on?

Lindsay looks to an ashen-faced Kim. There is an extended wait for a response.

(CONTINUED)

CONTINUED:

LINDSAY
(weakly)
Benton Harbor... Street.

A long pause as Lindsay gulps air. A menacing look slowly emerges on Cookie's face. She and Arlo both turn on Kim. Suddenly, all hell breaks loose.

ARLO
I knew it. I told you.

COOKIE
You're a lying brat!

KIM
I'm not lying. You guys just can't believe that I can make a friend who's rich and smart!

COOKIE
She's not rich!

KIM
No, she's rich. I swear.

COOKIE
She's a bum - like all your other friends!

Lindsay is dumbstruck, terrified. Cookie and Kim jump to their feet. On the couch, Chip stirs, confused by the commotion.

CHIP
What's happening?

COOKIE
It's that car. You're driving around town, tramping it up in that car. I know what you do, Kim.

KIM
Well, you should. I learned it all from you! Whore!

COOKIE
What did you call me?!

ARLO
You're grounded for good! You got me?

(CONTINUED)

CONTINUED: (2)

KIM
Newsflash. You're not my father, fat-ass.

COOKIE
That's it. I'm selling that car!

KIM
(emotional)
Nuh-uh. That's my car. Aunt Cathy gave me that car.

COOKIE
Well, your Aunt Cathy spent a thousand dollars of my money and snorted it up her nose - so as far as I'm concerned, that's my car.

KIM
Okay. I'm outta here. Let's go, Lindsay...

Lindsay stands. She follows Kim to the door.

COOKIE
No, you don't. No, no!
(to ARLO)
Get her keys.

Arlo intercepts Kim and pulls her back.

ARLO
Give me those keys.

Arlo tries to wrest Kim's car keys away from her. He overpowers her. She SCREAMS and bites his hand. He SCREAMS, releasing her hand but still holding her in a bear hug. Kim looks to Lindsay and tosses her the keys.

KIM
Get in the car, Lindsay!

ARLO
(to Lindsay)
Give me those keys!

Lindsay is frozen, panicking.

KIM
Go to the car! Now! Go!

(CONTINUED)

CONTINUED: (3)

Arlo moves toward Lindsay. Lindsay bolts from the house.

CUT TO:

EXT. KIM KELLY'S HOUSE - DAY

Lindsay runs from the house, to Kim's parked Gremlin. Arlo, then Kim, then Cookie follow, all YELLING.

Lindsay unlocks the car door and gets in the passenger side. She locks the door, just as Arlo pounces on the car, banging on the window.

INT. KIM'S GREMLIN - CONTINUOUS

Lindsay recoils with a SHRIEK.

ARLO
Open the door!

Arlo pounds on the window as Kim runs around to the driver's side. She hits on the driver's window.

KIM
Lindsay!

Lindsay unlocks the driver's side. Kim gets in. Lindsay hands Kim the keys. Kim, rattled, has trouble finding the right key to start the ignition.

COOKIE
You leave here now - you're never coming back!

Arlo is banging his fists on the passenger window. Suddenly, THE WINDOW CRACKS. Lindsay is horrified.

LINDSAY
Oh my god! Hurry!

Kim finally starts the engine and the car PEELS OUT, knocking Arlo to the asphalt.

EXT. KIM KELLY'S HOUSE - CONTINUOUS

Arlo rises. He and Cookie stand in the street, full of fury, watching the Gremlin disappear into the distance and we...

FADE OUT.

END OF ACT TWO

(CONTINUED)

CONTINUED:

ACT THREE

FADE IN:

INT. KIM'S GREMLIN - DAY

Kim has pulled over. Lindsay is stunned, breathless. Kim, reliving the fight in her mind, angrily pounds on her CAR HORN.

KIM
This is my car! Mine!  My car!

Exhausted, Kim reclines back in her seat.

LINDSAY
Are you okay?

KIM
(disgusted)
Benton Harbor Street?

LINDSAY
Look, I've never even been to Benton Harbor. You know, you should have told me you were just using me.

KIM
(defensive)
Yeah, well... they're always on my ass about where I'm going. She thinks I'm a loser and all my friends are losers. I just wanted to bring home someone like you.
(beat)
I'm sorry, okay? Happy now?

LINDSAY
(shrugs)
Whatever. I just wish I'd known.

KIM
My stepfather wants to sell my car? I don't think so. With all the dirt I have on him? He better just watch it, you know what I mean?

LINDSAY
What are you gonna do now?

(CONTINUED)

CONTINUED:

KIM
I gotta find Daniel. When he hears about this, he's gonna flip out.

Kim starts the engine and they pull out with a lurch.

CUT TO:

INT. SAM'S BEDROOM - NIGHT

Sam and Neal are on the brink of a fight. Bill watches, wide-eyed.

SAM
I hate to break it to you, but you're the geek.

NEAL
(in disbelief)
Me?

SAM
Yeah. You.

NEAL
I may be some things, but a geek? No. No way.

SAM
(imitating NEAL)
Let's make some acid and pour it on the sidewalk. Won't that be cool?

Sam picks up a couple beakers and mockingly pretends to mix chemicals. Neal grabs the beakers away.

NEAL
Watch it.  This stuff's expensive.

SAM
You're fourteen years old and you still play with chemistry sets. It's pathetic.

NEAL
Hey, nimrod. Adults play with chemistry sets, too. They're called scientists. However, I don't know many adults who still play with Tonka trucks.

(CONTINUED)

CONTINUED:

SAM
I don't play with Tonka trucks.

NEAL
You want to go on the record with that statement?

SAM
I gave my trucks away, like, years ago.

Neal walks over to the closet and pulls out a shoebox, filled with MATCHBOX CARS.

NEAL
May I direct the jury's attention to exhibit A.

SAM
(imitating)
"May I direct the jury's attention to exhibit A." You and your lame impersonations. Ever thought about teaching a class in Geek?

Neal is now stung. He lashes out.

NEAL
Well, at least I've got hair on my pits.

Neal raises his arm, pulls down his sleeve and shows off his patch of armpit hair. Sam looks to Bill.

SAM
All right, Bill. Who's the bigger geek - me or Neal? You decide.

Bill hesitates as Neal and Sam both glare at him.

BILL
I don't know. Neither.

NEAL
Come on, Bill. You've got to choose.

Locking eyes with Bill, Neal points insistently at Sam. Sam is oblivious.

(CONTINUED)

CONTINUED: (2)

BILL
(full of dread)
Umm. Uh... I don't know. What does geek mean anyway, you know? It's just a word.

SAM
Come on, Bill!

NEAL
Yeah! Just choose!

Neal continues pointing behind Sam's back, making crazed, insistent faces at Bill.

BILL
(more like a question)
I guess, uh... Sam?

Neal pumps his fists, victorious. Sam is enraged.

NEAL
And the verdict is in. Hey, you shouldn't be so ashamed. There's a lot of great geeks in history. Einstein. Gilligan. Gomer Pyle...

Suddenly, Neal, mid-sentence, is tackled by Sam. They begin punching and kicking each other. Bill moves to the corner of the room, to avoid the melee.

BILL
On, no. Here we go.

Sam gets Neal in a head-lock. Neal MOANS.

Neal, mustering his strength, breaks free from Sam's grip, by wrenching back Sam's fingers. Sam SCREAMS.

Sam clutches his hand in pain. Neal is flush with anger.

NEAL
Are you done with your little hissy fit now?!

Sam rushes Neal, with a FIGHTING YELL. He pounces on him. They both fall in a heap by the foot of the bed - on top of Neal's chemistry set. BEAKERS and TEST TUBES SHATTER under their weight. Neal is pinned under Sam. Neal's eyes bug out when he realizes what he's lying on.

(CONTINUED)

CONTINUED: (3)

NEAL (CONT'D)
Hey. Get off me!

Sam notices that his hand has been pierced by broken glass. There is a small cut on his palm - blood oozes.

SAM
Oh, no. Now look what you've done, you jerk.

NEAL
Get off my chemistry set.

Neal, still wedged under Sam, struggles to free himself. Bill sees there is something of even greater concern.

BILL
You guys. YOU GUYS!

Bill points to the floor - chemicals have mixed on Sam's carpet and are now emanating a COLORFUL SMOKE. Sam and Neal jump to their feet, shocked.

SAM
What is that?!

NEAL
I don't know.

BILL
Cover your flesh.

Bill, Neal and Sam watch in amazement. Finally, the chemical combustion dies down.

SAM
Okay, that's it. Both of you - get out.

EXT. KIM'S GREMLIN - TRAVELING - DUSK

Kim and Lindsay have been trolling for Daniel. Kim spots DANIEL'S CAR, parked near a public basketball court.

KIM
Hey. There's his car. Him and Nick come here to shoot baskets.

Kim slows down, scanning for Daniel. Then, both her and Lindsay's mouth simultaneously drop.

EXT. BASKETBALL COURT - SIMULTANEOUS

Nick is here, shooting baskets. But Daniel's attention is occupied by Karen Scarfolli. They both lean against a chain-link fence, flirting shamelessly.

INT. KIM'S GREMLIN - CONTINUOUS

Kim and Lindsay are mesmerized by this vision of betrayal.

EXT. BASKETBALL COURT - SIMULTANEOUS

Daniel traces Karen's lips with his finger, then sticks his finger into her mouth. She sucks on it, as he grins lasciviously.

INT. KIM'S GREMLIN - CONTINUOUS

Kim looks psychotic.

Lindsay is concerned.

LINDSAY
Kim?

EXT. BASKETBALL COURT SIMULTANEOUS

Daniel and Karen are about to kiss, when...

KIM'S CAR comes barreling towards them, the TIRES SCREECHING. Kim sticks her head out the window and yells at them.

KIM
YOU ARE DEAD! YOU ARE SO DEAD!!!

Just when it looks like she's about to run them down, the Gremlin swerves violently and speeds away.

Daniel, Karen - even Nick - are all stunned, speechless. It's a tableau of frozen terror except for Nick's basketball, which bounces a few times, then rolls slowly across the court.

OPTIONAL VERSION: Instead of a deafening silence--

DANIEL
I think she's pissed.

OR:

(CONTINUED)

CONTINUED:

NICK
Man, you better skip town.

CUT TO:

INT. SAM'S BEDROOM - DUSK

Sam, now alone, his hand bandaged, is picking up the shattered remains of Neal's chemistry set and stuffing them into a Hefty garbage bag. His attention turns to...

THE MATCHBOX CARS, collected in the shoebox on his bed.

After a moment of deliberation, Sam lifts the shoebox and empties the cars into the trash bag.

CUT TO:

EXT. WEIR HOUSE - DUSK

Sam has made another trip out to the TRASH CANS on the curb. He holds the garbage bag, filled with broken glass and Matchbox cars. He places the bag in the trash can.

He picks up a TONKA FIRE-TRUCK for one final viewing. Then he HEARS a car rapidly approaching.

Kim's Gremlin is speeding up the road. Sam drops the fire-truck and races into the house.

Kim's Gremlin pulls up to the Weir house, coming to an abrupt halt.

INT. KIM'S GREMLIN - CONTINUOUS

The car is parked. Kim is a wreck. Lindsay is relieved to have made it home in one piece. Lindsay attempts an empathetic smile.

LINDSAY
Maybe it's not what you think. Maybe they were just goofing around.

Kim gives Lindsay a repulsed look.

LINDSAY (CONT'D)
You never know.

Suddenly, Kim begins to emit a strange cry - like the sound of air escaping from a balloon. Her body begins to shake. She is sobbing.

(CONTINUED)

CONTINUED:

LINDSAY (CONT'D)
Gosh, Kim. I'm so sorry.

Lindsay puts a comforting hand on Kim's shoulder. Kim bristles, pulling away.

KIM
Don't touch me, all right!

Kim wipes away her tears.

KIM (CONT'D)
I don't want to ever see him again.

LINDSAY
Oh, I know.

KIM
He's just... he's nicer to me than any guy I've ever dated.

Lindsay finds this hard to believe.

KIM (CONT'D)
And he's such a babe, you know? I mean, he's sexier than Rod Stewart, don't you think?

LINDSAY
He's really good-looking, yeah.

Kim nods, glaring at Lindsay.

KIM
(paranoid)
You want to bag him.

LINDSAY
No, I don't.

KIM
Don't lie to me.

LINDSAY
I mean, he's cute. But I'm not looking to... bag anyone.

KIM
Daniel's a normal guy, you know? He'll screw anything that moves.
(MORE)

(CONTINUED)

40.

CONTINUED: (2)

KIM (CONT'D)
That's why I gotta stay alert, you know? That's why I gotta be a bitch.

Lindsay nods. Kim suddenly erupts in tears.

KIM (CONT'D)
My life sucks.

LINDSAY
No, it doesn't.

KIM
(through tears)
My parents hate me. I don't have any friends. You're like my only friend...

Kim locks eyes with Lindsay, who perks up at this compliment.

KIM (CONT'D)
...and you're a total loser. No offense.

Lindsay deflates.

LINDSAY
None taken.

CUT TO:

INT. WEIR DINING ROOM - MOMENTS LATER

HAROLD, Jean and Sam are at the dinner table. Sam is scarfing down his food. Jean is troubled.

JEAN
Sam, slow down. It's not a race.

HAROLD
What's the problem?

JEAN
Well, he usually never eats and just look at him.

HAROLD
You know who never eats? Karen Carpenter. You want our son to look like Karen Carpenter?
(OR: OPTIONAL LINE)
He's fine. He could use a little meat on those bones.

(CONTINUED)

CONTINUED:

JEAN
I'm just worried he might have worms. Sam, do you think you might have worms?

SAM
(mouth full)
No.

The door opens. Lindsay escorts a tearful Kim in the house.

JEAN
(excited)
Lindsay. Is this your new friend?

LINDSAY
Yeah. We're gonna be in my room, okay?

JEAN
Are you sure you don't want any dinner?

LINDSAY
No. We' re fine.

KIM
(through sniffles)
What'cha eating?

JEAN
Veal piccata.

KIM
Looks good.

JEAN
Well, sit down. I'll get you both a plate.

Kim plops down at the table. Lindsay looks dismayed.

INT. WEIR DINING ROOM - LATER

INSERT ON SAM'S PLATE - a fork reaches in and stabs at the last bite of veal.

Sam chews the bite slowly. He's over-eaten. He looks ill.

The rest of the Weirs closely observe Kim as she angrily cuts at her veal. Frustrated, she throws down her fork and knife with a CLANG. Jean and Harold are disturbed.

(CONTINUED)

42.

CONTINUED:

JEAN
Is everything all right, Kim?

LINDSAY
She's having problems with her boyfriend, Mom. She doesn't want to talk about it.

Kim starts to cry at the table, burying her head in her hands. Harold, sitting next to Kim, grimaces at Jean. Jean motions for him to do something. Harold pats Kim awkwardly on the back.

HAROLD
There, there.

Kim looks up at Harold, wiping her nose.

KIM
You're a guy. Why are guys only interested in sex?! It's so sick!

Harold, confounded, looks to Lindsay.

HAROLD
Where'd you find this piece of work?

Lindsay mouths the words - "SHUT UP" to her father.

Suddenly, an inhuman noise captures everyone's attention. It is the sound of Sam BELCHING. Everyone turns.

Sam, green with nausea, lets out the most protracted BURP the Weirs have ever heard. The entire family is astonished.

KIM
Damn!

Sam looks like he's about to barf. He gags.

HAROLD
What is it, Sam?
(to JEAN)
Is he gonna blow-up?

Sam runs from the table, clutching his stomach.

HAROLD (CONT'D)
That's a perfectly good piece of veal wasted.

(CONTINUED)

CONTINUED: (2)

JEAN
I'm telling you, I think he might have a parasite.

The PHONE RINGS. Jean rises to her feet.

JEAN (CONT'D)
I'll get it.

INT. WEIR KITCHEN - CONTINUOUS

Jean answers the phone.

JEAN
Hello? This is she.

CUT TO:

INT. WEIR DINING ROOM - CONTINUOUS

Lindsay eavesdrops on Jean's call.

JEAN (O.S.)
Yes, they're both here. She is? She did? Oh, really. Oh, my.

Harold, alone with the girls, tries to make conversation.

HAROLD
You look familiar. Does your family shop at my store?

KIM
Yeah, but my mom hates going there 'cause it's so overpriced. You can get the same stuff at Sports Mart for a hell of a lot less.

HAROLD
(through clenched teeth)
You don't say.

JEAN (O.S.)
Well, thanks for letting me know. Okay. Okay. Good-bye.

Lindsay is panicking, fearing the worst. Jean enters.

JEAN (CONT'D)
Lindsy, can I talk to you in the kitchen for a second?

(CONTINUED)

CONTINUED:

Lindsay follows her mom into the kitchen.

CUT TO:

INT. WEIR KITCHEN - MOMENTS LATER

A distressed Jean has pulled Lindsay aside. They speak in loud whispers.

JEAN
That was Kim's mom on the phone. What's happening?

LINDSAY
What do you mean?

JEAN
She was yelling - at me. She says you told her we have a vacation house in Benton Harbor. That you and Kim stay out all night and sleep with boys and I shouldn't believe a word you say.

LINDSAY
Mom, none of that is true. Kim had a fight with her parents and Mrs. Kelly's just upset.

JEAN
Well, now I'm upset, too. Very upset.

LINDSAY
Mom, come on, I barely know Kim.

JEAN
Good. Maybe that's for the best. She doesn't seem like a very positive influence.

LINDSAY
Try to be a little understanding, okay? Kim's from a broken home. Her parents are deranged. Not everyone's family is like ours.

JEAN
I know that, but...

Suddenly, Kim pops her head in the kitchen, taking Lindsay and Jean by surprise.

(CONTINUED)

CONTINUED:

KIM
Thanks so much for dinner, Mrs. Weir. It was tasty. You guys have such a killer pad. Do you mind if I hang out a little while? My house is such a nightmare right now.

JEAN
Oh, not at all, Kim. Make yourself at home.

Kim smiles, then exits. Jean looks a bit guilt-stricken.

JEAN (CONT'D)
Do you think she might want some ice cream?

Lindsay smiles appreciatively and we...

FADE OUT.

END OF ACT THREE

ACT FOUR

FADE IN:

INT. WEIR LIVING ROOM - NIGHT

Kim, Lindsay, Harold and Jean eat bowls of ice cream, gathered around the television. They watch a COP SHOW. Kim seems to be feeling better, enjoying her ice cream.

KIM
I hate cop shows. Cops are pigs.

Harold leans in to Jean. They speak in whispers.

HAROLD
This girl's getting on my nerves.

JEAN
Harold, she's Lindsay's new friend.
(off Harold's grimace)
Well, I, for one, would like to get to know these new kids Lindsay's been spending all her time with.

HAROLD
(annoyed; checking his watch)
(MORE)

(CONTINUED)

CONTINUED:

HAROLD (CONT'D)
Fifteen more minutes. Then I'm kicking her out.

KIM
(spinning around)
My brother got ambushed by two cops. They beat him on the head with their billy clubs.

JEAN
Oh, my. What was your brother doing?

KIM
Nothing. He was just drunk, minding his own business. And the cops just went nuts on him.

JEAN
That's terrible.

KIM
Yeah. They really messed him up, too. Now, he sleeps on the couch all day. He never parties. I think he has brain damage.

LINDSAY
Your family should sue.

KIM
Believe me, we were going to. But, I don't know, we never got around to it.

HAROLD
In Algeria, they don't have cops. They have something else instead - it's called anarchy.

KIM
I'd like to find those cops and give them brain damage. See how they like it.

Kim wields her spoon for emphasis. Jean and Harold cringe.

JEAN
(changing the subject)
How's your ice cream?

KIM
It's really good. Thanks.

(CONTINUED)

CONTINUED: (2)

The DOOR BELL RINGS. Lindsay jumps up.

LINDSAY
I'll get it.

Lindsay walks to the door and opens it. It's Nick.

NICK
Hey, Lindsay.

LINDSAY
Hey. What's going on?

Nick points to an idling car out front.

NICK
Daniel's in the car. He wants to
talk to Kim.

LINDSAY
I'm not sure if now's the best
time. She's really mad.

In the living room, Kim peers her head around and spots Nick.

KIM
Oh, no!

Harold and Jean are aghast as an angry Kim jumps to her feet.

NICK
Hey, Kim. Thanks for almost running
me over back there.

KIM
What do you want?!

NICK
Daniel's out front. He wants to
talk to you.

KIM
What are you, his chore boy?!

NICK
Screw you.

KIM
Tell your master I don't ever want
to talk to him again! He's scum!

(CONTINUED)

CONTINUED: (3)

NICK
He's outside. Tell him yourself.

KIM
I'm not going out there! Forget it!
He can go to hell!

NICK
If you don't go out there, he's
just gonna come in here.

Harold and Jean don't like the sound of that.

HAROLD
Maybe you should just talk to the
boy. OUTSIDE.

JEAN
Yeah. Just tell him how you feel.

KIM
I'm never gonna talk to him - ever -
so you can all just bite me!

And with that, Kim runs from the room. Nick, Lindsay, Harold and Jean are all stunned. Harold looks to Lindsay.

HAROLD
If she's planning on sleeping over,
she can just forget it.

LINDSAY
(plaintive)
Dad.

CUT TO:

INT. SAM'S BEDROOM - MOMENTS LATER

Sam, feeling ill, is sitting at his desk, attempting to write his essay. Kim suddenly enters the room, locking the door behind her. Kim spins around and notices Sam for the first time. She GASPS.

KIM
You scared me!

Sam, confused, watches as Kim goes to his window and peers out...

EXT. WEIR HOM- STREET - SIMULTANEOUS

KIM'S POV - ON THE STREET

Daniel has parked his car. He gets out and approaches the house.

INT. SAM'S BEDROOM - CONTINUOUS

ON KIM

She quickly closes the curtains.

KIM
Oh, crap.

Sam is not happy to see her. He musters his courage to confront her.

SAM
Get out of my room.

KIM
What?

SAM
You heard me. Get out of here. You can't come in here... after everything you've done to me. This is my room. Get out.

KIM
What have I done to you?

SAM
(in disbelief)
What have you...? Well, first, you painted "Geek" on my locker.

KIM
I didn't do that. Karen did.

SAM
(wound up)
Well, she's your friend and you were laughing. How would you like that painted on your locker? It's not my fault I'm small. Now everyone's talking about it and I have to write this stupid essay.

(CONTINUED)

CONTINUED:

KIM
Hey, Karen is not my friend, okay? And tomorrow at school, she's gonna learn - what goes around, comes around.

Sam's anger dissipates. His curiosity is piqued.

SAM
What do you mean?

KIM
Don't worry about Karen. She's dead meat.

SAM
She is?

KIM
Yeah. She messed with the wrong person. So now I'm gonna have to break her arms.

Sam lets out a surprised gasp. He smiles.

SAM
Seriously?

KIM
(possessed)
And after I break her arms, I'm gonna get a wrench and I'm gonna pull her teeth out, one at a time. And then I'm gonna get a match and set her hair on fire.

Sam's smile fades.

SAM
Well, don't hurt her too bad.

KIM
Just wait. She's gonna wish she was never born.

Sam nods. He can't believe how awesome Kim Kelly is.

SAM
Cool.

CUT TO:

INT. WEIR HALLWAY - CONTINUOUS

Lindsay and Nick are in the hallway, searching for Kim.

LINDSAY
Kim? Kim!

NICK
So... how's it going, Linds?

LINDSAY
(upset)
How's it going? It's going bad.
Kim!

NICK
Hey, those guys are gonna make up.
Don't worry.

LINDSAY
Yeah, but Kim's really pissed.

NICK
She's always pissed. You just gotta
calm down.

LINDSAY
Yeah, I know. This night's just
been... really intense.

NICK
You seem stressed.

Nick starts to massage her shoulders. The moment is interrupted by a BLOOD-CURDLING SHRIEK coming from the kitchen.

CUT TO:

INT. WEIR KITCHEN - CONTINUOUS

Jean is the source of the shriek. Standing by the sink, a sponge in her hand, she has been startled by Daniel, who has entered from the back door.

DANIEL
Lady. I'm not gonna hurt you. I'm
just looking for my girlfriend.

Harold, Lindsay and Nick come running, converging in the kitchen. Daniel grins, amused.

(CONTINUED)

CONTINUED:

DANIEL (CONT'D)
Hey, Lindsay. I saw the door was open.

HAROLD
Who's this punk?!

LINDSAY
Dad, that's Daniel. He's a friend of mine from school.

HAROLD
Jeez, kid. Ever heard of a doorbell? People do have heart attacks, you know?

DANIEL
(all smiles)
Sorry, Pops.
(to LINDSAY)
Where's Kim?

LINDSAY
She doesn't want to see you.

Suddenly, Kim pops up behind Lindsay.

KIM
That's right! So get the hell out of here!

DANIEL
Kim. Would you let me explain?

KIM
Explain what? That I hate you?!

DANIEL
I didn't do nothing.

KIM
Oh, you didn't do anything?

DANIEL
Can you just calm down and not be a bitch for one second?!

KIM
What did you call me?! What did you call me?!

(CONTINUED)

CONTINUED: (2)

Kim starts pounding on his chest. He just takes it. Harold and Jean are overwhelmed, mesmerized.

HAROLD
Calm down! I said, calm down so I can explain to you. Are you listening?

KIM
I saw her sucking on your finger. What else has she sucked on, hunh?!

Nick, unfazed, starts looking through the pantry. He grabs the box of fruit roll-ups.

DANIEL
Are you high?!

KIM
No, I'm not high!

JEAN
Maybe you two should discuss this in private.

KIM
Don't, Daniel!

Kim slaps Daniel several times as she speaks. Daniel just takes it without even flinching.

KIM (CONT'D)
Don't lie to me! Because it doesn't work! I know you slept with her!

DANIEL
I didn't do nothing! It's true! Don't call me a liar!

Daniel stares into Kim's eyes, unafraid of the danger. It's as if he's hypnotizing her.

DANIEL (CONT'D)
There's nobody but you. Okay? There's nobody but you.

KIM
(softens)
God, you suck.

DANIEL
Okay?

(CONTINUED)

CONTINUED: (3)

KIM
No, it's not okay. I'm mad at you.
I'm really mad.

But Kim is starting to soften.

LINDSAY
Mom. Dad

Lindsay motions for her parents to follow her out. Harold and Jean get the hint.

CUT TO:

INT. DINING ROOM - MOMENTS LATER

Harold, Jean, Lindsay and Nick have gathered in the dining room. Nick is unwrapping a fruit roll-up.

LINDSAY
Mom, Dad, this is Nick.

NICK
(offering his hand)
Hey, Mr. Weir. Mrs. Weir. It's
really nice to meet you.
(pointing to LINDSAY)
Lindsay's great. She turned out
real great. Congratulations.

HAROLD
(suspicious)
Thanks.

NICK
Hey. You mind if I have one of
these?

JEAN
No, go right ahead.

Kim and Daniel can be heard in the kitchen.

KIM (O.S.)
Promise you'll never hang out with
her again.

DANIEL (O.S.)
I swear. I don't like her, you
know? I like somebody else.

(CONTINUED)

CONTINUED:

KIM
Who?!

DANIEL
Who do you think, moron?

Then silence.

JEAN
I think they've made up.

Jean smiles at the others, conspiratorially.

JEAN (CONT'D)
Let's go check on them.

LINDSAY
No, Mom.

JEAN
Oh, Lindsay. I think we deserve to a see a happy ending, don't you, Harold?

HAROLD
Are these friends of yours gonna be leaving our house in the near future?

Jean walks to the kitchen with the others in tow. Jean's girlish smile disappears when she sees...

INT. WEIR KITCHEN - CONTINUOUS

It's like a scene from "THE POSTMAN ALWAYS RINGS TWICE". Daniel has Kim backed against the kitchen table. They share a salacious, sloppy kiss. Kim moans, passionately.

ANGLE ON: JEAN AND OTHERS

JEAN
Oh, my.

Jean gulps air, mortified. They back out of the entry way, discomfited.

CUT TO:

EXT. WEIR HOUSE - NIGHT

The front door opens. Nick, Daniel and Kim, finally leaving, spill out on the lawn. Lindsay, Harold and Jean linger in the doorway.

NICK
Mr. Weir. I wanted to tell you, I really dig your store. It's got a lot of good stuff in it. I bought a great basketball there a few years ago. It still works.

Nick holds up the box of fruit roll-ups.

NICK
Hey. Mind if I take this?

JEAN
Oh. No. That's... fine.

Kim gives the frazzled Weirs a blithe smile, as if this night were nothing out of the ordinary.

KIM
It was really nice to meet you guys. Thanks for dinner and the ice cream and everything.

LINDSAY
Good luck with your parents.

KIM
Ugh. Don't remind me. Listen, do you think I can leave my car here? I'll pick it up tomorrow. We can hang out.

LINDSAY
Great.

KIM
Hey, maybe we can all have dinner.

Kim smiles at the thought. The Weirs react to this as Kim, Daniel and Nick turn and head for the street.

CUT TO:

INT. WEIR LIVING ROOM - CONTINUOUS

Harold shuts the door, decisively. Both Harold and Jean turn on Lindsay. She smiles disarmingly.

LINDSAY
Well, I've got a ton of homework. I better go hit the books. Right, Dad? Good-night.

She cheerfully walks away, leaving her parents reeling.

HAROLD
This isn't good.

FADE TO:

INT. MCKINLEY HIGH SCHOOL - MORNING

Sam is walking through the hallway before class. He runs into Neal. They have a momentary silent stand-off before...

SAM
Hey.

NEAL
Hey. Going to class?

SAM
Yeah.

They start to walk together, when Kowchevski intercepts them.

MR. KOWCHEVSKI
Sam Weir, where's that essay?

Sam holds out a piece of paper. Kowchevski scans it. He seems pleased.

MR. KOWCHEVSKI (CONT'D)
You know what we're gonna do with this? We're gonna post it on your locker so everyone at McKinley can learn from your mistake.

Sam and Neal follow Kowchevski to Sam's locker. They all stop in their tracks when they see...

Karen Scarfolli, standing before her locker - the word "SLUT" has been painted down the front of it. Karen is outraged.

Kowchevski shakes his head, resigned.

(CONTINUED)

CONTINUED:

MR. KOWCHEVSKI (CONT'D)
Oh, for god's sake.

He crumples up Sam's essay and walks off.

Karen turns on Sam and gives him a menacing look.

KAREN
Did you do this?!

Sam, frightened, shakes his head. Karen retracts her arm as if she's about to pummel him. But, then, a voice rings out.

KIM (O.S.)
I did it.

Karen, Sam and Neal turn to see... a vengeful Kim Kelly.

KIM (CONT'D)
Because you are a slut. And if you ever hit on my boyfriend again, I'll kill you.

KAREN
You're crazy.

KIM
Yeah. That's right. And when school lets out, you're gonna find out just how crazy I am.

Karen clearly doesn't like the sound of that. She puts on her best tough sneer though, then turns and walks away.

Sam, brimming over with satisfaction, approaches his new pal.

SAM
That was really cool. Thanks, Kim.

Kim, still shooting poison looks in Karen's direction, casually shrugs.

KIM
No problem, Geek.

Kim walks away. And off Sam's mixture of emotions we...

FADE TO BLACK.

THE END

# FREAKS AND GEEKS

"TESTS AND BREASTS"

Episode #5

Written by Bob Nickman

Directed by Ken Kwapis

When Judd asked me to write an intro for "Tests and Breasts" I wasn't sure exactly what to do, so I re-read the script. Although I felt pretty good about myself and my cohorts on the *Freaks and Geeks* writing staff after perusing the aforementioned document, I still was "drawing a blank." Then as I was driving the other day, I was hit with an image from my own high school days. It was A LOOK from my good friend Bruce that, at the time, I did not understand. But I do now. I'll tell you about it because it ties in rather nicely with the two stories in "Tests and Breasts." Those stories being cheating on tests and early sexual awakening.

Anyway, Bruce is doing horribly in some inane class and gets it in his head that getting a good grade on this big test will somehow turn his life around, get his parents off his back, make him happy...I don't know. He gets me and another friend of ours, Teddy, to act as lookouts while he steals a copy from the classroom.

So Teddy and I are standing in this nearly abandoned hallway during lunch hour and Bruce is busy fumbling around in Mr. Somebody's desk. We're joking about how funny it would be if Bruce got caught and young comedy geniuses that we were, we decide to scare him. Teddy throws open the door and I yell, "What the hell do you think you're doing?!" Bruce screams as he jams his finger in the desk drawer trying to shut it. He quickly gets "the joke" and utters the classic "You fuckers," as Teddy and I laugh. We quickly apologize for scaring the shit out of him and as he grabs the test saying, "Let's just get out of here," he gives us THIS LOOK. It was a combination of fear, relief and a certain familiarity and clarity that said he wouldn't mind it happening again. It confused me because I'm pretty sure I just would have been straight ahead pissed. Of course I didn't ask him about it. Why would I?

Cut to: Four years later. Bruce is telling me a story about banging his new college girlfriend in the library and almost getting caught by the librarian. He tells me the closer he got to being discovered, the more he enjoyed it. Then he brings up the test-stealing story and tells me after Teddy and I scared him, he was totally aroused. It was one of the first times he realized this correlation between fear and sexual excitement for him. Oh yeah, THE LOOK. He was laughing as he quoted Arthur Bremer (the nutjob who shot Presidential candidate

Governor George Wallace) "Fear gives me an erection." Then Bruce asked jokingly, "You don't think I'm that crazy, do you?" No, I thought, but I am a little nauseous.

Now, I don't know how this becomes a thing for some people and I'm not really interested in judging it, but I do find these little psychological tributaries fascinating. I'm also glad I didn't know what that LOOK meant when it happened. I couldn't have handled it. I was only in high school.

Teddy became a shrink.

—Bob Nickman

FREAKS AND GEEKS

"TESTS AND BREASTS"

**CAST LIST**

LINDSAY WEIR
SAM WEIR
HAROLD WEIR
JEAN WEIR
DANIEL DESARIO
NICK ANDOPOLIS
BILL HAVERCHUCK
NEAL SCHWEIBER
KIM KELLY
MILLIE KENTNER
CINDY SANDERS
MR. ROSS
MR. KOWCHEVSKI
MR. FREDRICKS
SEAN
ALAN
HARRIS
SHAUNA
MISS LANDIS
BRAD
DOLORES
JOCK #1
JOCK #2

FREAKS AND GEEKS

"TESTS AND BREASTS"

**SET LIST**

**INTERIORS:**

MCKINLEY HIGH SCHOOL
/HALLWAY
/CLASSROOM
/LIBRARY
/CAFETERIA
/SHOP CLASS
/MR. ROSSO'S OFFICE
/MR. ROSSO'S WAITING RM
/MR. KOWCHEVSKI'S OFFICE
/MR. FREDRICK'S OFFICE
/UNDER THE STAIRWELL
WEIR HOUSE
/DINING ROOM
/LIVING ROOM
/LINDSAY'S ROOM
/DOORWAY
NEAL'S BEDROOM

**EXTERIORS:**

MCKINLEY HIGH SCHOOL
/SMOKING PATIO
/PARKING LOT
/MR. ROSSO'S OFFICE
/SIDE OF SCHOOL
WEIR HOUSE
/BACKYARD

TEASER

FADE IN:

INT. CLASSROOM - DAY

The GEEKS are in the midst of their all male health class. MR. FREDRICKS, the gym teacher, reads lifelessly from a clinical book on human sexuality. On the wall behind Fredricks is a cut-away anatomical drawing of the female reproductive system.

MR. FREDRICKS
(reading)
Puberty usually begins between the ages of eleven and fourteen when profound hormonal changes occur. The onset of these changes is the function of a small gland located near the base of the skull called the pituitary.

Bill looks to Sam for a clue as to what Fredricks is talking about. Sam shrugs. He doesn't know what's going on either.

MR. FREDRICKS (CONT'D)
This gland sends chemical signals throughout the body, most notably resulting in height increase, changes in body shape and hair growth in the genital area.

Several students as well as the Geeks, giggle. Fredricks looks in their direction.

MR. FREDRICKS (CONT'D)
Hey, knock it off. You think this is funny? Just try me.

The Geeks look scared and stifle their laughter.

CLOSE on the poster - the caption beneath reads "FEMALE REPRODUCTIVE SYSTEM." It is a clinical multi-colored drawing that looks more like something from another planet than anything resembling a human body part.

MR. FREDRICKS (CONT'D)
Okay, this here is the female reproductive system...

ON STUDENTS - BILL, NEAL and SAM, stupefied by this weird drawing. Bill looks to Sam.

(CONTINUED)

CONTINUED:

BILL
Jeez. What the hell is that?

Sam shushes Bill.

MR. FREDRICKS
The uterus is composed of two main parts, the corpus or body of the organ, and it's cervix or neck, and it is capable of undergoing major changes during a woman's reproductive life.

Bill, disturbed, whispers to Sam.

BILL
It looks like it's from outer space.

SAM
(trying not to move his mouth)
Shut up.

Fredricks turns on them.

MR. FREDRICKS
Weir. You have something to say?

SAM
No, sir.

MR. FREDRICKS
Is this a big joke to you? When you get the clap because you didn't pay attention in health class are you gonna find that funny, too?

SAM
No.

Fredricks continues reading and pointing to the drawing.

MR. FREDRICKS
The cervix is shaped like a cylinder and is about 2.5 centimeters long.

Neal whispers to Sam.

(CONTINUED)

CONTINUED: (2)

NEAL
Didn't Sigourney Weaver kill that
in Alien?

MR. FREDRICKS
It has a fine canal running through
it, opening into the cavity of the
uterus above...

SAM
Quiet!

MR. FREDRICKS
During pregnancy, the uterus
expands to allow the fetus to grow,
and provides it with protection and
nutrition. At the same time, the
large muscle fibers are prevented
from contracting. The uterus
suddenly changes its role when the
fetus is mature and begins to
contract in order to open the
cervix and allow the baby and
placenta to pass through.

BILL
Remember when it jumped out of that
guy's stomach?

SAM
(whispering)
Shut up! You're gonna get me in
trouble!

Fredricks, hearing voices, looks up, fit to pop.

MR. FREDRICKS
All right, Weir. Since you seem to
know everything, I got an idea.
I'll just shut my big mouth and you
can teach the class. Why don't you
come up here?

Sam stays put, mortified.

MR. FREDRICKS (CONT'D)
I said, get up here.

Sam feebly walks to the front of the room. Fredricks hands
Sam the pointer. Fredricks then goes and sits in Sam's seat.

(CONTINUED)

CONTINUED: (3)

MR. FREDRICKS (CONT'D)
Um, excuse me? Dr. Love, can you show me where the ovaries are located?

SAM
The ovaries?

Bill is completely uncomfortable with Mr. Fredricks playing pretend next to him. Sam slowly lifts the pointer. He moves it around a little and finally points to the center of the drawing.

MR. FREDRICKS
No. That's the uterus.
(shakes his head)
What about the fallopian tubes? Do you know where that is?
(off Sam's blank look)
No? How about the cervix?
(nothing)
Fine, just show me where the vagina is. Every guy knows where that is. That's just basic. Point to it.

Sam is clearly in over his head. Nobody would know where the vagina is on this complex drawing. He looks at the drawings, then to Bill and Neal who look almost as afraid as Sam does.

Sam raises the pointer and slides it along the drawing not wanting to stop at the wrong place. He looks to Fredricks for any hint that he is close, but Fredricks just grins at him.

SAM
I don't know.

The class erupts into laughter. Fredricks gets up and takes the pointer away from a humiliated Sam.

MR. FREDRICKS
Mr. Weir, instead of yucking it up during class, you might wanna pay attention or you're going to have a very difficult life. Sit down, Dr. Love.

Sam, humiliated, returns to his seat, passing the gleeful sneers of his fellow classmates.

He passes one student, ALAN WHITE, who mutters, under his breath...

(CONTINUED)

CONTINUED: (4)

ALAN
Dr. Love.

The other students chortle. Sam cringes and we...

CUT TO:

MAIN TITLES

ACT ONE

FADE IN:

INT. HALLWAY - DAY

Students mill about between classes. Jocks posture, a group of girls giggle and MR. ROSSO makes his way down the hall trying to be everyone's buddy.

MR. ROSSO
(to a large jock)
Good game on Saturday, Eddie.
(to a bookish girl)
Jennifer, I'm hearing terrific things about you from my sources in the English department.

He winks, continuing on.

MR. ROSSO (CONT'D)
Haven't seen you in a while, Brad. Stop by the office. We'll rap.

The student, BRAD, standing with a group of his BUDDIES, nods affirmatively.

BRAD
Okay, Mr. Rosso.

But as Rosso turns his back, Brad rolls his eyes and makes a "get a load of this moron" gesture. He and his pals laugh.
ANGLE ON: LINDSAY, ACROSS THE HALL

Lindsay, at her locker, is approached by Kim.

KIM
Hey, Lindsay.

Lindsay, still a bit nervous around Kim, smiles.

LINDSAY
Hey. What's up?

(CONTINUED)

CONTINUED:

KIM
I prayed this morning.

LINDSAY
Really?

KIM
Yeah, I prayed my mom would get hit by a truck. The whore stole my make-up again. Got any mascara?

LINDSAY
No. Sorry.

Suddenly, Rosso appears.

MR. ROSSO
Hey. How are you ladies?

Kim just looks at him like he's from Mars.

MR. ROSSO (CONT'D)
How's my buddy, Lindsay?

LINDSAY
(embarrassed)
Fine.

MR. ROSSO
Mind if I kinda do my guidance counselor gig here for a minute? Show a little interest in a bright, young student.

LINDSAY
(acting cool for Kim)
Who did you have in mind?

Rosso laughs.

MR. ROSSO
Guess.
(he laughs again)
Anyway, we've gotta find you an extra curricular you can get excited about. How about Ecology Club? A lot of our more "counterculture" students love that club.

(CONTINUED)

CONTINUED: (2)

LINDSAY
Too busy. Not interested. Other plans. Pick one that makes you happy.

MR. ROSSO
(laughing)
Whoa. Burn. You think about it.

Lindsay and Kim roll their eyes.

KIM
Teachers are so lame.

Rosso continues on. He spots a long-haired student.

MR. ROSSO
Rock on, Kirby.

Rosso walks past MR. KOWCHEVSKI who has been watching Rosso. He rolls his eyes as we follow him toward his classroom. We HEAR THE BELL. Kowchevski spots DANIEL in the hallway.

MR. KOWCHEVSKI
(to Daniel)
Let's go, Mr. Desario, time for your favorite class.

They enter the classroom together. Daniel takes a seat.

CUT TO:

INT. CLASSROOM - DAY - CONTINUOUS

Mr. Kowchevski is at the front of his math class.

MR. KOWCHEVSKI
Just a reminder about tomorrow's algebra test. It's tomorrow.

The students groan.

DANIEL
Uh, Kowchevski.

MR. KOWCHEVSKI
(irritated; imitating)
Uh, Desario.

DANIEL
Didn't we just take a test like last week?

(CONTINUED)

CONTINUED:

MR. KOWCHEVSKI
What's your point?

DANIEL
I'm just wondering - how many tests do we have to take in here?

Several freak students laugh. Daniel smirks.

DANIEL (CONT'D)
Don't you ever show movies?

More laughter. Kowchevski, though, is not amused. He stares down the students.

MR. KOWCHEVSKI
In math, each week you build on what you learned the week before, okay? It's like a bus. If you keep missing it, you're never gonna catch up.

DANIEL
But I don't ride the bus, man.

The freaks really stifle laughter. A couple STUDENTS look annoyed. Kowchevski is flush with anger.

MR. KOWCHEVSKI
Flunk another test, Desario, and you're just gonna have to come back next year and ride this bus again. And if you keep missing the bus, I guarantee, one day you'll be driving a bus.

A few "oohs" from the crowd. Daniel is stung momentarily, but he quickly composes himself, shaking his head.

DANIEL
(to himself)
Through your yard.

CUT TO:

INT. CAFETERIA - DAY

Sam, Bill and Neal are in line at the cafeteria. They wait behind a JOCK, telling a dirty joke to one of his PALS. They eavesdrop.

(CONTINUED)

CONTINUED:

JOCK #1
...so the guy looks up at her and says "how do you think I rang the doorbell?"

Jock #2 laughs.

JOCK #2
Pretty good one.

ANGLE ON: THE GEEKS.

SAM
I don't get it.

NEAL
What's to get? Jocks don't know how to tell jokes.

SAM
(to Bill)
Did you get it?

BILL
I don't really like jokes. I don't think they're funny.

SAM
Maybe if we understood it, it would be funny. They were laughing pretty hard.

NEAL
Trust me, those guys are idiots. It's not funny.

Sam, still pondering the joke, walks with his tray across the cafeteria, away from Bill and Neal. He is intercepted by Cindy Sanders.

CINDY
Hi, Sam.

Sam gulps air, instantly nervous.

SAM
Oh, hey, Cindy. How are you doing?

CINDY
I'm good. You?

(CONTINUED)

CONTINUED: (2)

SAM
Good.
(awkward beat)
I like your sweater.

Cindy smiles big.

CINDY
Thanks. It's really comfy. So, you going to the Muscular Dystrophy Carnival? I'm in charge of the ice cream booth.

SAM
I heard about that.

SEAN approaches.

SEAN
Hey, Dr. Love, I can't find my girlfriend's cervix. Can you help me out?

Sean laughs and walks off.

CINDY
What was that about?

SAM
It's an inside joke. It's stupid.
(changing the subject)
Listen, if you need another volunteer at your ice cream booth, I'm around.

CINDY
Oh, thanks, but Betsy's already doing it. But make sure you stop by. See you later.

Sam watches her reverently as she goes to the next table.

CINDY (CONT'D)
Hey, Tommy. You coming to the Muscular Dystrophy Carnival?

As Sam realizes she is asking everyone, Alan approaches.

ALAN
Are you Dr. Love? Would you autograph my genitals?

(CONTINUED)

CONTINUED: (3)

Alan laughs. Off Sam's weary look we...

CUT TO:

EXT. SMOKING PATIO - DAY

Lindsay, Daniel, Kim and NICK are hanging out. Daniel seems a bit withdrawn. Nick is drinking soda with a straw.

KIM
So I took twenty bucks out of her purse and then my mom went nuts on my brother. Hit him with a spatula. It was hilarious.

LINDSAY
Sounds... it.

Nick mindlessly fills his straw with soda, then blows it out onto Kim's shirt. Kim is red-faced with rage.

KIM
YOU BASTARD. WHY'D YOU DO THAT?

NICK
(instantly regretting it)
No reason.

KIM
What are you, lit or something? What the hell?!

NICK
Really, I'm sorry. Mellow.

KIM
I don't care if you're sorry, jack ass! Now I've gotta walk around with pop all over my shirt!

Kim knocks Nick's coke into his lap, then bolts to go clean herself up. Nick looks to Daniel and Lindsay.

NICK
I get these weird urges sometimes.
(sigh)
I should probably go apologize.

Nick follows Kim, leaving Daniel and Lindsay alone. Lindsay looks at Daniel. He looks preoccupied.

(CONTINUED)

CONTINUED:

LINDSAY
You okay?

DANIEL
Yeah.
(beat)
Kowchevski says if I flunk this test tomorrow, he's gonna make me take algebra again.

LINDSAY
No way.

DANIEL
(getting fired up)
Yeah. He's such a power-tripper. Who does he think he is? The Ayatollah Khomeini?

LINDSAY
Do you think you might flunk it?

DANIEL
No. I'm definitely gonna flunk it.

Daniel scrutinizes her for a moment.

DANIEL (CONT'D)
Do you take algebra?

LINDSAY
(a little embarrassed)
No, I did, last year. I take uh, trig.

Daniel finds this amusing.

DANIEL
You must study a lot.

LINDSAY
Sort of. Not really. Math isn't this big deal everyone thinks it is. It's really just a few basic formulas and shortcuts and then you plug in some numbers.

DANIEL
Shortcuts, huh? Like tricks?

(CONTINUED)

CONTINUED: (2)

LINDSAY
I guess you could call them that. Yeah. You definitely could do it if you wanted to.

DANIEL
I mean, if I studied... I mean, I could do it. It's not like I'm some bus driver. It's just I'm not interested, you know? It's so lame. When am I ever gonna use "A" plus "B" equals "D"?

LINDSAY
Yeah. Oh, I know. But do you really want to take algebra with Kowchevski next year?

DANIEL
Hell, no. And see that guy's ugly mug again? I'd rather go to jail.

LINDSAY
I could help you study. It could be fun.

He and Lindsay both smile, locking eyes and we...

CUT TO:

EXT. SCHOOL - DAY

The Geeks have sought out HARRIS. Sam is finishing the "doorbell joke."

SAM
...and the guy says "how do you think I rang the doorbell?"

A long beat as the Geeks await Harris' response. Harris finally laughs.

NEAL
So, it <u>is</u> funny.

SAM
What does it mean?

HARRIS
You guys are so young.

(CONTINUED)

CONTINUED:

NEAL
You're only a year older than us.

BILL
Come on, Harris. What does it mean?

Harris holds up his hand, grins and shakes his head "no". He understands something that they are not ready for.

NEAL
He doesn't get it either.

HARRIS
Oh, I get it.

SAM
Then tell us.

HARRIS
I can't.

SAM
Why not?

HARRIS
'Cause then you'd know.

BILL
So?

HARRIS
You need to find out for yourselves.

A girl, JUDITH, sits down next to Harris.

SAM
That's why we're asking.

Harris laughs knowingly.

NEAL
I told you he doesn't know.

HARRIS
If I didn't, would I be with Judith, here?

He kisses his girlfriend. She smiles, a mouthful of metal.

(CONTINUED)

CONTINUED: (2)

JUDITH
Oh, Harris, you're so bad.

HARRIS
Love is just like homework. You've gotta study if you want to get an A.

Judith hands Harris a sandwich wrapped in cellophane.

JUDITH
I got you that tuna sandwich. Extra mayo.

HARRIS
Thanks, baby.

SAM
Let's get out of here.

NEAL
(to Harris)
Jerk.

They walk away.

BILL
I think he does know. His girlfriend is hot.

NEAL
Shut-up.

CUT TO:

INT. WEIR DINING ROOM - NIGHT

Sam, HAROLD, JEAN and Lindsay are sitting at the dinner table. It is the end of the meal and Harold is sipping coffee. Sam is once again, finishing the "doorbell joke."

SAM
And the guy says, "how do you think I rang the doorbell?"

Harold stops drinking abruptly, trying not to react.

SAM (CONT'D)
Do you get it?

JEAN
_I_ don't.

(CONTINUED)

CONTINUED:

SAM
Dad?

HAROLD
(lying)
No.

Sam is disappointed.

JEAN
You know who's funny? That Red Buttons.

The doorbell RINGS.

JEAN
Who could that be?

Lindsay stands up to get the door.

LINDSAY
Oh, it's Daniel.
(off their looks)
You met him. He's a friend of mine from school.

HAROLD
He's not that greasy guy who broke in here the other night?

LINDSAY
No. I mean, yes. He's not "greasy." I'm helping him on his algebra. Don't be so judgmental.

Harold stands up.

HAROLD
I'll get the door. It's dark and you're a girl.

CUT TO:

INT. WEIR HOUSE DOORWAY - CONTINUOUS

Harold opens the door to reveal Daniel, smiling, leaning against the doorjamb, smoking a cigarette.

DANIEL
Hi. Lindsay here?

(CONTINUED)

CONTINUED:

Off Harold's look, Daniel licks his finger and puts the cigarette out with it. He places the extinguished butt in his pocket for later.

CUT TO:

INT. LINDSAY'S ROOM - MOMENTS LATER

Lindsay sits at her desk. Daniel sits on her bed. There's a moment of awkward silence.

LINDSAY
So, how do you wanna do this?

DANIEL
I don't know. I've never done this before.

Daniel's goofy grin makes Lindsay laugh.

LINDSAY
Well, in your textbook... did you bring your textbook?

DANIEL
Oh, no. I probably should've, hunh?

LINDSAY
Well...

DANIEL
Oh, man. I already screwed up.

LINDSAY
That's okay. I think I still have mine. They have these practice tests in the back. They're kind of helpful.

Daniel nods, then flops back on the bed.

DANIEL
Oh, man, just the idea of studying makes me want to take a nap.
(looks up at ceiling)
Nice bed.

LINDSAY
Thanks.

Lindsay, watching him, looks anxious. Daniel sits up. He starts fishing out a cigarette. Daniel takes out a lighter.

(CONTINUED)

CONTINUED:

LINDSAY (CONT'D)
What are you doing?

DANIEL
What?

LINDSAY
You can't smoke in here. I mean, I don't care. It's just... my parents.

DANIEL
Oh, I got ya. Okay, here's the deal. I'm gonna go out and smoke this, but when I get back, we're gonna blaze through these tricks of yours. I'm gonna be like a lean, mean, math machine.

He grins. She laughs, clearly smitten by him.

CUT TO:

EXT. WEIR'S BACK YARD - MOMENTS LATER

Sam, a sneaky look on his face, creeps out onto the back patio, cradling a book. He sits down and takes out one of those anatomy books with the transparency overlays of internal body parts. Sam looks at a picture then puts the transparency over it and stares at it quizzically.

DANIEL (O.S.)
What you got there?

Sam looks at Daniel through the transparency. He sees Daniel light a cigarette in the dark. Sam's instinct is to cover the book.

SAM
Nothing.

Daniel takes the book and looks at it.

DANIEL
These kind of books just make me think about how much crap can go wrong inside of you.

SAM
Oh, uh, yeah.

(CONTINUED)

CONTINUED:

DANIEL
Why are you reading this?

SAM
Um, I'm taking sex ed with Mr. Fredricks.

Daniel nods, taking a drag from his cigarette. Sam looks Daniel over, deciding whether to trust him.

DANIEL
He's not a very good teacher.

SAM
He's a jerk. He embarrassed me in front of everybody just because I'm a little behind when it comes to this stuff.

DANIEL
Yeah, I know how that goes.

SAM
You do?

DANIEL
You know, you're not gonna learn anything you can really use from a book like that.

SAM
I'm not?

DANIEL
No.

There's a moment of silence before Daniel puts out his cigarette.

DANIEL (CONT'D)
Tell you what. You meet me at my locker at noon tomorrow and I'll set you up.

SAM
(tentative)
Um, okay.

Daniel exits. Sam is unsure what to expect.

CUT TO:

INT. LINDSAY'S ROOM - NIGHT

Lindsay and Daniel are seated close to each other, at her desk. They are going over a problem. Daniel's attention is beginning to wander.

LINDSAY
Okay. Let's try a different one. Now, how do you solve this type of problem?

DANIEL
You use the quadratic formula.

LINDSAY
(pleased)
Exactly. That's right. Now, what is the quadratic formula?

Daniel looks confused and frustrated.

LINDSAY (CONT'D)
"X" equals...

Lindsay pauses, hoping this will remind him. It doesn't.

LINDSAY (CONT'D)
Negative "B," plus or minus... the square root of...

DANIEL
Lindsay, when you said you were gonna teach me some tricks, I thought you meant like, real tricks.

LINDSAY
(joking)
Whaddya mean, like magic tricks?

DANIEL
Something like that. I mean, you're kind of just teaching me math.

LINDSAY
But you're gonna get it.

DANIEL
(pointing to textbook)
Yeah, but I can't learn all this. The test's tomorrow. There's no way.

(CONTINUED)

CONTINUED:

LINDSAY
Well... I don't know what else to do.

DANIEL
I'll be cool.

LINDSAY
Really?

DANIEL
Yeah. I'll figure something out. Hey, listen, sorry if I wasted your time.

LINDSAY
No. You didn't.

DANIEL
So... you wanna go do something?

LINDSAY
Oh, I don't think my parents would let me. School night and everything.

DANIEL
Oh. Right. Well, I'll see you tomorrow, Linds. Thanks, again.

She smiles. He gives her a peck on the cheek, then exits. Lindsay, now alone, cups her freshly-kissed cheek and off her contemplative expression, we cut to the hallway.

CUT TO:

INT. HALLWAY - CONTINUOUS

As Daniel exits the bedroom, he runs into Harold.

HAROLD
That was fast.

DANIEL
Hey, what can I say? Lindsay's a great teacher. Later.

Off Harold's look, we:

FADE OUT.

END OF ACT ONE

(CONTINUED)

CONTINUED:

ACT TWO

FADE IN:

INT. HALLWAY - MORNING

Sam, Bill and Neal are walking down the hall.

NEAL
The Hulk could kick the Thing's butt any day.

SAM
No way, the Thing could definitely take the Hulk. Even if the Hulk could beat him, all he'd have to do is wait until the Hulk turned back into Bill Bixby, then he could cream him, no problem.

NEAL
You know, you're right.

Daniel approaches, holding a brown paper bag.

DANIEL
Hey, Weir. I got something you might be interested in.

Sam, a bit surprised, takes the bag from Daniel.

DANIEL (CONT'D)
Check it out. But don't lose it.

SAM
Yeah, okay.

DANIEL
I want it back.

SAM
All right. Thanks.

Sam starts to look inside the bag.

DANIEL
(conspiratorially)
Don't open it here, man. I don't want it getting confiscated, you know what I'm saying?

(CONTINUED)

23.

CONTINUED:

NEAL
Confiscated?

Daniel heads off. Sam quickly hides the bag in his shirt.

BILL
I'm scared.

ON DANIEL - he crosses the hallway toward a bleary-eyed Nick.

DANIEL
Chump. I need your help.

NICK
What?

DANIEL
Come here.

Daniel leads Nick to a classroom.

DANIEL (CONT'D)
I gotta get something in here. If you see Kowchevski, bang on the door. Got me?

Nick nods.

DANIEL (CONT'D)
Don't screw me over. Look alive.

Daniel slaps Nick lightly on his cheek.

NICK
I'm alive, man. You don't have to hit me.

DANIEL
All right. I'll be out in a sec.

Daniel makes sure the coast is clear, then pops into the empty classroom. Nick scans the hallway, keeping watch. Suddenly, a pretty girl, SARA approaches.

SARA
Hey, Nick. What's up?

NICK
Oh, hey, Sara.

CUT TO:

INT. KOWCHEVSKI'S OFFICE - CONTINUOUS

Daniel rifles through Kowchevski's drawers, looking for the algebra test. He's not having much luck.

CUT TO:

INT. HALLWAY - DAY

Nick is distracted by Sara.

SARA
Danielle and I are gonna sing
"Souper Trouper" at the talent show
- we're gonna dress up like Abba.
Won't that be cool?

NICK
Yeah. Awesome.

Suddenly, Nick spots Kowchevski at the other end of the hall. His face drops. He starts banging on the office door.

SARA
What are you doing?

CUT TO:

INT. KOWCHEVSKI'S OFFICE - CONTINUOUS

Daniel has found the stack of ALGEBRA TESTS. He grabs one and puts it in his jacket, quickly heading for the door.

CUT TO:

INT. HALLWAY - CONTINUOUS

Daniel bolts from the office. Nick points in the direction of Kowchevski and the two dart away. Sara watches them go, confused.

SARA
Talk to you later.

CUT TO:

INT. ANOTHER PART OF HALLWAY - MOMENTS LATER

Daniel is inspecting the stolen test, looking frustrated. Nick stands beside him, looking at his own hand.

(CONTINUED)

25.

CONTINUED:

NICK
I think I'm getting a wart on my wrist.

DANIEL
(looking at the test)
This algebra test looks crazy. What language is this?

NICK
How do you get rid of a wart?

DANIEL
(barking)
Hey. Can't you see I'm thinking here?

NICK
Sorry.

Daniel considers his next move.

CUT TO:

INT. UNDER THE STAIRWELL - DAY

Sam, Bill and Neal pow-wow under the stairs. Sam opens the bag and removes a small metal reel.

SAM
It's a movie or something.

NEAL
Let me see that.

Neal takes the film, unwinds it from the spool and holds it up to a window. They all gather around.

NEAL
Oh, my god, it's a naked woman.

BILL
What's she doing?

NEAL
Who cares what she's doing? She's naked. It's a dirty movie, you idiot!

BILL
You mean, like a porno?!

(CONTINUED)

CONTINUED:

SAM
SHUT UP! Give it to me.

Sam grabs the movie back and puts it in the bag.

SAM
What am I supposed to do with a porno?

NEAL
What do you think? You watch it-- over and over.

SAM
Only perverts watch pornos.

NEAL
Well, then every guy in America is a pervert. The meaning of that joke is right here. You wanna keep living in the dark?

SAM
No. But how would I even watch it? I don't have a projector.

NEAL
Well, I do. So give it to me.
(grabbing the bag; decisively)
Okay. When school's over, we're gonna go to my house and we're gonna watch this movie from beginning to end. Agreed?

Bill and Sam both solemnly nod, then break out into a smile. Bill is white as a ghost. Neal seems satisfied.

BILL
Now I'm really scared.
(lifting his hands)
Look. My hands are shaking.

CUT TO:

INT. LIBRARY - LATER

Lindsay is reading a book as Daniel sits down beside her.

LINDSAY
Hey.

(CONTINUED)

CONTINUED:

DANIEL
I ganked the test...

He grins mischievously at her.

DANIEL (CONT'D)
...but I need your help, man. I can't figure any of this out.

LINDSAY
Wait. What?

DANIEL
I ganked the algebra test.

LINDSAY
You "ganked" it?

Daniel looks around for any potential eavesdroppers.

DANIEL
I stole it. From Kowchevski's office. He's got no clue.

But Daniel's grin fades when he sees her concerned expression.

DANIEL (CONT'D)
What?

LINDSAY
You stole a test? From his office?

DANIEL
Yeah, pretty cool, huh? I just need you to walk me through it.

LINDSAY
I... I can't.

DANIEL
Sure, you can. This stuff is easy for you.

LINDSAY
No. I mean... I shouldn't.

DANIEL
Why not?

Lindsay just stares at him, trying to find the right words. Daniel nods as if he understands.

(CONTINUED)

CONTINUED: (2)

DANIEL (CONT'D)
Hey. Don't worry. I'm not gonna be hitting you up every time I have a math test. I promise. It's just if I flunk this one, he's gonna make me take the class over, you know? I can't do that.

He takes out the test and points to the first problem.

DANIEL (CONT'D)
So for this one. What should I write?

Lindsay is uncomfortable. She looks around the library.

LINDSAY
I don't want to be uptight, but... I just...
(she thinks)
You know, why don't I talk to Kowchevski?

DANIEL
(eyes-bugging)
What? Why?

LINDSAY
I'll ask him for an extension. He gave me one once. And he likes me. I'll tell him that I'm tutoring you and that you're getting the hang of it, but you just need a little more time.

Lindsay likes her idea. Daniel grimaces.

DANIEL
Come on, just fill out this test.

LINDSAY
Let me go talk to him. Okay?

DANIEL
Hey, you don't want to get in trouble - that's cool. No big deal. I'll find somebody else...

LINDSAY
(firmly)
I'll get you an extension. We'll study. You'll pass the class.
(MORE)

(CONTINUED)

CONTINUED: (3)

LINDSAY (CONT'D)
Daniel, trust me. This is gonna work.

CUT TO:

INT. KOWCHEVSKI'S OFFICE - DAY

Lindsay sits across the desk from Mr. Kowchevski.

MR. KOWCHEVSKI
Forget it. I'm not giving that dirtbag an extension.

LINDSAY
But Mr. Kowchevski, I worked with him last night and he was really learning. He just needs more time. Daniel's the kind of student who needs more attention, you know?

MR. KOWCHEVSKI
Daniel's the kind of student who needs to just disappear.

LINDSAY
(astonished)
I can't believe you just said that.

MR. KOWCHEVSKI
He wastes class time. He wastes my time. Now, he's wasting your time.

LINDSAY
He's not wasting anybody's time. I mean, isn't your job to teach?

MR. KOWCHEVSKI
My job is to teach the students who want to get taught. Daniel's a lost cause. He doesn't want to learn.

LINDSAY
So you're just gonna flunk him?

MR. KOWCHEVSKI
Hey, it's not like I want to have him back in my algebra class another year. He's a nightmare, but rules are rules.

LINDSAY
I'm just asking for a few more days.

(CONTINUED)

CONTINUED:

MR. KOWCHEVSKI
Lindsay, I know Daniel's cute with his bedroom eyes and his stringy hair, but... he's a loser. And losers pull down winners. You're a smart girl. Don't let your hormones get in the way.

Lindsay is stunned and angry.

LINDSAY
Excuse me?

CUT TO:

INT. OUTSIDE KOWCHEVSKI'S OFFICE - CONTINUOUS

Lindsay, flush with anger, comes storming out of Kowchevski's office. Daniel is waiting for her.

LINDSAY
Where's that test?

DANIEL
In my coat.

LINDSAY
Let's go.

Lindsay storms down the hallway. A smile curls on Daniel's lips, then he follows.

CUT TO:

INT. LIBRARY - MOMENTS LATER

Lindsay dictates to Daniel as he fills out the test.

LINDSAY
Seventy-four times twenty-three - put that in parentheses - then X equals nineteen Y. Y equals... eight.

DANIEL
Damn. It's weird you can do all this in your head. You're like a brainiac or something.

LINDSAY
(sarcastic)
Thanks.

(CONTINUED)

CONTINUED:

DANIEL
(genuine)
No. I mean, you're like... smart.

LINDSAY
It's not that hard. It just takes a little... effort.

Daniel, finished with the test, puts it away, excited.

DANIEL
You rock. I owe you.

LINDSAY
That's okay.

DANIEL
I can't wait to see Kowchevski's face when he gives this test back to me. He's gonna lose his mind.

LINDSAY
But Daniel... this isn't over, right? I'm gonna tutor you after this so you don't have to keep stealing tests.

DANIEL
Oh, yeah. Definitely. Yeah. I'm gonna be like a kid with one of those things.

LINDSAY
An abacus.

DANIEL
Yeah.
(pantomiming)
Seven, y, four, x, equals, nine.

Daniel gives her a wink and a grin. Lindsay is charmed. The SCHOOL BELL RINGS.

DANIEL (CONT'D)
Oh, man. Here we go.

Lindsay watches as Daniel gingerly crosses himself.

CUT TO:

INT. CLASSROOM - LATER

MUSIC UP: CURTIS MAYFIELD'S "SUPERFLY."

Daniel is taking the test. He discreetly replaces the one on his desk with the previously filled out test, which is rolled up in his sleeve. Grinning, he pretends to continue to take the test.

CUT TO:

EXT. SIDE OF SCHOOL - DAY

We see the doors of the school as we HEAR the final BELL RING.

MUSIC UP: AC/DC's "HIGHWAY TO HELL."

The doors fly open. Bill, Sam and Neal come running out full gallop, headed toward camera.

Other students now exit the school as the Geeks bound home, Sam clutching the bag in his hand. As they run, Bill falls. They stop. Neal helps him to his feet and they continue running.

CUT TO:

INT. KOWCHEVSKI'S OFFICE - DAY

Kowchevski is grading Daniel's test, a big fat RED MARKER in his hand. His smile disappears when he sees the first answer is correct. He skims the entire test. He's stunned.

CUT TO:

INT. HALLWAY - LATER

The halls are emptying out as only students involved in extracurricular remain. Lindsay is at her locker when Mr. Kowchevski approaches her from behind.

MR. KOWCHEVSKI
Lindsay.

She spins around. She turns ashen when she sees him.

MR. KOWCHEVSKI (CONT'D)
I guess Daniel didn't need that extension after all. He got an A on his test.

(CONTINUED)

CONTINUED:

LINDSAY
Well... uh... I told you, I helped him study.

MR. KOWCHEVSKI
Did you help him cheat?

Lindsay hesitates under Kowchevski's glare, then quickly regroups.

LINDSAY
(barely audible)
No.

MR. KOWCHEVSKI
Well, I got an anonymous note that says you did.

LINDSAY
I... I didn't cheat Mr. Kowchevski.
(off his skeptical look)
I didn't.

MR. KOWCHEVSKI
Well, I think you did.

Lindsay just stares, but is unable to speak. Mr. Kowchevski gives her a disapproving look.

MR. KOWCHEVSKI (CONT'D)
We'll deal with this tomorrow. You're in a lot of trouble, young lady.

He walks away. Lindsay, reeling, slumps against her locker. Suddenly, an overly chipper MILLIE appears beside her.

MILLIE
Why were you talking to Mr. Kowchevski?

LINDSAY
(lost in her own world)
Hunh?

MILLIE
(excited)
Are you joining the Mathletes again?

(CONTINUED)

CONTINUED: (2)

LINDSAY
(looking nauseous)
No.

Lindsay, in a dark fog, stumbles away. Millie is offended.

MILLIE
Jeez. Sorry I asked.

And off Millie's shrug, we...

FADE OUT.

END OF ACT TWO

ACT THREE

FADE IN:

EXT. PARKING LOT - DAY

Lindsay and Daniel are standing beside Daniel's Trans Am. Lindsay is panicked.

DANIEL
An anonymous note? That's so lame.

LINDSAY
Oh, god. I'm so dead.

DANIEL
What did you say to Kowchevski?

LINDSAY
Nothing. My dad's gonna murder me.

DANIEL
Did you tell him we cheated?

LINDSAY
No, but he could see it all over my face.

DANIEL
(hopeful)
Okay, well, then it's not over. An anonymous note - that means nothing, man. And as long as we don't, you know, admit it... they don't have jack on us.

(CONTINUED)

CONTINUED:

LINDSAY
We're gonna deny it?

DANIEL
Yeah. Definitely.

LINDSAY
(shaking her head)
Daniel...

DANIEL
Listen to me. You're good at math, okay? I'm good at this sort of thing. When something like this happens, you just gotta deny everything, okay?

LINDSAY
But I'm not a good liar.

DANIEL
Well, then this'll be good practice for you.
(off her look)
Lindsay, I got you into this and I'm gonna get you out, but you gotta trust me, all right?

Daniel shoots her his most effective puppy-dog look.

DANIEL
We're in this together.

He gives her a reassuring smile. Off Lindsay's worried look, we...

CUT TO:

INT. NEAL'S BASEMENT - DAY

Neal is threading the projector, as Sam and Bill eagerly anticipate their first stag film.

SAM
This is taking forever.

NEAL
Hey, do you want to let the projector eat the film and have Daniel kill you? 'Cause we can do that, too.

(CONTINUED)

CONTINUED:

The film begins to be projected.

NEAL (CONT'D)
There!

SAM
Kill the lights.

NEAL
Aye, aye, sir.

Neal salutes and turns off the lights as the projector rolls. We ANGLE ON THE GEEKS watching the film. They are illuminated only by the glow of the Bell and Howell.

NEAL (CONT'D)
Here we go.

SAM
WOW.

BILL
Hel-lo.

NEAL
How'd you like to come home to that every night?

SAM
Yeah.

BILL
He's in good shape.

DISSOLVE TO:

INT. NEAL'S BASEMENT - MOMENTS LATER

The room is silent except for the sound of the projector. Bill and Sam's expression of excitement are gone. They now just look confused. Neal seems intrigued.

VARIOUS CLOSE-UPS of SAM AND BILL looking disturbed. NEAL has a glint in his eye.

NEAL
What is she <u>doing</u>?

DISSOLVE TO:

INT. NEAL'S BASEMENT - MOMENTS LATER

Bill and Sam now look horrified and disgusted. Their chairs have been moved farther apart from each other. Neal is intent.

SAM
Oh my god.

Suddenly, their eyes go wide. Then Sam and Bill close their eyes. They're speechless, stunned. Neal seems almost transported. The film ends, flapping against the projector.

NEAL
(eager)
So, thread it up again?

BILL
I think I'm gonna be sick.

Bill bolts from the room as Sam shakes his head in horror.

NEAL
...or no?

CUT TO:

INT. WEIR DINING ROOM - NIGHT

Lindsay, Sam and Jean are finishing dinner. Sam is ashen. He can barely eat.

JEAN
Sam, you've barely touched your cutlets. Aren't you feeling well?

SAM
I had a big snack at Neal's after school. May I be excused?

JEAN
Okay, but I've got chocolate coconut squares for dessert.

SAM
Maybe later.

Sam exits in silence.

JEAN
He's at that stage.

(CONTINUED)

CONTINUED:

Harold enters from the kitchen, looking very disturbed. He takes a seat at the table and stares at Lindsay for a few beats. Brow furrowed.

HAROLD
That was Mr. Kowchevski on the phone.

Lindsay's face drops.

HAROLD (CONT'D)
Apparently, my daughter is now a cheater.

JEAN
(gasps)
My Aunt Sally.

HAROLD
She cheated on a math test with that hoodlum she brought over here the other night. Now, she's facing suspension.

JEAN
Lindsay?!

Lindsay stares at their angry faces. Finds her resolve.

LINDSAY
(feeble)
Well... it's not true.

HAROLD
Don't lie to me, Lindsay.

LINDSAY
I'm not.

JEAN
But why? You're a good student. I don't understand why you have to cheat.

HAROLD
She's falling in with the wrong crowd. She's lying and cheating and next thing you know, she's Patty Hearst and she's got a gun to our heads.

LINDSAY
Dad, I just told you, it's not true.

(CONTINUED)

CONTINUED: (2)

HAROLD
Maybe I don't believe you.

LINDSAY
I didn't cheat. I... I helped Daniel study. He got a good grade on his test and Mr. Kowchevski just can't handle it.
(stammering; standing up)
The teachers at McKinley are, you know, they don't trust the students. They just want to punish people. Just like you guys! You don't even ask me my side - you just jump to conclusions and start yelling. It's so sick! I'm your daughter and you're gonna believe some stranger over me? Just because he's an adult?
(shaking her head; upset)
Hey, believe what you want. I don't even care. Punish me. Fine. Whatever. Thanks for all the support!

Lindsay storms off to her room. Harold and Jean are stunned.

CUT TO:

INT. LINDSAY'S ROOM - NIGHT - MINUTES LATER

Lindsay sits on her bed. There is a knock on the door.

LINDSAY
Yeah.

JEAN (O.S.)
Can we come in?

LINDSAY
I guess.

Harold and Jean enter, contrite.

JEAN
Your father and I just want to say... we're sorry, and we believe you.

HAROLD
(with some trouble)
It was an upsetting call, but I should have asked for your side of the story. And I don't think you're gonna turn out like Patty Hearst.

(CONTINUED)

CONTINUED:

Harold and Jean exchange upset looks, then head for the door. Lindsay is silent.

JEAN
You want me to bring up a coconut square, sweetie?

LINDSAY
No, that's okay.

After her parents exit, a guilty looking Lindsay buries her head in her hands.

CUT TO:

INT. HALLWAY - DAY

A concerned Millie approaches Lindsay in the hall.

MILLIE
Lindsay, I need to talk to you. Some of the Mathletes have been saying things. Awful things... about you.

LINDSAY
Like what?

MILLIE
There's a rumor going around that you cheated on a math test. Just so you know, I defended you. I told them, "That's impossible. Even though Lindsay's not a Mathlete anymore, she would never break the league's code of honor."

LINDSAY
Millie, guess what? I did cheat. I lied and I cheated. Then, I lied some more. Deal with it.

Millie stares at her a beat.

MILLIE
You're funny Lindsay. I knew it wasn't true.

Millie exits.

CUT TO:

INT. CAFETERIA - DAY

Sam, Neal and Bill are having an awkwardly silent lunch. No one wants to say anything for fear of bringing up last night's dirty movie. Finally Neal speaks.

NEAL
Anyone see Dukes of Hazzard last night?

SAM
Yeah.

BILL
It was a good one.

Back to silent eating.

NEAL
Boss Hogg is really funny.
(imitating)
"I'll bet there's a reward in this big enough to choke a plow horse. "

SAM/BILL
Yeah./Yeah.

Cindy Sanders comes over to the table next to them and BENDS OVER to talk to some friends.

Sam stares at her, then grimaces, quickly going back to his lunch. Suddenly, Cindy appears above him.

CINDY
Hi, Sam.

Sam cannot make eye contact and answers quietly.

SAM
Oh, god. Well, what do you want?

CINDY
I was wondering if you could run the ice cream booth with me. Betsy can't make it to the Carnival.

Sam's thoughts are torturing him. He has to get rid of Cindy.

SAM
I'm not going to be able to make it either, I found out.

(CONTINUED)

CONTINUED:

CINDY
Oh. That's too bad.

SAM
I'm kind of busy right now, okay?

CINDY
(confused)
Yeah, sure.

Sam stares at her.

CINDY (CONT'D)
I'll see ya' later.

Sam watches Cindy walk away. There is an awkward moment.

NEAL
How great was that when them Dukes handcuffed Roscoe, Enos and Boss Hogg together?

BILL
Yeah... that was pretty funny.

Sam is in his own world, troubled. Simultaneously, they all go back to eating their meals in silence.

CUT TO:

INT. MR. ROSSO'S OFFICE - CONTINUOUS

Lindsay sits across from Mr. Rosso.

MR. ROSSO
Is there anything you want to tell me before the meeting this afternoon? Something you can't say in front of Daniel and Mr. Kowchevski?

LINDSAY
Uh, just, uh... I didn't cheat.

MR. ROSSO
Well, no one wants that to be true more than I do.
(beat)
You know, something like this happened to me when I was in high school. Got a minute?

(CONTINUED)

CONTINUED:

LINDSAY
I guess.

MR. ROSSO
I felt bad for this kid, Bruce Conforti, so I'd kinda "help" him on biology tests. Okay, we cheated. But, after a while, I realized he was the one who was being cheated out of something priceless. Knowledge. So, one day I just told him I wasn't gonna do that anymore and...

LINDSAY
(tired of Rosso pontificating)
...and he studied and got straight A's on his own.

MR. ROSSO
No, he beat the stuffing out of me, because I became his crutch. You understand?

LINDSAY
All I did was help Daniel study.

MR. ROSSO
Well, I hope you're telling the truth. There's nothing that makes me happier than seeing students helping other students. That's why I got into this game.

LINDSAY
That's all I was trying to do.

MR. ROSSO
Right on.

LINDSAY
Thanks, Mr. Rosso.

Lindsay gets up to leave.

MR. ROSSO
Hey. Just remember this afternoon, I'm not your judge or your executioner. I'm your friend. So do me a favor and don't give up on us adults, okay?

(CONTINUED)

CONTINUED: (2)

Rosso gives Lindsay a black handshake.

LINDSAY
(finally, a smile)
Okay.

Lindsay exits. Rosso looks quite pleased with himself.

CUT TO:

INT. HALLWAY - DAY

Bill is walking down the hall when a teacher, MISS LANDIS, approaches and puts her arm around his shoulder.

MISS LANDIS
Bill, I just read your paper on the Aborigines. Excellent job. Keep up the good work.

Bill is totally uncomfortable with her touching him. He makes a strange whimpering noise and runs away.

MISS LANDIS (CONT'D)
I said I <u>liked</u> it.

CUT TO:

EXT. SMOKING PATIO - DAY

Kim is chilling on the smoking patio, when a stressed Lindsay sits down.

LINDSAY
Hey. Where's Daniel?

KIM
Beats me.

LINDSAY
We have a disciplinary meeting after school.

KIM
You nervous?
(off Lindsay's nod)
Don't worry. Daniel gets out of stuff like this all the time. Just let him do the talking.

(CONTINUED)

CONTINUED:

LINDSAY
I shouldn't feel bad, right? I mean, Kowchevski is a jerk and I'll, you know, tutor Daniel - he'll pass the class. It's all gonna work out.
(full of doubt)
Right?

KIM
What, you think you and Daniel are gonna be like study buddies?

Kim laughs.

LINDSAY
What?

KIM
He's not gonna study. He already passed the test.

LINDSAY
Yeah, he still wants to learn. What about the next test?

KIM
He'll get somebody else to give him the answers. He always does.

Kim laughs. Lindsay stares at her, unsure of what to think. Lindsay looks unsettled, when Daniel appears on the patio.

DANIEL
What's up with you?

KIM
Hey, we were just talking about you.

DANIEL
(coy)
Yeah? What were you saying?

KIM
(flirtatious)
I was saying, you're hot.

DANIEL
Oh, yeah?

She nods. Daniel pounces on her, playfully.

(CONTINUED)

CONTINUED: (2)

DANIEL (CONT'D)
So, Linds. Ready to stick it to the Man?

She gives a very half-hearted smile.

DANIEL (CONT'D)
All right. Partners in crime. Give me five.

Daniel raises his hand. But she just stares at him, blankly.

DANIEL (CONT'D)
Hey. Don't leave me hangin'.

Lindsay gives him a feeble high-five.

FADE OUT.

<u>END OF ACT THREE</u>

<u>ACT FOUR</u>

FADE IN:

INT. SHOP CLASS - DAY

Daniel is prepping Lindsay for their meeting. They huddle in the empty shop class.

DANIEL
Another thing they do is an old cop trick. They'll get you alone and they'll tell you I confessed. Don't buy it. I'll never confess, okay? Never.

LINDSAY
Well, <u>I'm</u> going to. I can't keep lying.

DANIEL
What? Why not?

LINDSAY
What is this, a big game to you? You got me to cheat and lie to my parents and to Mr. Rosso. I've become this like pathological liar in one day.

(CONTINUED)

CONTINUED:

DANIEL
Well, so... why stop now? I mean, we're almost home free.

Lindsay just stares at him. He'll never get it. Frustrated, Lindsay leans against one of the stripped cars. After a moment, Daniel sits beside her.

DANIEL (CONT'D)
Hey. I get it. You care about your grades and your transcript. But look, if you get suspended, that's gonna go on your transcript. Then you really will be screwed. So let's just stick to the program, okay?

Lindsay looks at him, warily.

LINDSAY
You're manipulating me.

DANIEL
What?

LINDSAY
You're manipulating me.

DANIEL
No, I'm not.

LINDSAY
Yes, you are. And it's just... it's very hard for me to say no to you, but... I have to. I can't go in there and lie. I'm sorry. I can't.

Daniel looks stumped. After a moment...

DANIEL
(getting angry)
You know what, fine, don't lie.

LINDSAY
What?

DANIEL
No. Forget it. You're right. Let's just tell them what we did. What the hell's the difference? You'll get a slap on the wrist, I'll get suspended--expelled.

(CONTINUED)

CONTINUED: (2)

LINDSAY
That's not fair. Don't do that to me.

DANIEL
What do you think, I want to be terrible at school?! You think I like it?! I wish I was as smart as you. I wish this all came easy to me, but it doesn't. When I was in sixth grade they told us that when we got to junior high we'd be in track one, track two or track three. Track one was the smart kids, track two were the normal kids and track three was the dumb kids. Where do you think I ended up? You know how that feels to be told that you're dumb when you're eleven years old.
(starts to cry)
Where are you supposed to go from there?

Daniel looks away, shaking his head.

LINDSAY
You're not dumb.

DANIEL
Everybody thinks I am. Kowchevski thinks I am. And I just wanted to prove him wrong, you know? Just once. Even if I am cheating.

Lindsay gives him a sympathetic smile. Then, for a moment, they sit in contemplative silence.

CUT TO:

INT. HALLWAY - DAY

Neal is telling the "doorbell joke" to several other guys.

NEAL
...and the guy says, "how do you think I rang the doorbell?"

The guys laugh. Neal beams.

(CONTINUED)

CONTINUED:

NEAL (CONT'D)
Good one, huh?

CUT TO:

INT. CLASSROOM - DAY

Bill, Neal and Sam are in health class. Mr. Fredricks is holding a small handful of papers. He reads from one of them.

MR. FREDRICKS
If a pregnant woman has sex, can the baby get poked?

Laughter. Fredricks is annoyed.

MR. FREDRICKS (CONT'D)
Hey, hyenas, can I get through one question without you guys getting hysterical on me? Jeez.

The class shuts up.

MR. FREDRICKS (CONT'D)
Sex is completely safe for the fetus. It's not gonna come out with dents in it's head, looking like a golf ball.

The SCHOOL BELL RINGS.

MR. FREDRICKS (CONT'D)
Okay, Casanovas, that's all for today.

As the boys file out, Fredricks stops Sam.

MR. FREDRICKS (CONT'D)
Sam, can I talk to you?

SAM
Sure.

MR. FREDRICKS
In my office.

Sam shoots a fearful look at Neal and Bill.

CUT TO:

INT. FREDRICKS'S OFFICE - MOMENTS LATER

A tiny, cramped office next to the classroom. Both Sam and Fredricks are uncomfortable.

(CONTINUED)

CONTINUED:

MR. FREDRICKS
When I was going through the questions, I was a little disturbed by yours.

SAM
How do you know which one was my question? They were anonymous.

MR. FREDRICKS
You're the only one who has Star Trek notebook paper.

SAM
Oh.

MR. FREDRICKS
Where did you find out about this "activity?"

SAM
Uh, I saw a... movie.

MR. FREDRICKS
I see. Sometimes those kinds of... movies - they sensationalize certain... things. But in reality, those things don't usually happen. Do you understand what I'm saying?

But Sam stares at him blankly. Fredricks sighs, then seems to lose the teacher side of his personality.

MR. FREDRICKS (CONT'D)
Okay. I'll tell you the truth, in plain language, but you can't tell anyone we had this talk. Your permission slip for sex ed doesn't cover this and I could get in a lot of trouble for what I'm about to say. Okay?

SAM
(scared)
Okay.

MR. FREDRICKS
Certain men, <u>not me</u>, but certain men do certain things for the purpose of arousal...

As Fredricks talks, his dialogue fades out.

(CONTINUED)

CONTINUED: (2)

MUSIC UP: BARRY WHITE'S "LOVE'S THEME"

CLOSE on Fredricks' mouth as he discusses bizarre sexual practices to a wide-eyed, nodding Sam.

A series of DISSOLVES: Fredricks gesturing, Sam laughing, Sam and Fredricks shaking hands.

MUSIC OUT.

MR. FREDRICKS (CONT'D)
But they're just things people do in these kinds of movies. That's not reality. If it was, I'd be as freaked out as you. Okay?

SAM
(relieved)
Yeah. Thanks, Mr. Fredricks.

MR. FREDRICKS
No problem. Now, get outta here, cowboy.

SAM
I just have one more question.

MR. FREDRICKS
What is it?

SAM
Could you explain this joke to me? You see, there's this guy who has no arms and no legs...

CUT TO:

INT. WAITING ROOM - DAY

Lindsay and Daniel sit outside Mr. Rosso's office.

DANIEL
(in a whisper)
Hey, if you want to just tell the truth, that's cool. Whatever you want.

LINDSAY
No, Daniel. Let's just stick to our story.

DANIEL
You sure?

(CONTINUED)

CONTINUED:

LINDSAY
Yeah.

They exchange a sweet smile.

DANIEL
But when we're inside, let me handle it, okay?

She nods. Daniel gives her the thumbs-up just as Lindsay's parents walk in the door. Lindsay turns white as a sheet.

LINDSAY
Mom? Dad? What are you doing here?

JEAN
We feel terrible about last night. You've always been truthful with us and we should never have doubted you.

HAROLD
Nobody falsely accuses my daughter.

LINDSAY
It's okay. It happens.

HAROLD
Not to any member of this family, it doesn't. I want to give this Kowchevski joker a piece of my mind.

LINDSAY
You don't have to do that.

HAROLD
Yes, I do. I don't pay taxes so my daughter can get railroaded.

JEAN
Your father even closed the store.

Lindsay tries to muster an appreciative smile.

CUT TO:

INT. MR. KOWCHEVSKI'S CLASSROOM - DAY - SIMULTANEOUS

Rosso and Kowchevski discuss the impending meeting.

(CONTINUED)

CONTINUED:

MR. ROSSO
Now, let's be patient and hear everyone out. Try to be a team. We don't actually know that anyone cheated.

MR. KOWCHEVSKI
I do.

MR. ROSSO
Fine. Unfortunately an anonymous note isn't sufficient proof. Let's see it.

MR. KOWCHEVSKI
There is no note.

MR. ROSSO
There's no note?

MR. KOWCHEVSKI
No, sometimes I use that as a ploy to get a confession. It works, you'll see.

MR. ROSSO
How do you expect to have real relationships with these kids, if you're lying to them?

MR. KOWCHEVSKI
Well, I'm not here to have "real relationships" with these kids, thank God. I'm here to teach.

MR. ROSSO
That's terrible.

MR. KOWCHEVSKI
Oh, stop it with that liberal crap. You're being snowed.

MR. ROSSO
No, I'm not. These kids just need someone to believe in them.

MR. KOWCHEVSKI
Oh, please. I knew guys like Daniel in Vietnam. They're the kind of guys who get you killed.

Rosso is reeling. A perky secretary, DOLORES, enters, interrupting them.

(CONTINUED)

CONTINUED: (2)

DOLORES
Everyone's here.

CUT TO:

INT. CAFETERIA - DAY

Cindy Sanders and some of her friends are making posters for the carnival on the floor of the empty cafeteria. Sam watches her for a moment, before she spots him.

CINDY
Hey, Sam.

SAM
Oh, hey, Cindy. Listen, sorry if I was acting weird at lunch.

CINDY
Were you acting weird?

SAM
Well, anyway, it turns out I can go to the Carnival. So, if you still need a scooper, I'm available.

CINDY
Jeanine's gonna help me. But we can always use another scooper.

SAM
Great. So, what time should I be there?

As they make plans, we reveal that Bill has been watching them through the cafeteria doors.

BILL
Eww.

CUT TO:

INT. ROSSO'S OFFICE - LATER

Harold is teeing off on Mr. Kowchevski as Lindsay, Daniel, Mr. Rosso and Jean look on.

HAROLD
...she's a good student, she's never been in trouble before and if she says she didn't help this kid cheat, then she didn't.

(CONTINUED)

CONTINUED:

JEAN
She tutored him and it worked.

HAROLD
You shouldn't be punishing her. You should be paying her for doing your job.

Mr. Kowchevski responds with an irritated look.

MR. ROSSO
Mr. Weir... Harold. It's recently come to my attention that there was no anonymous note written.

JEAN
There was no note?

MR. ROSSO
No. It was a forgery. I apologize.

HAROLD
See, I told ya'.

MR. KOWCHEVSKI
But we're still not convinced that these two didn't cheat.

HAROLD
So, in other words, you wanna punish my daughter for cheating, but you have no proof?

MR. ROSSO
Look, Mr. Weir, it should have never come to this. I've talked to Lindsay. I know she didn't do anything. Daniel, did you... cheat on this test?

DANIEL
No.

MR. ROSSO
Good. Then, I'm satisfied.

MR. KOWCHEVSKI
You're satisfied? Well, I'm not.

MR. ROSSO
(to Mr. K)
Give it up Frank, it's over.

(CONTINUED)

CONTINUED: (2)

HAROLD
What is going on here? I took off
work for this!

MR. ROSSO
I apologize for the inconvenience.

MR. KOWCHEVSKI
Hold on a second. I've got an idea.
Right here is the algebra test
Daniel took. He got a perfect
score. If he can do the first
problem - just the first problem, I
will not only get down on my hands
and knees and beg for forgiveness,
I will also quit. I'll... resign.
I'll never teach again.

Everyone is stunned.

HAROLD
Well, that'd be a start.

Kowchevski hands the test and a pen over to Daniel.

DANIEL
I already took the test. You can't
make me take it again.

MR. KOWCHEVSKI
Yes, I can. One easy little problem
and this all goes away.

HAROLD
Come on, son.

MR. ROSSO
Go ahead, Daniel.

Daniel looks first to Lindsay, who grimaces. He then looks down at the test.

DANIEL
Okay, I just need to use the
quadratic formula.

He begins to write. Harold and Rosso smirk at Kowchevski, totally confident Daniel will come through. Lindsay looks concerned.

Daniel looks up, finished.

(CONTINUED)

CONTINUED: (3)

The others stare down at the test.

ON TEST - Instead of figuring out the problem, Daniel has drawn the "ROLLING STONES" LOGO.

Everyone's faces drop. Daniel looks like the cat who ate the canary.

JEAN
What is that?

MR. KOWCHEVSKI
That's a student Mr. Rosso believes in.

Harold and Jean look at Lindsay, both mortified.

HAROLD
What the hell?

JEAN
Lindsay, you lied to us!

LINDSAY
Mom, I...

DANIEL
Look, don't blame Lindsay. It's not her fault.

Daniel thinks for a moment, then comes up with something.

DANIEL (CONT'D)
It's mine. She was just trying to help me. No one else ever does! What do you think I want to be terrible at school?! You think I like it?!

Lindsay raises an eyebrow.

DANIEL (CONT'D)
I wish I was smart. I wish this all came easy to me, but it doesn't. When I was in sixth grade they told us that when we got to junior high we'd be in track one, track two or track three. Track one was the smart kids, track two were the normal kids and track three was the dumb kids. Where do you think I ended up?
(MORE)

(CONTINUED)

CONTINUED: (4)

DANIEL (CONT'D)
You know how that feels to be told, in ink, that you're dumb when you're eleven years old.
(starts to cry)
Where are you supposed to go from there?

Everyone is engrossed by the story. Jean seems moved. Rosso puts his hand on Daniel's shoulder to comfort him.

Suddenly, LINDSAY BURSTS OUT LAUGHING at the absurdity. This quiets the room as they all turn toward her.

LINDSAY
I'm sorry. I'm sorry.

Lindsay tries to compose herself, but then she bursts out in another peal of laughter.

JEAN
Lindsay?

MR. KOWCHEVSKI
She's probably high as a kite.

HAROLD
My daughter is not high!

This makes Lindsay laugh even harder.

JEAN
Harold, what's happening?

DANIEL
(under his breath)
Lindsay, be cool.

Lindsay completely loses it. As the adults continue to argue, we:

FADE OUT.

THE END

# FREAKS AND GEEKS

"I'M WITH THE BAND"

Episode #6

Written by Gabe Sachs & Jeff Judah

Directed by Judd Apatow

This episode was a blast to write!!! We all knew we wanted to do a band episode at some point, and Jeff and I knew we wanted to write it. I was in a band in high school and we all had friends who were in bands in high school, but the challenge was to make the dialogue as real as possible, and Judd really kicked ass in bringing this script to life.

Everyone in high school took their bands way too seriously which caused all kinds of arguments between band members. We really wanted to capture those stupid but passionate arguments. On the geeks' side, we wanted to really get to what would actually happen if you were a geek who suddenly got that confidence to take a shower. Well, the truth was, you'd still be a geek and you would probably be picked on even more. We wanted to write conversations between the geeks that would really show their lot in life as in the curb scene where they talk about if they're ever really going to meet girls. That was the reality of our show. The geeks had small victories, and that's what made the show real and special...and canceled. Ugh!

Even when we were starting to talk about this episode, we realized that our first challenge was that none of the actors *really* played instruments that well, so we had to figure that out quickly. I showed Jason Segel a bunch of stuff on the drums and we practiced to Rush in his dressing room and at his house. Jason picked it up WAY faster than I did when I started playing. My brother Jon Sachs taught James Franco and continues to give Franco lessons to this day. Shaun played a little bass and Seth, well, Seth was literally afraid to sing during rehearsals. He just sort of mumbled into the microphone but when we were shooting, he suddenly became Joe Cocker and belted it out. Ya couldn't shut him up. Anyway, when our band got together for practice, it was great. They worked really hard and quickly saw how the dynamics of a high school band work...like oil and water. The fact that all the actors had their own personalities and quirks made all the real frustrations about being in a band really shine through. I mean, when you're in a band in high school, you always think you're kicking ass the louder you play, when in reality you're just covering for your lack of skill. Our freak band was no exception. But they had a lot of heart, damn it!

On the geeks' side, the fear of taking a shower was part of all of our lives. This idea first came up because it was a huge fear for Paul, as most things were to Paul in high school, but this was really big. I remember Paul telling us the horror story about bullies picking on some kids by piling on them naked in the showers. This was evidently called a dog-pile. Paul talked about this a lot...quite frankly a little too much. We fortunately couldn't re-create that in our episode, and to this day we can't get that image out of our heads; Paul at the bottom of a dozen naked boys.

When we shot the locker room scenes it was insanity. We were trying to re-create the last scene in *Bonnie & Clyde*. Extras were *really* whipping our actors with towels, and our geeks became the *real* geeks amongst the extras and everyone was happy to pick on them. Especially Levine. The big challenge of the episode was that we wrote that Sam was running down the halls naked, but how were we really going to shoot it? The big blue dot solved the problem. John Daley was amazing and quite frankly happily walked around the set in his underwear.

Jeff and I were really excited that Judd was going to direct the episode, and that it was the first episode that would really bring Nick and Lindsay together. Their first kiss. It was also going to really establish Nick and what his passions were. I remember that the first thing we shot for that show is Nick and Lindsay's kiss after his hellish audition. It was as awkward and sweet as we had imagined, and Jeff and I like to think that we contributed to that "real life" relationship in some small way.

Judd knows what he wants when he directs and knew the characters so well that it really helped make everything pop. Judd and Paul are great with notes, although Paul is a bit more forgiving and will make you feel good about your writing even if he wasn't crazy about something. Paul always let you down in a nice way. Judd really just kicks your ass as a writer. He's really direct, and gentle is not his style. He often wrote things on our scripts that made Jeff and I very nauseated and have irritable bowels. Jeff and I remember getting his notes one day on our script. Next to a paragraph of dialogue it said: IF YOU WRITE THIS, PEOPLE WILL STOP WATCHING THE SHOW!! And of course when you ask Judd about it he says; "Did I really write that? I gotta stop doing notes at 5 a.m." But on the other side, Judd gave everyone the chance to be as involved in the producing end as possible, which is very rare. Jeff and I really appreciated that and learned a ton from being on the set as much as we were.

As you've probably seen, Jeff and I had cameos in Nick's audition scene, as did Mike our composer and Paul. Mike was the lead singer, and Paul played the bass. I was on drums, and Jeff was working the mixing board. The funny thing was that Judd made Paul try and flirt with Lindsay. The operative word here is try. It creeped Paul out because he is such a nice guy that his sleaziness never truly came through. It turned into a nod and was just awkward enough to make it work.

The creative process on that show was amazingly unique, and we know it. We were very lucky to be writers there. The types of relationships we had there may never be created again. We truly were like a family but a real family who argued and laughed and would absolutely do anything for each other no matter what. It was an amazing experience, and Jeff and I are very thankful to Paul and Judd for letting us be a part of it. We hope we can try and bring that quality of storytelling to everything we do in the future.

—Gabe Sachs and Jeff Judah

FREAKS AND GEEKS

"I'M WITH THE BAND"

**CAST LIST**

LINDSAY WEIR
SAM WEIR
HAROLD WEIR
JEAN WEIR
DANIEL DESARIO
NICK ANDOPOLIS
BILL HAVERCHUCK
NEAL SCHWEIBER
KEN MILLER
KIM KELLY
MILLIE KENTNER
CINDY SANDERS
ALAN WHITE
MR. KOWCHEVSKI
MR. FREDRICKS
SEAN
HARRIS
COLIN
MR. ANDOPOLIS
MR. CASPER
NURSE HEIN
GORDON CRISP
SCOTT
ALEX
DRUMMER #2
MARK
GEEK #1
BULLY #1

FREAKS AND GEEKS

"I'M WITH THE BAND"

**SET LIST**

**INTERIORS:**

MCKINLEY HIGH SCHOOL
/GYM
/LOCKER ROOM
/SHOWER AREA
/CLASSROOM
/NURSE'S OFFICE
/SCHOOL BATHROOM
/HALLWAY
/PRINCPAL'S RECEPTION AREA
/CAFETERIA
NICK'S HOUSE
/BASEMENT
/LIVING ROOM
WEIR HOUSE
/DINING ROOM
/SAM'S ROOM
REHEARSAL HALL

**EXTERIORS:**

MCKINLEY HIGH SCHOOL
/SMOKING PATIO
/OUTSIDE GYM DOORS
NICK'S HOUSE
/FRONT YARD
NEIGHBORHOOD STREET
ALLEY BEHIND REHEARSAL STUDIO
NICK'S STREET
NEAL'S DRIVEWAY

TEASER

FADE IN:

INT. NICK'S BASEMENT - LATE AFTERNOON

The neat basement has been converted into a rec room with wood paneling and industrial gray carpeting.

CLOSE UP of a hand putting an eight-track in the stereo. A KITCHEN GLOVE reaches into a bucket and pulls out a piece of DRY ICE. The dry ice is placed into a bucket. It begins to immediately produce a fog.

We hear crowd noise from Rush's live version of "Spirit of the Radio." We see NICK, wearing headphones, behind his massive drum set, but in his mind he is on stage before an adoring crowd.

Nick reaches down and flicks one of the three switches on a Radio Shack style SWITCH BOX. A SPIN WHEEL behind him starts producing red, green and blue flares of light.

Nick starts to play along with the song. He stops for a moment to turn on another switch, the one that activates THE STROBE LIGHT. He then rejoins the track. Nick sounds like he is amazing.

He is completely into it. There is a mirror to his side where he can check himself out as he plays.

Nick's father, MR. ANDOPOLIS, comes down the stairs and watches Nick. From Mr. Andopolis' POV we SOUND DISSOLVE TO...

The reality of Nick drumming along with the record... it's mediocre banging. Nick never sees his dad watching. Mr. Andopolis returns upstairs.

BACK TO RUSH VERSION OF SONG. Nick tries to twirl one of the sticks which falls out of his hand to the floor.

He pulls another stick out of his stick bag and continues playing.

CUT TO:

MAIN TITLE

ACT ONE

FADE IN:

INT. MCKINLEY HIGH SCHOOL GYM - DAY

The CAMERA DOLLIES past kids lined up for gym class. There is a general rowdiness.

As we DOLLY past GORDON CRISP and HARRIS, we hear...

HARRIS
Women prefer guys with a sense of humor over looks.

GORDON
Really?

HARRIS
I read it in McCall's, so it must be true.

We CONTINUE TO DOLLY. We see ALAN WHITE abusing a kid in a vicious game of "hand slap," while BULLY #1 watches.

SAM, NEAL and BILL are near the end of the line. Bill is wearing black dress socks. Sam and Neal are staring at Bill's socks.

NEAL
Why don't you just put a sign on your back that says "Kick Me Really Hard"?

BILL
My mom didn't do laundry. What am I supposed to do, not wear any socks?

SAM
You kinda look like my grandpa.

BILL
Oh? Is your grandpa super cool?

SAM
Maybe you should roll them down a little bit.

MR. FREDRICKS walks onto the gym floor and blows his whistle.

(CONTINUED)

CONTINUED:

MR. FREDRICKS
All right, all right. Settle down, petunias.

MR. FREDRICKS (CONT'D)
We've got a busy week ahead of us. It's time to start training for the President's Physical Fitness Test.

The class moans and boos.

ALAN
Jimmy Carter's a wimp.

MR. FREDRICKS
Can it, White. This is important. Strong bodies lead to strong minds. Your mind must be weak. Now, we're going to start by building your upper body strength with some rope climbing.

NEAL
(to Sam and Bill)
Oh, yeah. This'll help us get into a good college.

MR. FREDRICKS
Schweiber. You want to bring the rest of us into your little hen party?

Neal shakes his head. He can't believe Fredricks even heard him.

MR. FREDRICKS (CONT'D)
All right, let's go. Oh... and one more thing, stink dogs. There's a new district policy that EVERYBODY must take a shower after class. Starting today.

The class GROANS.

ANGLE ON: Sam's face. He suddenly goes white. He looks completely freaked.

MR. FREDRICKS (CONT'D O.C.)
And I'm going to be checking for wet hair, so don't think you can pull a fast one.

(CONTINUED)

CONTINUED: (2)

Sam looks around at his classmates in a panic. Alan leans into Sam.

ALAN
Is Weir allowed to shower with us? Because he's a flat-chested girl.

DISSOLVE TO:

INT. GYM - MINUTES LATER

Various STUDENTS in groups at different ropes that hang from the top of the gym. Sam and Neal are at the bottom of their rope holding it steady for Bill.

On the rope to the left of Bill, Alan White and Bully #1 are holding the rope for Harris, who is climbing the rope. They shake the rope and laugh.

Fredricks is making Gordon climb the rope. Gordon is two feet up the rope and not going any further. Two KIDS nervously spot him.

MR. FREDRICKS
That's it, you can do it Gordon. There is no such word as "can't." You know what "can't" means? Won't.

GORDON
(under his breath)
I thought there was no such word as "can't. "

BACK ON SAM, BILL AND NEAL

SAM
They can't make us shower.

NEAL
This is school. They can make us do anything.

ANGLE ON: BILL

BILL
What are you guys talking about? Don't look up my shorts.

BACK ON SAM AND NEAL

SAM
(ignoring Bill)
Don't you think it's weird they want us to get naked?

(CONTINUED)

CONTINUED: (3)

NEAL
It's not a burlesque show, Sam.
They just want us to shower.

ANGLE ON: HARRIS. He clings to the rope like a Koala on a tree branch. He is afraid to go any higher or any lower. Alan and his buddies are laughing.

MR. FREDRICKS
What is the matter? You can't stay up there forever. Other people want to climb the rope.

HARRIS
Help me. I can't get down.

ALAN
I can get him down.

Mr. Fredricks slaps Alan in the back of the head.

MR. FREDRICKS
You want me to hang you with that rope?

ANGLE ON: SAM AND NEAL

SAM
I'm not doing it.

NEAL
Is it because you don't have any pit hair?

SAM
I have pit hair. And I think it's pretty weird that you want to get naked in front of a bunch of guys.

NEAL
Hey, I didn't say I was looking forward to it.

Alan has climbed up another rope and yells at Neal from the top.

ALAN
Hey, Schweiber. You gonna show us your circumcision?

SAM
C'mon. Let's not do it.

(CONTINUED)

CONTINUED: (4)

NEAL
(getting worried)
Well... I guess it is kind of weird...

Now Neal's concerned.

SAM
Then that settles it. We're not doing it.

Bill comes down from the rope. He pushes the rope towards Sam and Neal but neither makes a move for it. Mr. Fredricks looks over.

BILL
Okay, I'm done. Take it.

MR. FREDRICKS
Let's go, Haverchuck. Up the rope, already!

BILL
I was just up the rope.

MR. FREDRICKS
Did you touch the ceiling?

BILL
No.

MR. FREDRICKS
Up, Princess.

Bill struggles to climb the rope.

CUT TO:

INT. MCKINLEY HIGH CAFETERIA - DAY

We weave through the cafeteria where we see a table of FRESHMAN GEEKS listening to a joke.

GEEK #1
...so the guy says, "how do you think I rang the doorbell?"

All laugh.

We see MR. KOWCHEVSKI trying to get everyone's attention.

(CONTINUED)

CONTINUED:

MR. KOWCHEVSKI
All right, everybody. Be quiet. The drama club has a special announcement, so listen up.

MILLIE, playing the lead character, Laurie, is dressed in a blue bonnet with a blonde wig and character dress.

She is joined by COLIN, dressed in cowboy garb, playing the role of Curly.

MILLIE
(to Colin)
Well now, who are all these kind folk?

COLIN
(to Millie)
I think they're fixin' to hear about our little get together.

MILLIE
(to Colin)
Well then, I better tell them.
(to audience)
Hi, everybody. If you're just a boy or a girl who can't say no...

COLIN
Then you won't be able to say no to tickets to the McKinley drama club's presentation of...

MILLIE/COLIN
Oklahoma!

COLIN (CONT'D)
So come on down, pard'ner, and leave the ducks and geese at home.

MILLIE
Oh, what a beautiful evening you'll have.

MILLIE/COLIN
Yee-ha!

They bow and dosido out of the cafeteria. There is a spattering of applause.

(CONTINUED)

CONTINUED: (2)

MR. KOWCHEVSKI
Tickets are on sale, two dollars, in the administration office.

The camera pulls back behind the FREAKS who turn away from the performance and toward the direction of the camera. They are eating their lunches.

NICK
Hey, you guys wanna jam today?

SEAN
Hell, yeah.

NICK
(excited)
Yeah! How about three?

DANIEL
Nah, that's too early. I got to do something with Kim at three.

KEN
Then how about 3:01?

DANIEL
I gotta jump start her car, dim-wad.

Lindsay wants to be involved.

LINDSAY
Is this your guys' rock band?

NICK
Yeah. We're auditioning for a Battle of the Bands next month. Winner gets three hundred bucks.

LINDSAY
So, how come you never invite me to watch?

NICK
Well, why don't you stop by today?

LINDAY
Okay. Cool. So are you guys really good?

(CONTINUED)

CONTINUED: (3)

SEAN
We only reduce the house to rubble
when we rock.

LINDSAY
Do you guys have a name?

NICK
Yeah. Creation.

DANIEL
No. We don't have a name.

NICK
(to the guys)
So, how about we get together at
3:30?

DANIEL
Hey, man, we'll get there when we
get there. What, you got something
better to do?

Nick just laughs and nods at Daniel's burn. Lindsay looks excited.

CUT TO:

INT. MCKINLEY HIGH LOCKER ROOM - DAY

A rowdy locker room. Kids in various states of dress, from being wrapped in towels as they cross to others already fully dressed.

Passing through, Alan pursues a shirtless Gordon Crisp.

ALAN
Hey, Gordon, why don't you put a
bra on those puppies?

GORDON
(unphased)
He's hilarious. A regular Gary
Muldeer.

Gordon walks into the bathroom and into a stall and closes the door. We find Sam, Neal and Bill at the sinks washing up. They all have their heads soaking under faucets.

(CONTINUED)

CONTINUED:

BILL
You know, to be honest, I don't smell so good. I could probably use a shower.

SAM
No. We have to stick together.

NEAL
(joking)
Hey, if we don't shower, we <u>are</u> going to stick together. Get it? Get it?

Sam and Neal turn around first and see Mr. Fredricks standing behind them. Bill continues to wet his hair for a beat.

MR. FREDRICKS
Haverchuck.

Bill, startled, hits his head on the faucet and turns to face the coach. His wet hair drips throughout the scene.

MR. FREDRICKS (CONT'D)
You ladies having a nice time at the beauty parlor?

NEAL
Uh... well, ya see it's like this. We wanted to make sure our hair was extra clean after our shower and...

MR. FREDRICKS
Schweiber, save the sales pitch for when you're selling used cars. I told you guys that everybody has to shower.

A couple of kids have drifted over and stand and watch. Neal looks around and sees them. He's suddenly self-conscious.

SAM
But we didn't even sweat. Smell us.

MR. FREDRICKS
You know what, Weir? I'll put that on my "To Do" list. Now, hit the showers.

The bell rings signaling the end of class. Sam looks at Mr. Fredricks with hopeful anticipation as everyone scurries out of the locker room.

(CONTINUED)

CONTINUED: (2)

SAM
But we'll be late for class and I have a quiz in Algebra and I won't be able to make it up and--

Mr. Fredricks sighs. He stops Sam. He doesn't want to deal with all of this now.

MR. FREDRICKS
Just...go to class. But tomorrow you will all be getting in the showers. And if you don't, I will know about it.

Mr. Fredricks exits. Neal glares at Sam.

BILL
That guy's really into making guys shower.

CUT TO:

INT. NICK'S BASEMENT - LATE AFTERNOON

The guys are playing Cream's "Sunshine of Your Love." Nick is on the drums in his own world. Daniel plays a really beat up guitar covered with dents. Sean's bass guitar is covered with Van Halen, The Who and Stones stickers. Ken is singing lead.

The music isn't very good but the guys are having a blast.

ANGLE ON: KIM AND LINDSAY

They are listening on the couch. Kim is dancing around as she sits. Lindsay's laughing at the guys' antics.

As the guys play, Ken keeps hitting Nick's crash cymbal with his hand, thinking this is hilarious.

They finish the song with a long drawn-out ending. They jump around even more. Daniel pretends that he's going to smash his guitar against the wall as Nick stands and does the final cymbal crash.

Lindsay and Kim clap and "WOOOO" as if they were at a rock concert. Lindsay looks like she's having a blast.

NICK
That was smoking!

(CONTINUED)

12.

CONTINUED:

KIM
(to Daniel)
That was so amazing. You look so hot when you play.

Daniel sits down.

DANIEL
Man, I wish I could smash this thing for real.

KIM
Do it. Do it.

Nick walks out from behind the drum kit and stands in front of the group.

NICK
So, what did you think, Lindsay? Pretty amazing, huh?

LINDSAY
That was really wild. Did you guys write that?

Room killer. The guys all stare at Lindsay.

DANIEL
That's "Sunshine of Your Love."

SEAN
Cream?

LINDSAY
That's "Sunshine of Your Love"? Oh... well, when you rehearse it more, it'll be really great.

KEN
Gee, thanks. Be sure to let us know when that review comes out in Rolling Stone.

Daniel laughs hard and the rest join in. An awkward beat of silence. Nick tries to help.

NICK
Hey, Lindsay came up with some great names for the band.

Ken and Sean sit down on the bar stools at the bar.

(CONTINUED)

CONTINUED: (2)

KEN
Gosh, I hope it's something catchy... like The Math-letes.

DANIEL
Let's hear 'em.

LINDSAY
Well, I was thinking that you guys needed to have a name that said not only who you were, but what you want to represent to the audience. So, I--

KEN
Is this going to happen soon? 'Cause I've got to go do a solo on the porcelain drum throne.

Lindsay takes a moment for dramatic effect.

LINDSAY
Okay. Here's one. Mission Control.

DANIEL
(fast)
No way.

NICK
Why not?

DANIEL
It sounds like some...space thing.

NICK
What's wrong with that?

KEN
Space blows.

Lindsay can't believe this. Nick tries to be supportive.

NICK
(to Lindsay)
Tell them the next one, they'll love it.

LINDSAY
Okay. Anarchy's Child.

DANIEL
Next.

(CONTINUED)

CONTINUED: (3)

Lindsay's becoming unnerved.

SEAN
Really? I liked that one.

DANIEL
Then start your own band. What else you got?

LINDSAY
Oh... well... um... I like this one but you might not 'cause it may not be right for you...

KEN
Say it.

LINDSAY
Ichabod Crane.

DANIEL
God no.

SEAN
Boo.

NICK
I don't see you guys coming up with any good names.

KIM
(to Lindsay)
You do know you can't get extra credit here, right?

NICK'S FATHER comes down the steps. He is a dry, no-nonsense military man. He wears an army officer's uniform. However, his jacket is off and his tie is pulled loose.

MR. ANDOPOLIS
Hello, boys.

All sit up straight when he enters. Daniel and Kim untangle themselves. This is a guy even the freaks don't mess with. He casually sniffs the air in search of any mysterious pot odors.

ALL
(flatly)
Hello, Mr. Andopolis.

MR. ANDOPOLIS
Nick, can I talk to you for a moment?

(CONTINUED)

CONTINUED: (4)

Mr. Andopolis looks pointedly at his watch.

NICK
Yes, sir.

MR. ANDOPOLIS
I'll be upstairs. Nice seeing you boys. And ladies.

All ad-lib good-byes. Father exits.

DANIEL
We're outta here.

NICK
I'll just be a minute.

DANIEL
Yeah. But he won't.

KIM
I'm hungry. Let's eat.

DANIEL
Yeah. Let's go.
(to Sean)
You working the drive-thru tonight?

SEAN
Yeah. In an hour.

DANIEL
(to Kim)
Let's wait 'til then and he'll give us a bag full of free crap.

SEAN
You got to at least buy a pop, man, or I'll get caught.

DANIEL
That sucks.

NICK
Can't you guys wait for me?

DANIEL
Just meet us there.

The freaks start to head out.

(CONTINUED)

CONTINUED: (5)

LINDSAY
I'll wait for you.

NICK
Oh, okay. Cool.
(to the departing freaks)
We'll meet you guys there.

But they're gone. Nick gives Lindsay an "oh, those guys" smile. Lindsay smiles back, feeling bad for him.

CUT TO:

INT. NICK'S LIVING ROOM - DUSK

Mr. Andopolis is pouring himself a scotch. Nick approaches sheepishly.

NICK (CONT'D)
Dad, I know we're not supposed to play past five. I'm really sorry.

MR. ANDOPOLIS
(putting down paper and drink)
Yeah, I know you are. That's why you do this every day.

NICK
I forgot to look at the clock.

MR. ANDOPOLIS
And I forgot to pay the mortgage, so now we have to live on the street.

Nick looks down. He knows there's nothing right he can say.

MR. ANDOPOLIS (CONT'D)
You're killing me here, Nick. I keep trying to be a good guy but you're pushing me.

NICK
I'm not pushing you, dad.

MR. ANDOPOLIS
You're pushing me.

Nick backs off. Mr. Andopolis sits down in his recliner and starts to read.

(CONTINUED)

17.

CONTINUED: (6)

MR. ANDOPOLIS (CONT'D)
I want your drums out of the basement.

CUT TO:

INT. NICK'S BASEMENT - DUSK

Lindsay is listening at the bottom of the stairs where she can hear every word. She grimaces in pain for Nick, walks over to the drum kit and sits down.

CUT TO:

INT. NICK'S LIVING ROOM - DUSK

NICK
What? But you already made me move them out of the garage. Where am I supposed to put them?

Mr. Andopolis puts his paper aside and stands up. Faces Nick. Nick knows what's coming.

MR. ANDOPOLIS
Why don't you set them up in the living room? That way you can buy some more drums and set them up in our bedroom. And then your mother and I can sleep on the front lawn so we don't get in your way. That sound like a good plan? That work for you?

NICK
(quietly)
Dad...

MR. ANDOPOLIS
(pointing a finger at Nick)
Nick, instead of practicing with your friends, why don't you practice getting your grades up? 'Cause your eighteenth birthday is coming up fast and if you're not keeping a C+ average, you're enlisting. You know our deal.

Nick is looking down, completely cowed. He nods, knowing he can't win.

(CONTINUED)

CONTINUED:

He starts to walk away as his dad sits back down and takes a drink. Nick stops and turns back, mustering his courage.

NICK
Dad, I really think I can make it as a drummer.

MR. ANDOPOLIS
Well, son, I really thought I was gonna walk on the moon but you don't see any moon rocks around here, do you?

CUT TO:

INT. NICK'S BASEMENT - DUSK

Lindsay is sitting at the drum kit, fiddling with the drum sticks as Nick enters agitated and emotional. He walks over to the couch, picks up a pillow and SCREAMS INTO IT, muffling his voice.

LINDSAY
You okay?

Nick throws the pillow back on the couch, then sits down heavily. He's gone to a dark place.

NICK
Yeah.
(then)
Why don't you go meet up with those guys?

Lindsay looks at Nick. He's staring into space, lost in angry thought. Lindsay doesn't know what to do.

LINDSAY
...Okay.

Lindsay gets up and heads to the stairs, then turns back.

LINDSAY (CONT'D)
Nick, I couldn't help overhearing and maybe it's none of my business, but you're the one who told me when I first met you that the drums are your reason for living. Well, you can't let anyone talk you out of that. You just gotta stick with it and prove everyone wrong.

Nick stares at Lindsay, thinking. Lindsay sits down behind the drum kit.

(CONTINUED)

CONTINUED: (2)

NICK
Ya think?

LINDSAY
Absolutely.

He nods, then gives a grateful smile.

NICK
Thanks, Lindsay.
(stares at her)
You're the only person who's ever gotten what I'm about.

LINDSAY
Hey, we're not that different.
(smiling)
Except that you're gonna be a famous drummer.

Lindsay whacks the drum with the drum sticks. Lindsay and Nick laugh.

MR. ANDOPOLIS
(yelling from upstairs)
NICK!!!

NICK
Uh... let's get outta here.

Lindsay nods and they bolt off up the stairs.

FADE OUT.

END OF ACT ONE

ACT TWO

FADE IN:

INT. MCKINLEY HIGH GYM - DAY

FROM A HIGH ANGLE CRANE SHOT. A giant Earth Ball floats down from the ceiling descending upon a massive group of students, packed together on their backs in crab like positions waiting to kick it.

Sam, Neal and Bill are on the edge of the circle trying to avoid the ball landing on them and being kicked.

(CONTINUED)

CONTINUED:

NEAL
(looking at the ball)
Don't come near me. Don't come near me.

The ball is kicked towards Sam, Neal and Bill, who are unsuccessful at keeping the ball alive. The enormous sphere ends up landing on them. They are now getting kicked by everyone. Mr. Fredricks BLOWS THE WHISTLE.

MR. FREDRICKS
Good work today, guys. Hit the showers.

We notice that all of the jocks have been working out while the rest of the students have been playing earth ball. They all get up and head to the locker room, except the geeks who linger for a moment. Neal looks at his hands. They are disgusting from crawling around on the gym floor.

NEAL
This is ridiculous. My hands are filthy.

BILL
I'm kind of looking forward to showering.

Sam is extremely panicked.

SAM
You can't.

NEAL
You're on your own. I'm farshtinkiner and I'm showering.

SAM
Just one more day. Please?

NEAL
Will you quit being such a baby? Just close your eyes and it will be over before you know it.

CUT TO:

INT. MCKINLEY HIGH LOCKER ROOM - DAY

SLOW MOTION as Sam pushes open the door to the locker room and enters carefully. His face is filled with terror.

(CONTINUED)

CONTINUED:

SAM'S POV: There is danger everywhere. Older, muscular students without shirts stare at Sam. Guys in their underwear punching each other. No one seems to be phased by being undressed.

Sam stares at it all with dread. A hand taps him on the shoulder. Sam jumps and turns. End of SLOW MOTION.

It's Harris. We can tell that he's completely nude from Sam's uncomfortable reaction. Harris is completely comfortable with his body. Sam avoids looking at him.

HARRIS
Are you taking French next semester?

Shot from behind the lower part of Harris's back.

SAM
Uh... I... I don't know.

HARRIS
I was thinking about taking German since I'm one quarter German.

SAM
Uh, could you put a towel on?

HARRIS
Sam, our bodies are only a shell which surround our heavenly souls. No need to get uptight. Auf Wiedersehn.

Harris exits to the showers.

Neal and Bill come around the corner on the opposite side of the locker room from where the shower is. Bill is wearing a short, thin velour robe and Neal is wrapped in a massive "Virginia is for Lovers" beach towel around his waist.

SAM
You have chest hair. When did you get that?

Neal starts to proudly stroke his small patch of chest hair.

NEAL
My armpit hair got lonely. Thank you for noticing.

(CONTINUED)

22.

CONTINUED: (2)

BILL
It's gonna slow you down in the pool.

SAM
So you guys are really gonna do it? You're gonna shower?

NEAL
Hey, it's only water. What could happen?

SMASH CUT TO:

INT. MCKINLEY HIGH LOCKER SHOWER AREA - MINUTES LATER

ANGLE ON: the opening to the shower. Neal and Bill emerge with wet hair. There are a couple of kids in the background.

NEAL
Oh, shoot, I was gonna bring some cologne. I completely forgot.

As Bill and Neal walk toward Sam, Alan and several other KIDS twirl their towels and proceed to whip them from behind. Neal and Bill start running toward the other end of the row of lockers. As they do, more and more kids whip them as they pass.

Neal and Bill reach the end of the row of lockers. The snapping ends.

BILL
I hope I can still have children.

NEAL
You got hit in the groin, you moron. You didn't have a hysterectomy.

ANGLE ON: SAM. He is dressed and headed for the exit. Fredricks comes around the corner.

MR. FREDRICKS
Weir? What are you doing? Let's go. I'm not going through this again. Off with your uniform and get in the shower.

SAM
No.

(CONTINUED)

CONTINUED:

MR. FREDRICKS
What?

SAM
I, uh... oh, I don't feel well

MR. FREDRICKS
Do you think I'm new? Don't pull that fake sick crap on me.

SAM
I am sick. I feel like I'm going to barf.

MR. FREDRICKS
Well, that's fine. That's what drains are for.

SAM
But I'm dizzy and I have a headache and I'm nauseous...

Sam puts his hand up to his mouth like he's going to barf. Mr. Fredricks takes the path of least resistance.

MR. FREDRICKS
All right, Weir. Just... go to the nurse's office.

Sam gets up slowly, grabs his clothes out of his locker and walks away. Mr. Fredricks looks at Neal.

MR. FREDRICKS (CONT'D)
And Schweiber, put on some clothes. You look like a fifty year old man.

CUT TO:

INT. CLASSROOM - DAY

Lindsay and Nick are in English class together, sitting a few rows apart. Nick is reading a special issue of a Modern Drummer about the life and death of John Bonham while absent mindedly drumming lightly on his desk with a pencil.

Lindsay is trying to make eye contact with Nick to get him to pay attention in class. She clears her throat, Nick looks up. She mouths "C+" at him then looks at him to stop tapping the pencil. He nods, stops tapping, then goes right back to his magazine. Lindsay sighs.

(CONTINUED)

CONTINUED:

The teacher, MR. CASPER, is an excessively passionate, flamboyant teacher who loves the sound of his own voice. He wears an oversized shawl-collared, button-down reindeer sweater.

MR. CASPER
So, what do we know about Jay Gatsby? Besides his obvious physical beauty.
(no response from class)
It's that he is obsessed with Daisy. She's right there. So painfully close that-- oh, my God -- he can almost reach out and touch her.

Several students in the class are trying not to laugh. Mr. Casper knows this but doesn't care. He continues down the aisle, heading toward Nick.

MR. CASPER (CONT'D)
And yet, he's restrained by his inability to act on his desires.

And with this, Mr. Casper pulls Nick's magazine away. The class LAUGHS. Lindsay is mortified.

MR. CASPER (CONT'D)
I'm sorry if I'm boring you, Mr. Andopolis. Should I wait till you're done with your periodical?

Mr. Casper looks at it.

MR. CASPER (CONT'D)
And what is so fascinating?

NICK
I'm reading about John Bonham.

MR. CASPER
Hmmm. He looks like a lovely fellow.

NICK
Yeah, well, he's dead.

MR. CASPER
Hard to believe, 'cause he looks like he's in such wonderful shape. And what interests you about this fellow?

(CONTINUED)

CONTINUED: (2)

NICK
He was the greatest drummer in the world.

MR. CASPER
And what happened to him?

NICK
What? What do you mean?

MR. CASPER
How did he depart this Earth?

NICK
(embarrassed, long pause)
He drank too much and... choked on his... vomit.

The entire class laughs.

MR. CASPER
(gives him the magazine)
Then please keep reading. A man of such quality is clearly more important than F. Scott FitzGerald.

Nick gives Lindsay a look like "can you believe this guy." Lindsay just looks pained.

CUT TO:

INT. MCKINLEY HIGH NURSE'S OFFICE - DAY

Sam is sitting on the nurse's cot with a thermometer in his mouth. There are several sick kids in the room, including one who holds a bucket in case he throws up, another with ice on his forehead, and a girl doubled over with cramps.

The nurse, NURSE HEIN, takes the thermometer from Sam's mouth and examines it.

NURSE HEIN
Well, you're not running a temperature, sweetie. Maybe it's something you ate.

SAM
Yeah. Maybe.

Mr. Fredricks enters. Nurse Hein's eyes light up.

(CONTINUED)

CONTINUED:

NURSE HEIN
Oh, hello, Coach Fredricks.

MR. FREDRICKS
(the attraction is not mutual)
Oh... hi, Nurse Hein. How is he?

NURSE HEIN
He seems to feel better. It was probably just a little indigestion.
(in a creepy baby voice)
I think that someone's been eating too many french fries, huh?

She squeezes Sam's cheek, laughs, then looks at Fredricks for approval. Fredricks forces a smile, weirded out. Sam starts to get up.

SAM
I should get to class.

MR. FREDRICKS
Hold up, soldier. Nurse Hein, could I have a moment alone with Mr. Weir?

NURSE HEIN
Certainly... Ben.

MR. FREDRICKS
(in pain)
Thank you... Nurse Hein.

Nurse Hein gives Fredricks a flirty smile and exits. Mr. Fredricks sits on the cot across from Sam. There is a sick kid lying on it.

SAM
I think Nurse Hein was right. It was something I ate.

MR. FREDRICKS
Weir, it doesn't take a rocket scientist to see what's going on here.

SAM
I had too many french fries.

(CONTINUED)

CONTINUED: (2)

MR. FREDRICKS
Look. I know you're uncomfortable about getting naked in front of the other boys.

We see reaction shots of other sick kids. Sam looks at him, completely embarrassed.

MR. FREDRICKS (CONT'D)
When I was your age, I was just as scrawny and underdeveloped and as hairless as you are. I know what it's like to be afraid. But, if you face your fears, people will respect you.

SAM
(quietly)
Well, could I just wear a bathing suit?

MR. FREDRICKS
So you'd rather be the dork who wears the bathing suit in the shower? No. Don't be the guy who won't take a shower, Sam. Believe me, you don't want to be that guy. There will be plenty of times in your life when you'll want to make a stand, but this isn't one of them. Do you understand me?

SAM
(just wanting to escape)
Yes.

CUT TO:

EXT. NICK'S STREET - DAY

Nick is shooting baskets in his driveway. There is a mini bike leaning against the garage. Lindsay approaches.

NICK
Hey.

LINDSAY
Hey. I thought you guys were practicing today.

NICK
Yeah, well, I don't know if they're coming or not.
(MORE)

(CONTINUED)

CONTINUED:

NICK (CONT'D)
They went to some junk yard looking for a carburetor for Kim's Gremlin. So, that might take a while.

LINDSAY
Oh. Okay.

NICK
What?

LINDSAY
I don't know. I thought you guys had an audition for the Battle of the Bands coming up.

NICK
Yeah, we do. We're ready.
(no response from Lindsay)
What?

LINDSAY
I just think you guys need to rehearse more.

NICK
You said we were good.

LINDSAY
Yeah, but you guys aren't good enough to win any contests.

NICK
Thanks a lot.

LINDSAY
Well, it's true, Nick. If you want to show your dad he's wrong, the band has to really be great.
(then; embarrassed)
Or he's gonna make you join the army.

Nick looks like he's about to take offense. Then he deflates, knowing Lindsay's right.

NICK
...Yeah. I know.
(angry)
God, my stupid dad.

(CONTINUED)

CONTINUED: (2)

LINDSAY
Yeah, but just think about how dumb he'll feel after your band blows everyone away. You just need to work harder.

NICK
You think so?

LINDSAY
Yeah. When I was in the Math-letes, we did logarithms like almost until our fingers bled. But it paid off. We were state champions.

NICK
But Daniel isn't really into practicing.

LINDSAY
Who's the leader of this band? You or Daniel?

CUT TO:

EXT. NEAL'S DRIVEWAY - AFTERNOON

The boys are walking away from an ICE CREAM TRUCK. Sam has purchased a Push-Up, Neal has the Rocket Ship and Bill a Nuddy Buddy.

The truck pulls away and rings it's bells.

SAM/NEAL/BILL
See ya, Ralph.

As they sit down on the curb they see a car pull into the driveway across the street.

TWO JOCKS exit the car with three PRETTY GIRLS, two of whom are dressed as cheerleaders. One of the jocks picks one of the girls up and twirls her around. Another jock tickles the two other girls. They all share a giddy laugh.

NEAL
I don't get it. What do they have that we don't?

Neal takes a bite of his Rocket Ship.

(CONTINUED)

CONTINUED:

SAM
Good bodies. It's so stupid. So he can throw her over his shoulder. Big deal.

BILL
He should use his legs more or he's going to throw out his back.

NEAL
My mom says that women prefer guys with a good sense of humor.

BILL
But you're not funny.

NEAL
Screw you, I'm hilarious.

BILL
Oooh, how witty. Get this guy on "Hollywood Squares."

SAM
I overheard Todd Schellinger say that he takes off his shirt when he makes out with a girl. Why would he do that?

BILL
Why would anybody do that?

NEAL
Probably to show off his chest hair. I know that's what I'm going to do.

Sam and Bill laugh.

NEAL (CONT'D)
Go ahead and laugh, but all of the cool guys have hairy chests. Selleck, Reynolds... Rockford.

BILL
Don't forget Mork. That guy has more hair on his hand than Sam has on his pits.

SAM
Shut up.

(CONTINUED)

CONTINUED: (2)

BILL
I meant that as a compliment. Who wants hairy hands?

SAM
Are girls ever going to like us?

NEAL
No. Not those kinds of girls. I think our best play is to go for the smart, sexy librarian type. You know, she seems sweet and shy, but then she takes off her glasses and...

Neal makes a growling noise. All of the boys laugh.

BILL
Like Baily on WKRP in Cincinnati.

NEAL
Yeah.

SAM
But Cindy Sanders is the librarian type.

NEAL
Yeah, the librarian for the Playboy Mansion.

In the process of his gesturing, Neal's Rocket Ship falls to the street.

NEAL (CONT'D)
(beat)
Come on, you've got to admit that joke was funny.

Bill picks it up and hands it to Neal, who waves him off.

SAM
Gross.

BILL
Fine, I'll eat it.

Bill takes a bite without wiping it off.

CUT TO:

INT. NICK'S BASEMENT - LATE AFTERNOON

Lindsay and Kim watch as the band is playing the end of "Sunshine of Your Love." The guys are goofing around the same as before. The song sounds just as messy.

Nick is looking very intense, not the free wheeling drummer he was. He is really studying what the other guys are doing.

Kim is dancing around in her seat again like a groupie. Lindsay, however, now watches the band judgementally.

The guys finish, doing another long drawn out ending. Nick doesn't participate. The guitars finally hit a final chord as Daniel, Ken and Sean do a final Pete Townsend jump.

All the guys ad-lib praise to each other. Nick subtly looks at Lindsay who gives him a look that says the song wasn't too good.

KIM
WOOOOO!!! You rock, baby!
(excited)
I think you guys should all grow your hair past your butt. Wouldn't that be crazy sexy, Lindsay?

Lindsay forces a smile. Nick takes a deep breath and dives in.

NICK
Okay, guys. That wasn't very good. Let's try again.

KEN
What?

NICK
Come on. Let's just try it again from the top.

DANIEL
Why would we do it again? We just did it.

NICK
Because it wasn't right. We were playing way too sloppy.

DANIEL
We sounded like we always sound.

(CONTINUED)

CONTINUED:

Daniel starts off the opening riff of some random chords. Sean and Ken join.

NICK
(standing up)
Hold it. Hold it.

They stop. Look at Nick like he's crazy. Then Ken and Sean look at Daniel to see what he'll do.

DANIEL
What's your problem?

NICK
Let's do "Sunshine of Your Love" again.

DANIEL
I said we just played it, man. you deaf or something?

NICK
We've gotta do it right once. Now c'mon. Let's go.

SEAN
Whatever you say, Keith Moon.

The guys exchange looks. Daniel rolls his eyes and gives in. He starts to play the opening chords. Nick stops him.

NICK
Did you hear any sticks? Wait for my count. Here we go. 1-2-3-4.

Nick starts playing. The guys jump in. Right away, Sean and Daniel start jumping around and crash into Nick's cymbals.

NICK
DAMN IT!

The guys continue playing. Nick throws a stick at Sean. Lindsay looks surprised. Sean stops playing.

SEAN
Are you insane?!

NICK
Stay away from my cymbals!

(CONTINUED)

CONTINUED: (2)

SEAN
Well, you got fifty of them. how can I?

NICK
I don't bang into your guitar. Now come on. 1-2-3-4.

Daniel gives Nick a disapproving look, then shrugs at the guys that it's okay to play. The guys start playing.

DANIEL
What is with you?

NICK
You missed your cue.

DANIEL
What cue?

NICK
You're supposed to be playing the same thing as Sean. Listen to the record.

DANIEL
I don't care what the record sounds like, man. We play it the way we play it. If it doesn't sound like the record who gives a crap?

KEN
(to Nick)
Are you still buying pot from the same guy?

SEAN
You mean me?

NICK
Look. We have to play it the right way or it isn't gonna work.

DANIEL
Any way we play it is the right way.

NICK
Not if we wanna get into the Battle of the Bands, man. We've gotta nail these songs.

(CONTINUED)

CONTINUED: (3)

DANIEL
I don't give a crap if we get into the stupid Battle of the Bands. Who cares, man?

Nick huffs at Daniel.

NICK
You were right, Lindsay.

Lindsay goes white. Daniel looks at Lindsay.

DANIEL
Right about what?

KEN
Yes, do tell.

NICK
(losing it)
That you guys don't care. Maybe you're just screwin' around but I want us to be good. I'm tired of sucking at everything in my life. I wanna nail that audition but we're not gonna nail anything unless we play these songs over and over again until they're perfect. So, c'mon, let's just do this and play it right.

Nick stares Daniel down. Daniel gives him a look that says "you've obviously got something going on, so I'm not going to kill you yet." All look at Daniel for his reaction.

DANIEL
All right. Let's play the stupid song.

NICK
(upset)
Thank you.

KEN
(after a beat)
Gee, this is really fun. I'm glad we have a band.

(CONTINUED)

CONTINUED: (4)

Lindsay looks on uncomfortably, surprised by all the aggression in the room, and now seemingly focused on her. Nick tensely counts off the band as we...

FADE OUT.

END OF ACT TWO

ACT THREE

FADE IN:

INT. NICK'S BASEMENT - LATE AFTERNOON

We hear the end of an uninspired "Sunshine of Your Love." No fun. No spontaneity. Daniel is playing while kicked back on the couch next to Kim. Sean is leaning against the wall and Ken is sitting backwards on a chair. The song ends.

SEAN
Well, that sucked.

NICK
No. It sounded better.

LINDSAY
It really did sound better this time.

DANIEL
Oh, did it? You approve, Linds?

LINDSAY
Oh, come on, Daniel.

DANIEL
I'm outta here.

KIM
(to Lindsay)
You're a piece of work.

Daniel starts packing up his guitar. Ken and Sean are looking unhappy at this turn of events.

NICK
Wait. Where are you going?

DANIEL
Anywhere.

(CONTINUED)

CONTINUED:

NICK
But we need to rehearse more.

DANIEL
No. You need to rehearse more. We need to get the hell out of here.

KEN
I hate this song now. We've played it like six times. I never want to hear it again.

NICK
But it sounded better.

SEAN
Who cares? We're in a paneled basement, not the Silver Dome.

DANIEL
You and Yoko turned music into school. What are you going to do, start assigning band homework?

NICK
I just want us to play it right.

KIM
Then go join the marching band... geek.

The guys and Kim laugh.

NICK
Well, at least the marching band knows how to play something the same way twice in a row.

Daniel slams his guitar case shut.

DANIEL
You're a dumb ass, Andopolis. Rock & Roll doesn't come from the brain, it comes from the crotch. If you ever got laid, you'd know that.
(to Ken and Sean)
Let's get outta here, man. I quit.

Ken and Sean look at each other, shrug and start packing their guitars, too, as Daniel starts for the stairs.

(CONTINUED)

CONTINUED: (2)

Lindsay doesn't know what to say. Daniel stares at her for a beat, then shakes his head, laughs to himself and heads up the stairs. Lindsay looks like she wants to die. They exit. Only Nick and Lindsay remain.

Nick looks at Lindsay.

NICK
Thanks for your help.

CUT TO:

INT. MCKINLEY HIGH GYM - DAY

The next day. The gym class is line up. Mr. Fredricks is calling roll.

MR. FREDRICKS
Schweiber.

NEAL
Here.

MR. FREDRICKS
Trinsky.

HARRIS
(in a German accent)
Ich bin hier.

Mr. Fredricks rolls his eyes.

MR. FREDRICKS
Weir.

Silence. Mr. Fredricks looks up. Sam is nowhere to be seen.

MR. FREDRICKS (CONT'D)
Weir? Has anybody seen Weir today?

Neal and Bill avoid the gaze of Mr. Fredricks. Mr. Fredricks sighs and shakes his head to himself.

CUT TO:

INT. SCHOOL BATHROOM - DAY

ANGLE ON: SAM

Who is hiding in a bathroom stall.

MARK and another STUDENT talk by the urinals.

(CONTINUED)

CONTINUED:

MARK
...then the little kid goes "Red-rum...red-rum."

Mr. Kowchevski enters on hall patrol.

MR. KOWCHEVSKI
Hey. Let's go. Finish your business and hit the bricks. This ain't tea with the queen.

They hurriedly exit.

ANGLE ON: SAM

Who gets a panicked look when he hears Kowchevski's voice. Sam slowly picks his feet up to hide, trying not to make any noise.

ANGLE ON: KOWCHEVSKI

Kowchevski, thinking he's alone, leans into the mirror to check out his bald spot. He takes out a comb, wets it, then tries to comb his hair in different ways to cover the balding area.

Some of this is through Sam's POV.

Kowchevski goes to the urinal to take a pea. He makes really weird sounds.

ANGLE ON: SAM

Sam's foot slips on the toilet seat and goes into the bowl. There is a loud noise and splash which alerts Kowchevski. Sam keeps his leg in the toilet hoping not to make anymore noise.

Kowchevski turns and goes over to the stall and bangs on the door.

MR. KOWCHEVSKI (CONT'D)
Who's in there?

Sam remains quietly terrified.

Kowchevski looks over the top and sees Sam standing on and in the toilet. Sam stares up at him. Busted.

(CONTINUED)

CONTINUED: (2)

MR. KOWCHEVSKI (CONT'D)
You know it's a little easier if you sit down and drop your pants.

CUT TO:

EXT. MCKINLEY HIGH SMOKING PATIO - DAY

Lindsay walks out onto the patio. Only Ken is sitting in the usual spot. He is eating and spitting sunflower seeds. She hesitates, screws up her courage, then goes over to him.

LINDSAY
Hey.

Ken nods, then spits. An awkward pause.

LINDSAY (CONT'D)
So, where is everybody?

KEN
No idea.

LINDSAY
That's kinda weird, isn't it?

Ken just stares at Lindsay, making her very uncomfortable.

LINDSAY (CONT'D)
I mean that no one is around, not that you don't have any idea where anyone is.

Ken continues to stare.

LINDSAY (CONT'D)
I'm going to go.

Lindsay turns and starts to walk away.

KEN
Hey...
(Lindsay turns back)
Thanks for breaking up the band.

Lindsay stops.

LINDSAY
What?

(CONTINUED)

CONTINUED:

KEN
(mockingly)
What?

LINDSAY
I didn't break up the band. I thought you should learn one song.

KEN
So, you admit it.

LINDSAY
Yes! Yes, I admit it.

Daniel enters the smoking patio.

LINDSAY (CONT'D)
How could I have done such an awful thing like suggesting that you actually play an entire song correctly, all the way through? God knows Zeppelin only plays half of "Stairway to Heaven" and The Who never even practices "Teenage Wasteland."

KEN
Baba O'Riley.

LINDSAY
What?

Ken gets up.

KEN
(disgusted)
The name of the song is "Baba O'Riley."

Ken exits. Lindsay turns and sees Daniel standing near. She's becoming upset.

LINDSAY
I didn't break up the band. I wanted to help Nick.

DANIEL
Nick doesn't need any help.

(CONTINUED)

CONTINUED: (2)

LINDSAY
How can you say that? If he doesn't get a job as a drummer he has to go in the army.

DANIEL
He's never going to get a job as a drummer. So why don't you let the guy have fun before he joins the army? 'Cause he ain't gonna get his life together and he sure as hell ain't gonna make it as a drummer.

LINDSAY
How do you know?

DANIEL
I know.

LINDSAY
You sound like his dad.

DANIEL
Maybe his dad is right.

LINDSAY
I can't believe you're saying that.

DANIEL
Look around you, Lindsay. We're not going to be doctors, or lawyers... or drummers. So if Nick's got some place to go that'll take care of him, don't get in his way.

LINDSAY
But that's not how it has to be.

DANIEL
(laughing at her innocence)
Oh. Okay.

The bell rings. Daniel walks away.

CUT TO:

INT. PRINCIPAL'S RECEPTION AREA - AFTERNOON

A nervous Sam is sitting in the Principal's office waiting area. His pant cuff is wet. He is next to Geek #1 who is crying uncontrollably.

CUT TO:

EXT. NICK'S FRONT YARD - AFTERNOON

Nick is mowing his front lawn. Lindsay approaches.

LINDSAY
Hey.

NICK
Hey.

LINDSAY
So... why weren't you in English?

NICK
I bailed. I couldn't deal with it. This whole band breaking up thing has kinda got me pretty down, you know?

LINDSAY
Well, it shouldn't. It wasn't a real band. Those guys were just screwing around. You're the only one trying to be a professional.

NICK
Yeah... well. I still don't have a band.

Lindsay takes a moment. She hands a piece of paper to Nick.

LINDSAY
Well, maybe you can join this one.

Nick gives her a puzzled look. She nods toward the paper. He reads it.

NICK
(excited)
Whoa, Dimension is looking for a drummer?!

LINDSAY
It was up at the record store.

(CONTINUED)

CONTINUED:

NICK
They're like the top working band
in Detroit. I saw them open for
Jethro Tull at CoBo Hall last year.
Tull could barely follow them.

Nick's excitement is tempered by his worry at the scale of this audition and what it would mean for his life.

LINDSAY
You could be getting paid to drum.
Like a real job.

NICK
Hell, yeah.

Nick is suddenly full of energy. He drops the rake.

NICK (CONT'D)
I gotta call these guys and set up
an audition. And then I better go
practice.
(stops)
It's not five yet, is it?

LINDSAY
You've got two hours.

NICK
Great!

Lindsay laughs as Nick sprints off toward the house. He stops and runs back to Lindsay.

NICK (CONT'D)
Hey, you wanna come with me to the
audition?

LINDSAY
Wouldn't I make you nervous?

NICK
Are you kidding?

LINDSAY
(smiles at him a beat)
Sure, Nick. I'd love to.

NICK
Cool!

(CONTINUED)

CONTINUED: (2)

Lindsay looks very pleased with herself. He smiles at her another beat, then gives her an awkward hug and runs back to the house.

CUT TO:

INT. WEIR DINING ROOM - NIGHT

The Weir's are sitting around the dining room table having dinner. Sam's obviously in the doghouse. Lindsay is in a happy mood, eating and enjoying the fact that Sam's in trouble and she's not.

HAROLD
(to Sam)
What is wrong with you? Physical fitness is very important, Sam. You don't take care of your body, there's going to come a day when doctors are trying to stick a monkey heart in your chest. And that's if you can get on the waiting list.

JEAN
Can you at least tell us why you don't want to go to gym class? You're so good at gym.

Sam looks down, completely embarrassed. The family just stares at him. He knows he has to respond.

SAM
They make us take showers.

HAROLD
That's it?

SAM
(with great effort)
I don't want to be naked in front of... other guys.

Lindsay gives Sam a sympathetic look. After a beat...

HAROLD
Well, who does? Do you know how many naked men I've seen in my life?

The family stares at Harold quizzically. He gives them a look.

(CONTINUED)

CONTINUED:

HAROLD (CONT'D)
In the Army.

SAM
I don't want to be teased.

JEAN
Oh, who would tease you?

HAROLD
You know what you do? You tell them you're proud of your body. That'll show 'em.

JEAN
You have a beautiful body, Sam. Doesn't he, Harold?

HAROLD
(Joe improvs descriptions about the beautiful aspects of Sam's body)
Oh, yes. Very... beautiful.

JEAN
Those other boys are probably just jealous. Lindsay, tell your brother he has a beautiful body.

LINDSAY
Mom!

SAM
MOM!

HAROLD
Lindsay.

LINDSAY
What?

HAROLD
Your mother asked you to tell your brother that he has a beautiful body.

LINDSAY
This is so stupid.

HAROLD
Lindsay.

(CONTINUED)

CONTINUED: (2)

LINDSAY
It's not going to help him.

JEAN
Just say the words honey, it will make him feel so much better.

Because of Lindsay's good mood and because the whole situation seems funny to her, Lindsay dives in.

LINDSAY
You have a beautiful body, Sam. You're really, really hot. You're an Adonis. A slab of beef. If you weren't my brother, oh my God--

HAROLD
Lindsay.

JEAN
See, Sweetheart?

Sam is absolutely dying of embarrassment. He gets up.

SAM
Can I be excused?

HAROLD
No. We're eating.

SAM
(desperate)
Dad, I'll shower, okay? I'm proud of my body. Can I be please be excused?

HAROLD
Fine.

Sam hightails it out of there, thoroughly humiliated.

HAROLD (CONT'D)
(to Lindsay)
You were a real help.

CUT TO:

INT. REHEARSAL HALL - LATE AFTERNOON

Dimension is finishing an ORIGINAL SONG. The guitarist is doing an amazing guitar riff and the drummer is really good. He's playing on a very small set but makes it sound big. They are all older than Nick.

(CONTINUED)

CONTINUED:

Nick and Lindsay are sitting on a couch, watching.

LINDSAY
These guys are amazing.

NICK
(very nervous)
Yeah. I never played on a drum set that small before.

The band finishes the song. Scott, the cool band leader, dismisses the drummer.

SCOTT
Okay. Great job, Paul. You really nailed it. We'll be in touch.
(turning to Nick)
Are you Nick?

NICK
(jumping up)
Yeah.

The other band members, ALEX and VANCE approach. Nick goes to shake Scott's hand, then pulls it back to wipe the sweat off it. Then he shakes the band's hands.

SCOTT
I'm Scott. This is Vance and that's Alex.

NICK
Scott, Vance, Alex...

ALEX
Thanks for coming down, man. I hope that kit's okay for you.

NICK
Oh, well... the kit I normally play's a lot bigger.

ALEX
How many pieces?

NICK
Twenty-nine.

The guys all stop and stare at Nick. Then they burst out in amazed laughter.

(CONTINUED)

CONTINUED: (2)

SCOTT
Oh, man! A twenty-nine piece kit? What are you doing here? You should be auditioning us.

The guys all laugh. Nick relaxes a bit.

NICK
(laughs)
Are you kidding, man? You guys are great. I saw you at Cobo Hall last year. You blew Tull away!

ALEX
You musta been there Friday night. Saturday we got booed off the stage.

The guys laugh again. Nick looks like he's having fun. Lindsay watches, looking happy for him.

SCOTT
Well, whaddaya say, Nick? You ready to jam or what?

NICK
Yeah. Let's rock it.

Nick heads over to the drums and sits behind them as the guys grab their instruments. Nick looks at Lindsay, who gives him a secret thumbs-up. Nick smiles, looking nervous but happy.

Lindsay sits on a folding chair in the corner.

SCOTT
Name the song, Nick.

NICK
How about some Cream?

SCOTT
"Crossroads" it is.

NICK
Uh... how about "Sunshine of Your Love?"

SCOTT
No, we do "Crossroads" live. Count it off, my man.

Nick takes a breath, then clicks his sticks really hard.

(CONTINUED)

50.

CONTINUED: (3)

NICK
1-2-3-4.

The band starts in for a few measures.

SCOTT
Hold it. Just a little tighter, buddy.

NICK
Cool. 1-2-3-4.

Nick starts. They get five seconds into the song.

SCOTT
Wait. A little quicker pace, Nick.

NICK
Quicker. Got it.

Nick starts again. He is really sweating.

The bass player is giving Lindsay a flirty smile and plays to her with a Eddie Van Halen grin. This makes her uncomfortable.

SCOTT
(singing)
I go down to the crossroads...

Lindsay sees Nick getting frustrated and that these guys are in another league as they play. The song sounds great... but the drums aren't steady. Lindsay looks at the sound guy.

Nick sees the guys looking at each other in a "this guy isn't very good" kind of way. Vance, the bass player, keeps nodding his head for Nick to pick up the pace.

They play for a little bit, then Scott stops them.

SCOTT (CONT'D)
(super friendly)
Okay. That's it. Thanks for coming down, Nick.

NICK
That's it?

SCOTT
Yeah, we got what we needed. So we'll make the decision and let you know.

(CONTINUED)

CONTINUED: (4)

We can see that Nick is trying everything in his power to keep from breaking down. He forces smiles at them but can't even speak. He stands up and awkwardly hands the sticks to Scott.

ALEX
(trying to be nice)
Hey, man, take good care of that twenty-nine piecer. Maybe someday you'll get it to an even thirty.

The guys laugh. Nick forces a smile. He can't even look at Lindsay.

ANGLE ON: Lindsay is in shock. This is all her fault.

Nick exits quickly. Lindsay follows behind.

FADE OUT.

END OF ACT THREE

ACT FOUR

FADE IN:

INT. WEIR HOUSE SAM'S ROOM - DUSK

Sam, wearing a cut-off T-shirt, is in his bedroom looking in the mirror. He reaches under his bed and pulls out a couple of dumbbells and starts doing intensely fast curls.

He stops, looks in the mirror to check out the results. then picks up a bar bell and presses it over his head.

CUT TO:

EXT. ALLEY BEHIND REHEARSAL STUDIO - DUSK

Nick is leaning against his car, devastated. He stares straight ahead, wearing the blank expression of the living dead. Lindsay has no idea what to say to make Nick feel better.

LINDSAY
Nick...

NICK
Lindsay... don't even say anything, please.

(CONTINUED)

CONTINUED:

Another drummer, DRUMMER #2, coming for the audition, walks by.

DRUMMER #2
(to Nick)
You go already?

NICK
Yeah.

DRUMMER #2
How'd it go?

NICK
Good.

DRUMMER #2
Well, hopefully not too good.

Drummer #2 then enters the rehearsal hall.

LINDSAY
So... what are you gonna do now?

NICK
Join the army, I guess.

LINDSAY
(forcing a laugh)
No, I meant right now. You want to go to the record store or any...

She trails off. Nick stares at her like a man who's lost everything.

NICK
I suck, Lindsay.

LINDSAY
That's not true.

NICK
You were there. You heard. I'm a joke. I shoulda got stoned. What was I thinking?

LINDSAY
You know, those guys are like at least five years older than you. I'll bet in five years you'll be way better than they are now.

(CONTINUED)

CONTINUED: (2)

Nick turns away, in his own world.

NICK
No, I won't. You know, sometimes I go down in my basement, put on a live album and I see myself on that stage, playing a ten minute solo. I'm on one of those hydraulic risers that make the drum set go way up like Peter Criss. People are screaming, explosions, and fireworks are going off...

Nick starts to sink deeper. Lindsay just stares at him. Nick shakes his head slowly.

NICK (CONT'D)
But, I'm never gonna be that guy. I'll be lucky if I'm the guy who pushes the button to make the riser go up. But I won't be that guy either, because I can't even keep a C+ average.

LINDSAY
I'll help get your grades up.

NICK
What's the point? He's going to make me join the army. And then I'll be surrounded by psycho guys like my brothers. And there'll be a war with Russia and I'll get shot and paralyzed and I won't even be able to feed myself.

Lindsay leans towards Nick.

LINDSAY
Nick. That's not going to happen. You're too special. I won't let it.

NICK
You can't help me. No one can. I'm done.

Nick is in a dark place. His eyes are dead and black. He's given up.

Lindsay leans in to Nick. She gently kisses him on the lips. His eyes go wide. She's controlling the kiss.

(CONTINUED)

CONTINUED: (3)

Then Nick realizes what's happening and kisses her back. Hard. Now he's controlling the kiss.

CUT TO:

INT. MCKINLEY HIGH LOCKER ROOM - DAY

MUSIC UP: ALLMAN BROTHERS "WHIPPING POST"

We are looking at the locker room door. IN SLOW MOTION, it pushes open and an intense looking Sam, in his gym clothes, enters.

He walks into the locker room. Other guys come in the door behind him and walk past him, some immediately pulling their shirts off.

SLOW MOTION as Neal and Bill walk out of the showers in their locker room garb and walk in Sam's direction. From in front of them, Alan and his cronies whip Neal and then whip Bill, who flies back against the locker. He is immediately surrounded by a sea of white towels which repeatedly snap at his body, simulating Sonny Corleone's death scene in "The Godfather."

ANGLE ON: NEAL abandoning him and running away.

BILL gets snapped some more, then falls to the ground out of frame. END OF SEQUENCE.

ANGLE ON: SAM, who is now wearing nothing but his Star Wars towel. Neal and Bill walk over to him.

NEAL
How can they still find this funny? I can see how it would be funny the first day or two, but how can it still be funny?

BILL
If it wasn't happening to us, it would probably still be funny.

Bill sees Bully #1 coming up behind Neal with a towel in snap position. Bill takes his towel, pulls it back and nails Neal on the butt really hard. SNAP! Neal HOWLS IN PAIN as Alan cracks up.

BULLY #1
Good one, Haverchuck.

(CONTINUED)

CONTINUED:

BILL
Thanks.
(quietly, to Neal)
That was for your own protection.
He was about to nail you.

NEAL
Well, I wish he had. You hit me
harder than he does.

BILL
Sorry. I thought your chest hair
would protect you.

Bill turns and smiles to himself.

Harris passes by, shot from the waist up, but seemingly nude. And as always, very confident.

HARRIS
(to Bill and Neal)
Afternoon, Gentlemen.

Neal looks at Sam.

NEAL
Did you lose weight?

SAM
Shut up. Now, get outta my way. I'm
headed to the showers.

Sam slowly walks toward the shower. Alan and his crony see Sam in his towel.

ALAN
Hey, look who's finally decided to
take a shower. Nice pecks, Weir.
You look like a flat-chested girl.

Sam girds himself. He looks Alan in the eye.

SAM
Yeah, well... I'm proud of my body.

Alan and his crony crack up. Sam just glares at them, defiantly.

ALAN
Oh, you're proud, are you? Then
maybe you should show it to
everybody.

(CONTINUED)

CONTINUED: (2)

And with this, the crony pulls open the locker room door and Alan pushes Sam out the door. Alan and his crony then push the door shut and hold it closed.

CUT TO:

INT. MCKINLEY HIGH HALLWAY OUTSIDE LOCKER ROOM - CONTINUOUS

The halls are empty. Sam is banging on the locker room door in a nightmare. He's terrified and almost naked.

SAM
Let me in. Let me in. Come on, open up. Mr. Fredricks! MR. FREDRICKS!

INT. MCKINLEY HIGH GYM - CONTINUOUS

Mr. Fredricks is putting the moves on some young pretty student gym teacher.

MR. FREDRICKS
So, how long are you going to be student-teaching here?

CUT TO:

INT. MCKINLEY HIGH HALLWAY OUTSIDE LOCKER ROOM - CONTINUOUS

Sam continues to pound on the door. Suddenly, the bell rings. Sam's eyes go wide in terror.

Suddenly, the locker room door opens back up. Sam breathes a sigh of relief. Alan sticks his head out.

ALAN
Oh, I'm sorry, Rear. I forgot to take this.

RIP! Alan snatches Sam's towel off and slams the door closed, leaving a naked and shocked Sam trapped.

Hundreds of kids start pouring into the halls. Sam looks around and sees all the kids. He has no idea where to hide. The students all stop and stare at Sam.

MUSIC UP: COMPOSER

In a panic, Sam runs down the hall as fast as he can. The halls are filled with shrieks, screams and laughter.

(CONTINUED)

CONTINUED:

SEAN
Streaker!

Sam starts down another hallway, but sees Cindy at her locker. She doesn't see him. He stops, turns, and runs back the way he came.

COLIN
Go, Sam, go!

ANGLE ON: Lindsay, who is coming out of a classroom. Nick walks over to her.

NICK
Hey, Lindsay.

LINDSAY
(feeling a little weird)
Hi, Nick.

Sam bolts by her in the background. They don't see him.

CUT TO:

EXT. MCKINLEY HIGH OUTSIDE GYM DOORS - CONTINUOUS

Sam has doubled-backed to the gym. He opens the huge outside door and enters. THE MUSIC ENDS.

CUT TO:

INT. GYM - CONTINUOUS

Sam enters the gym. Mr. Fredricks is still talking to the girls gym teacher. They both see Sam, standing before them like a frightened Chihuahua. Sam's lower body is obscured by the giant Earth Ball. Sam is beyond tears with anger.

SAM
Well, what the hell are you looking at?

CUT TO:

INT. MCKINLEY HIGH HALLWAY - DAY

Lindsay is walking down the hall with Nick.

NICK
Listen. I just wanted you to know I was thinking about that kiss all night.

(CONTINUED)

CONTINUED:

LINDSAY
Oh... good.

NICK
It really meant a lot to me.

LINDSAY
I'm... glad.

NICK
Hey, come on. Let's head out to the patio.

LINDSAY
The patio? Aren't you fighting with those guys?

NICK
Naaaaaah. I mean we were, but not now. We fight like that all the time. It doesn't mean anything.

LINDSAY
Oh.

NICK
They heard what happened at the audition so they all came over last night. We're cool.

They walk toward the exit.

CUT TO:

EXT. SMOKING PATIO - DAY

Nick and Lindsay approach the freaks. All ad lib greetings. They start abusing Nick. All is well again in the freak world. Daniel gives Nick a friendly slug to the shoulder.

DANIEL
Glad you could make it, Ringo.

KEN
Well, you finally got your wish. You're as good a drummer as John Bonham. Of course, he had to be dead first.

Ken puts Nick in a playful headlock.

(CONTINUED)

CONTINUED:

NICK
Hey, I heard they burned the drum set I used 'cause I stunk it up so bad.

SEAN
Is Dimension going to charge you for the pee stain you left on the drum seat?

NICK
Okay, enough.

DANIEL
Dimension sucks, man. You're too good for those guys. I saw them open for Tull and they got booed off the stage.

Kim catches Lindsay's eye and mouths to her almost inaudibly.

KIM
We have to talk. You are such a slut.

Lindsay looks at Kim. Kim makes a face that says she thinks that Lindsay and Nick got it on. Lindsay's face falls.

DANIEL
So, can we rehearse at your place today or is your old man gonna pop a vein?

NICK
We just got to be out by five, so we should start at three.

DANIEL
Make it four. I've got to re-wire Kim's dashboard.

KEN
Why don't you just shoot that thing and put it out of our misery.

DANIEL
Hey, let's play some real music for once. I wrote out some Iggy Pop and The Ramones songs.

(CONTINUED)

CONTINUED: (2)

NICK
The Ramones? They only play like
three chords.

DANIEL
So I'll learn a third one.

Daniel smiles. The guys all laugh and start trying to punch each other. Lindsay just watches them as if she were watching an alien race. Has no idea what to think. Daniel and Lindsay make eye contact. He knows what she's feeling.

Kim whispers to Lindsay.

KIM
I heard you jumped him.

CUT TO:

EXT. NEIGHBORHOOD STREET - AFTERNOON

Sam, Neal and Bill are walking down the street.

NEAL
I'm pretty sure Cindy didn't see
you. If she did, it was just with
her peripheral vision.

BILL
I wouldn't mind people seeing my
back. But my front, that's a whole
different deal.

SAM
Maybe I could transfer to another
school.

Alan comes riding by on his bike.

ALAN
Hey, Weird. That was fun today, gym
class, huh?

SAM
Leave me alone.

ALAN
I heard that they're bringing in a
psychiatrist to help the kids who
had to see you naked.

(CONTINUED)

CONTINUED:

SAM
Shut up, Alan.

Just then, a car full of cheerleaders drives by and slows down.

CINDY
Hey Sam... I heard you streaked.
Way to go.

They all cheer for Sam and honk as they pull away. Alan is stunned. Sam waves to them like a celebrity. Neal and Bill just turn and look at Sam in awe.

NEAL
All right, Sam.

ALAN
You guys are losers and you always will be.

Alan rides off, sulking.

NEAL
Then how come you're the guy riding home with no friends?

BILL
Wow, you're gonna be a legend.
People are going to worship you.

SAM
Yeah. Until they see me in my bathing suit tomorrow.

CUT TO:

INT. NICK'S BASEMENT - DUSK

Nick is playing the drums. He is drumming wildly, showing off with a cacophonous sounding solo. Lindsay looks a little pained.

NICK
Here's the really cool part, Linds.

She forces a smile. Nick bangs even louder and faster.

LINDSAY
(yelling over drums)
Yeah. It's really cool.

(CONTINUED)

62.

CONTINUED:

He nods. Then he stops suddenly. Lindsay is relieved that the noise has stopped.

NICK
Hey. I just thought of a great name for the band.

LINDSAY
Really?

NICK
(smiles; pointed)
Yeah. "First Kiss."

Lindsay is dying inside and gives a forced smile. Nick is ecstatic and starts a huge noisy drum solo, crashing cymbals and drums as wild as he can.

FADE OUT.

THE END

# FREAKS AND GEEKS

"CARDED AND DISCARDED"

Episode #7

Written by Judd Apatow and Paul Feig

Directed by Judd Apatow

This episode was written in a bit of a panic. Judd decided that we needed a new episode for our big Monday night relaunch after being pulled from NBC's schedule for two months. The episode scheduled to run was "Girlfriends and Boyfriends," which was the middle episode of a three-show arc about Lindsay and Nick dating, and Judd was nervous that whatever new audience our relaunch was going to bring us wouldn't have a clue what was going on.

And so we locked ourselves and all the writers and producers in the writers' room and brainstormed. We looked through old lists of story ideas that all of us had written in the carefree weeks when we were first bonding as a staff and the show wasn't yet in production. And out of these ideas came this episode, which Judd and I then wrote.

I know, I know, that's not a very exciting intro to this script. But there're not a lot of stories to tell about this one. It was fun to write, the Rusty Nail and the Iron Horse Inn were both places that existed in my hometown, and Jason Schwartzman and Kevin Corrigan were kind enough to lend their immense talents to our cast. That's kinda it.

Oh, wait. There is one other thing that happened:

When Judd and I were in my office working on this script, a bear burst through the door and tried to kill us. Fortunately, Judd and I were able to disorient it by running around it very quickly while singing the *Queen* song "We Will Rock You." The bear became so dizzy that he fell over onto the display cast that hosts my vast collection of Hummel figurines, destroying them. When the authorities came and took the bear away, they said that they had no idea how he had gotten into our building but that it probably had something to do with the fact that Mike White had left an open jar of honey on his desk.

Weird, huh? I can't believe that I almost forgot to tell you that.

And now, please enjoy our script....

—Paul Feig

FREAKS AND GEEKS

"CARDED AND DISCARDED"

**CAST LIST**

LINDSAY WEIR
SAM WEIR
HAROLD WEIR
JEAN WEIR
DANIEL DESARIO
NICK ANDOPOLIS
BILL HAVERCHUCK
NEAL SCHWEIBER
KEN MILLER
KIM KELLY
MILLIE KENTNER
CINDY SANDERS
MR. ROSSO
MR. KOWCHEVSKI
ALAN WHITE
HARRIS
ELI
GORDON CRISP
VICKI APPLEBY
MR. LACOVARA
MAUREEN
HOWIE
TOBY
BOUNCER
WAITER
SALESMAN

FREAKS AND GEEKS

"CARDED AND DISCARDED"

**SET LIST**

**INTERIORS:**

MCKINLEY HIGH SCHOOL
/HALLWAY
/CAFETERIA
/COUNSELING OFFICE
/BIOLOGY CLASSROOM
WEIR HOUSE
/LIVING ROOM
/KITCHEN
/DINING ROOM
/LINDSAY'S ROOM
TOBY'S HOUSE
/BEDROOM
DANIEL'S TRANS AM
THE IRON HORSE RESTAURANT
THE RUSTY NAIL BAR
SILVERMAN'S MENS CLOTHING

**EXTERIORS:**

MCKINLEY HIGH SCHOOL
/SMOKING PATIO
/QUAD
EMPTY PARKING LOT
WOODED PATH
SEEDY STREET
THE RUSTY NAIL BAR
DANIEL'S TRANS AM

TEASER

FADE IN:

INT. MCKINLEY HIGH SCHOOL HALLWAY - DAY

MUSIC UP: GEEK MUSIC

BILL is walking down the hallway with ELI.

ELI
"Three's Company" was so funny last night. I couldn't stop laughing.

BILL
I know. It's so much better than "What's Happening." Dwayne drags the whole show down with him.

ALAN WHITE and his BUDDY walk past.

ALAN
Hey, what are you doing hanging out with that retard...
(turns to Eli)
...Eli?

Alan cracks up and keeps walking.

BILL
That was hilarious the first ten times you said it.
(to Eli)
Doesn't that drive you crazy?

ELI
What?

BILL
What he just said.

ELI
What did he say?

BILL
Forget it.

ELI
I'll walk you to your next class. Meet me right here. Bye, Bill.

BILL
Bye, Eli.

(CONTINUED)

CONTINUED:

Eli walks away. Bill walks up to Sam and Neal at Sam's locker.

NEAL
Did you hear? Vicki Appleby's having a party.

SAM
Where'd you hear that?

BILL
Not from Vicki Appleby.

NEAL
I say we go.

SAM
We can't go to a party that we weren't invited to.

NEAL
People do it all the time. It's called crashing. Half the people at my Bar Mitzvah were from a wedding down the hall. Besides, if we lay low nobody will notice.

BILL
Great idea, Neal. Let's go to a party and hide.

Lindsay and Nick walk by.

LINDSAY
Hey, Sam.

SAM
Hey, Lindsay.

MUSIC UP: FREAK MUSIC

NICK
Oh, Lindsay, I got you something.

LINDSAY
(excited)
Really? What?

Nick pulls out a candy bar.

(CONTINUED)

CONTINUED: (2)

NICK
It's a candy bar. The drama club was selling them.

LINDSAY
Oh... great.

NICK
It's white chocolate. It's really good and white chocolate doesn't make you break out. Not that you would. You have nice skin.

Ken walks over with Daniel and Kim.

KEN
What about my skin? I use Camay.

NICK
Your skin is as smooth as a baby's butt.

DANIEL
A baby with horrible acne of the ass. Hey, we're cutting out of here. Want to come?

LINDSAY
I have a test.

KIM
Yeah, so do we. That's why we're cutting.

LINDSAY
Uh... okay. I guess so.

The bell RINGS. Students start to run for their classes. The hall starts to empty as the freaks keep walking toward the front doors.

NICK
So, do you want to go to my house and watch TV? Nobody's home.

DANIEL
Nah, let's go to the Dairy Queen. I'm dying for a Brazier Burger.

They casually exit the building. A beat later, Mr. Kowchevski comes running down the hall as fast as he can. He yells into the principal's waiting area.

(CONTINUED)

CONTINUED: (3)

MR. KOWCHEVSKI
Hey, Rosso, get the hair out of your eyes! We've got five kids going A.W.O.L.!

He and Rosso bolt out the front door after the freaks.

MR. KOWCHEVSKI (CONT'D)
Excuse me!

CUT TO:

MAIN TITLES

ACT ONE

FADE IN:

INT. WEIR DINING ROOM - NIGHT

The Weirs are sitting around the table eating dinner. Lindsay and Sam look bored.

JEAN
Hey, Lindsay, Aunt Judy and Uncle Gary sent you a birthday card.

Jean hands her the card. Lindsay opens it.

SAM
What is it?

LINDSAY
Oh my god. She sent me three hundred dollars cash for my college fund.

HAROLD
Through the mail? She's lucky that didn't get intercepted by some junkie who works for the post office.

JEAN
Hey, kids. Your father brought us home a little treat. Harold?

(CONTINUED)

CONTINUED:

HAROLD
(very pleased)
I was visiting Mr. Prieh's today over at his store and he was selling a game that my family and I used to play every Friday night when I was a kid. Pit.

LINDSAY
Pit?

HAROLD
Pit.

SAM
(joking)
Sounds like fun.

HAROLD
It is. It's a stock trading game. We all yell across the table at each other trying to get the other players to trade stocks with us.

Harold gives them a look that says "doesn't that sound great?" Lindsay and Sam exchange a look.

LINDSAY
So we're gonna sit around the table and you're gonna yell at us?

SAM
Sounds like a fun game, Dad.

JEAN
I think it sounds fun.

LINDSAY
Yeah, well. Have a good time. I'm going out Friday night.

SAM
Me, too.

Harold's face goes flat. He looks like they just broke his last straw.

HAROLD
(stewing)
You know what? I am sick and tired of you two acting like you're not part of a family.
(MORE)

(CONTINUED)

6.

CONTINUED: (2)

HAROLD (CONT'D)
You act like you're staying in a hotel and we're your employees. Well, guess what? We are not your employees. We are your parents. We created you and we deserve respect.

LINDSAY
We respect you.

HAROLD
Oh, you can barely stand to be around us. When you two were kids, you used to run around naked and lay in bed with us all night. We bathed you, cleaned your butts when you pooped and we loved it.

Lindsay looks down at her plate, grossed out.

HAROLD (CONT'D)
Now, if I so much as try to pat you on the head you run for the hills. Well, I'm fed up. We're gonna be close from now on, whether you like it or not. We're going to spend more quality time together and we're going to enjoy it, dammit.

Harold throws his napkin on the table and gets up.

HAROLD (CONT'D)
This Friday the Weirs are playing Pit. Get used to it.

And with this, he storms out of the room. Silence.

SAM
Wow, that's the first time I've seen dad run away from the table.

JEAN
Your father's just very tired from work. Now, I want you two to go in the other room and give him a hug.

SAM
Mom...

JEAN
Honey, your father loves you so much, it drives him crazy.

(CONTINUED)

CONTINUED: (3)

LINDSAY
Apparently.

JEAN
Go on.

Lindsay and Sam exchange pained looks, then get up and start the long walk to go hug dad.

CUT TO:

INT. BIOLOGY CLASS - DAY

MR. LACOVARA is in front of the class lecturing. The geeks are sitting around at their lab tables, looking bored. Neal and Bill are sitting together at one table. Cindy sits at another table.

MR. LACOVARA
Natural selection is a process by which weak and inferior genes are weeded out of the gene pool. Many of you might know this concept by its more popular nom-de-plume, "Survival of the Fittest."

Just then, there's a knock on the door.

MR. LACOVARA (CONT'D)
That might be Mr. Darwin right now.

Mr. Lacovara chuckles at his lame joke as he opens the door. Standing there is MAUREEN SAMPSON, a pretty new freshman. She hands Mr. Lacovara a slip of paper.

MAUREEN
Hi, I'm Maureen Sampson. I'm a transfer student.

MR. LACOVARA
Oh, well, go find yourself an empty seat. Always room for another head on the chopping block.

He chuckles at his doofy joke. Maureen steps in. Every male eye in the room goes wide.

MUSIC UP: THE WHO'S "SEE ME, FEEL ME, TOUCH ME, HEAL ME" OR BILLY JOEL "SHE'S ALWAYS A WOMAN."

ANGLE ON: The geeks see Maureen. They look like their eyes are going to pop out of their heads.

(CONTINUED)

Maureen walks to the only empty seat, a lab table in the back with one NERDY KID sitting at it. She sits down next to him. He looks at her as if a queen had just sat next to him.

MAUREEN
(to nerdy kid)
Hi.

The nerdy kid just stares at her, terrified. She opens her binder and takes a pencil out of a pencil pocket as the nerdy kid looks back up to the front of the class, his eyes constantly darting back to Maureen.

The geeks turn and exchange looks. Neal looks at Bill, who's sitting next to him.

NEAL
You had to be sitting next to me, didn't you?

CUT TO:

INT. COUNSELING OFFICE - DAY

The freaks are sitting in one of the school's counseling offices. They have their chairs in a semi-circle. Mr. Rosso sits in front of them. Serious.

MR. ROSSO
Hey, the last thing I want to be is the guy who chases you down and sends you back to class.

DANIEL
Then don't chase us.

MR. ROSSO
Guys, there's two ways you can look at anything in this world. Take my job, for instance. I could get up every morning and go, "Boo hoo, I don't want to go in and try to help a bunch of kids. I'm tired." But I don't. I put on my shirt and my tie and I say to myself, "Hot dog, let me in there. Let me at 'em."

KEN
Do you really say 'hot dog'?

(CONTINUED)

CONTINUED:

MR. ROSSO
(pointedly)
Yes. I do. I know you guys are struggling. That's what they made guidance counselors for. To help you. I understand, you've just gotten through puberty. And man, what a long, strange trip that was. And now you've got these adult bodies, but you've still got the minds of little kids. And it's weird. You're alone and you're confused and you don't think anyone understands. Well, I do. Lots of people do. Even Mr. Alice Cooper. And I bet you don't think he's a square.

Rosso reaches over and retrieves an acoustic guitar from behind a desk. He plays the opening lick of "Eighteen." The freaks look pained and horrified. As Rosso sings, he directs each of the lyrics toward the freaks.

MR. ROSSO (CONT'D)
(singing)
"Lines form on my face and hands/Lines form on the left and right/I'm in the middle without any plans/I'm a boy" -- or girl -- "and I'm a man" -- or woman...

He gives them a wise smile, sure this is working on them. Then he strums the guitar hard and gets into it.

MR. ROSSO (CONT'D)
"I'm eighteen, I get confused everyday/Eighteen, I just don't know what to say/Eighteen, I've gotta get away!"

He continues to play as the freaks exchange looks. Ken's eyes are watering from trying not to burst out laughing.

CUT TO:

EXT. HALLWAY - DAY

The freaks are walking out of the office, looking shell-shocked.

DANIEL
That was brutal.

(CONTINUED)

CONTINUED:

KEN
I've never hated Alice Cooper more than I do right now.

NICK
Rosso's pretty good at the guitar. Some of those chords are hard.

They start down the hall. Rosso comes out and stops Lindsay, holding her back.

MR. ROSSO
Lindsay.

She stops. Everyone else heads out.

LINDSAY
What?

MR. ROSSO
I was trying to have fun in there, but I'm worried about you.

LINDSAY
Why?

MR. ROSSO
Because you're not one of them. You're a different breed.

LINDSAY
Oh, really? What breed am I?

MR. ROSSO
You're the kind of person who changes this world. You're Betty Freidan. Gloria Steinem. Golda Meir. You're whoever you want to be.

LINDSAY
You told Millie she was like Eleanor Roosevelt.

MR. ROSSO
And I believe that. I'm just worried because before you know it you're going to have to apply to colleges and if you keep going the way you're going, some of those colleges may not want you.

(CONTINUED)

CONTINUED: (2)

LINDSAY
Maybe I don't want them. You know who didn't go to college? Einstein. Jesus Christ.

MR. ROSSO
Frank.

LINDSAY
Frank, who?

MR. ROSSO
The dude who pumps my gas. Just saying.

She exits.

INT. CAFETERIA - DAY

The geeks are walking through the cafeteria with their hot lunch trays.

BILL
I saw Ronald Reagan kissing a monkey on TV last night.

NEAL
On the news?

BILL
No, in a movie. He's a really good actor. The monkey was great too.

They walk up to their table and find that Maureen is sitting there. They freeze, unsure what to do.

SAM
Uh... hi.

MAUREEN
Oh, I'm sorry. Is this your table?

BILL
Well, we don't own it but we kinda like sit here every day.

MAUREEN
I can sit somewhere else.

NEAL
No, no. Please join us.

(CONTINUED)

CONTINUED:

They sit and stare at her for a couple of beats.

SAM
So, where did you come from?

MAUREEN
Florida. My dad was transferred here to work at General Motors.

NEAL
Hey, my dad drives a Coupe de Ville, so we're practically related.

Maureen laughs, politely. There is an awkward silence.

MAUREEN
So, are people nice here?

BILL
Sometimes.

NEAL
You've gotta be careful who you hang out with. There are some real characters in this school.

SAM
We saw you in our biology class. How'd you like it?

MAUREEN
It's okay. The teacher's kinda weird, though.

BILL
You know, once he ran over an old lady, but he blamed it on the car. He said his accelerator got stuck.

MAUREEN
Really? We had a teacher at our school, and this guy broke into his house, and the teacher shot him.

BILL
With a gun?

(CONTINUED)

13.

CONTINUED: (2)

MAUREEN
Yeah, but he didn't go to jail because I guess if somebody breaks into your house you're allowed to shoot them.

BILL
Our shop teacher got his hair caught in the lathe and got his scalp torn off. Now he has to wear a wig.

MAUREEN
Our shop teacher cut his pinky off with the radial arm saw and they had to helicopter him and his finger to the hospital but when they tried to sew it back on it didn't fit anymore, so now everybody calls him Pinky Tuscadero.

The geeks laugh at this.

SAM
I wonder if he kept it.

Maureen looks at them, smiling.

MAUREEN
I'm glad I sat here. You guys are nice.

NEAL
You're really nice.

MAUREEN
Would you mind showing me the ropes around here?

NEAL
We could show you...the ropes.

MAUREEN
But if I start bugging you guys, be sure to let me know.

SAM
Don't worry, we'd never let you bug us.

Maureen smiles at them. The three geeks melt.

CUT TO:

EXT. SMOKING PATIO - DAY

The freaks are sitting around their picnic table. Nick and Lindsay sit next to each other.

NICK
I feel kinda funny after watching Rosso sing and stuff. It's like when I walked in on my parents having sex. I can't get it out of my head.

LINDSAY
I can't wait until I get older so I don't have to get lectured anymore.

DANIEL
Every old person thinks they're smart. Like what, there are no dumb old people?

KEN
I just wanna be older so I can go to bars. Everything fun in this world happens in bars.

NICK
Yeah, no kidding, man. There's this kick ass band called Feedback playing at the Rusty Nail tomorrow night, but I hear they card.

KIM
(taunting)
Oh, maybe I'll go.

NICK
Shut up. Just because you've got a fake ID, don't go lording it over us.

LINDSAY
You've got a fake ID?

KIM
Yeah, check it out.
(as she gets it out of her coat pocket)
It's my cousin's old drivers license.

Kim hands it to Lindsay. Lindsay studies it intensely.

(CONTINUED)

15.

CONTINUED:

LINDSAY
Wow, your cousin looks just like you. But it says you're twenty four.

KIM
Yeah, so? I look mature. Nobody ever stops me.

LINDSAY
(to Daniel)
Do you have one?

DANIEL
Not anymore. Some bouncer asked me what my star sign was and I didn't know so he snagged it.

KIM
Oh, poor baby.

DANIEL
I hate astrology. How can everyone born in the same month have the same life?

LINDSAY
We should get some fake I.D.s so we can go see Feedback.

NICK
Howie Gelfand sells 'em. But he charges a ton.

LINDSAY
Well, I just happen to have come into a little cash. I can lend you some.

Lindsay takes out the greeting card.

KEN
I don't know why, but I'm liking her more and more every day.

Nick looks at Lindsay with love in his eyes.

NICK
Join the club.

CUT TO:

INT. SCHOOL HALLWAY - DAY

MUSIC UP: BILLY JOEL "BIG SHOT"

The end of the school day. Students are heading out. The geeks round the corner with Maureen. The geeks have never looked happier. They walk with confident gaits and are putting on quite a show of talking to Maureen.

They pass Gordon Crisp and Harris, who are having a conversation by a locker.

BILL
(calling out loudly)
Hello, Gordon! Hello, Harris! How are you both today? Do you know our friend Maureen?

GORDON
Hi.

MAUREEN
Hi.

Harris attempts to walk with them.

HARRIS
Are you new to our school? You should stop by the A.V. room. We just got a new Beta machine--

NEAL
Okay, thank you, Harris. We're very late, though.

The geeks speed up and leave Harris in the dust.

SAM
Oh, Maureen, by the way, tomorrow is Pizza Day in the cafeteria.

BILL
It's made with real tomato sauce and everything.

As they walk past Cindy...

CINDY
Hi, Sam.

SAM
Hey.

(CONTINUED)

CONTINUED:

MAUREEN
So, what are you guys doing after school? You want to do something?

They are all frozen for a moment.

BILL
Yes.

MAUREEN
I don't have to be home until dinner.

NEAL
I don't have to be home ever.

The geeks all beam as they strut out the door with Maureen. Cindy watches Sam, surprised at having been blown off.

FADE OUT.

END OF ACT ONE

ACT TWO

FADE IN:

INT. SILVERMAN'S MEN'S CLOTHING - DAY

The freaks are standing around in Silverman's Men's store. HOWIE, a young guy dressed in slick clothes, is standing in front of them.

DANIEL
Hey, I hear you know how to get your hands on some fake I.D.'s.

HOWIE
Shhhhh. I work here.

Howie pulls them over to the side of the store, between two silver naked man mannequins.

HOWIE (CONT'D)
How many do you need?

DANIEL
Four. All of us except Kim.

HOWIE
I thought I just got you one. You get it pulled?

(CONTINUED)

CONTINUED:

DANIEL
I'm not into astrology.

HOWIE
I told you, man, you gotta memorize that stuff. Where'd you lose it at?

DANIEL
The Oktoberfest.

HOWIE
What, you're that hard up for beer you gotta go sit in a tent with a bunch of old fat Nazi's singing Oompah songs?

DANIEL
Hey, I've had enough lectures for one day. You wanna get us these or not?

Howie just gives Daniel a disapproving look and looks at Lindsay.

HOWIE
Who's the chick?

NICK
Hey, her name is Lindsay.

HOWIE
Sorry, Bill Laimbeer. You've got good timing. I'm getting a shipment of genuine Delaware drivers licenses. Okay, let me memorize your faces so I can find a match.

Howie studies all their faces, then closes his eyes, as if he's taken a mental picture. He holds his eyes closed for a second, then opens again.

HOWIE (CONT'D)
Okay, I got it. That will be a hundred dollars. Half in advance.

LINDSAY
Not a problem.

She takes out the Hallmark Card and pulls a hundred dollar bill out of it. Howie looks impressed.

(CONTINUED)

CONTINUED: (2)

HOWIE
A chick with money.
(refers to Nick)
You've got good taste, stretch.

Just then, the other SALESMAN yells back at them from the register.

SALESMAN
Hey, Gelfand, there's a box of Parisian nightsuits in the back that aren't going to unpack themselves.

HOWIE
(very polite)
I'll be right there, sir.
(quietly to the freaks)
Okay, tomorrow at eleven o'clock. Be on time.

Howie heads into the back room to unpack Parisian nightsuits. The freaks look happy. Lindsay looks especially pleased.

CUT TO:

EXT. EMPTY PARKING LOT - DAY

The geeks are standing in the middle of the parking lot. Each man holds a rocket. Bill's rocket is enormous.

NEAL
You had to bring the big rocket, didn't you?

BILL
What? So, I have a big rocket. What do you want me to do, cut it in half?

Maureen comes around the corner of a nearby building. They talk out of the corner of their mouths so she can't tell that they're talking about her.

SAM
There she is.

NEAL
She's beautiful.

BILL
I can't believe she's going to hang out with us.

(CONTINUED)

CONTINUED:

NEAL
What if I'm actually asleep right now and this is just my dream, and in a few moments Maureen and I are going to make love?

BILL
Euuw.

SAM
Then what are we doing here?

BILL
Maybe it's my nightmare.

Maureen starts running to them.

NEAL
Oh my God, she's running to get to us.

Maureen walks up to them.

MAUREEN
Hi, guys.

SAM
Hi, Maureen.

MAUREEN
Your rockets look great. God, Bill, your rocket is huge.

BILL
Oh, is it? I hadn't noticed.

MAUREEN
I've never shot off a rocket before. This is gonna be fun.

SAM
Well, what do you usually do for fun?

MAUREEN
Well, I used to be way into ballet. I still do it sometimes but, I don't know, I don't think I want to be a ballerina anymore.

SAM
I bet you were good.

(CONTINUED)

CONTINUED: (2)

MAUREEN
Yeah, I was okay. My feet weren't really big enough, though.

BILL
Ballerinas have big feet?

MAUREEN
The good ones do. They have to.

NEAL
Hey, Bill, I think we just found a career for you and those gunboats of yours.

Neal laughs. Maureen takes him serious, though.

MAUREEN
Hey, you should do it, Bill. You have the body for it. Men make great ballet dancers. It's really sexy.

BILL
Oh, really? Maybe I will.

Bill makes a face at Neal that says "your put-down didn't work."

SAM
Cape Canaveral, ready for lift off.
(turns to Maureen)
You ready to shoot off some rockets?

MAUREEN
Heck, yeah.

Maureen looks excited by this new activity. The geeks beam, unable to believe they've met a girl who actually gets excited about Estes rockets.

MONTAGE MUSIC UP: BILLY JOEL "ROSALINDA'S EYES" OR "GET IT RIGHT THE FIRST TIME"

1) The geeks are setting up the launch pad as Maureen kneels with them watching. They are all pointing and showing her stuff, each trying to teach her something.

2) The geeks walk over to the rockets. Maureen chooses Bill's rocket to launch first. Bill smiles.

(CONTINUED)

3) The geeks prepare for the launch. They load the engine (a little cardboard tube) into the rocket. They put the rocket onto the launch pad post. They unspool the wires of the controller. Maureen is watching them with interest, asking questions. The geeks look beyond happy to explain.

4) The geeks and Maureen stand far back from the launch pad, doing a countdown in unison. Bill's large rocket is on there. Maureen has her fingers in her ears, not sure what to expect. The geeks look at her and exchange knowing chuckles.

Three, two, one. Neal allows Maureen to push the button on the control box.

The rocket fizzles, and then bursts into flames. Bill looks horrified. Maureen starts to laugh, then they all laugh with her.

5) They launch Neal and Sam's rockets.

CUT TO:

EXT. WOODED PATH - DAY

The freaks are walking down the road. Kim and Lindsay are walking ahead of Daniel, Nick and Ken. Each group is having their own conversation.

KIM
Lindsay, that was cool you fronting everybody the cash.

LINDSAY
You gotta help your friends when you can.

KIM
Where'd you get it? You take it out of your mom's wallet?

LINDSAY
No. College fund. I figure if I don't go, the money's mine anyway.

KIM
So, going to the Rusty Nail with Nick. This is gonna be like your first real date, huh?

LINDSAY
I don't know. Not really. We're not going out or anything.

(CONTINUED)

23.

CONTINUED:

KIM
Yeah, but you're not just friends anymore.

LINDSAY
(smiles, embarrassed)
Kim, I don't know. I just kissed him once. Don't make such a big deal out of it.

Behind them, the guys are mid-conversation.

NICK
There's a real connection, man. I'm telling you, she digs me.

DANIEL
So, are you guys like going out?

NICK
You know, we're not into labelling things. We have a more mature relationship than that. Let's just say that we have an understanding.

KEN
I'm glad you have an understanding 'cause I don't know what the hell you're talking about.

CUT TO:

INT. WEIR LIVING ROOM - DAY

The geeks are sitting around the living room, basking in the afterglow of their day with Maureen.

SAM
Is this what having a girlfriend is gonna be like? She's your best friend and she's beautiful and you can say and do anything in front of her?

NEAL
My dad always says that's what women want you to think before you marry them. That's how they suck you in.

(CONTINUED)

CONTINUED:

BILL
She's the kind of woman you can cut the cheese in front of.

SAM
Yeah, Bill, that's what love is all about.

BILL
It is. You wouldn't be able to be in love with somebody if you couldn't. Think about it.

NEAL
That is true. You have to sleep with your wife every night of your life. If you couldn't blast one in bed, you'd get physically ill.

SAM
You can't fart in front of a woman.

BILL
What do you think you do? Get up and run outside every time you have to let one go? You'd never get any sleep.

The geeks all think about this.

SAM
I think I might like her, too.

BILL
I thought you liked Cindy Sanders.

SAM
I do. But... Maureen talks to us. She's not as scary.

NEAL
I'm going to ask Maureen out. She clearly likes me best.

SAM
How do you know?

NEAL
You see the way she looks at me? It's like she can barely contain herself.

(CONTINUED)

CONTINUED: (2)

BILL
You're just looking at her when she's thinking about me.

NEAL
She doesn't like you. She feels sorry for you.

BILL
If she felt sorry for me, would she tell me I should be a ballerina?

Sam and Neal stare at Bill.

BILL (CONT'D)
Um, let me re-phrase that.

SAM
Look, we're all in love with her and she obviously likes all of us. So, we've just got to decide who gets her.

BILL
How're we gonna do that?

NEAL
The same way we decided who was going to have to stand in line for "Empire Strikes Back" tickets.

SAM
I'll get the hat.

They look at each other and seem to make a decision. Sam grabs his notebook and tears out some paper. They start to write on the papers. Harold walks past them from the bedroom.

HAROLD
Hey, Sam, you excited about the big Pit game on Friday?

SAM
I guess I have to be.

Jean walks in from the kitchen.

JEAN
Harold, come over here.

Harold follows Jean into the kitchen.

CUT TO:

INT. WEIR KITCHEN - CONTINUOUS

Harold and Jean enter the kitchen.

JEAN
You cannot force these kids to spend time with us. We can't force them to do anything anymore.

HAROLD
Did you know in other cultures, if your children shame you, you're allowed to have them executed? Well, I feel shamed.

JEAN
Oh, Harold.

HAROLD
Well, I'm not swinging an ax. I just want them to play Pit with me. Is that so horrible? Unbelievable. I'm supposed to let them treat me like dirt, then pay for their college educations?

JEAN
Honey, it's like the old saying. If you love something, set it free. Maybe if we don't try to force it, they'll come to us.

HAROLD
Well, they better... by Friday.

CUT TO:

INT. WEIR LIVING ROOM - SAME TIME

The geeks are standing. Sam holds a hat as they all hold their folded-up pieces of paper. They put the papers in the hat. Sam tosses them by jiggling the hat. Neal and Bill look nervous, as does Sam. Sam holds the hat up above their heads.

SAM
All right, Bill. You pick.

NEAL
Why does he get to pick?

SAM
'Cause I don't trust you.

(CONTINUED)

CONTINUED:

Neal doesn't look happy with this explanation but accepts it. Bill moves his hand around in the hat.

NEAL
Do it fast. Don't try to feel for your paper.

BILL
I'm not. I'm just trying to grab one. Quit being so paranoid.

Bill pulls out a paper and hands it to Neal. Neal looks at them, takes a nervous breath.

NEAL
The words on this paper could potentially change our lives. You both know that, don't--

SAM
Just open it, Neal.

Neal nervously opens the paper.

ANGLE ON: The paper is opened. It reads "BILL THE STUD."

NEAL
Oh, no! Not him.

Sam's face falls. Bill gets a huge smile.

BILL
I'm the happiest man in the world.

SAM
Oh, great, now you can go and fart in front of her. You'll make quite an impression.

NEAL
He wet his paper with spit. That's why he wins all the time. He just feels for the wet one.

BILL
Mrs. Maureen Haverchuck. Has a nice ring to it, don't you think?

Bill smiles, cocky. Sam and Neal look bummed out.

FADE OUT.

END OF ACT TWO

ACT THREE

FADE IN:

INT. SCHOOL HALLWAY - DAY

Students are entering McKinley, starting another day. Lindsay enters, just as Mr. Rosso is coming out of the front office.

MR. ROSSO
Hey, Lindsay. How are we this morning? I've got some new brochures from some Ivy league schools. Several are in color.

LINDSAY
Mr. Rosso, why can't you just leave me alone?

Lindsay gives Rosso an angry look.

MR. ROSSO
Because it's my job. I'm a guidance counselor. I'm trying to guide you.

LINDSAY
Well, guide someone else.

Mr. Rosso stares at her.

LINDSAY (CONT'D)
What?

MR. ROSSO
I heard the words but your eyes said something different. They said, "I'm lost. I need your help. Don't listen to me. Guide me."

LINDSAY
I don't need your help.

MR. ROSSO
Okay, then I guess I should just wait until you ask me for help. 'Cause then I can show up at the prison and give you some really good advice. You know, should you get shanked in the yard or in the dining hall?
(MORE)

(CONTINUED)

29.

CONTINUED:

MR. ROSSO (CONT'D)
When you have your baby, which prison guard should take care of it? That kind of thing. That'd be a great way to do my job, don't you think?

LINDSAY
Only time will tell. See you in the prison yard.

Lindsay heads off, at her wit's end with Rosso. He watches her go, concerned.

ANGLE ON: ANOTHER PART OF THE HALLWAY

The geeks are standing off to the side, prepping Bill.

SAM
All right. Are you ready to get yourself a girlfriend?

BILL
I've never been readier.

NEAL
What are you gonna say to her?

BILL
I don't know. I'm just gonna let the love flow.

NEAL
This is so unfair.

SAM
Here she comes.

Maureen has just rounded the corner. Bill's eyes go wide.

BILL
(terrified)
Oh, man. I gotta get something out of my locker.

SAM
Go on.

Sam and Neal push him into the center of the hall. Maureen sees him and smiles.

MAUREEN
Hi, Bill.

(CONTINUED)

CONTINUED: (2)

BILL
Oh, uh... hi.

MAUREEN
What're you doing?

BILL
Nothing.

MAUREEN
I really had fun yesterday. I told my dad all about the rockets. He said that he used to do that when he was in high school too.

BILL
(completely nervous)
You don't say.

Bill just stands there, uncomfortable, breathing loudly. All his ease from yesterday gone. Maureen stares at him, waiting for him to say something. Finally...

MAUREEN
Well, I'd better get to class. Don't want to be late my second day.

BILL
Good idea.

MAUREEN
See ya.

And she heads off. Sam and Neal come out to Bill.

NEAL
What the hell was that?

BILL
I choked. It was easier talking to her yesterday when she wasn't the future Mrs. Haverchuck.

SAM
It's okay, Bill. I would have gotten nervous too.

NEAL
Yeah, and that's why you guys should let me have her. I know what to say to a woman.

(CONTINUED)

31.

CONTINUED: (3)

Neal looks off after Maureen. His face falls.

ANGLE ON: Maureen is now standing talking to VICKI APPLEBY, a pretty, popular girl who is also head cheerleader. Vicki is welcoming her to the school.

VICKI
So, you're new. How do you like it here?

MAUREEN
It's great. I've met some really nice people.

Neal looks panicked. He turns to Sam and Bill.

NEAL
Oh, no. Maureen's talking to Vicki Appleby.

SAM
So?

NEAL
So... the minute she starts getting in with the popular crowd, we've lost her forever. You think she's gonna hang out with us after she's been around all those jocks and cheerleaders?

BILL
Why wouldn't she?

NEAL
Because they're pod people. It's like "Invasion of the Body Snatchers." They'll turn her into one of them. We'll see her in a week and she'll be like...

He does an impression of the end of "The Invasion of the Body Snatchers." He holds out his hands and makes a screeching sound.

SAM
Oh, man, we've gotta get her away from Vicki.

BILL
What do we do?

(CONTINUED)

CONTINUED: (4)

They look around in a panic. Then, Neal sees Eli walking down the hall toward them.

NEAL
(calling out)
Eli! Come here.

Eli sees them and happily comes over.

ELI
Hi, Neal. Hi, Sam. Hi, Bill!

SAM/BILL
Hey.

NEAL
Eli, Vicki Appleby told me that she doesn't think "Three's Company" is funny.

ELI
But it's the funniest show on TV.

NEAL
That's what I told her.

ELI
I better go talk to her.

Eli quickly heads off, on a mission. He walks right up to Vicki and Maureen as the geeks watch with bated breath.

ELI (CONT'D)
Vicki, "Three's Company" is the funniest show on TV.

VICKI
(surprised)
Oh... really?

ELI
Yes. The Ropers don't want Jack to live with two girls because he doesn't want dirty stuff to happen in his apartment building.

As Eli corners Vicki, the geeks quickly scoot over and grab Maureen.

SAM
Hey, Maureen, we'll walk with you to class.

(CONTINUED)

CONTINUED: (5)

MAUREEN
Oh, okay. I'll see you later, Vicki.

VICKI
Um, okay. See you later.

ANGLE ON: ELI AND VICKI

ELI
And Jack pretends that he likes boys but he doesn't really because he likes to look at Chrissy when she is in her bathing suit.

As Eli keeps rambling, the geeks hustle Maureen off down the hall.

CUT TO:

EXT. SMOKING PATIO - DAY

Lindsay, Daniel, Ken and Nick are off in a corner of the smoking patio, talking to Howie. Lindsay looks excited.

HOWIE
You got the money?

Lindsay takes her card out again. It's getting a little ragged.

LINDSAY
(handing him the money)
Yeah, here. You got our I.D.'s?

Howie takes the money and counts it.

HOWIE
(pulls out IDs)
Okay, here you go.

They reach for them, but he pulls them back.

HOWIE (CONT'D)
Before I give them to you let me give you the owner's manual. First, take all other forms of ID out of your wallet. Memorize everything on the ID. Date of birth, hair color, weight. Proper spellings. Address. You are no longer from Michigan. You are from Delaware. Live as these people. Call each other by these names. They are you.
(MORE)

(CONTINUED)

CONTINUED:

HOWIE (CONT'D)
You are them. Your previous identities no longer exist.

KEN
We just want a beer. We didn't inform on the mob.

HOWIE
Fine, don't listen. Be like Daniel. Don't memorize your zodiac sign. See where it gets ya.

Howie sorts through them, handing each one to a specific person.

HOWIE (CONT'D)
Congratulations, you are now all of age.

The freaks happily take their cards, then their faces fall.

KEN
Who the hell is Jesus Garcia?

HOWIE
It's pronounced Hay-soos. And it's your new identity. Tell me that picture doesn't look like you.

KEN
This picture doesn't look like me.

HOWIE
Sure it does.

Nick peers over at Ken's ID.

NICK
You know what? It does kinda look like you. Except for the mustache and the mole.

DANIEL
It's gotta be better than mine. The guy on this card's got blonde hair and a huge nose.

NICK
Yeah, and mine looks kinda Chinese.

Lindsay glances at theirs, then holds her's out.

(CONTINUED)

CONTINUED: (2)

LINDSAY
At least yours are the right age. Mine says I'm twenty-nine.

HOWIE
Hey, you can never be too old with these things. Mine says I'm thirty-four and I've never had a problem.

DANIEL
Give us the money back.

HOWIE
Hey, this is top grade stuff. You don't get any refunds.

NICK
Give us the money back!

Howie sighs, and pulls out the cash.

HOWIE
All right. You know how hard it is to find matches for you guys? People in Delaware don't look like you.

KEN
You know what? I'm gonna go with Hay-soos here. I think I can pull it off.

HOWIE
Finally, a sane man.

He hands them the money back.

HOWIE (CONT'D)
By the way, Silverman's has got a big sale tomorrow. Fifty percent off all dress shirts. Stop by, I'll hook you up.

He exits.

LINDSAY
So, that's it? We don't get I.D.'s? The band's playing tonight.

DANIEL
That was my only contact.

NICK
I don't know anyone.

(CONTINUED)

CONTINUED: (3)

LINDSAY
Wait. I think I do.

CUT TO:

INT. CAFETERIA - DAY

The geeks are eating their lunches, deep in conversation.

SAM
There's gotta be something we can do. Maybe we can split up the day and make sure that at least one of us is with her between each class. Then we can make sure she doesn't talk to anyone but us.

BILL
But what about during class?

NEAL
She's a good student. She'll be focused on the teacher.

The geeks look over to see Maureen walking away from the cashier. Vicki Appleby is waving her over. Maureen nods and starts toward the popular table.

NEAL (CONT'D)
Oh, no! it's Vicky!

BILL
Where's Eli?

NEAL
Sam, go talk to her about Three's Company.

Sam jumps up and runs over to Maureen as she's halfway to the popular table.

SAM
Maureen! Hey, you wanna sit with us?

MAUREEN
Oh. Okay.
(calling to Vicki)
I'll talk to you in Algebra.

Vicki gives her a friendly wave and goes back to her friends. Sam escorts Maureen over.

(CONTINUED)

CONTINUED:

SAM
Hey, you got chocolate pudding. I like that, too.

MAUREEN
Yeah, I like it when it's been sitting around for a while and it gets that skin on the top.

They sit at the geek table. Neal and Bill give her big smiles. She smiles back.

BILL
Hi, Maureen, good to see you again.

NEAL
How's your day going?

MAUREEN
Great. I've met tons of new people.

The geeks look panicked.

BILL
What are you doing this weekend?

SAM
We're thinking of buying a Star Trek Enterprise and launching it.

NEAL
It's got a top difficulty rating.

MAUREEN
Oh, that sounds cool but I've gotta help my family unpack all weekend. I won't be able to go out.

The geeks look at each other, relieved.

MAUREEN (CONT'D)
Except Saturday Night. Vicki invited me to her party. Wasn't that nice of her?

The geeks look like their stomachs have fallen into their shoes. They exchange sick looks, then force smiles at Maureen.

CUT TO:

(CONTINUED)

CONTINUED: (2)

INT. SCHOOL HALLWAY - DAY

Lindsay walks up to Millie as they are walking down the hall.

LINDSAY
Hey, Millie. What's up?

MILLIE
Nothing. I'm just heading to Mathlete practice. We've got a scrimmage coming up against North Lake next week. You wanna come watch?

LINDSAY
Oh, no thanks. Hey, do you ever talk to your cousin Toby anymore?

MILLIE
No way. Not since he went to jail.

LINDSAY
He's in jail?

MILLIE
He was. He got caught stealing hood ornaments off of cars. They weren't gonna lock him up but he called the policeman a bad word.

LINDSAY
Does he still make fake I.D.'s?

MILLIE
I don't know. Our family doesn't talk to him anymore. He's adopted, you know. My uncle said it was the biggest mistake their family ever made.
(then)
Why, do you want a fake ID? So you can drink even more?

LINDSAY
No, we just want to go see this band play.

MILLIE
That's what records are for.

LINDSAY
Do you have his number?

(CONTINUED)

CONTINUED: (3)

MILLIE
I'm not going to be an accessory to this crime. You know where he lives. Do it yourself.

CUT TO:

EXT. SEEDY STREET - DAY

Daniel's Trans Am rumbles up in a run-down neighborhood. Lindsay, Daniel and Nick get out of the car.

LINDSAY
Okay, it's up this path.

They head up a dirt path toward a very crummy looking house.

NICK
How do you know this guy?

LINDSAY
He's Millie's cousin. I knew him when I was really little. But he's kind of scary now.

DANIEL
I think we can handle it.

LINDSAY
I wish we lived in a state where the drinking age was eighteen. It'd be way easier to get into places.

NICK
Yeah, I know. Why's it even different in every state?

DANIEL
'Cause some states are more fascist than others.

NICK
I think I heard the drinking age is something like ten in Idaho.

LINDSAY
I don't think that's right.

DANIEL
Canada's cool. Their drinking age is nineteen. Canadians rock.

(CONTINUED)

CONTINUED:

NICK
We should go to Canada, man. Then we could hang out with Rush. And April Wine.

They look at the place and take a deep breath, a little nervous.

DANIEL
Well, here goes nothing.

Daniel knocks on the door.

VOICE (O.S.)
(through door)
What?

DANIEL
We're here about the I.D.'s.

VOICE (O.S.)
Only one person's allowed inside at a time.

NICK
You can go first.

A nervous Daniel walks inside.

FADE OUT.

END OF ACT THREE

ACT FOUR

FADE IN:

INT. SCHOOL HALLWAY - DAY

The geeks are talking to Harris.

SAM
Well, what are we going to do?

HARRIS
Why should I help you? You wouldn't share her the other day.

NEAL
Would you share her with us?

(CONTINUED)

CONTINUED:

HARRIS
(after a beat)
Touche.

BILL
So, what do we do?

HARRIS
If she's going to be at Vicki Appleby's party on Saturday then you need to hang out with her on Friday. And if you show her the time of her life then maybe, just maybe, she will continue to base herself out of your lunch table.

SAM
What are our chances?

HARRIS
You don't want to know.

NEAL
Where do we take her?

HARRIS
There's only one place that might be able to compete with a Vicki Appleby party. All-you-can-eat night at The Iron Horse Restaurant.

They all throw their arms up in the air at this obviously perfect suggestion.

CUT TO:

INT. TOBY'S HOUSE - CONTINUOUS

Daniel walks into the very cluttered and unkempt house of Toby. There's all kinds of contraband piled everywhere. Car stereos, boxes of auto parts, plastic bags of stuffed animals (the crappy kinds they give away at carnivals) and other nameless boxes that look like they fell off the back of a train.

Daniel looks around as Toby goes into another room off to the side.

DANIEL
Man, you got a lot of stuff.

(CONTINUED)

CONTINUED:

TOBY
Don't look at that stuff, please. Okay? I'm just holding it for somebody.

Daniel runs his finger across one of the boxes. There's about an inch of dust on the box.

DANIEL
Looks like you've been holding it for a long time.

TOBY
Am I speaking Swahili? Don't look at that stuff. I don't like people eyeballing the contents of my house. No offense.

DANIEL
None taken.

TOBY
Now, let me find some film.

He opens up a closet door. The closet is filled with bright grow lights and potted plants.

DANIEL
What's that?

TOBY
I've got a green thumb. Don't worry about it. Do you have the money?

DANIEL
Lindsay's got it.

TOBY
(stares at Daniel a beat)
You're not messing with me, are you? Please don't mess with me. I've really got a major headache going.

DANIEL
I swear she has it. I think she busted a bond or something.

TOBY
That's sad. I hope it was mature. You shouldn't bust a bond if it's not mature.
(MORE)

(CONTINUED)

CONTINUED: (2)

TOBY (CONT'D)
Somebody should talk to her about that. All right, come in here. And don't look around.

Toby waves Daniel into the other room. Daniel walks across the living room and into

THE BEDROOM

Daniel stops and stares, a little in awe.

DANIEL
Man, that's pretty cool.

ANGLE ON: The back wall of the very messy bedroom is dedicated to a giant poster of an Ohio driver's license. There's also a big empty spot where a person's picture should go.

There's a camera and a flash umbrella set up to take a person's picture when they stand in front of the empty picture spot.

DANIEL (CONT'D)
Why does it say Ohio?

TOBY
'Cause it passes easier in Michigan. Ohio might as well be Africa to a dumb bouncer.

DANIEL
Oh.

TOBY
You have to promise me you'll forget about all this once you leave.

DANIEL
Yeah, sure.

TOBY
This is my livelihood. I don't need you giving the idea to potential rivals.

As he talks, he moves Daniel into position, putting Daniel's face where it will be on the license. Daniel has to squat down a bit to line himself up. Toby gets behind the camera.

(CONTINUED)

CONTINUED: (3)

TOBY (CONT'D)
All right, Desario, look like you don't want to have your picture taken.

Daniel makes a face that looks like a terrible drivers license picture. FLASH!

CUT TO:

EXT. MCKINLEY HIGH SCHOOL QUAD - DAY

Sam is sitting on a bench in the quad, staring at Cindy sitting on the other side of the quad. Maureen walks up.

MAUREEN
(busting him)
What are you doing? Oh, my God. You're in love with that girl.

SAM
What, what are you talking about?

MAUREEN
Oh, please, Sam.

SAM
Well, I mean, I like her.

MAUREEN
Does she like you?

SAM
I don't know. I haven't talked to her much. It's hard to tell.

MAUREEN
You wanna make out and see if she gets jealous?

Sam looks at her, suddenly white as a ghost.

MAUREEN (CONT'D)
I'm just kidding, Sam.

SAM
Oh, ha ha. I knew that.

MAUREEN
Well, you should find out if she likes you.
(MORE)

(CONTINUED)

CONTINUED:

MAUREEN (CONT'D)
I always had a crush on this guy and two years later he told me he always liked me but by then it was too late. He already had a girlfriend.

SAM
What if she doesn't like me?

MAUREEN
Well, then she's dumb.

Just then, a guy starts talking to Cindy.

MAUREEN
Who's that guy talking to her? Is that her boyfriend?

SAM
No, it's Jeffery Futeran. He used to be one of my best friends but we don't talk anymore.

MAUREEN
What happened?

SAM
I don't know. We got to junior high and he started hanging out with other kids. Now we never even say "hi" anymore.

MAUREEN
That's sad.

SAM
Yeah, it is.

They sit in silence for a second.

SAM (CONT'D)
Are you doing anything tonight? Bill and Neal and I were thinking of going to the Iron Horse. It's All-U-Can-Eat night. We go in there and try to put the place out of business.

MAUREEN
Then I'm not eating lunch. That restaurant is in trouble.

(CONTINUED)

CONTINUED: (2)

Sam laughs.

CUT TO:

INT. TOBY'S HOUSE - DAY

Nick comes out of the bedroom, having just had his picture taken. Toby calls from the bedroom.

TOBY (O.S.)
All right. Tell Lindsay she can come in.

Nick looks back at the bedroom nervously, then goes to the door and opens it.

NICK
Come on in, Lindsay.

Lindsay enters and takes in the place.

LINDSAY
Wow. This looks like my dad's warehouse.

NICK
Oh, uh... you're not supposed to look around. It's kinda like a rule or something.

Just then, Toby comes out of the bedroom.

TOBY
Hey, man, you've gotta get out. You know the rule. One person at a time. That's the only way I can guarantee security.

NICK
Hey, if you don't mind, I'd like to stay here with Lindsay. She's kinda nervous.

TOBY
(hurt)
Nervous about what? We're old friends. We played as children.
(looks at her)
You've grown up nice, Linds.

LINDSAY
So did you.

(CONTINUED)

CONTINUED:

TOBY
You don't even need ID. You look very womanly. Bouncers never stop women who look like you. That's how they get men into the bar.

LINDSAY
Thanks.

Toby heads to the bedroom. Lindsay throws a look at Nick. He signals her to go, that he'll be right behind her. She gives him a nervous smile and heads to the bedroom.

CUT TO:

INT./EXT. DANIEL'S TRANS AM - CONTINUOUS

Daniel and Kim are in the car. Kim holds Daniel's ID, which is in his wallet.

KIM
That looks pretty real.

DANIEL
It better work.

KIM
Look how much hotter you look than your real drivers license.
(looks at it)
Is this one fake, too?

DANIEL
No, why?

KIM
It says you're eighteen.

Daniel looks upset.

DANIEL
So? I got left back.

KIM
I know. But still...

DANIEL
Fine. I got left back twice. Are you happy? Now there's no secrets between us.

(CONTINUED)

CONTINUED:

KIM
Yeah! I'm dating a man.

CUT TO:

INT. TOBY'S HOUSE - MOMENTS LATER

Nick and Lindsay are standing around a card table as Toby cuts the pictures and prepares them. There's a large laminating machine and a typewriter on the table. Toby keeps eyeballing Lindsay as he works.

TOBY
You're a beautiful girl. You go to McKinley? It's a pretty good school. I almost graduated a few years back.

LINDSAY
Oh, really.

TOBY
Yeah. You want something to eat? I've got some Freihoffer's cookies. They're from the East Coast. They're really hard to get. You should try one.

LINDSAY
No thanks. I'm not really hungry.

NICK
Hey, is this gonna take a long time?

TOBY
Be cool, man. The laminating machine's still warming up.
(back to Lindsay)
I got tickets for Yes at Cobo. You wanna go? Richie Blackmore's Rainbow is opening up. We could catch up.

LINDSAY
Oh, no, that's okay.

Lindsay just nods uncomfortably. Toby goes back to trimming the IDs with an Exacto knife.

(CONTINUED)

CONTINUED:

TOBY
So, would you mind giving me your home phone number? I could give you a call sometime.

NICK
Man, she's kinda my girlfriend. Could you stop hitting on her?

TOBY
No, she's not.

LINDSAY
(quickly)
No, I'm his girlfriend.

Nick looks at her, surprised. She makes a face that says "I am right now." Nick looks happy. Toby puts down his Exacto knife and sits back. Stares at them, upset.

TOBY
That's not cool, man. Now you make me feel like a fool. Asking for your phone number.

LINDSAY
(getting worried)
You can have my number. I just have a boyfriend.

TOBY
I don't need to ask. I could get it from Millie. I was trying to be polite.
(gets up)
Let's just get this over with. That'll be seventy-five each.

NICK
You said it was forty.

TOBY
Oh, did I? I'm sorry, a hundred.

LINDSAY
Let's just do it and get out of here.

Lindsay takes out her Hallmark card and pulls out the money.

TOBY
What's that?

(CONTINUED)

CONTINUED: (2)

LINDSAY
It's nothing.

Toby takes the Hallmark card and starts to read from it.

TOBY
"Happy Birthday, Lindsay. We are so very proud of you. Here's a little something to help you fulfill your dream of going to Harvard. We know you can do it. Aunt Judy and Uncle Gary."

Toby hands the IDs and the money with the card back to Lindsay.

LINDSAY
What are you doing?

TOBY
Just take it. I would never take college money from Aunt Judy and Uncle Gary. What kind of guy do you think I am? Now get out of here before I change my mind.

Nick and Lindsay exit.

CUT TO:

INT. LINDSAY'S ROOM - NIGHT

Lindsay sits in her room staring at her fake ID. Sam walks in wearing a bathrobe. He has wet hair.

SAM
Do you have the blow dryer?

LINDSAY
Yeah.

She hands it to him.

SAM
What's that?

LINDSAY
You can't tell Mom and Dad. It's a fake I.D. Check it out.

(CONTINUED)

CONTINUED:

SAM
Oh my God. That looks so real. It says you're twenty-two.

LINDSAY
If it said I'm twenty-one, it's really obvious it's fake. You've gotta throw them off a little.

SAM
You're not gonna drink, are you?

LINDSAY
No. We're just going to see this band. What're you doing?

SAM
Me, Neal and Bill are taking a girl to the Iron Horse.

LINDSAY
Oooh, All-You-Can-Eat. Sounds serious.

SAM
Believe me, it is.

LINDSAY
Well, good luck.

Lindsay heads out of the bathroom. Sam gives himself a final once-over, then heads out too.

CUT TO:

INT. WEIR DINING ROOM - CONTINUOUS

Harold and Jean are sitting at the dining room table playing Pit. They look they're having a great time, laughing.

JEAN
I've got corn! I need two corns!

HAROLD
How about some barley? I'll give you two barleys for your corn.

JEAN
You're on!

They happily swap cards and laugh. Lindsay and Sam walk by.

(CONTINUED)

CONTINUED:

HAROLD
Hey, you two, pull up a chair. We've got a lot of high stakes stock trading happening here in the pit.

LINDSAY
Dad, I told you. I'm going out.

SAM
Me, too.

Lindsay comes over and kisses Harold on the cheek goodbye.

LINDSAY
Have a fun night.

HAROLD
Don't you worry. We will.

JEAN
Be careful.

Sam waves goodbye too, and they head out the front door. Jean starts to play again, happy as a clam.

JEAN (CONT'D)
All right, I need some oats!

Harold's demeanor immediately changes. He tosses down his cards, upset.

HAROLD
See, I told you we should have forced them to stay with us.

JEAN
Harold, we can't force them to do anything. You want to keep playing Pit?

HAROLD
(throwing his cards down)
No. This game's terrible with just two people.

JEAN
(after a beat)
Nobody's home. You want to have sex?

Harold gets up and stalks.

(CONTINUED)

CONTINUED: (2)

HAROLD
I'm not in the mood. I'm all agitated. Check with me in an hour. I'm gonna watch TV and try to relax.

CUT TO:

EXT. THE RUSTY NAIL BAR - NIGHT

The freaks walk up to the bar. There's a small line-up of people waiting to get in. A large BOUNCER is checking IDs.

LINDSAY
Oh, man, I'm nervous.

KIM
Just do it the way we discussed.

They are now up to the bouncer. Kim tries to stand with an adult posture. The bouncer waves her in.

BOUNCER
(to Daniel)
Let's see some I.D.

DANIEL
What? Really? Oh, yeah.

Daniel makes a big show out of looking for his ID. The bouncer just watches him, impassively.

DANIEL (CONT'D)
Shoot, man. I didn't know you guys were gonna be carding tonight. I hope I brought it.

BOUNCER
The suspense is killing me.

DANIEL
(finding it)
Oh, here it is. Being a Sagittarius, I'm always forgetting things.

Daniel hands the bouncer the ID. The bouncer studies it. Looks skeptical. Then he hands Daniel his ID back.

BOUNCER
Go on.

(CONTINUED)

CONTINUED:

The bouncer takes Ken's card. Looks at the card, then Ken, then back at the card.

BOUNCER (CONT'D)
Where's your mustache, Jesus?

KEN
It's Hay-soos and I shaved it.

BOUNCER
Too bad. You looked better with it.

KEN
Gracias.

Ken heads in. Nick comes up. He looks quite nervous. Hands the bouncer his ID.

NICK
I can't believe you're carding me. That's so great. I haven't been carded in years. Man, you make me feel like a kid again. Thanks. I really appreciate it.

The bouncer just hands Nick his card back, weirded out. Nick takes it, gives the guy a big smile and walks in, still looking nervous. Lindsay steps up.

LINDSAY
Hi. How are you tonight?

BOUNCER
All right, come on in.

LINDSAY
Don't you need to see my ID?

BOUNCER
No, you're good.

Lindsay doesn't know whether to be happy or offended. Nick puts his arm around her and they walk in. The bouncer turns to another bouncer.

BOUNCER (CONT'D)
Those I.D.'s looked nuts. Business must be pretty bad if we're supposed to let them in.

CUT TO:

(CONTINUED)

CONTINUED: (2)

INT. THE IRON HORSE RESTAURANT - NIGHT

All-U-Can-Eat Night at the Iron Horse, a dark wood old man restaurant. The place is crowded with diners. The geeks and Maureen are sitting at a table, eating mountains of food. Empty plates are pushed off to the side.

MAUREEN
So, how does this work?

NEAL
Well, we order a lot of food, then we keep asking for more food until they go out of business.

BILL
My mom says it takes a while for your stomach to tell your brain it's full. That's why it's important to eat really fast.

SAM
But the problem is the service is usually slow.

NEAL
They take forever on purpose so you'll get full while you wait. Watch how much bread they give us.

MAUREEN
I'm not eating bread. I'm here to eat ribs.

The waiter walks over.

WAITER
Good evening. Welcome to the Iron Horse.

MAUREEN
I hear the service is really bad because you don't want us to eat much.

WAITER
What? I don't own the place. I don't care how much you eat.

MAUREEN
Are you sure?

(CONTINUED)

CONTINUED: (3)

WAITER
No, I'm a millionaire and I do this for fun.

BILL
Really?

SAM
We just want to get our money's worth.

WAITER
I'll bring 'em faster than you can eat 'em, but I want a twenty percent tip.

BILL
Twenty? I thought ten was standard.

WAITER
Fifteen is standard. Twenty is classy.

NEAL
Twenty it is. Why are we still talking? I want some ribs.

The waiter exits.

MAUREEN
This is gonna be the best night ever.

The geeks exchange happy looks. The waiter returns.

WAITER
Oh, I forgot your bread.

He drops two huge baskets of bread on the table. Neal looks annoyed.

CUT TO:

INT. THE RUSTY NAIL BAR - NIGHT

The bar is crowded. The freaks are sitting around a table, waiting for the band to start. Ken is looking around for a waitress.

(CONTINUED)

CONTINUED:

KEN
Where's the waitress when you need her? I've got to take advantage of this evening.

LINDSAY
This is so exciting. I've always wondered what it was like in here. We've driven past this place on our way to church every Sunday since I was a kid.

NICK
This is gonna rock. I am so ready to rock.

On stage, the band gets up and puts on their instruments. They are in the dark and we can only see their silhouettes.

LINDSAY
This is so cool. Thanks for letting me be part of this.

DANIEL
Hey, good to have you here. Welcome to the real world.

The band strums an amplified chord. The crowd CHEERS. The freaks look excited. Lindsay grabs Nick's arm, beaming.

LINDSAY
This is gonna be so much fun.

NICK
We're only here because of you, Lindsay. Thanks.

They share a big smile.

VOICE
(over the loudspeaker)
Good evening, everybody. Are you ready to rock?

CROWD
YEAH!

VOICE
Then put your hands together for...FEEDBACK!!!

(CONTINUED)

58.

CONTINUED: (2)

The crowd CHEERS again. THE BAND KICKS IN. The lights pop on. The music is loud. They're playing Alice Cooper's "Eighteen."

The freaks jump up, excited, then their faces fall.

On stage, behind a keyboard and about to sing lead vocals is... MR. ROSSO!

MR. ROSSO
I hope there's a lot of party people out there tonight 'cause we are gonna PARTEEEEEEE!!!!
(starts singing)
"Lines form on my face and hands/Lines form on the left and right..."

The freaks exchange looks and slowly sink back down into their seats.

CUT TO:

INT. THE IRON HORSE RESTAURANT - NIGHT

MUSIC UP: BILLY JOEL "STILETTO"

We see a montage of Maureen and the three geeks eating ribs. Maureen has no trouble keeping up. Soon, they are surrounded by plates piled high with bones. Their faces are covered in barbecue sauce.

END OF MONTAGE.

The four look very full, but satisfied. The waiter comes over carrying two plates of ribs.

WAITER
Ready for more ribs?

They stare at the ribs, completely full.

NEAL
Could you put those in a doggy bag?

CUT TO:

INT. THE RUSTY NAIL BAR - NIGHT

The freaks are sitting at their table, watching as Rosso's band finishes "Eighteen." The crowd is rocking. The freaks are into it, too.

(CONTINUED)

CONTINUED:

The song ends. The crowd CHEERS.

MR. ROSSO
All right, everybody. I've got a hard working group of rockers behind me and I'd like to introduce them all to you but first, we've got some special guests in the audience I'd like to introduce.

A waitress is coming toward the freak table with a tray full of beers.

MR. ROSSO (CONT'D)
All the way from McKinley High School, we've got the key members of another smoking band we like to call "Creation." Daniel Desario, Ken Miller, Nick Andopolis, Kim Kelly and their manager, Miss Lindsay Weir. Give 'em a big hand.

The crowd claps as the freaks exchange looks. They're completely busted. Just then, the waitress sets her tray on their table and is about to give them their beers.

MR. ROSSO (CONT'D)
Hold on, Sue. I can't let you serve our guests plain old beer. Why don't you bring them some of your finest Pop, on the house?

The waitress nods to Rosso, shrugs to the freaks, and takes the beers back. The freaks look up at Rosso, who gives them a big thumbs up. Busted. Rosso and the band start a blues standard.

KEN
Pop. Perfect. I was just about to say instead of having eight beers each, let's have Pop.

CUT TO:

INT. THE IRON HORSE RESTAURANT - NIGHT

The geeks are by the front door of the restaurant. They are all grabbing for mints and toothpicks. Maureen is messing around with the specials chalk board.

(CONTINUED)

60.

CONTINUED:

MAUREEN
I had a really good time. We should do it again.

SAM
That'd be great.

HONK HONK. They all look to the door.

MAUREEN
Oh, that's my dad. I'd better get going. Thanks again. You sure you don't want any money.

NEAL
No, no, no, it's on us.

MAUREEN
Hey, check it out.

She has changed a special from 'Pan Fried Bass' to 'Pan Fried Ass.' The geeks walk over and laugh. She exits.

MAUREEN (CONT'D)
Okay, well, I'll see you guys Monday.

She gives them a wave and runs out the door. They watch after her as the door slowly closes. They don't move.

BILL
How are we not supposed to be in love with her?

SAM
You think we'll ever see her again?

NEAL
Oh, yeah, we'll see her plenty. Sitting at the popular table.

BILL
No way. She's cool. We're gonna be friends with her for a long time.

SAM
I hope so.

CUT TO:

INT. THE RUSTY NAIL BAR - NIGHT

Feedback plays The Band's "Up On Cripple Creek."

ANGLE ON: The freaks, watching.

NICK
Mr. Rosso kind of rocks.

LINDSAY
This was fun. I don't mind not drinking. I'm just glad we got in.

The band finishes their set.

DANIEL
Are you guys about ready to go?

KEN
Why? I was gonna be bad and see if they'd let me have some cranberry juice.

They all walk to the exit. Mr. Rosso finishes the song then runs to the exit.

MR. ROSSO
Did you have fun, kids?

NICK
Yeah. You guys rock pretty hard.

MR. ROSSO
Thanks. I really appreciate you guys showing up to see us. That was way cool.

KEN
We're Feedback groupies.

MR. ROSSO
Can't get enough of those.

DANIEL
You should play the electric guitar at the rap sessions.

MR. ROSSO
And get fired by the man? No, thank you. Did you have fun, Lindsay?

(CONTINUED)

CONTINUED:

LINDSAY
I wish I could say no, but I did.

MR. ROSSO
Cool, well I'll see ya' at McKinley High.

They start to exit.

MR. ROSSO (CONT'D)
Oh, before you leave, I'm gonna need those fake I.D.'s.

LINDSAY
Don't, Mr. Rosso.

MR. ROSSO
I swore an oath. Well, my own personal oath.
(taking the ID's)
But if you want to see Feedback rock out again, we'll be playing the Junior High School prom.

KEN
You are a vicious man.

MR. ROSSO
I promise, I'll give these back to you when you turn twenty one. And then Jesus Garcia will ride again. Don't feel bad. Just know, everyone in this bar is jealous of your youth.

KIM
And we're jealous of their hangovers.

They all walk toward the exit.

KEN
Hey, Lindsay. Since all these I.D.'s have been confiscated, do we still have to pay you back?

CUT TO:

INT. CAFETERIA - DAY

The geeks are seated. Maureen walks over with her tray. She does not sit.

(CONTINUED)

CONTINUED:

MAUREEN
Hey, guys.

They all say hello.

MAUREEN (CONT'D)
Hey, you mind if I go over there and sit with those guys today?

She points to Vicki's table of popular kids.

SAM
No, not at all.

MAUREEN
Do you want to sit over there with me?

BILL
Over there?

MAUREEN
Yeah, come on. You don't have to sit here forever if you don't want to.

SAM
No, we like it here.

NEAL
Go on. Have fun with your friends. We'll be right here if you need us.

MAUREEN
Okay.

SAM
Before you do. Remember, those jocks are only after one thing.

NEAL
And be careful around Vicki. She's a wolf in sheep's clothing.

BILL
And remember, don't believe everything they say about...people in the school. Sometimes they don't bother to get to know everyone.

(CONTINUED)

64.

CONTINUED: (2)

MAUREEN
I'm just sitting three tables over.
I'm not moving back to Florida.

SAM
We know.

MAUREEN
I'll see you in biology class.

SAM
See ya' in biology class.

MUSIC UP: BILLY JOEL "YOU WERE THE ONE"

The geeks watch her go. She walks away in SLOW MOTION. The geeks look like proud/scared parents sending their child off to school for the first time.

They are silent until Eli walks over to the table.

ELI
Is this seat taken?

NEAL
Yes it is. By you, my good man.

Eli sits down.

ELI
Did you see "Three's Company" last
night? Mr. Furley is crazy.

BILL
I like his leisure suits.

ELI
Last night it was green. There was
this one scene where...

They settle in as Eli begins telling them the storyline from last night's episode.

FADE TO BLACK.

THE END

# FREAKS AND GEEKS

"GIRLFRIENDS AND BOYFRIENDS"

Episode #8

Written by Patty Lin & Paul Feig

Directed by Lesli Glatter

Writing this episode with Paul Feig was pure joy. Instead of monopolizing the script as many showrunners might do, Paul gave me complete freedom to be creative with the characters and use my own personal experience in the writing. For the first draft, Paul wrote the freak scenes and I wrote the geek scenes. Then in subsequent drafts we both worked on each other's scenes, often writing together in Paul's office, making each other laugh.

I pitched the idea for Sam's story because I wanted to show a different side of the Cindy Sanders character. Up to this point, she was the popular, pretty, perfect cheerleader. I thought, wouldn't it be funny if Sam found out she was kind of disgusting? The original pitch involved Cindy having facial hair and eating like a pig. The mustache was cut, but the eating disorder remained—for anyone who suspected that Cindy might be bulimic when she scarfed that Stackey burger, you get points for reading between the lines. Judd Apatow was the one who suggested that Cindy should fart—and here's the brilliant part—blame it on the chair. I still remember my shock and elation when I realized that I was being paid to write about farts. In one of the early drafts, after Cindy left the room, Bill actually smelled the chair. But I guess you've got to draw the line somewhere.

Another note about the fart: In the scene where Sam, Bill and Neal are discussing Cindy's fart at school, we had to change the word "fart" to "cut the cheese" for standards & practices reasons. But "cut the cheese" turned out to be even funnier than "fart," especially because they repeated it about five hundred times in one conversation.

Here are some personal notes about the script:

Cindy's depressing yearbook poem was based on some bad poetry I wrote in high school.

Jean's advice to Lindsay, "Your virginity is a gift," was a direct quote from my mom, which she told me when I was about 25.

Gordon Crisp was a kid in my high school.

Mr. Lacovara was my biology teacher.

Mr. Mainzer was my art teacher.

Todd Schellinger was a cute production assistant at *Martial Law*, the first show I wrote for.

—Patty Lin

## Addendum to Patty Lin's "Girlfriends and Boyfriends" Intro

I love Patty Lin. I think she's one of the most talented writers I've ever met. And she's also a great person. True, she does have a few food issues that made ordering lunch each day a bit of an ordeal, but she's got a heart of gold. And we had a blast writing this episode, making each other laugh every time we sat down to work on it. I just wanted to let you all know that "standards & practices" is TV-speak for "the censors," that fine group of people who make sure that you don't say bad words on TV or do anything else that might offend your audience or the FCC.

That's all I wanted to say. Sorry for interrupting. Just pretend that I'm not here.

—Paul Feig

FREAKS AND GEEKS

"GIRLFRIENDS AND BOYFRIENDS"

**CAST LIST**

LINDSAY WEIR
SAM WEIR
HAROLD WEIR
JEAN WEIR
DANIEL DESARIO
NICK ANDOPOLIS
BILL HAVERCHUCK
NEAL SCHWEIBER
KIM KELLY
MILLIE KENTNER
CINDY SANDERS
MR. ROSSO
MR. KOWCHEVSKI
SEAN
GORDON CRISP
MR. LACOVARA
MR. MAINZER
OWNER
FUNERAL DIRECTOR
TODD SCHELLINGER
MR. YEATS*
MR. SAMPSON*

FREAKS AND GEEKS

"GIRLFRIENDS AND BOYFRIENDS"

**SET LIST**

**INTERIORS:**

MCKINLEY HIGH SCHOOL
/HALLWAY
/STUDY HALL
/BIOLOGY CLASS
/FRONT OFFICE
/MR. ROSSO'S OFFICE
/CAFETERIA
/GIRLS BATHROOM
/UNDER THE STAIRS
/CLASSROOM
WEIR HOUSE
/FRONT DOOR
/KITCHEN
/SAM'S ROOM
/DINING ROOM
/LIVING ROOM
/LINDSAY'S ROOM
CINDY'S BEDROOM
NICK'S HOUSE
/BASEMENT
/LIVING ROOM
HAROLD WEIR'S STORE
AUTO REPAIR SHOP
FUNERAL HOME
STACKEY'S BURGER RESTAURANT

**EXTERIORS:**

MCKINLEY HIGH SCHOOL
/UNDER THE BLEACHERS
NICK'S HOUSE
NEIGHBORHOOD STREET

TEASER

FADE IN:

INT. MCKINLEY HIGH SCHOOL HALLWAY - MORNING

MUSIC UP: THE ALLMAN BROTHERS' "WHIPPING POST"

The halls are filled with students heading to their lockers, walking to classes, trapped in a typical morning malaise. We MOVE through them toward the double doors that lead outside.

We ARRIVE just as LINDSAY enters the building. She stops and scans the scene before her. Takes it all in. It's obviously not where she wants to be.

She makes a face and wades into the activity. We MOVE AROUND AND BEHIND her and FOLLOW her through the school. She walks past students engaged in all sorts of social interaction.

Band kids talking, excited, holding their instrument cases. Jocks joking and having punching contests. Teachers interacting with clean-cut students.

Lindsay turns a corner into an emptier hallway.

AN ATTRACTIVE COUPLE

is making out heavily against a locker. Lindsay can't help but stare as he walks past them and continues down the hall.

CUT TO:

EXT. UNDER THE BLEACHERS - MORNING

Several FREAKS are hanging out under the bleachers before school. DANIEL and KIM are there. Daniel is watching Kim put on lip gloss.

NICK approaches from the parking lot, sees Lindsay approaching from the opposite direction and runs over to her.

LINDSAY

Oh, hey.

NICK

Hey, Linds. I was just coming to look for you.

Lindsay seems pleased. Nick smiles, helps Lindsay up to the bleacher area and puts his arm around her. They walk up to Daniel and Kim.

(CONTINUED)

CONTINUED:

DANIEL
Hey. What's up?

NICK
(super cool)
Nothing. Just hanging with Linds.

KIM
So are you guys going out or what?

NICK
Hey, I don't kiss and tell.

Everybody laughs. Nick smiles at Lindsay. She blushes despite herself.

DANIEL
Cool, man. Cool.

Daniel pulls Kim onto his lap. Nick pulls Lindsay a little closer. Lindsay smiles, psyched to be part of the group in this new way.

Nick slips his hand into Lindsay's back pocket. Lindsay, caught off-guard, instinctively stiffens. Just then, SEAN walks by.

SEAN
Hey, Nick. Grab me a piece.

NICK
Shut up, man.
(to Lindsay)
Sorry.

Nick gingerly extracts his hand from Lindsay's pocket. She looks relieved.

CUT TO:

<u>MAIN TITLES</u>

<u>ACT ONE</u>

FADE IN:

INT. MCKINLEY HIGH SCHOOL HALLWAY - MORNING

Lindsay and Nick are walking down the hallway. Nick has his arm draped around her shoulders.

(CONTINUED)

3.

CONTINUED:

NICK
Remember those guys from the band Dimension? They found a drummer.

LINDSAY
Really?

NICK
Yeah, I heard he dropped a stick soloing on "Black Dog" at their first gig.
(quickly)
I'm not jealous. The truth is I'm glad I bombed that audition. 'Cause if I didn't, we might never have kissed.

Nick gazes into Lindsay's eyes. She's flattered and a little embarrassed.

LINDSAY

Well, I've gotta get to study hall. I need to cram for my English quiz.

NICK
Okay. See ya later.

Lindsay starts to leave, but Nick quickly leans in to kiss her, catching her off-guard. He ends up getting her ear.

They laugh awkwardly, then re-adjust and give each other a peck on the lips. Nick smiles and heads off.

Lindsay turns to go, finding herself face-to-face with MILLIE.

MILLIE
Lindsay, you just kissed Nick.

LINDSAY
Yeah. So?

MILLIE
(sincere)
Is he your boyfriend?

Lindsay thinks for a second. Should she tell Millie?

LINDSAY
No. We haven't even gone on a date or anything.
(MORE)

(CONTINUED)

CONTINUED: (2)

LINDSAY (CONT'D)
(off Millie's look)
It's just... we were at his house the other day and he was really depressed... and we kissed. It's no big deal.

Millie makes a disapproving face.

LINDSAY (CONT'D)
What? You've got a boyfriend.

MILLIE
Yeah, but Tommy goes to church. Nick is a freak.

LINDSAY
So what?

MILLIE
So, this. Freaks only date freak girls. And you're not a freak girl.

LINDSAY
How do you know?

MILLIE
Because freak girls go all the way.

LINDSAY
Millie, you have no idea what you're talking about.

MILLIE
What about Patty Felker? She's a freak girl and she has a baby. But I guess that's "no big deal."

Lindsay stares at Millie, unnerved.

LINDSAY
Millie... mind your own business, okay?

Lindsay heads off. Millie watches after her, concerned, then turns and walks away.

We FOLLOW HER as she walks past SAM, who is pulling books from his locker. BILL and NEAL stand next to him. The BELL RINGS.

BILL
Hurry up. I don't want to be late for bio again.

(CONTINUED)

CONTINUED: (3)

NEAL
What's the big deal?

BILL
Yesterday I came in late and everyone looked at me.

Sam nods. Point taken. He closes his locker, then turns to see CINDY, heading in his direction. She looks more beautiful than ever. Sam gawks as Cindy approaches.

CINDY
Hi, Sam.

SAM
Hi, Cindy!

And she walks past, leaving Sam staring after her.

NEAL
Gee, Sam, you're a real Don Juan.

SAM
Well, it's not like I'm gonna have a deep conversation with her in front of all these people.

Sam, Neal and Bill start walking to class.

NEAL
Have you ever had a deep conversation with Cindy Sanders?

SAM
Not exactly. But we've talked twenty-one times.
(determined)
If I could just spend some time alone with her, she'd really get to know me. And then maybe she'd like me.

BILL
Yeah. Remember when Bugs Bunny and Christopher Columbus were stranded on a ship and they didn't have any food? And Christopher Columbus was so hungry that he thought Bugs Bunny looked like a chicken with those chef's hats on his hands and feet, and he started chasing him around?

(CONTINUED)

CONTINUED: (4)

SAM
Yeah, so?

BILL
Well, weird things happen when you're alone with somebody for a long time.

NEAL
Bill, that was a cartoon.

BILL
Okay, well, remember that one "Love Boat?"

Sam and Neal roll their eyes and walk off.

BILL (CONT'D)
Where're you going?

CUT TO:

INT. STUDY HALL - DAY

Daniel and Lindsay are sitting across the row from each other. Daniel's kicked back, doodling. Lindsay's reading "Wuthering Heights." MS. YEATS, a pretty female teacher, is at the front of the room, grading papers.

Daniel leans over to Lindsay. Their whole conversation is whispered.

DANIEL
Hey, Lindsay. I think it's really cool that you and Nick are going out.

LINDSAY
Yeah, me too.

DANIEL
I mean it. Nick's a great guy. We like to give him a hard time, but you know... he's the man. It's just really good you guys are going out.

Lindsay smiles. Daniel gets a very sincere look. Almost lecturing Lindsay.

DANIEL (CONT'D)
He's really a great guy.

(CONTINUED)

7.

CONTINUED:

LINDSAY
Yeah, I know.

Lindsay nods, then goes back to her book. Daniel just stares at her, thinking. He gets an odd smile.

After a beat, Lindsay feels Daniel staring and looks over again. He nods at her.

DANIEL
Nick's a stud, you know. He may not seem like it, but he is.

MS. YEATS
Mr. Desario, don't you have something to do?

DANIEL
Yeah, but I can't do it here.

Daniel makes a kissy face at the teacher. Some students laugh as Daniel throws Lindsay a big "I'm pretty funny, ain't I?" look. Lindsay smiles, then looks away, a little confused.

CUT TO:

INT. BIOLOGY CLASS - DAY

Class is about to begin. Students sit at lab tables, talking and goofing off. Sam and Bill are at the first table. Neal is at the table behind them. Cindy's sitting a couple of tables away.

GORDON CRISP, a stinky, overweight kid, enters. Students part like the Red Sea as he walks by. He passes Sam, Bill and Neal. They hold their breath. Neal leans up.

NEAL
Oh, man. Gordon reeks. Do you think he ever takes a shower?

SAM
Maybe he takes baths instead. My mom says they don't really get you clean.

BILL
Yeah. You just sit in your own filth.

Gordon sits down. The PRISSY GIRL next to him gets up and moves. The teacher, MR. LACOVARA, shouts over the noise.

(CONTINUED)

CONTINUED:

MR. LACOVARA
All right, settle down. We've got a lot to do today. We're going to be dissecting kittens.

Suddenly, the whole class goes silent. Repulsion on everyone's faces. Mr. Lacovara chuckles.

MR. LACOVARA (CONT'D)
Just trying to get your attention.
(the class GROANS)
But you will be getting your lab partners today.

Sam hears this and perks up. Mr. Lacovara walks into the lab table next to Sam and Bill.

MR. LACOVARA (CONT'D)
McKenna, you'll be partnered with Boyle.

SAM
(quietly to Bill)
I hope I get to be partners with Cindy.

BILL
What about me?

SAM
(whispers)
Please let it be Cindy.

Sam crosses his fingers. Mr. Lacovara comes up to Sam and Bill's table. He consults his list.

MR. LACOVARA
All right, Weir. Your lab partner will be... Gordon Crisp.

Sam's face falls. A few students SNICKER. Sam looks over at Gordon who holds up his hand, revealing a huge sweat stain under his arm. Mr. Lacovara turns to Bill.

MR. LACOVARA (CONT'D)
Bill, you'll be partnered with...
(scans list)
...Cindy Sanders.

Sam's eyes gc wide. He turns to Bill in disbelief. Bill stands up and gathers his books.

(CONTINUED)

CONTINUED: (2)

BILL
Oh, how interesting. Me and Cindy. You and Gordon. Oh, well, I guess I'd better go sit next to my lab partner.

Sam watches, upset, as Bill heads for Cindy's table. Bill approaches her, smiling.

NEAL
(to Sam)
Well, there goes Cindy's grade point average.

BILL
Excuse me, madam. Is this seat taken?

Bill laughs at his joke and sits down. He throws a cocky look to Sam, then reaches behind Cindy and pretends to grab her ass.

OFF Sam, miserable.

CUT TO:

INT. FRONT OFFICE/MR. ROSSO'S OFFICE - DAY

Lindsay is sitting in the front office waiting chairs, looking confused. Mr. Rosso comes out of his hallway.

MR. ROSSO
Come on back, Lindsay.

Lindsay gets up and follows him toward his office.

LINDSAY
Is anything wrong?

MR. ROSSO
No. I'm just checking in on my good friend Lindsay Weir. Anything wrong with that?

LINDSAY
(wary)
I guess not.

MR. ROSSO
So, how's everything going? Classes keeping you interested?

LINDSAY
Yeah, sure.

(CONTINUED)

CONTINUED:

They enter Mr. Rosso's office. He closes the door. Lindsay sits in the chair across from him.

MR. ROSSO
Hey, have you checked out the new Rush album? I've gotta say, it rocks pretty heavily. And that's coming from a guy who's seen Hendrix live.

LINDSAY
(in pain)
Yeah, I heard it's good.

Rosso sits behind his desk. Takes a beat.

MR. ROSSO
So... I understand you and Nick Andopolis are getting pretty tight. How's that going?

Lindsay immediately knows what this whole meeting is about. She gets defensive.

LINDSAY
Mr. Rosso, Nick and I are just friends. That's all.

MR. ROSSO
Hey, no need to explain anything to me. I got it on in a van at Woodstock, so I'm not judging anybody.

Lindsay makes a face. She can't deal with the thought of Rosso "getting it on."

MR. ROSSO (CONT'D)
I just want to make sure that you know what you're getting yourself into. I mean, when you're a teenager, your emotions are running high and it's easy to get confused.

Mr. Rosso takes a breath, then opens his desk drawer. He pulls out a pamphlet that seems to be deliberately hidden.

MR. ROSSO (CONT'D)
I want you to have this.

He holds the pamphlet out to Lindsay. It reads "DATING, SEX AND YOU." Lindsay looks like she wants to die.

(CONTINUED)

CONTINUED: (2)

LINDSAY
...oh my God.

MR. ROSSO
Don't let the pamphlet freak you out. There's some good stuff in there. It's just that you've gotta be careful these days.

LINDSAY
(desperate to get him to stop)
I know, I know.

MR. ROSSO
Do you?
(then, soberly)
I thought I did, too. Until one night I was checking out this discotheque. The one in the bowling alley on 15 mile? I met this girl who seemed really nice, we danced a bit, I kissed her, one thing led to another..and now I get sores on my lip once a month.
(a deep breath)
I have herpes. It doesn't hurt that much, but believe me, you don't want it.

Lindsay just stares at him, horrified.

LINDSAY
Can I go? Please?

MR. ROSSO
Did I just blow your mind?

LINDSAY
No, no. I just don't want to be late for lunch.

MR. ROSSO
Okay. Just use your head, Linds. That's all I ask.

LINDSAY
You got it.

(CONTINUED)

CONTINUED: (3)

Mr. Rosso nods and gives her a supportive smile. Lindsay takes the pamphlet and heads out, completely unnerved.

CUT TO:

INT. CAFETERIA - DAY

Sam, Neal and Bill are having lunch. Sam stares at an untouched sandwich in front of him. He looks nauseous.

NEAL
How come you're not eating?

SAM
This tuna salad smells like Gordon.

BILL
You know, Cindy smells too...
(grins)
...like flowers.

NEAL
(laughs; then)
You know what's ironic, Sam? In one class, Bill spent more time with Cindy than you have in your entire life.

SAM
Did she say anything about me?

BILL
I couldn't tell you. Her tongue was in my ear.

SAM
Shut up!

Sam punches Bill on the arm.

BILL
Oww!
(rubbing his arm)
Now I'll have to get Cindy to kiss it and make it better.

Bill and Neal laugh. Sam doesn't. Just then, Cindy approaches their table. Sam tries to be cool.

SAM
Hey, Cindy.

(CONTINUED)

CONTINUED:

CINDY
Oh, hi Sam. Hey, Nate.

NEAL
Uh, it's Neal.

Cindy doesn't hear him. She turns to Bill.

CINDY
So Bill, we should get started on our lab assignment. I've got cheerleading practice at three and French club at three forty-five, but can you come over at four-thirty?

BILL
To your house?

Cindy nods. Bill glances at Sam, then smiles a Cindy.

BILL (CONT'D)
I think I can squeeze you in.

CINDY
Great, I'll see you then. Bye, Sam.

Cindy takes off. Sam and Neal exchange a look of disbelief. Bill goes back to his lunch, cocky.

BILL
Should I splash on some Hi Karate or Old Spice?

CUT TO:

INT. HALLWAY - DAY

Students are milling about, killing time between classes. We find Daniel, Kim, Nick and Lindsay walking down the hall.

DANIEL
(seeing a banner)
Hey, check it out. Donkey Basketball game's next week. I love those things.

LINDSAY
I think they're mean.

KIM
Oh, yeah, like donkeys really give.

(CONTINUED)

14.

CONTINUED:

LINDSAY
How'd you like some big fat teacher sitting on your back and making you run around on a slippery gym floor?

DANIEL
(to Kim)
Yeah, how did your date with Fredricks go?

Kim jumps at Daniel and starts punching him playfully. Nick and Lindsay are left alone for the moment. The BELL RINGS.

NICK
So, I was wondering if you wanted to hang out Friday night.

LINDSAY
Oh. Sure.

NICK
Cool.

LINDSAY
Have you seen "The Elephant Man?"

Nick looks around, confused.

LINDSAY
The movie.

NICK
Oh, the one about the deformed guy? No, why?

LINDSAY
'Cause I was thinking maybe we could go see it.

Mr. Kowchevski comes down the hall.

MR. KOWCHEVSKI
The bell has rung, people. Stop dilly-dallying and get to class.
(to Daniel and Kim)
Hey, Lord and Lady Skips-a-lot. Let's go.

Daniel makes a face behind his back, then heads off to class with Kim. Lindsay's starting to get antsy.

(CONTINUED)

15.

CONTINUED: (2)

NICK
Well, actually, I was thinking you could come over to my house. My parents are going out for the night and my brothers aren't around, so we can just, I don't know... hang out.

Lindsay's caught off-guard. Mr. Kowchevski heads toward them.

MR. KOWCHEVSKI
(clapping)
I'm not joking people.

Lindsay looks at Mr. Kowchevski, then turns back to Nick, who's looking at her expectantly.

NICK
So, Friday night? My house?

LINDSAY
Oh... um, okay.

NICK
Cool.

Mr. Kowchevski walks right up to Nick and Lindsay.

MR. KOWCHEVSKI
Hey, Romeo and Juliet, get a move on. Last one to class, first one on welfare.

As Lindsay turns and heads off to class, the second BELL RINGS. And OFF Lindsay's worried expression...

FADE OUT.

END OF ACT ONE

ACT TWO

FADE IN:

INT. SAM'S BEDROOM - DAY

Sam enters, carrying his books. He looks less than enthusiastic. REVEAL Gordon, coming in behind him. Gordon looks around.

GORDON
I like your room, Sam.

(CONTINUED)

CONTINUED:

SAM
Thanks.

Gordon sees Sam's Star Wars bedspread. He lights up.

GORDON
Whoa. Cool bed!

Before Sam can stop him, Gordon heads for Sam's bed and plops down on it. Sam cringes.

GORDON (CONT'D)
May the force be with you.

Sam forces a smile. He carefully sits on the other end of the bed. Gordon opens his notebook.

GORDON (CONT'D)
Okay, let's see. I already started the plant cell diagram. It's the animal cell that's tricky.

SAM
I know. I couldn't tell what was going on under that microscope.

GORDON
(laughs)
Can I borrow your pencil?

SAM
Uh... sure...

Sam hands Gordon his PENCIL. Gordon chews on the pencil, thinking. Then he picks his ear with it. He finally makes some notes and hands the pencil back to Sam.

GORDON
Here you go. Thanks.

Sam stares at his pencil, disgusted. He looks like he's about to vomit.

GORDON (CONT'D)
What's the matter, Sam?

SAM
(lying badly)
Nothing.

Gordon studies Sam.

(CONTINUED)

CONTINUED: (2)

GORDON
I know what's bugging you. You didn't want to be my lab partner.

Sam averts his eyes, racked with guilt.

SAM
Well...

GORDON
You wanted to be with Cindy Sanders.

Sam looks up, relieved.

SAM
(too eagerly)
Yeah, how did you know?

GORDON
It's obvious you like her.

SAM
(suddenly worried)
It is? Do you think she likes me?

GORDON
I don't know. Cheerleaders are hard to read that way.

SAM
Oh.

GORDON
But you and Cindy would make a good couple. I mean, she's really popular and everything, but she needs someone like you. I think you'd be good for her.

SAM
Really?

Gordon nods. Sam considers this, pleased. He smiles at Gordon, seeing him in a bit of a new light.

CUT TO:

INT. CINDY'S BEDROOM - DAY

PAN ACROSS a traditional girl's room. Canopy bed, stuffed animals. Everything's pink and white and incredibly neat.

(CONTINUED)

CONTINUED:

We FIND Bill, sitting on a pink beanbag, uncomfortable. He picks up a BOOK from Cindy's nightstand.

ANGLE ON: The book is "Miss Piggy's Guide to Life."

Bill tosses the book away, weirded out. Just then, Cindy enters, carrying a tray of food.

CINDY
I'm so bad. I can't do homework without having a snack.

Cindy puts down the tray, revealing carrot sticks and sliced apples. Bill is disappointed.

BILL
Do you have any chips or cookies?

CINDY
No, sorry. My parents don't let us eat junk food.

Cindy sits down on a vinyl-covered chair and starts scarfing carrot sticks. Bill looks at his watch.

BILL
Do you think we could turn on the TV? "Welcome Back Kotter" is on.

He does the obnoxious, deep-throated Horshack laugh. Cindy looks at him strangely.

CINDY
Are you okay?

BILL
That's Horshack. From the show.

CINDY
Oh. I've never seen it before.

BILL
(horrified)
Really?

CINDY
I don't really watch TV. Except for "The Muppet Show."
(beat)
Oh, I'm sorry. I've been hogging these.

(CONTINUED)

CONTINUED: (2)

Cindy stops eating and holds out the plate of carrot sticks. Bill hesitantly takes one and tries it. He looks like he's chewing a piece of cardboard.

CINDY (CONT'D)
Did you want something to drink?

BILL
(mouth full)
Mm-hm.

CINDY
I'll get some lemonade.

As Cindy starts to get up from her vinyl chair, we HEAR a short, distinct FARTING NOISE. Cindy looks at Bill, embarrassed.

CINDY (CONT'D)
This stupid chair... it always does that. I'll be right back.

Cindy leaves the room. Bill looks horrified. He waits a few seconds, then cautiously approaches Cindy's chair.

He sits down and tries to recreate the farting noise, using several different positions and methods of standing up. But no matter what he does, he just can't make that noise.

Bill stares after Cindy in disbelief, trying to process this.

CUT TO:

INT. SAM'S BEDROOM - DAY

Sam and Gordon are still hanging out. Gordon's lecturing to an interested Sam.

GORDON
This is what you should do. Find out her schedule and memorize it. That way you can bump into her and say hi. Compliment her hair. Then the next time you see her, go, "Hey, did you change your hair?" Pretty soon you'll have tons of stuff to talk about.

SAM
Good idea...

(CONTINUED)

CONTINUED:

GORDON
And join all her after-school clubs. "A," you'll get to hang out with her more. "B," you'll learn more about her interests, so you can pretend they're your interests, too.

SAM
That makes sense.

GORDON
And "C"-- very important-- you can make sure she's not falling in love with some other guy. Like your friend Bill.

Sam looks up, worried.

SAM
You think Cindy's gonna fall in love with Bill?

GORDON
(shrugs)
I don't know. Being lab partners is like getting stranded on a desert island. You never know what might happen.

Sam absorbs this, deeply concerned.

CUT TO:

INT. MCKINLEY HIGH SCHOOL - UNDER THE STAIRS - DAY

Nick and Daniel are hanging out under the stairwell, cutting class.

NICK
Hey, I heard Kim got an A on her World Civ test.

Daniel's confused. Nick breaks out into a shit-eating grin.

NICK (CONT'D)
Oh, I'm sorry. That was my girlfriend.

DANIEL
(sarcastic)
That's really funny.

(CONTINUED)

CONTINUED:

NICK
Did you know Lindsay got detention for saying the "F" word to her gym teacher?
(beat)
Oh, wait. That was your girlfriend.

DANIEL
You know what? I heard Kim punched you in the chest, really hard.
(beat)
Oh, whoops. That was me.

Daniel slugs Nick in the chest. Nick coughs, the wind knocked out of him, then smiles and points at Daniel like, "Good burn."

CUT TO:

INT. GIRLS' BATHROOM - DAY

Kim and KAREN are butting out their cigarettes in the sink. The bathroom is smoky.

KIM
C'mon, let's go hit the record store.

They head for the door, just as Lindsay enters.

KIM (CONT'D)
(to Karen)
I'll meet you in the parking lot.

Karen looks at Lindsay coldly and exits. Kim acts friendly.

KIM (CONT'D)
Hey, I just wanted to tell you, I think it's really cool that you and Nick are going out. He's...

LINDSAY
A really great guy?

KIM
Exactly. Nick's a sweetheart. He's not like Daniel. Daniel's a total dog. You know, two months after we started going out, me and my mom went up north for a week. I came back and found out Daniel was sleeping with my next-door neighbor the whole time.

(CONTINUED)

22.

CONTINUED:

LINDSAY
And you stayed with him?

KIM
Yeah, I know. But he's just so hot. And all guys are like that. They want to have sex all the time.

LINDSAY
(nervous)
Like, how often?

KIM
You have no idea. And I thought I was horny.
(then, casual)
I gotta go to the can.

And Kim disappears into a stall, leaving Lindsay completely freaked.

CUT TO:

INT. HALLWAY - DAY

Sam, Neal and Bill are walking to class.

BILL
I'm telling you, she's abnormal. She eats carrot sticks, she likes Miss Piggy...

SAM
(defensive)
Big deal. The Muppets are cool.

BILL
The Swedish Chef is kinda cool. Miss Piggy is lame.

NEAL
Professor Honeydew is hysterical.

SAM
Cindy is not abnormal.

BILL
Oh, yeah? Well, guess what? She cut the cheese.

NEAL
Oh my God.

(CONTINUED)

CONTINUED:

SAM
That's not funny.

BILL
I swear. I heard it. She blamed it on the chair, but... she cut the cheese.

NEAL
Did it smell?

BILL
No, but it was a loud one.

SAM
Some chairs do make weird sounds, you know. What kind of chair was it?

BILL
I don't know. Vinyl.

SAM
Well, vinyl chairs always squeak.

BILL
It wasn't a squeak. It was the sound of cheese being cut.

Bill and Neal crack up. Sam stops walking, angry.

SAM
I think you're making all this stuff up so I'll stop liking her-- 'cause you like her now.

BILL
What?

Just then, they HEAR:

CINDY (O.S.)
Bill!

They turn to see Cindy approaching. Sam's face turns red with embarrassment, but Cindy is oblivious.

CINDY (CONT'D)
Hey guys, what's up?

(CONTINUED)

CONTINUED: (2)

SAM
Hey, Cindy. You, um, changed your hair.

Cindy touches her hair self-consciously.

CINDY
It just looks really flat today. I didn't have time to wash it this morning 'cause my alarm clock didn't go off and I got up late.
(to Bill)
Oh, I wanted to tell you, I've got a yearbook meeting after school. But we can work on our lab assignment afterwards.

Sam takes this in, his mind racing. Bill throws a look at Sam, then lays it on thick.

BILL
I can't wait. Maybe this time you can come over to my house.

CINDY
Okay. Oh, and by the way, I finally saw "Welcome Back Kotter." You're right -- Mr. Woodman is so funny.

BILL
Yeah. I'm telling you. He's totally underrated.

Cindy and Bill head off. Neal and Sam watch after them. Neal gives Sam a pat on the back.

NEAL
Well, all's fair in love and war.

Neal takes off. Sam stares after Bill and Cindy, upset.

CUT TO:

INT. CLASSROOM - DAY

Students are quietly taking a test. Lindsay finishes early. She goes up to MR. SAMPSON'S desk and hands in her test.

(CONTINUED)

25.

CONTINUED:

MR. SAMPSON
Lindsay, it's a test, not a race. But if it were a race, Millie already beat you.

Mr. Sampson smiles, but Lindsay is too preoccupied to respond. On her way back to her seat, she walks past Millie, who is now leisurely reading "The Dog Days of Arthur Cane."

Lindsay hesitates, then sits down at the desk behind Millie. She leans forward like she's in a confessional.

LINDSAY
(quietly)
Millie. I need to talk to you.

MILLIE
Why?

LINDSAY
I just do.

Millie puts down her book but keeps facing forward as Lindsay talks over her shoulder with quiet desperation.

MILLIE
Yes?

Lindsay searches for the right words. Then...

LINDSAY
Remember how we used to love Leif Garrett and we'd take out my Dynamite magazines and kiss his picture?

MILLIE
Yeah, and then we went to see him at the State Fair and got all the way to the front row and it turned out to be Jack Albertson from "Chico and the Man"?

LINDSAY
(remembering)
Oh, yeah... That sucked.

MILLIE
It wasn't so bad. He was funny.

(CONTINUED)

CONTINUED: (2)

LINDSAY
Millie, I'm just saying... we always dreamed of having a boyfriend. And I think I finally have one. And I think he wants to have sex.

MILLIE
You can't have sex with Nick. Once you do, you'll never be the same again.
(beat)
Plus, no one'll want to marry you. Why should they buy the cow when they can get the milk for free?

Lindsay leans back, considering this. quietly goes back to her seat. Then she gets up and quitely goes back to her seat.

INT. CAFETERIA - DAY

The yearbook staff meeting. MR. MAINZER, the photography teacher, talks to several students, including Cindy. Possible YEARBOOK THEMES are listed on a chalkboard: "The '50s," "World Peace," "The Environment," "Space Age."

MR. MAINZER
Some of you will be happy to see that after several complaints, I eliminated "Disco Days" from the running.

A few Students APPLAUD. As the meeting continues, Sam enters. He spots Cindy and casually sits near her. Cindy is surprised to see him.

SAM
Hey, Cindy.

CINDY
I didn't know you were on yearbook. Did you just join?

SAM
Um, yeah... I'm trying to get more involved in after-school activities.

CINDY
Oh, that's cool.

(CONTINUED)

27.

CONTINUED:

Cindy turns her attention back to Mr. Mainzer. Sam smiles to himself. He's making progress.

MR. MAINZER
Any more article ideas?

Cindy raises her hand.

MR. MAINZER (CONT'D)
Cindy?

CINDY
It's called "Diary of a McKinley Student." It describes a student's high school experience. I started it, if you want to see.

MR. MAINZER
Go ahead, read it.

Cindy pulls out a typed poem. Stands. Reads to the class.

CINDY
"September 3rd, 1980. Freshman year. Dear Diary. High school. So cavernous, cold, uninviting. Starting over, no identity. Everyone looking. Everyone judging. Their eyes pierce my soul."

ANGLE ON: Various students staring at Cindy, confused and weirded out.

ANGLE ON: Sam gazing at Cindy in awe, amazed by how deep she is. He's falling more in love with her with every word.

CINDY (CONT'D)
"Aimless youth. All trapped together, but no one connecting. Education or isolation? Class dismissed."

Cindy puts down her paper, waiting for approval. Sam APPLAUDS loudly. The rest of the class is silent.

MR. MAINZER
O-kay. Thank you, Sylvia Plath. It's a little too dark. We want to sell yearbooks, not tell the truth.

The class laughs. Cindy blushes and sits.

(CONTINUED)

CONTINUED: (2)

CINDY
(hurt but hiding it)
Oh... okay. It was just an idea.

MR. MAINZER
(moving on)
All right, photography
department...

Sam looks at Cindy, feeling bad for her.

CUT TO:

INT. WEIR HOUSE - DAY

Lindsay comes in the front door, looking preoccupied.

JEAN (O.C.)
(singsongy)
Lind-say. I've got something to
show you.

Confused, Lindsay heads into the kitchen.

CUT TO:

INT. WEIR KITCHEN - CONTINUOUS

Lindsay enters the kitchen to find Jean with a goofy smile on her face.

LINDSAY
What's up?

JEAN
Somebody likes you. That's what's
up.

Jean motions her head toward the kitchen counter.

LINDSAY'S POV: A single red ROSE lays on the counter. A card in a small envelope is attached by a red ribbon.

Lindsay stares at the rose, surprised. Jean flutters over to her, excited and girly.

JEAN (CONT'D)
You didn't tell me you had a
boyfriend. So, what's his name?
What's he like? I want to know
everything.

(CONTINUED)

CONTINUED:

LINDSAY
He's just a friend.

JEAN
A "friend"? Do I know him?

LINDSAY
Mom...

Lindsay clearly does not want to talk about this.

JEAN
Well, open the card.

Lindsay takes the rose and heads out of the kitchen. Jean watches her go, dying of curiosity.

INT. LINDSAY'S BEDROOM - MOMENTS LATER

Lindsay enters her room, shuts the door and sits on the bed. She pulls the card out of its little envelope.

CU - INSERT The note says, "CAN'T WATE TILL TOMOROW NITE -- NICK." The chicken-scratch handwriting is barely legible.

LINDSAY
W-A-T-E?

Lindsay stares at the misspelled note, then looks up, turned off and full of dread.

CUT TO:

INT. CAFETERIA - DAY

The yearbook meeting is still in progress.

MR. MAINZER
The next thing we need to talk about is ad sales.
(the Students GROAN)
I know, it's no fun, it's not creative... But if we don't sell the rest of this ad space by tomorrow, we won't have enough money for printing.

He starts passing out lists.

MR. MAINZER (CONT'D)
Here's a list of the local merchants we haven't hit yet.

(CONTINUED)

30.

CONTINUED:

Sam raises his hand, eager to be useful.

SAM
My dad owns A-1 Sporting Goods.

Mr. Mainzer studies Sam, clearly not recognizing him. Hands him a list anyway.

MR. MAINZER
Great, you can start with your dad's store. Why don't you pair up with Cindy?

SAM
Sure.

MR. MAINZER
Greg, you pair up with Karen...

Sam is stoked. Cindy turns to Sam, lamenting.

CINDY
Can you believe we have to sell ads?

SAM
(trying to be cool)
Yeah, that really sucks.

Sam turns away, hiding a huge smile. He couldn't be happier.

FADE OUT.

END OF ACT TWO

ACT THREE

FADE IN:

EXT. STREET - DAY

Sam and Cindy are walking down a neighborhood street. Sam is trying his best to seem relaxed.

SAM
My dad's store is right up the next block.

CINDY
Oh, yeah? Great.

Sam takes a moment to muster his courage. Then...

(CONTINUED)

CONTINUED:

SAM
I liked what you wrote for the yearbook. It was cool. Mr. Mainzer doesn't know what he's talking about.

CINDY
(flattered)
Thanks.

SAM
You're right. Being a freshman sucks.

CINDY
The worst part is everyone pigeonholes you and expects you to act a certain way. Like if you're a cheerleader, you have to be in a good mood like all the time.

SAM
That must be tough.

CINDY
It's like, I'm sorry, but there are just some days when I feel a little cranky. Like today. I just got my period. So what? Deal with it.

Sam's freaked out. He desperately tries to change the topic.

SAM
So how's your lab assignment going?

CINDY
Pretty good.

SAM
Too bad you have to be partners with Bill. He's really lazy. I bet he's making you do all the work.

CINDY
Not really.

SAM
Oh, then you'd better be careful. 'Cause he's not too smart. Make sure you double-check his spelling.

(CONTINUED)

CONTINUED: (2)

CINDY
(confused)
I thought Bill was your friend.

Sam, caught, quickly tries to backtrack.

SAM
He is. We just goof on each other a lot.

CUT TO:

INT. NICK'S BASEMENT - DAY

Nick is practicing his drums. He sounds terrible, but he's totally into it. He stops when he sees Lindsay coming down the stairs.

NICK
(surprised)
Hey, Lindsay.

LINDSAY
Hi. I rang the doorbell, but I heard you drumming so I just came down.

Nick holds up his drumsticks.

NICK
Sorry, I was jamming.

LINDSAY
That's okay.

Nick breaks into a big smile. He gets up and approaches Lindsay.

NICK
So, I take it you liked the rose?

LINDSAY
Um, yeah. It was nice.

NICK
You're welcome.

Nick starts to move in for a kiss. Lindsay panics.

LINDSAY
(quickly)
Did you get another drum?

(CONTINUED)

CONTINUED:

NICK
Uh, no.

ANGLE ON: Nick's 29-piece drum kit. There's no way she could possibly tell if there was a new drum.

Lindsay backs away from Nick and sits down behind the drums.

NICK (CONT'D)
You look cute behind my drums.

Nick smiles and starts to move toward her. Lindsay grabs the drumsticks and starts banging on the drums wildly. She finally stops.

LINDSAY
Sorry. I just felt the urge.

NICK
No, that was pretty good. You're a natural.

Lindsay looks pained as Nick reaches over and holds her hand. She struggles for a moment, figuring out how to put this.

LINDSAY
Nick... I know that for guys, sex is no big deal. And for some girls, it's no big deal. And maybe I'm like a prude, but... I'm just not ready to move this fast. I mean, all we've done is kiss. You don't go from algebra to calculus in one week--

NICK
(interrupting her)
Lindsay, Lindsay-- I'm not even thinking about sex.

LINDSAY
You're not?

NICK
That's not what our relationship is about.

Lindsay exhales and tosses the drumsticks aside, relieved.

(CONTINUED)

CONTINUED: (2)

LINDSAY
I am so glad to hear you say that. 'Cause you know, everybody's just assuming things.

NICK
(rolls his eyes)
Who? Daniel and Kim?

LINDSAY
Well, yeah.

NICK
Don't listen to those boneheads. Just 'cause they hump every five minutes.

Lindsay laughs. Nick looks at Lindsay, sincere.

NICK (CONT'D)
Me and my last girlfriend Heidi rushed into sex and it ruined everything. Which is fine, 'cause if I was still with her, I wouldn't have met you.

Lindsay smiles.

NICK (CONT'D)
So, are we cool?

LINDSAY
Yeah. Definitely.

Lindsay and Nick share a relieved smile. A huge weight has been lifted.

CUT TO:

INT. HAROLD WEIR'S STORE - DAY

A small sporting goods store. It's pretty busy. HAROLD finishes ringing up a sale just as Sam and Cindy enter. Harold's in total work mode.

HAROLD
Sam! I thought you were going to help me out today.

SAM
Oh, uh... I had a yearbook meeting.

(CONTINUED)

CONTINUED:

HAROLD
Yearbook? When the heck did you join that?

SAM
Uh, today. This is my friend, Cindy.

CINDY
Nice to meet you.

HAROLD
Hello. Sam, you've got to put in your hours. I'm trying to teach you a work ethic here. If you want to buy those crazy Micronaut things, you've got to earn the money for them.
(seeing something)
Oh, for cryin' out loud...

Harold walks out into the store to pick up a football that's fallen on the floor.

CINDY
You have a really nice store, Mr. Weir.

Harold doesn't hear as Sam and Cindy follow him.

SAM
Hey, Dad, Cindy and I, um... we have to sell these yearbook ads. An eighth of a page is twenty-five dollars. Do you think you could buy one?

HAROLD
That's highway robbery. I could buy a full page in the Sunday paper for a hundred.

SAM
Dad. It's really important for Cindy and me to sell these.

Sam gives Harold a meaningful look. Harold looks at Sam, then Cindy, finally getting it. He winks at Sam.

HAROLD
Tell you what. Give me a full page.

(CONTINUED)

36.

CONTINUED: (2)

CINDY
Wow. Thanks, Mr. Weir.

HAROLD
No problem. You know, Sam's the
best salesman I've got.

CINDY
Really?

Cindy smiles at Sam, impressed. Behind her back, Harold gives Sam the thumbs-up. As Harold takes cash out of the register, Cindy confers with Sam.

CINDY (CONT'D)
Okay, we've got sixteen more ads.
We should try the big stores first,
since they'll probably buy more
space.

SAM
The small stores close earlier,
though.

HAROLD
You're squandering your manpower.
You should split up and take
separate routes so you can cover
more ground.

Sam glares at Harold. Realizing his mistake, Harold tries to backtrack.

HAROLD (CONT'D)
But then again, some of the
greatest salesmen worked in teams.

SAM
Yeah, maybe we should stick
together.

CINDY
But we'll both finish sooner if we
split up, don't you think?

SAM
(defeated)
I guess.

Sam shoots a "thanks a lot" look at Harold. Harold makes an apologetic face.

(CONTINUED)

CONTINUED: (3)

SAM (CONT'D)
(angry)
See ya, Dad.

CUT TO:

INT. AUTO REPAIR SHOP - DAY

Cindy walks past several MECHANICS working on cars. She approaches the OWNER, a balding man in his 60's.

CINDY
Excuse me, sir. I know you're busy, but if I could just have a minute...

OWNER
(immediately charmed)
What can I do for you?

CINDY
I'm selling ad space in my yearbook...

OWNER
Sign me up.

Cindy smiles, triumphant. Easy as pie.

CUT TO:

INT. FUNERAL HOME - DAY

Sam is nervously giving his sales pitch. He keeps sneaking terrified glances at something off-screen.

SAM
I go to McKinley... it's a high school... and we have this yearbook with advertisements in the back...

PULL BACK to reveal he's standing next to an open coffin. Sam keeps looking inside (at a dead guy?). He's talking to a FUNERAL DIRECTOR, who sighs impatiently.

SAM (CONT'D)
Anyway, I was wondering if maybe you wanted to buy an ad...

Sam trails off, anxious.

(CONTINUED)

CONTINUED:

FUNERAL DIRECTOR
Have you sold any ads to other funeral homes?

SAM
No.

FUNERAL DIRECTOR
That's because this is the only funeral home in town. You know what that means? It means I don't need advertising.

SAM
(quickly)
Okay, bye.

Sam immediately bolts out.

CUT TO:

INT. WEIR DINING ROOM - DUSK

Harold, Jean and Lindsay are having dinner. Jean keeps glancing at Lindsay. The curiosity is killing her.

HAROLD
So, I saw Sam's yearbook partner at the store today. Quite a cute little number.

LINDSAY
(put off)
God, Dad.

HAROLD
What? What's wrong with that? She's cute. Am I supposed to call her Ms. or something?

Lindsay rolls her eyes. Jean smiles at Lindsay.

JEAN
See, Lindsay? Sam's not afraid to show off his girlfriend.

LINDSAY
Mom...

Lindsay shoots Jean a pre-emptive look. Jean looks at Harold, a big goofy grin on her face.

(CONTINUED)

CONTINUED:

HAROLD
What's eating you?

JEAN
(bursts)
Lindsay's got a boyfriend!

LINDSAY
Oh my God...

HAROLD
What? Who?

JEAN
Someone sent her a red rose.
(giggly; to Lindsay)
He must be quite a Romeo.

HAROLD
I'll say he is. Who the hell is this joker?

LINDSAY
He's just a friend.

HAROLD
Nobody who's "just a friend" sends a single red rose. I know all about single red roses. I sent one to your mother and I know when and why I sent it.

JEAN
Oh, Harold.
(trying to coax Lindsay)
You can tell us who it is, honey. We won't make a big deal out of it.

LINDSAY
Okay, okay. It's Nick.

HAROLD
(alarmed)
Nick? Not another one of those burn-outs! Did he make you cheat, too?

LINDSAY
No!

(CONTINUED)

CONTINUED: (2)

HAROLD
Look, I don't know what happened between you and this Nick character but I'm telling you right now, I don't want you dating any of that group, you hear me?

JEAN
(trying to remember)
Nick. Is he the one who ate all my fruit roll-ups?

LINDSAY
You said he could have them.

HAROLD
You'd better know right now, your mother and I are not going to take care of some wedlock baby while you're off gallivanting at college.

LINDSAY
Dad!

HAROLD
I'm warning you, Lindsay. I absolutely forbid you from dating this boy. The last thing I want is you turning into some tramp like that Kim Kelly.

Lindsay glares at Harold. Without a word, she slowly puts down her fork, gets up and walks out. Harold and Jean exchange a look.

HAROLD (CONT'D)
At least she didn't yell.

They both get up and follow after Lindsay.

CUT TO:

INT. WEIR LIVING ROOM - CONTINUOUS

Lindsay's sitting on the couch, arms folded, stewing as she watches TV. Harold and Jean come in, shut off the TV, and sit down on both sides of her.

HAROLD
You don't know what it's like to have a daughter and want to protect her. I mean, you will someday.
(MORE)

(CONTINUED)

CONTINUED:

HAROLD (CONT'D)
But I'd like that day to be a long time from now.

JEAN
We just want to make sure this boy respects you. Not all of them do.

HAROLD
Trust me, I know what they're like. I was one of them.

JEAN
He was.

Lindsay gets a skeptical look on her face.

HAROLD
I know it's hard to believe, but I did some stupid things when I was young.

JEAN
(to Harold)
Tell her about Korea.

HAROLD
(a deep breath, then)
Once I had a weekend pass into Seoul. I went to this bar, had a few too many...then I followed a couple of my buddies to the red light district...

Harold trails off, trying to find the right words.

JEAN
His first time wasn't special and he's always regretted it.

HAROLD
That was the worst five dollars I've ever spent.
(meaningful)
And I wish I could get that five dollars back.

JEAN
(quiet, serious)
Lindsay, what your father' s trying to say is... your virginity is a gift.

Lindsay's truly in pain. She can't take anymore.

(CONTINUED)

CONTINUED: (2)

LINDSAY
Oh my God. Please stop.
(then, calm)
Nick and I are not going to have sex. We've already talked about it and decided we're not ready.

Harold and Jean take this in, shocked.

HAROLD
Good Lord. You've talked about it?

LINDSAY
Yes. And Nick was the one who said that our relationship isn't about sex.

Harold makes a face.

HAROLD
And you bought that?

LINDSAY
It's true!

HAROLD
I hope it is.

Harold and Jean exchange a concerned look. Jean gives Lindsay a tentative pat on the arm. Lindsay forces a smile.

CUT TO:

EXT. NEIGHBORHOOD STREET - DUSK

Sam is walking home, exhausted, the old yearbook tucked under his arm. He suddenly realizes he's outside Bill's house and peers up at the window.

SAM'S POV: Bill and Cindy are studying in Bill's room. Bill keeps tapping Cindy's head with a pencil, then acts innocent when she look up. She laughs hysterically.

ANGLE ON: Sam watching them from the curb, completely depressed.

FADE OUT.

END OF ACT THREE

ACT FOUR

FADE IN:

INT. MCKINLEY HIGH SCHOOL HALLWAY - DAY

Daniel, Kim, Nick and Lindsay are walking down the hall. Kim is digging in her purse, irritated.

KIM
Where are my smokes?
(accusing Daniel)
Did you take 'em?

Daniel shakes his head, then rolls his eyes to Nick and Lindsay like, "What an addict."

DANIEL
Hey, we're all going to Dez's tonight. You coming?

NICK
Nah. Linds and I are hanging out.

DANIEL
(nodding smiling)
All right. Make it happen.

NICK
Shut up, man.

Nick and Lindsay share a knowing look.

KIM
(teasing)
Tonight's the night, huh?

DANIEL
For Kim, every night's the night.

Kim shoves Daniel. They both head off, laughing. Nick and Lindsay look at each other, shy and excited.

NICK
So, I'm really psyched about tonight.

LINDSAY
Yeah. Me, too.

NICK
You sure it's okay? I mean, you coming over to my house? 'Cause if you feel weird about it...

(CONTINUED)

CONTINUED:

LINDSAY
(completely genuine)
No, not at all.

NICK
Okay. Cool.

Lindsay stops walking, pulls Nick to her and kisses him on the mouth. It's a great kiss, their best one yet. Nick is ecstatic. We PAN OVER to

SAM AND NEAL

walking to class. Sam looks tired and upset. He's in the middle of a huge yawn.

NEAL
You keep yawning like that, you're gonna dislocate your jaw.

Bill catches up to them.

BILL
Hey, guys, wait up.

Sam looks at Bill coldly, then keeps walking. Bill follows.

BILL (CONT'D)
Sam, you know what Cindy said last night?

SAM
(erupts)
What? That she's in love with you 'cause you're so smart and funny and you don't care that she cuts the cheese? You know what, Bill? Just go out with her! Go ahead and marry her! I don't care anymore!

Bill and Neal are stunned by Sam's anger.

BILL
I was gonna tell you that Cindy said you were the nicest guy in the school.

SAM
She said that?

BILL
Yeah.

(CONTINUED)

CONTINUED: (2)

NEAL
I guess she was wrong.

A beat as this sinks in on Sam.

SAM
So, you don't like Cindy?

BILL
No. I was just messing with you.

NEAL
Sam, Bill's been in love with Melissa Karpinsky, ever since he stood behind her at the Dairy Queen.

BILL
She was wearing a halter top.

NEAL
She is one foxy lady.

BILL
And she doesn't cut the cheese.

Sam gives Bill a look, then laughs and shakes his head. They start walking to class together.

SAM
Melissa Karpinsky is way out of your league. She likes big football players.

BILL
Hey, I just haven't filled out yet. My cousin Jeff was a shrimp till he turned sixteen. Then he got all tall and muscular in like a month. Now he looks like the Hulk.

SAM
Really? You think I'll fill out?

BILL
Yeah. Not like me, though. Three years. You'll see. I'll be huge.

NEAL
(confident)
Oh yeah. Me, too. My dad's 6'3".

(CONTINUED)

46.

CONTINUED: (3)

SAM
Hey, you guys wanna go see "Airplane" again on Saturday? Surely you do.

BILL
Yeah, okay. And stop calling me Shirley.

NEAL
I would, but I have a drinking problem.

Neal pantomimes throwing a glass of water against his forehead a la Robert Hayes in "Airplane." The geeks laugh.

Just then, Sam sees Gordon a few feet ahead, heading into the classroom.

SAM (CONT'D)
You wanna ask Gordon to come?

NEAL
(confused, not mean)
But... he smells.

SAM
(sincere)
I know, but he's actually pretty cool. Maybe he doesn't know he smells.

BILL
So, are you gonna tell him?

CUT TO:

INT. BIOLOGY CLASS - MOMENTS LATER

Students are entering, getting ready for class to begin. Bill and Neal sit down together. Sam sits down next to Gordon. Gives him a friendly smile.

SAM
Hey, Gordon.

GORDON
Hi, Sam. How's it going with you-know-who? Did you join her clubs?

(CONTINUED)

CONTINUED:

SAM
Yeah. And I got to hang out with her. Sort of.

GORDON
Cool.

SAM
(trying to be casual)
And you know, she smelled really great. I think it was her shampoo. Or maybe, you know... her deodorant. What kind do you use?

Gordon immediately catches on. He's very matter-of-fact.

GORDON
I know I smell.

SAM
What? What are you talking about?

GORDON
C'mon, Sam. I may be smelly, but I'm not stupid.

SAM
Yeah, so... what is that?

GORDON
I have a medical condition. It's called trimethylaminuria. It's genetic.

SAM
Wow. Is there a cure?

GORDON
Not yet. But research is progressing.

SAM
So you're just gonna smell for the rest of your life?

GORDON
Uh-huh. But. I don't mind. Nice people don't care. It weeds out the jerks. My mom says it's a gift.

Sam considers this. After a beat...

(CONTINUED)

CONTINUED: (2)

SAM
You wanna go to the movies with me and Bill this weekend?

GORDON
(happy)
Okay. I'll try not to stink up the joint. Just kidding.

They both laugh. Just then, Cindy enters and approaches Sam.

CINDY
How'd it go? Did you sell all your ads?

SAM
(embarrassed)
No, not really.

CINDY
That's okay. No one else did, except me. I'm glad you joined yearbook. I had fun yesterday.

Sam perks up.

SAM
Yeah. Me, too.

CINDY
What are you doing after school?

SAM
(cautious)
Why, is there another yearbook meeting?

CINDY
Oh, no. I was just gonna go to Stackey's later and I was wondering if you wanted to come.

Sam is stunned. He glances over at Bill and Neal, expecting to find out this is a joke. They're both oblivious. Bill is trying to touch Neal's hair. Neal slaps his hand away.

NEAL
Don't touch the hair.

Sam turns back to Cindy.

(CONTINUED)

49.

CONTINUED: (3)

SAM
Uh, sure. I'll go.

CINDY
Great. Well, I'd better sit down.
See you after school okay?

Sam nods, smiling as this sinks in. Gordon grins and nudges Sam, leaning in very close.

GORDON
"See you after school."

Sam smiles, then turns away, gasping for breath.

CUT TO:

INT. STACKEY'S BURGER RESTURANT - DAY

A tray heaped with burgers, fries, Cokes and milkshakes. REVEAL Sam, carrying the feast over to Cindy's table.

CINDY
Thanks, Sam. Are you sure you don't
need any money?

SAM
Yeah, I'm fine.

Sam stuffs his measly change in his pocket and sits down. Cindy starts chowing on a burger.

CINDY
Mmmm. I love bacon cheeseburgers.

SAM
Really? I kinda pictured you eating
healthy stuff. Like carrots.

CINDY
Yuck. If I never saw another carrot
again, it would be too soon. My
parents never take us to Stackey's.
That's why I have to sneak over
here after school.

Cindy takes a huge, bulimic bite of her cheeseburger. Sam offers her his fries.

SAM
Want some?

(CONTINUED)

CONTINUED:

CINDY
Sure. Thanks.

Cindy and Sam start sharing their fries. Sam eats but keeps sneaking glances up at Cindy. She looks pretty. Sam looks happy but nervous.

Just then, TODD SCHELLINGER, a tall, handsome jock, walks by with his buddies.

TODD
So, I'm running down court and Nickman's running next to me, smiling and nodding like he wants me to pass to him, right? So I throw him the ball and he ducks like a girl.

The jocks crack up and get in line. Cindy watches Todd, then turns to Sam.

CINDY
Do you know Todd Schellinger?

SAM
Um, yeah. Well, not personally. Why?

CINDY
I don't know. He's kinda cute, don't you think?

Sam's devastated, but tries to hide it.

SAM
I guess...

CINDY
I never told anybody this before, but... I have the hugest crush on him. At last week's game? He asked my friend Jill for my phone number. You think that means he likes me?

SAM
He asked for your phone number?

CINDY
Yeah, but he never called. And every time I see him, he acts like he doesn't even know I exist.

(CONTINUED)

CONTINUED: (2)

SAM
Maybe he's just shy.

CINDY
You think? I'm always so nervous
around him, I never know what to say.
(sincere)
It's not like with you. You're so
easy to talk to.

Sam, completely crushed, forces a smile.

SAM
Thanks.

CINDY
(excited)
Oh my God, did he just look at me?

OFF Sam, his heart in pieces.

CUT TO:

INT. WEIR LIVING ROOM - NIGHT

Harold and Jean are sitting on the couch. Harold's watching "The Jeffersons" on TV while Jean knits.

Behind them, Lindsay enters quietly, primped for her date. She quickly heads for the front door. Harold and Jean both turn around. Jean tries to give Lindsay a supportive smile.

JEAN
Have a nice time, honey.

HAROLD
Don't stay out too late.

LINDSAY
I won't. Bye.

Lindsay exits. As soon as she's gone, Jean and Harold both turn back around, filled with a mixture of parental emotions. It's too much for them to articulate. After a beat...

JEAN
(calls out)
Sam!

HAROLD
Hey, son!

(CONTINUED)

CONTINUED:

Sam emerges from his room and enters the living room.

SAM
Yeah?

HAROLD
Why don't you come on over here and join your mom and dad.

SAM
(puzzled)
Why? What did I do?

Harold and Jean laugh adoringly.

JEAN
Nothing, silly. Just get your butt over here.

Sam obeys. Jean and Harold make room for him on the couch. Sam sits down between them. They immediately put their arms around him, smothering him.

Then they happily go back to watching "The Jeffersons." Sam is completely weirded out by this display of affection.

SAM
Um... I have to do my homework.

JEAN
You can do it tomorrow.

HAROLD
Family time is more important.

Sam's stuck. He reluctantly leans back into his parents' arms and stares at the TV.

CUT TO:

EXT. NICK'S HOUSE - NIGHT

Lindsay walks up to the front door. She checks her hair, then rings the doorbell. Nick opens the door immediately.

LINDSAY
(startled)
Oh! Hi. You must have been right there.

NICK
Perfect timing.

(CONTINUED)

CONTINUED:

He smiles and motions for Lindsay to enter.

CUT TO:

INT. NICK'S LIVING ROOM - CONTINUOUS

MUSIC UP: THE MOODY BLUES' "KNIGHTS IN WHITE SATIN"

Nick watches expectantly as Lindsay enters.

LINDSAY'S POV: The living room is bathed in dim mood lighting. The lights on the stereo are visible in the dark.

Lindsay stares at the scene, a bit stunned. Nick has obviously put a lot of planning into this.

NICK
I hope you like the Moody Blues.

LINDSAY
Yeah, they're really good.

NICK
I mean, they're a little wimpy but their songs are okay.

LINDSAY
Yeah.

There's an uncomfortable silence. Lindsay scans the room. She looks down at a bunch of basketball trophies on a nearby table.

LINDSAY (CONT'D)
Wow, whose basketball trophies?

NICK
Oh, uh, mine. I used to play.

LINDSAY
Why'd you quit?

NICK
(casual)
I got caught with a dimebag in my locker. They kicked me off the team. And then I lost interest.
(then)
Hey. Uh... you wanna hang out downstairs for a while?

(CONTINUED)

CONTINUED:

LINDSAY
Uh... yeah... okay.

Nick leads her to the stairs. Lindsay's starting to look nervous.

CUT TO:

INT. NICK'S BASEMENT - CONTINUOUS

Nick ushers Lindsay in. Instead of the usual drum and band mess, the room has been turned into a romantic love nest. Lit candles abound, red scarves cover the lampshades and the normally ratty couch is draped with a quilt and several extra pillows.

Lindsay looks around. Nick takes her hand and ushers her to the couch. Lindsay sits down. Nick sits next to her and gazes intensely into her eyes.

LINDSAY
(nervous)
Nick, what is all this? I thought we decided we weren't gonna, you know, rush things.

NICK
Oh.. no. That's not why I brought you down here.

Nick reaches over to his stereo. He opens the turntable and puts the needle on an album.

STYX'S "LADY" comes on. Nick leans toward Lindsay intently. He talks softly over the intro.

NICK (CONT'D)
Lindsay, this song says a lot of the things I haven't been able to say to you. It's kinda corny, but I mean it.

The singer on the record starts to sing. Nick half sings, half lip-syncs.

NICK (CONT'D)
"Lady, when you're with me I'm smiling..."
(points to himself)
"Give me all your love..."
(grabs her hand)
(MORE)

(CONTINUED)

CONTINUED:

NICK (CONT'D)
"Your hands build me up when I'm sinking..."
(brings her hand to his chest)
"Touch me and my troubles all fade..."

Lindsay stares at Nick, weirded out. Nick lowers the volume and talks over the next verse.

NICK (CONT'D)
You see, Linds, nothing about me and you should ever be rushed. Me and Heidi made that mistake. But I'm not gonna do that with you. 'Cause we've got plenty of time. We've got all the time in the world. You know why? 'Cause--

Nick points at Lindsay as he sings:

NICK (CONT'D)
(singing)
"You're my la-dy of the morning/Love shines in your eyes!"

As Nick continues to sing to a horrified Lindsay...

CUT TO:

INT. WEIR KITCHEN - NIGHT

Sam is now sitting alone at the kitchen table, eating a Ding Dong and drinking a glass of milk. He looks really depressed.

The PHONE RINGS. He goes over and picks it up.

SAM
Hello? Hey, Cindy. Oh, Todd called you? Great. Yeah, I can't believe it, either. He said that?

Sam lowers the phone and covers his face, wallowing in misery. After a few beats, he brings the phone back up to his ear...

SAM (CONT'D)
Uh-huh. No, I'm not busy. Tell me everything.

(CONTINUED)

CONTINUED:

Then he lowers the phone again, letting Cindy jabber on. And as we leave Sam in Platonic Friend Hell...

SLOW DISSOLVE TO:

INT. WEIR KITCHEN - NIGHT (ALTERNATE ENDING)

Sam is now sitting alone at the kitchen table, eating a Ding Dong and drinking a glass of milk. He looks really depressed. Lindsay comes in. She looks a little shellshocked.

LINDSAY
Hey.

SAM
Hey.

LINDSAY
Are there any more Ding Dongs?

SAM
One more. You want it?

LINDSAY
Yeah.

Sam takes the silver-wrapped Ding Dong out and slides it over to Lindsay. She sits down across the table from him. She picks up the Ding Dong and looks at it. Puts it back down.

SAM
How was your date?

LINDSAY
It was okay. What did you do?

SAM
Mom and Dad made me watch TV with them all night. They were weird.

LINDSAY
Yeah, what else is new.

SAM
(after a beat)
Is Nick your boyfriend now?

LINDSAY
I don't know.

(CONTINUED)

CONTINUED:

SAM
But he really likes you, right?

LINDSAY
Oh, yeah.

SAM
I wish Cindy liked me.

LINDSAY
(supportive)
She likes you.

SAM
Yeah, like a "friend."

LINDSAY
Ooh. That stinks.

SAM
I know. I don't need another friend. I've already got two. How many friends does a guy need?

ALTERNATE LINE:

SAM
I know. I don't need another friend. I've already got Bill and Neal. And at least they don't want to talk about boys all day.

They both laugh. The PHONE RINGS. He picks up the phone.

SAM (CONT'D)
Hello? Hey, Cindy. Oh, Todd called you?

Sam makes a face at Lindsay. Lindsay smiles sympathetically and leaves, taking the Ding Dong with her.

SAM (CONT'D)
Great. Yeah, I can't believe it, either. He said that?

Sam lowers the phone and covers his face, wallowing in misery. After a few beats, he brings the phone back up to his ear...

SAM (CONT'D)
Uh-huh. No, I'm not busy. Tell me everything.

(CONTINUED)

CONTINUED: (2)

Then he lowers the phone again, letting Cindy jabber on. And as we leave Sam in Platonic Friend Hell...

FADE OUT.

INT. NICK'S BASEMENT - NIGHT

Nick's still sitting next to Lindsay. The end of "LADY" plays softly in the background.

NICK
You see, we're made for each other, Lindsay. We're soulmates. You and me... we're forever. You know what I mean?

Lindsay is now completely freaked. She desperately tries to diffuse Nick's intensity.

LINDSAY
Nick... you want to make out or something?

NICK
No. All guys want to make out. But not me. I just want to hold you.

Nick wraps his arms around Lindsay and gently lays down on the couch with her. We CUT TO--

CEILING POV: Lindsay, trapped in Nick's arms, is staring up at the ceiling, wide-eyed. Nick smiles blissfully.

NICK (CONT'D)
What's better than this?

OFF Lindsay's horrified expression...

FADE OUT.

THE END

# <u>FREAKS AND GEEKS</u>

"WE'VE GOT SPIRIT"

Episode #9

Written by Mike White

Directed by Danny Leiner

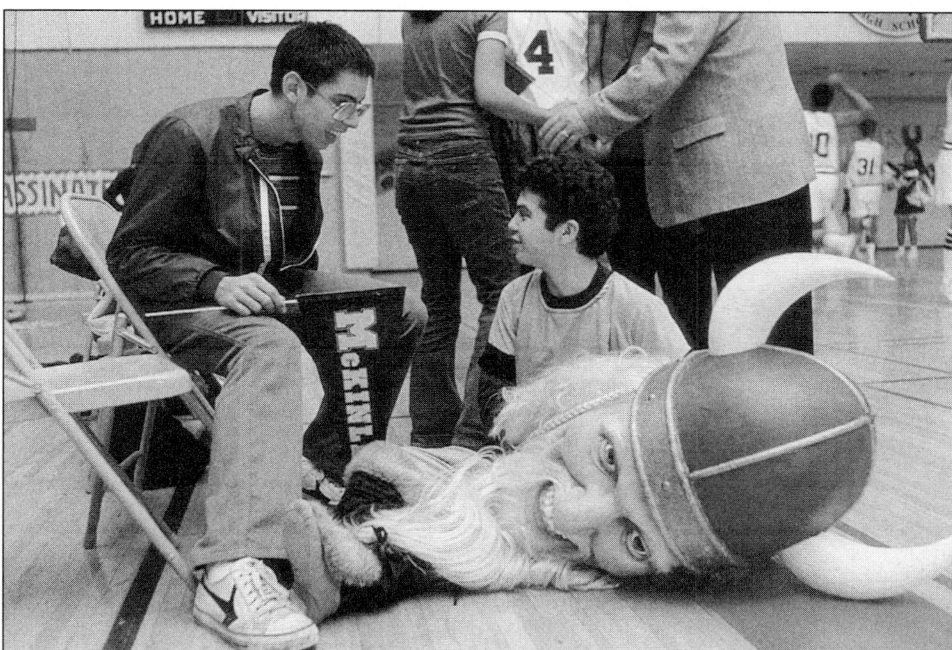

The first job I ever landed was writing for the flagship teen soap opera for the WB called *Dawson's Creek*. It wasn't my sensibility—pretty people exchanging platitudes in picturesque places—but it paid. The writer's room on that show was like a king's court, rife with blood feuds, back-stabbings, and *coups d'etat*. After surviving two cut-throat seasons, I inevitably found my head on the chopping block.

Disheartened by the experience, I swore off television, until the pilot of *Freaks and Geeks* found its way to me. Here was a show I could relate to—funny-looking people struggling to express themselves in awkward situations. I signed on with enthusiasm. I was even more stoked when I realized this writer's room was blessedly free of intrigue. The actors weren't pitted against the staff writers, and the writers weren't pitted against each other. We were a freaky geeky team.

It's difficult to write on someone else's show, especially when that show is borne out of the creator's personal life experience. Think of it like an extended stay at a friend's house—they want you there, but be careful not to rearrange the furniture. Fortunately, Paul Feig is the nicest guy you'll ever meet—even when you were pitching an idea he hated, he'd smile and bite his tongue until the blood was seeping down his shirt. I liked his style. Maybe it wasn't my house, but I believed I could make it my home.

But my cock-eyed optimism was short-lived. For me, it was easier writing for the freaks than the geeks. The geeks were Paul's exclusive domain. In the writer's room, Paul could channel thirteen-year-old geeks like Linda Blair could channel Satan. And it was almost as scary. His head would cock back and his eyes would cross as a little geek ghost from decades past would inhabit his body and out of his mouth would come this hilarious and strange geek speak.

Besides being intimidated by Paul's supernatural inspiration, my other problem writing for the geeks was that most of their scenes had no story. It was just three dorks sitting around shooting the shit, swapping observations about Steve Martin and pubic hair. It was Beckett meets Charlie Brown meets Paul's adolescence. And it was those scenes more than any that gave the show its wonderful specificity—but I didn't have a knack for them.

I don't remember much about this episode, except that after a read-through, Paul looked anxious. Then, I overheard Judd say to Paul—"Well, it's not totally wrong." It was at that moment I started eyeing the back door. I realized I couldn't keep living in other people's houses—even if they were cool and friendly. I had to bust out and build a house of my own.

—Mike White

FREAKS AND GEEKS

"WE'VE GOT SPIRIT"

**CAST LIST**

LINDSAY WEIR
SAM WEIR
HAROLD WEIR
JEAN WEIR
DANIEL DESARIO
NICK ANDOPOLIS
BILL HAVERCHUCK
NEAL SCHWEIBER
KEN MILLER
KIM KELLY
CINDY SANDERS
MR. FREDRICKS
COLIN
TODD SCHELLINGER
HEIDI HENDERSON
VICKI
HERBERT
COUNCILMAN RITCHIE
PRETTY GIRL
CHEERLEADER #1
TEENAGE GUY #1
TEENAGE GUY #2

FREAKS AND GEEKS

"WE'VE GOT SPIRIT"

**SET LIST**

**INTERIORS:**

NICK'S HOUSE
/BASEMENT
MCKINLEY HIGH SCHOOL
/HALLWAY
/HALLWAY NEAR THE GYM
/GYM
/UNDER THE STAIRS
/CAFETERIA
/LOCKER ROOM
/BLEACHERS
/BASKETBALL COURT
/BIOLOGY CLASS
WEIR HOUSE
/KITCHEN
/DINING ROOM
/PARENT'S BEDROOM
/LINDSAY'S BEDROOM
NICK'S CAR
DANIEL'S CAR

**EXTERIORS:**

MCKINLEY HIGH SCHOOL
/PARKING LOT
/OUTSIDE SCHOOL
STREET

TEASER

FADE IN:

INT. NICK'S BASEMENT - EVENING

LINDSAY and NICK are listening to music, relaxing side-by side on his ratty basement couch.

NICK
Hey, Lindsay, do you ever think about heavy stuff?

LINDSAY
Heavy stuff?

NICK
Death. Meaning of life.

LINDSAY
Yeah. I mean, when my grandmother died, I took it pretty hard. I was depressed for a while and...

NICK
(excited; interrupting)
See. I knew it. I knew you were like me. I can't talk to those other guys. Ken and Daniel.
(suddenly ranting)
They're jokers. They don't think about anything. They don't ever think about the meaning of stuff - why we're here - the point of it all. They never think about the point of it all, Linds. But I do. I do all the time. My mind.

He pounds on his temple for emphasis.

LINDSAY
Are you stoned?

NICK
Little bit. Wanna get high?

LINDSAY
No, thanks.

NICK
You know what I've been thinking? Where is John Bonham right now?

(CONTINUED)

CONTINUED:

LINDSAY
The drummer for Led Zeppelin? I thought he was dead.

NICK
Yeah, but where is he? Is he rotting away in the ground? Or maybe he's up in heaven, partying with Jimi and Janis?

LINDSAY
Maybe he's in Hell.

NICK
Jeez. I hope not.

Lindsay turns her attention to a PHOTO ALBUM on the table.

LINDSAY
Oh, look at you. You were so cute.

She points to a baby picture of Nick.

NICK
I was really happy back then.

Lindsay flips through the book.

ON ALBUM - She comes upon a PHOTO of Nick, in a basketball uniform, holding up a trophy. In the picture, a girl stands beside him - BUT HER HEAD HAS BEEN METHODICALLY CUT OUT.

Lindsay looks baffled. Nick is slightly proud.

NICK (CONT'D)
That was the year I won MVP.

LINDSAY
(pointing to photo)
Who's this?

NICK
Who's who?

LINDSAY
Who's this girl here?

NICK
(nonchalant)
Oh, yeah, that's Heidi Henderson. I dated her for a while. Before you came along.
(MORE)

(CONTINUED)

CONTINUED: (2)

NICK (CONT'D)
(changing the subject)
Hey. You wanna watch me play "Kashmir"?

LINDSAY
(distracted)
Sure.

Nick goes over to his drumset. Lindsay stares back...

AT THE PHOTO.

She traces her finger around the missing head.

And off Lindsay's confused look, we...

CUT TO:

MAIN TITLES

ACT ONE

FADE IN:

INT. MCKINLEY HIGH SCHOOL HALLWAY - DAY

The hallway is crowded with STUDENTS, congregating before school. TWO CHEERLEADERS, (one of them, VICKI, the pretty team captain), are taping up a banner to the wall. It reads - "ASSASSINATE LINCOLN!" KEN walks by.

KEN
Who's Lincoln?

VICKI
("duh")
Our rivals.

CHEERLEADER #1
We made regionals. Isn't that cool?

KEN
(dry)
Yeah. I'm thrilled. In what?

VICKI
Basketball.

Vicki suddenly turns on the other cheerleader.

(CONTINUED)

4.

CONTINUED:

VICKI (CONT'D)
Would you quit jerking it out of my hand? You're gonna rip it.

Ken continues on down the hall. There are visual reminders of the upcoming BASKETBALL GAME everywhere. He approaches DANIEL and KIM, hanging by the lockers.

KEN
(sarcastic)
Heard about the basketball team? Pretty exciting.

DANIEL
I'm sick of all this "rah-rah" crud everywhere. It's giving me a pain in my eyeballs.

KIM
Aww, poor baby.

DANIEL
These jocks think they're such bad-asses. Walking around like they cured cancer. They're just monkeys.

TWO JOCKS walk by. Daniel makes a monkey noise. Kim laughs.

Lindsay approaches, troubled. They all greet her.

LINDSAY
Hey, guys.

DANIEL
Where's loverboy?

LINDSAY
Nick? I don't know.

KEN
I thought you two were joined at the tongue.

LINDSAY
(serious)
Kim, can I talk to you for a second?

Ken and Daniel stare at Lindsay, curious.

KEN
Uh, O-oh. Are you pregnant?

(CONTINUED)

CONTINUED: (2)

LINDSAY
No.

KIM
Hey. Don't be a pig. She wants to talk to me. In private. Come on, Lindsay.

Kim leads Lindsay away from them.

KIM (CONT'D)
What's the problem?

LINDSAY
I'm thinking about breaking up with Nick.

KIM
(grave)
Why?

LINDSAY
Well, I like him, but he's just so...intense. He's always high. I'm starting to think I don't know him as well as I thought. It just doesn't feel right.

KIM
Don't do it, Lindsay. Give him another chance.

LINDSAY
(surprised)
What?

KIM
Let me set him straight. I'll beat some sense into him.

LINDSAY
No, Kim. Don't make a big deal out of this. I'll figure it out.

KIM
Just don't dump him, okay? The last time he got dumped - he went berserk.

LINDSAY
You mean, with Heidi Henderson?

(CONTINUED)

CONTINUED: (3)

KIM
He told you about that?

LINDSAY
No. Why? What happened?

KIM
(clearly lying)
Nothing. I don't know.

Suddenly, Nick appears behind Lindsay, giving her a big bear hug. Lindsay is startled.

NICK
Hey. I've been looking for you.

LINDSAY
Well, here I am.

KIM
(acting blithe)
I'll see ya guys later.

As Kim walks away, her smile fades into a look of doom. We FOLLOW Kim down the hallway, until she passes by CINDY SANDERS, in her cheerleading uniform.

We STAY on Cindy as she puts the final decorating touches on a hallway locker. She has taped-up miniature plastic basketballs, as well as colorful cardboard letters, spelling out motivational phrases ("GO TODD" ; "YAY, NORSEMEN!"). She is taping up the last basketball, when SAM approaches.

SAM
Hey, Cindy. What are you doing?

CINDY
We decided to decorate the players' lockers. We're pumping them up for the big game.

Finished, she steps back and looks at the locker.

CINDY (CONT'D)
Sam, if that was your locker, would you be pumped?

SAM
Yeah. I'd be really pumped.

Cindy turns to Sam, excited.

(CONTINUED)

7.

CONTINUED: (4)

CINDY
You think Todd'll be pumped? It's his locker.

SAM
Well, it looks...really good.

CINDY
(in a whisper)
All the girls wanted to decorate it. I had to beg them to let me do it. I've been here since six in the morning.

Suddenly, Cindy turns ashen.

CINDY (CONT'D)
Oh my God. Here he comes, here he comes.

The studly TODD SCHELLINGER approaches. He is surprised by his decorated locker.

CINDY (CONT'D)
(nervous)
Hey, Todd. Me and all the cheerleaders wanted to pump you up for the big game.

TODD
(unenthused)
Oh. Cool.

In order to open his locker, Todd has to yank off a basketball.

CINDY
I'll take that. Sorry.

Todd grabs a book out of his locker, then closes it.

TODD
Later.

Todd walks away. Cindy is agitated.

CINDY
He didn't seem very pumped.

(CONTINUED)

CONTINUED: (5)

SAM
Well, he should be. I would've been happy if I was him. I think it's really nice that you did that.

CINDY
Thanks, Sam. You're sweet.

Sam gives her an "aw, shucks" smile. He's trying to worm his way into Cindy's heart. Then...

CINDY (CONT'D)
Sam, you know how I told you I had a crush on Todd? Well, I don't.

SAM
(hopeful)
You don't?

CINDY
No. It's not a crush. It's an obsession. Last night, I lit a love candle for him. I watched it burn until my eyes hurt.

Cindy shakes her head at the gravity of her situation.

SAM
Well... I better get to class.

Sam turns and walks away, devastated.

CUT TO:

INT. CAFETERIA - LATER

CLOSE on the CHEERLEADERS, including Cindy Sanders. They are shouting a cheer at the top of their lungs, their faces distorted, their veins bulging.

CHEERLEADERS
Give me an N!!!

Reveal that we are in the cafeteria. People are eating. The cheerleaders are by the front of the cafeteria. Students with trays struggle to get around them.

ANGLE ON: A table full of JOCKS (including Todd) is watching, way into it.

JOCKS
N!!!

(CONTINUED)

CONTINUED:

PULL BACK TO REVEAL Sam, NEAL and BILL are sitting at the geek table which is right in front of the jock table. Bill, pained by the shouts of the jocks, covers his ears.

CHEERLEADERS
What does that spell?!

JOCKS
NORSEMEN!!!

Bill cringes from the noise.

BILL
Oww. Jeez. Quit yelling.

The NORSEMAN MASCOT, (in a pint-sized warrior costume with an OVERSIZED head), runs out from behind them and thrusts a PHONY DAGGER in the air.

CHEERLEADERS
Who's gonna win?!

Near the back, Kim, Daniel and Ken sit watching at their table. Ken puts the heels of his hands on his mouth and does a huge fart noise along with the crowd's response.

CROWD
NORSEMEN!!

Kim and Daniel laugh at Ken's fart.

The cheerleaders erupt into a frenzy of leg-kicks and fist-pumping. The jocks and students who are into it APPLAUD.

At the geek table, NEAL shakes his head.

NEAL
That mascot is depressing me.

The Mascot stands in front of the cheerleaders, running in place.

NEAL (CONT'D)
Look at him. He's running in place. What is that? Is that supposed to be funny?

BILL
He's trying to get us excited.

NEAL
Well, I'm not excited.

(CONTINUED)

CONTINUED: (2)

SAM
I wish he'd sit down. He's blocking Cindy.

Vicki, the head cheerleader, steps forward.

VICKI
That's the spirit! And now, let's hear a big McKinley cheer for our own Coach Fredricks!

The mascot continues to run in place. MR. FREDRICKS steps over and taps the mascot on the shoulder. The mascot stops and turns his giant head to look at Fredricks. Fredricks gives him the "cut it" sign. The mascot signals "sorry."

Neal sees this and makes a "what an idiot" face to himself.

MR. FREDRICKS
(emotional)
We haven't made regionals since 1971. Saturday is an important day for our school. We've worked our butts off for you all season, so I want to see some butts in those bleachers on Saturday. Now, I'd like to bring up my team captain and my friend - Todd Schellinger. Come on up here, son.

Todd steps forward. A lot of whistles and cat-calls from the girls in the audience.

Sam, however, looks forlorn. He stares at Cindy, who claps enthusiastically for Todd, dreamy-eyed.

TODD
Thanks, Coach. I just want to say this season's been fantastic and you fans have been great.

Students clap. Sam watches Todd with disgust.

SAM
Why does Cindy like him? He's such a jerk. He's not even nice to her.

NEAL
Because cheerleaders have to date athletes. It's the law.

(CONTINUED)

CONTINUED: (3)

BILL
Hey, Sam, if you want to get in with Cindy, you should join the basketball team. Are you any good?

Sam gives Bill a "you've gotta be kidding" look.

BILL (CONT'D)
Uh... never mind.

TODD
And everybody should come out on Saturday and watch us destroy Lincoln!

The CROWD goes WILD. Daniel looks annoyed.

DANIEL
(to no one in particular)
Shut up.
(annoyed, to KEN)
Let's get out of here. Where's Nick?

KEN
I'll give you one guess.

SMASH CUT TO:

INT. UNDER THE STAIRS - CONTINUOUS

Nick and Lindsay are alone, under the stairwell. Not another student in sight. Nick rests his head on Lindsay's lap.

LINDSAY
Didn't you tell Daniel we were gonna meet him for lunch?

NICK
I don't care about him. I just want to be with you. I feel like I could just lie here with you forever.

Lindsay's not sure she likes the sound of that.

LINDSAY
Well... I have a class in ten minutes.

(CONTINUED)

CONTINUED:

NICK
Then I'll just have to cherish
these next ten minutes.

CUT BACK TO:

INT. CAFETERIA - CONTINUOUS

The cheerleaders are energizing the crowd.

CHEERLEADERS
What do we got?

CROWD
SPIRIT!

CHEERLEADERS
That's S-P-I-R-I-T.

The cheerleaders begin to sell out "Spirit" with their arms.

Ken, Kim and Daniel are the only ones in the cafeteria seated. A PRETTY GIRL next to them, looks down and sneers.

PRETTY GIRL
Why don't you guys stand up?

DANIEL
Why don't you pay me?

PRETTY GIRL
Would it kill you to have a little
pride in your school?

KEN
Yeah.

KIM
Hey, sunshine - take a hike.

The Cheerleaders start dancing and cheering. As they do, the mascot jumps up on a table and starts jumping up and down, trying to get the crowd to stand up and cheer.

CHEERLEADERS
That's spirit. For victory.
That's spirit. To win this game.
So come on, Norsemen, put Lincoln
to shame!!!!

(CONTINUED)

CONTINUED:

As the mascot jumps, he gets too close to the edge of the table. He jumps up and lands right on the edge, causing the table to flip up, smack him in the head and dump him on the floor with a LOUD THUD and a CRACK.

The Cheerleaders SHRIEK. Everyone goes silent.

MASCOT
(panicking; muffled)
Get the head off! Get the head off!

Several cheerleaders attempt to remove his head.

ON THE FREAKS

They laugh at this. The Pretty Girl looks over.

KEN
Ouch.

PRETTY GIRL
You guys are sick.

ANGLE ON: THE GEEKS

Neal shakes his head, then turns to Bill and Sam.

NEAL
He can't even fall funny.

CUT TO:

INT. HALLWAY - LATER

Sam and Bill are walking down the hall. Cindy Sanders walks over to them. She is holding a poster board which says, "Mascot Auditions Sign-Up Sheet".

CINDY
Hey, Sam.

SAM
Hey, Cindy. How' s everything?

CINDY
Not good. The mascot broke his arm and he got a concussion, too. His mom won't let him go to sleep tonight 'cause she's afraid he'll go into a coma.

(CONTINUED)

CONTINUED:

BILL
My cousin was in a coma. When he woke up, he spoke fluent Spanish.

CINDY
Well, we're all freaking out. We really need a mascot.

Cindy pins up the sign-up sheet.

CINDY (CONT'D)
See you later, Sam.

Cindy walks away.

BILL
I think that was a subliminal message. She wants you to be the new mascot.

SAM
What?

BILL
We really need a mascot. I really need a mascot. I really need Sam to be the mascot. I really need Sam to be my lover.

Neal approaches.

SAM
Do you really think I should try out?

BILL
Open your eyes, Sam. That was the biggest come on I've ever seen. She was practically kissing you.

As they're talking, Neal walks up to the sign-up sheet and writes down his name.

SAM
What are you doing?

NEAL
I'm going to become the new Norseman.

BILL
You can't. Sam is gonna do it.

(CONTINUED)

CONTINUED: (2)

NEAL
But Sam isn't funny.

SAM
Yes, I am. And Cindy just asked me to do it. I think if I spend more time with her, she might start liking me.

NEAL
You are so selfish. You wanna deny the whole school big laughs just so you can hit on a girl?

SAM
Come on, Neal. This is my chance. You know how important this is to me.

NEAL
This is important to me, too. Being the school mascot has always been a dream of mine.

BILL
Yeah, since lunch.

SAM
C'mon, Neal.

NEAL
I don't know.

SAM
(thinks; then)
"Help me, Obi Wan Kenobi. You're my only hope."

NEAL
(about to protest; stops)
You had to go and quote Star Wars, didn't you?

Neal makes a conciliatory shrug. Sam laughs and pats him "thank you" on the back.

CUT TO:

INT. WEIR DINING ROOM - NIGHT

Lindsay, Sam, HAROLD and JEAN are around the dinner table.

(CONTINUED)

CONTINUED:

SAM
In the cafeteria today, the school mascot fell and broke his arm. It was pretty scary.

JEAN
Aww. Poor thing.

SAM
They need a new mascot for the game. I'm gonna audition.

JEAN
That'll be fun. You know how I love to watch you kids perform.

LINDSAY
(full of dread)
You're not coming to the game, are you?

HAROLD
Of course we are. It's a big community event.

LINDSAY
So?

HAROLD
I'm expected to be there. I'm a community leader.

LINDSAY
Since when?

Harold's eyes bug-out. Lindsay realizes her faux-pas.

LINDSAY (CONT'D)
It's just some dumb basketball game, Dad.

JEAN
(gingerly)
I know why you don't want us to go. You've got a date with your new boyfriend. We're gonna get to know him sooner or later, Lindsay. So why don't we all just go together?

LINDSAY
No way.

(CONTINUED)

CONTINUED: (2)

JEAN
How's it going with you two?

LINDSAY
Mom. No.

Jean is disappointed. Harold is still stewing.

HAROLD
I'm a member of the Rotary, you know. And the Masons. And Councilman Ritchie just last week said I should run for the school board. What do you have to say about that?

LINDSAY
That's great, Dad.

HAROLD
I could be the mayor and I wouldn't get any respect around this house.

CUT TO:

INT. LINDSAY'S BEDROOM - NIGHT

The lights are out. Lindsay is in bed, wide-awake. She is contemplating her relationship when she hears a TAPPING. She looks to the window and sees ....

NICK, wearing a hooded sweatshirt, grinning back at her.

Lindsay gasps, sitting up in bed.

Nick points insistently in the direction of the back door, then disappears.

Lindsay, sits for a moment, confounded.

CUT TO:

INT. WEIR KITCHEN - MOMENTS LATER

Lindsay, in an oversized T-shirt, has opened the back door to let Nick in. They speak in whispers.

LINDSAY
Nick. What are you doing?

NICK
Can I come in?

(CONTINUED)

CONTINUED:

LINDSAY
No. It's one in the morning. My dad'll flip out.

NICK
I'm sorry. I couldn't sleep. I couldn't stop thinking about you. I just had to see your face.

He stares intently at her face for a moment, then...

NICK (CONT'D)
(satisfied)
Okay. That's good. I don't want to get you in trouble.

Nick gives her a quick kiss.

NICK (CONT'D)
Nice. Sleep tight. Don't let the bugs bite.

LINDSAY
Thanks. Bye, Nick.

She shuts the door on his face. He enthusiastically waves good-bye through the window, then disappears. Lindsay shakes her head, disturbed and we...

FADE OUT.

END OF ACT ONE

ACT TWO

FADE IN:

INT. BIOLOGY CLASSROOM - MORNING

Students are assembling before class, chatting with each other. Sam and Bill stand together.

BILL
I heard the mascot has to change with the cheerleaders in the girl's locker room.

SAM
Really? That doesn't sound right.

Sam looks and sees Cindy approaching.

(CONTINUED)

CONTINUED:

SAM (CONT'D)
Cindy?

CINDY
Oh. Hey, Sam.

SAM
Hey. Umm... guess what? I'm gonna audition for school mascot.

CINDY
Really?
(off his nod)
Sam, being a mascot is harder than it looks. You have to be super coordinated.

SAM
Oh, I'm really coordinated. You'd be surprised.

CINDY
That's cool. But it's not up to me. Vicki's the head cheerleader.

SAM
Oh, okay. Well, put in a good word for me, will ya?

CINDY
Okay, but Vicki's not my best friend. She's kind of... bossy. But I'll do what I can. See you at auditions.

SAM
Okay.

Cindy walks away. Sam looks nervous.

SAM (CONT'D)
You think there was a subliminal message in there somewhere?

BILL
For your sake, I hope not.

Sam bites his lip, troubled.

CUT TO:

INT. MCKINLEY HIGH SCHOOL HALLWAY - DAY

Lindsay hesitantly approaches a Senior girl, HEIDI HENDERSON, at her locker. She's a hard-looking rocker chick.

LINDSAY
Heidi? I'm Lindsay. I'm in your Spanish class.

Heidi nods, expressionless.

LINDSAY (CONT'D)
You went out with Nick Andopolis, right?

HEIDI
Ugh. Don't remind me.

LINDSAY
Do you mind me asking - what happened?

HEIDI
Are you dating him or something?

LINDSAY
Sort of.

HEIDI
(suddenly intense)
You better ditch him. He's crazy.

LINDSAY
He is?

HEIDI
Breaking up with him was a nightmare. He started stalking me. He broke into my house. He got in this insane fight with my dad. Oh god.

Heidi sees Nick approaching. She scurries off.

NICK
(suspicious)
Hey. Why were you just talking to Heidi?

LINDSAY
We're in Spanish together.

(CONTINUED)

CONTINUED:

NICK
What were you talking about?

LINDSAY
Spanish stuff.

NICK
Just be careful with her. She's a liar. She loves to screw people over.

Nick tries to lighten the mood with a big smile.

NICK (CONT'D)
Wanna go to class?

LINDSAY
Okay.

Nick puts his arm around Lindsay and they walk off down the hall.

CUT TO:

INT. CAFETERIA - DAY

Vicki and the other cheerleaders, including Cindy, watch as Sam and a handful of GEEKS (including COLIN) and some other students perform a routine for their mascot audition. Colin really hams it up with all his "Oklahoma" moves. Sam appears to be better than the other klutzy students.

GEEKS
Chewin' tobacco, chewin' tobacco - spit, spit, spit. We make Lincoln look like... shift to the left, shift to the right. Stand up, sit down. Fight, fight, FIGHT!!!

They freeze. Colin ends in a one-knee-on-the-floor, thumbs-under-his-armpits musical theatre pose.

VICKI
All right. Good work. Take a break.

CINDY
Nice job, Sam!
(turning to VICKI)
Sam's really good, isn't he?

(CONTINUED)

CONTINUED:

VICKI
Cindy, if I want your opinion, I'll ask for it. Let's see how he does with "Funky Chicken".

ANGLE ON: Sam and Colin, catching their breath.

COLIN
You have pretty good moves, Sam. You should try out for the musical. We're doing "Fiddler". You could be a dancing Yeshiva student.

Standing against the wall, Neal and Bill are observing. They stand near a small, spaced-out kid, HERBERT, who sports an arm cast and a bandaged forehead.

BILL
Sam's pretty good.

NEAL
Yeah, but he's not very funny, but at least he's better than the old mascot. That guy was as funny as a car wreck.

Herbert looks over at them.

HERBERT
Hey!

Neal and Bill recoil, embarrassed.

NEAL
Just kidding.

BILL
(to Herbert)
Hey, Herbert, you didn't sleep last night, did you?

HERBERT
No, and my mom's not gonna let me sleep tonight either. She's really nervous I might fall into a coma.

BILL
Every time you feel tired, pull out one of your nose hairs. You'll wake right up.

CUT TO:

INT. CAFETERIA - MINUTES LATER

Vicki, holding her clipboard, approaches the assembled geek auditioners.

VICKI
This was not an easy decision for me. The Norseman head could have rested nicely on any one of you. However, our next school mascot will be... Sam Weir.

Sam is excited. Cindy lets out a squeal of glee.

Bill and Neal look a little surprised.

The other Geeks take it hard, some grumbling.

COLIN
(to other geeks)
It's all politics.

VICKI
The rest of you - don't give up on your dreams. In junior high, I didn't make the squad, but then I spent a summer at cheerleading camp and now, here I am.

COLIN
Is there a camp for mascots?

VICKI
Probably not.

The Geeks disperse. Cindy, overjoyed, runs to Sam.

CINDY
Sam - you're so coordinated. I had no idea. This is gonna be so much fun. I can teach you all our routines.

SAM
Cool. When do we start?

Cindy gives him a hug. Sam is elated. He looks over at...

NEAL AND BILL - Neal gives a begrudging thumbs-up. Nearby, Herbert has fallen asleep. Bill immediately taps him on the shoulder.

(CONTINUED)

CONTINUED:

BILL
Hey man, get up!

Herbert springs back to life.

CUT TO:

INT. HALLWAY - DAY

Ken, Daniel, Kim and Lindsay are hanging out. A bunch of SPIRITED GIRLS run by, shouting...

SPIRIT GIRLS
Assassinate Lincoln! Yeah!

DANIEL
This place is turning into a cult. These jocks - they throw a ball through a hoop. Whoop-de-freakin'-do. They're not gods.

KIM
Jealous, maybe?

DANIEL
Oh, yeah. I want to be a monkey who dribbles. You know, this whole team thing is what's wrong with this society, man. Lincoln - McKinley. U.S.A. - Soviet Union. Same thing. This is how wars get started.

LINDSAY
My parents are making me go with them to the game. They're so into it.

KEN
I'm going.

LINDSAY/KIM
Really?/ What?

KEN
I hear we're gonna lose. I like it when jocks cry.
(imitates a blubbering jock)
They cheated, man!

The others laugh. They see Nick approaching.

(CONTINUED)

CONTINUED:

DANIEL
Here comes Nick. Hey, Lindsay, what's up with you and Nick?

LINDSAY
Nothing.

KEN
Kim says you're gonna dump him.

Lindsay shoots a look at Kim, who shrugs.

DANIEL
Oh, no. Don't do it.

But just then, Nick joins them.

NICK
(ignoring the others)
Hey Linds.

KEN
Hey, Nick. I'm great. Thanks for asking.

NICK
Hey, Ken. Hey, guys.

LINDSAY
Nick, do you think you could give me a ride home?

The Freaks exchange looks of dread.

NICK
Sure. No problem. You wanna go now?

LINDSAY
Yeah.
(standing)
See you guys later.

NICK
(full of pride)
I'm gonna give Lindsay a ride home. Later.

DANIEL
Hey, Lindsay!

She looks back. Daniel makes prayer-hands and mouths "Don't do it." Nick is oblivious.

(CONTINUED)

CONTINUED: (2)

KEN
You kids have fun!
(to KIM and DANIEL)
I wouldn't want to be his drumset tonight.

CUT TO:

INT. NICK'S CAR - DAY

Nick and Lindsay sit in Nick's car, parked in the school lot.

LINDSAY
Nick, I need to talk to you.

Nick's face falls, already fearing the worst.

NICK
What?

LINDSAY
Ever since we started hanging out, you've been really... intense.

NICK
Intense?
(off her nod; upset)
This is me, Lindsay. This is who I am. Are you saying you don't like who I am?

LINDSAY
No, I'm not saying that.

NICK
It sounds like you're saying that.

LINDSAY
Maybe it's just you're stoned all the time. And I'm not.

NICK
Oh, so now I'm stoned all the time?

LINDSAY
Well, aren't you?

NICK
This has something to do with Heidi Henderson, doesn't it? She said something to you.

(CONTINUED)

27.

CONTINUED: (3)

LINDSAY
Well... sort of.

NICK
(blowing up)
I told you, Lindsay, she's a liar! God, I'm sick of trying to defend myself when it comes to Heidi Henderson! It's ancient history! I wish she'd just graduate already.

Lindsay is stunned by his outburst. Nick composes himself. He manages a feeble smile.

NICK (CONT'D)
I'm sorry. Look, I don't want to fight.

LINDSAY
Neither do I.

NICK
It's just that I really like you. And I can't stand the thought of you not liking me.

LINDSAY
I do like you, Nick.

Nick lets out a sigh of relief. He smiles at her.

LINDSAY (CONT'D)
But I...

But before she can finish her sentence, Nick kisses her, then rests his head on her shoulder, a satisfied smile on his face.

NICK
Let's never fight again.

And off Lindsay's distressed expression we...

CUT TO:

EXT. OUTSIDE SCHOOL - DAY

Ken, Daniel and Kim are still hanging out by Daniel's car. A PICK-UP TRUCK pulls up beside them. THREE TEENAGE JOCKS are inside. One of them sticks his head out the window.

(CONTINUED)

CONTINUED:

DANIEL
(taking a big whiff)
I love the smell of gasoline.

KIM
Yeah? It gives you brain damage.

DANIEL
Really?

TEENAGE GUY #1
You guys go to McKinley?

KIM
Yeah.

TEENAGE GUY #I
Norsemen suck!

Suddenly, Ken, Daniel and Kim are all pegged by WATER BALLOONS.

The teenage marauders burst into maniacal laughter and peel out with a SCREECH. One of them yells out...

TEENAGE GUY #2
Lincoln rules!!!

The Freaks chase after the truck, but to no avail. Kim is drenched. Daniel is pissed.

KIM
Dammit, I'm soaked. Daniel - do something.

DANIEL
What do you want me to do? Blow on you?

CUT TO:

INT. CAFETERIA - DAY

The cheerleaders are practicing. Sam is running up and down, waving his arms to pump up an invisible crowd. He's really chugging.

(CONTINUED)

CONTINUED:

VICKI
Wave your arms more! Work it! Get those people to cheer!
(Sam runs harder)
Funky chicken! Let's see it.

Sam starts doing the funky chicken.

VICKI (CONT'D)
Not funky enough!

ANGLE ON:

Bill and Neal, who are still observing. They sit with a groggy Herbert.

HERBERT
You know, I wanted to be funny. But Vicki didn't want comedy. It was always cheers, cheers, cheers.

NEAL
Hey, Herbert. You're drooling.

BACK ON MASCOT PRACTICE

Vicki, the head cheerleader, approaches a breathless Sam.

VICKI
Pretty good. It'll be better when you have your head on.

SAM
Can I try it on today?

VICKI
No, it's still being fixed. Now, are you ready to try the pyramid?

SAM
(panting)
Ummm, okay.

Vicki re-joins the other cheerleaders. They start forming the pyramid.

HERBERT
Uh, oh. The pyramid. He's gonna need some pointers.

Herbert runs over to Sam.

(CONTINUED)

CONTINUED: (2)

HERBERT (CONT'D)
Hey. When you're climbing them, be careful not to pull their hair. 'Cause they'll jerk up and you'll fall.

SAM
Right. Okay.

HERBERT
Oh, and don't pull on their bra straps, 'cause they'll start wiggling and you'll fall.

The cheerleaders are in their pyramid, ready for Sam.

HERBERT (CONT'D)
And if you do fall, tuck your head so you don't break your neck.

Herbert clutches his own head to emphasize his point.

Sam anxiously approaches the pyramid of cheerleaders.

SUSPENSEFUL MUSIC as Sam scans the tower of blondes. He begins to scale - one level of kneeling cheerleaders after another.

His arms quiver - he is half-way there. The cheerleaders look like they might buckle underneath him.

He climbs upon the backs of the two cheerleaders at the very top. One of them is Cindy Sanders.

SLOW-MOTION REACTIONS OF SAM AND CINDY - As Sam's knee digs into Cindy's back, his expression is one of fear and excitement. Cindy is in pain, but hides it beneath her painted smile.

Sam lifts his torso and throws his arms into the air, signaling victory. Cindy's head retracts to look at him, her eyes toward heaven - a distorted smile on her face.

IN THE BLEACHERS - Neal and Bill are transfixed by this vision of Sam and Cindy.

BACK ON SAM AND CINDY - THE MUSIC SWELLS on this tableau of ecstatic achievement. Sam and Cindy both simultaneously let out a...

(CONTINUED)

CONTINUED: (3)

SAM/CINDY
WHOOO!!!

CUT TO:

INT. CAFETERIA - MOMENTS LATER

Cindy Sanders and Sam, both pleasantly exhausted, share a post-jubilant moment, sitting side-by-side on the floor.

CINDY
Sam, that was amazing.

SAM
Thanks, Cindy.

CINDY
It kinda hurt when you were getting on. But it's great you stayed up for so long.

SAM
I guess I have a knack for it.

CINDY
I'll say.

They lock eyes and share a sweet smile.

CUT TO:

INT. WEIR KITCHEN -- NIGHT

Lindsay and Jean are doing dishes together, when the PHONE RINGS. Jean answers it.

JEAN
Hello? Oh, hi, Nick. How are you?

Lindsay waves her arms, shaking her head. Jean is confused.

LINDSAY
(whispering)
I'm not here.

JEAN
(into phone)
Oh, I'm glad to hear that. You know, she's not. She's... she's out with her father. Yeah, they're, uh...
(MORE)

(CONTINUED)

CONTINUED:

JEAN (CONT'D)
I don't know what they're doing but they're doing something. I'll tell her you called. Okay. Buh-bye.

Jean puts down the phone.

JEAN (CONT'D)
Lindsay, I don't like to lie.

LINDSAY
I know. I'm sorry.

Lindsay returns to dish-washing. Jean joins her at the sink.

JEAN
So - are you gonna tell me what's going on?

LINDSAY
Mom, it's complicated.

JEAN
(stung)
I see.

They continue washing dishes in silence. Then...

LINDSAY
I want to break up with Nick.

JEAN
You do? Why?

LINDSAY
It's just... going too fast. I just need my space, you know? But every time I try to break up with him, I chicken out. I'm afraid of hurting his feelings and what he might do.

JEAN
Well, honey, you don't keep going steady with a boy just to be nice. If it's not going to work out, then you need to muster your courage and tell him it's over. The longer you let it drag on, the more hurt he's gonna be when it does end.

Lindsay considers this, then nods emphatically.

(CONTINUED)

CONTINUED: (2)

LINDSAY
You're so right.

JEAN
Yeah?

LINDSAY
No. You are so right. I've just gotta do it. I'm gonna call him right now.

Lindsay, in deep thought, walks from the room. Jean watches her go, amazed by their interaction.

CUT TO:

INT. HAROLD AND JEAN'S BEDROOM - MOMENTS LATER

Harold is reading in bed, when Jean bursts in, euphoric.

JEAN
Harold!

HAROLD
What is it?

Jean sits down on the bed, grinning.

JEAN
I just had a conversation with Lindsay about, her love life. She doesn't like her boyfriend. She's gonna break it off.

HAROLD
Well, praise God.

JEAN
She confided in me, Harold. And she took my advice. I feel like... a mother. I feel like a mother.

Jean is positively glowing. Harold is unsettled.

HAROLD
Well, you look like a nutbag.

But Jean ignores this. She smiles to herself.

JEAN
It's the little things in life, you know?

(CONTINUED)

CONTINUED:

HAROLD
Yeah. You're on my leg.

JEAN
(hopping up)
Oh, sorry, honey. I'm just so tickled.

Jean literally bounces out of the room. Harold watches her go, then turns his attention back to his book.

CUT TO:

INT. LINDSAY'S BEDROOM - CONTINUOUS

Lindsay is on her bed, cradling the telephone. She takes a deep breath, lifts the receiver and dials Nick's number.

CUT TO:

INT. NICK'S BASEMENT - CONTINUOUS

Nick sits merrily at his drumset. He dips an OREO into a glass of milk. The PHONE RINGS, near him. He shoves the Oreo in his mouth, and picks up the phone.

NICK
(mouth full of food)
Hello? Hello? Hello?

CUT TO:

INT. LINDSAY'S BEDROOM - CONTINUOUS

Suddenly, Lindsay loses her nerve. She slams down the phone.

Jean passes by the room, popping her head in.

JEAN
How'd it go?

LINDSAY
(weakly)
I think I should tell him in person, don't you?

JEAN
Remember - you have to do what's best for you.

(CONTINUED)

CONTINUED:

LINDSAY
I'll do it tomorrow. Before the game.

JEAN
Okay. Good night, Lindsay. If there's anything else you want to talk over, I'm always here for you.

Jean makes a cheerful exit. Lindsay stares at the phone, her mind racing.

CUT TO:

INT. NICK'S BASEMENT - CONTINUOUS

Nick is still cradling the phone, suddenly paranoid.

NICK
Hello? If this is you, Ken, you were supposed to be here an hour ago. I don't like waiting around. I got stuff to do. Hello?

Nick slams the phone down. All is silent in his room. He looks disturbed as he contemplates the hang-up.

FADE OUT.

END OF ACT TWO

ACT THREE

FADE IN:

INT. WEIR KITCHEN - MORNING

Jean is bustling around the kitchen. Harold and Lindsay are eating breakfast. Lindsay is lost in thought.

JEAN
Lindsay, do you want to drive with your father to the game?

HAROLD
Yeah. I'd like to introduce you to the pillars of the community - also known as my friends.

LINDSAY
I'll meet you guys there. I've got something to take care of first.

(CONTINUED)

CONTINUED:

JEAN
(remembering)
Oh, that's right.

Jean sits down next to Lindsay, full of compassion.

JEAN (CONT'D)
What are you gonna say to him?

LINDSAY
(slightly annoyed)
Mom, I don't know.

HAROLD
Why don't you tell him he's a greasebag and you deserve better?

JEAN/LINDSAY
Harold!/Dad.

Harold shrugs, unapologetic. Lindsay stands, full of dread.

LINDSAY (CONT'D)
I'll see you at the game.

JEAN
Good luck, honey.

Lindsay exits, passing Sam on her way out. Sam is hobbling, all of his muscles aching. With much labor, Sam sits down at the table.

HAROLD
What's wrong with you?

SAM
I had mascot practice yesterday. I'm sore.

Sam stares at his father, a strange smile on his face.

SAM (CONT'D)
Dad, I think Cindy Sanders likes me.

HAROLD
Oh, yeah?

SAM
I formed a human pyramid on top of her.

(CONTINUED)

CONTINUED: (2)

HAROLD
Yep. That would do it.

Harold does a double-take as he processes this exchange. Sam blithely pours himself a bowl of cereal.

CUT TO:

EXT. STREET - DAY

Kim watches as Daniel and Ken work on Daniel's car.

KIM
Nick's cool. But he gets a girlfriend and goes psycho.

KEN
Maybe he gets so horny, his brain... fries.

DANIEL
Dumbest thing you can do is show a girl how much you like her. Then they run.

KIM
Is that why you're such a bastard to me?

DANIEL
You're still here, aren't you?
(off her sneer)
Try the engine.

Kim steps around to get in the car, when a PICK-UP TRUCK passes by. Kim's eyes-widen.

KIM
(pointing)
Daniel! That's the truck.

KEN
What truck?

KIM
Those jocks from Lincoln that nailed us. There they are!

DANIEL
She's right. Oh, man. Get in the car!

(CONTINUED)

CONTINUED:

Daniel slams down the hood and they all pile into his car. Kim tries the engine - it starts.

KIM
Go. Before they get away.

Daniel follows.

CUT TO:

INT. GYM - DAY

The cheerleaders have assembled for practice. Sam saunters up to Cindy Sanders, who is stretching. He smiles at her, coyly.

SAM
Hey, Cindy. So I guess today's the big day. This has been a fun week.

But Cindy is all worries.

CINDY
Sam. Vicki told me that Todd Schellinger called her last night, and it wasn't about the game. Do you think that's true or is Vicki a big, fat liar?

SAM
Vicki? Uh... I don't know.

The wind is taken out of Sam's sails. Vicki interrupts them.

VICKI
Can everybody please focus?! Let's run through all the cheers one more time - make sure we have them down, all right? Get into position.

Cindy glares contemptuously at Vicki. She whispers to Sam.

CINDY
I'm really sick of her telling me what to do, aren't you?

SAM
Well...

VICKI
Let's start with 'funky chicken'!

(CONTINUED)

CONTINUED:

Sam sighs deeply as he gets into position.

SAM
Oh, no. Not 'funky chicken'.

ON THE BLEACHERS

Bill and Neal watch the practice.

CHEERLEADERS (O.S.)
How funky is your chicken?! How loose is your goose?! So come on everybody - and shake your caboose!

Neal is shaking his head to himself.

NEAL
See that phony dagger? That's a great prop and he's not even using it.

BILL
What do you do with a phony dagger?

NEAL
A million things. You fall on it. You stab yourself. You stab the other mascot.

BILL
That's not funny.

NEAL
It is if you do it right. The Norseman should be doing shtick. Zany dance moves. Like this.

Neal stands and acts like he's in a chorus line, waving a top hat.

BILL
Why is that funny?

NEAL
'Cause I'm a Norseman in a chorus line. Or check out this one.

Neal acts like he's performing at a Hawaiian hula show.

CUT TO:

INT. NICK'S BASEMENT - MOMENTS LATER

Nick is practicing his drums when Lindsay enters. It takes him a moment to notice her.

NICK
Oh, hey!

LINDSAY
Hey. Your dad let me in.

Nick gets up from his drumset and walks over to her.

LINDSAY (CONT'D)
I don't have a lot of time. I told my parents I'd meet them at the game.

NICK
Cool. I'll come with you.

LINDSAY
Well, listen, Nick--

NICK
Lindsay, I need to talk to you. I was up all night feeling bad about our fight, you know? I realized if we're gonna go out, we should know everything about each other. I want you to know the truth about what happened between me and Heidi.

LINDSAY
You don't have to do that.

NICK
No, I want to. See, I had this huge crush on her. And when she broke up with her boyfriend, we went out for like a week. I thought I was in love. I wrote her all these poems and stuff. I guess they were pretty cheesy. Anyway, turns out she was just on the rebound and she was trying to make her boyfriend jealous. She didn't like me at all. They got back together and she showed him my poems. Pretty soon she was showing them to everybody. It was humiliating.

(CONTINUED)

CONTINUED:

LINDSAY
God. That's so mean.

NICK
So one night I went to her house, while she was gone. I wanted to get the poems back. Her dad walked in on me. He started yelling. Everything got blown out of proportion. The whole thing's made me really insecure, you know, when it comes to girls. Maybe that's why I get so... intense.

LINDSAY
God, Nick, I had no idea.

NICK
It's pretty embarrassing.

LINDSAY
I'm sorry. I'm glad you told me.

NICK
I was hoping you'd understand.

Nick smiles at her, appreciatively. Lindsay smiles back, genuinely relieved - now is not the time for the big talk.

CUT TO:

INT. GYM - DAY

The cheerleaders have congregated in the gym. Vicki is looking them over.

VICKI
Shelley, you've got a huge stain on your sweater. I told you guys not to wear them when you eat.

A distracted Cindy stands off to the side with Sam. The BASKETBALL PLAYERS are warming up in the b.g.

SAM
You know, Cindy, you'd make a great head cheerleader. You're way nicer than Vicki.

(CONTINUED)

CONTINUED:

CINDY
Thanks, Sam. I know, she's so rude sometimes. I mean, we're all just here to have fun, you know?

Just then, Todd Schellinger walks past them, bouncing a basketball.

TODD
(casual)
Hey, Cindy.

CINDY
(nervous)
Oh, hey, Todd. Have a great game.

TODD
Thanks.
(keeps going; turns back)
Oh, hey, Cindy?

CINDY
Yeah?

MR. FREDRICKS
(calling from across court)
Schellinger! Chat up the ladies on your own time. Now, get over here!

TODD
(to Cindy)
Never mind. Wasn't important.

CINDY
Oh, right. Okay. Good luck.

Todd hustles away. Cindy's head is spinning.

CINDY (CONT'D)
Oh my god. What do you think he wanted? Do you think he was going to ask me out?

Sam acts like a caring friend.

SAM
I don't think so. He didn't seem like it.

(CONTINUED)

CONTINUED: (2)

CINDY
Yeah, but what if he was going to? Should I try to talk to him after practice? Oh, this is going to make me crazy. I'm not gonna be able to remember my cheers.

SAM
(hesitates a beat)
Cindy, maybe Todd doesn't like you... you know, in that way. I think he probably has a lot of girlfriends.

CINDY
Sam, don't say that.

SAM
Well, It's just... Todd's a really popular guy. I don't think you should get too hung up on him. You know, in case he doesn't ask you out or something.

CINDY
Yeah, I don't know. I guess. Maybe you're right.
(sighs; distracted)
I'll talk to you later.

Cindy wanders away, looking depressed and confused. Sam watches after her, unsure if he's made an impression or not.

CUT TO:

EXT. STREET - DAY

Daniel's car creeps up next to the parked pick-up truck, pulling up alongside it. Ken, Daniel and Kim hop out. They scan the scene.

KIM
Go for it.

DANIEL
Why don't you do it?

KIM
'Cause I'm a girl.

Daniel, wielding a spray can, paints "LINCOLN SUCKS" across the side of the pick-up. Kim and Ken look on.

(CONTINUED)

CONTINUED:

KEN
Hurry, man.

Suddenly, the car's owner, TEENAGE GUY #1, appears behind them. Daniel's surprised. He looks a little freaked.

TEENAGE GUY #1
What are you doing?!

KIM
(not missing a beat)
We're giving your car a new paint job. What are you gonna do about it?

TEENAGE GUY #1
What the hell?!

KIM
This is what you get for throwing water balloons at us.

But suddenly FOUR MORE GUYS, all of them big and burly, approach. They all sport "LINCOLN" JERSEYS.

KEN
Something tells me it's time to go.

KIM
Kick their asses, you guys.

Daniel and Ken give her a "Hey, shut up" look.

TEENAGE GUY #1
(to his buddies)
Hey, these losers are from McKinley. Look what their bitch just did to my car.

KIM
You're the bitch, man!

Kim grabs the guy's hair, yanking his head around. Angry and embarrassed, the TEENAGE GUY responds by pushing her to the ground.

Daniel and Ken exchange a look. Now they have no choice but to fight. They prepare to throw down.

And with that, the FOUR LINCOLN THUGS menacingly advance. Daniel and Ken put up their dukes. They try to conceal their fear, without much success.

(CONTINUED)

CONTINUED: (2)

DANIEL
(under his breath)
Tell my mother I loved her.

Off their looks of doom, we...

CUT TO:

INT. GYM - DAY

A CROWD is starting to arrive for the game. Sam is approached by Vicki, who carries the oversized Viking head.

VICKI
Okay, Sam. Here's your head. Please don't break it. It cost six-hundred dollars.

She hands Sam the head. He is surprised by its weight.

SAM
Jeez. It's heavy. It's gonna be harder to do the cheers with this on.

VICKI
No duh. That's why you better stay focused. Why don't you put it on and walk around so you can get used to it?

She walks off. Sam puts the head on. He starts to walk with the mask on, but he looks tentative, changing directions, almost stumbling.

SAM'S POV: Inside the mask, all is dark, except for two small eye holes, where figures can be made out only vaguely. We HEAR Sam's heavy breathing.

He takes a few paces, then immediately bumps into another CHEERLEADER.

CHEERLEADER #1
Hey. Watch it.

He turns around and walks off, stumbling a bit. He holds his hands out in front of him, trying to get his bearing.

SAM'S POV: Everything looks weird from inside the head. He sees snippets of the bleachers, the wall. BREATHING.

(CONTINUED)

CONTINUED:

Sam is about to walk into the wall when he stops, then turns and exits the gym.

CUT TO:

INT. HALLWAY NEAR GYM - CONTINUOUS

Sam is getting steadier but he still walks a bit drunkenly. He turns again.

SAM'S POV: Through the small eyeholes, Sam sees Cindy Sanders and Todd SHARING A SWEET KISS.

Sam stops in his tracks. We can't see his expression because of the mask but we can only imagine that it's not a happy one.

Suddenly, Todd breaks away from Cindy and gives her a good-bye smile. He turns to leave and sees Sam as the Norseman.

TODD
Oh, hey, man. Give me five for luck.

Todd holds out his hand. Sam the Norseman gives him a very unenthusiastic five. Todd slaps him on the back and runs to the locker room.

Cindy, exuberant, approaches Sam as Sam pulls the head off. He looks like he just had his heart ripped out.

CINDY
Oh my gosh. Sam, you won't believe it. Todd asked me out. He says he really likes me. I told him I like him too and then... he kissed me. And he told me he doesn't have a girlfriend.
(playfully)
So, seeee? You were wrong.

Sam stares at her, stunned and stewing for a beat. Then...

SAM
Todd's a jerk.

CINDY
What?

(CONTINUED)

CONTINUED:

SAM
He's a jerk. I hate to say it, but it's true. He's not even nice to you. He's all cocky.

CINDY
Sam!

SAM
Well, it's stupid that you like him. Just 'cause he's a jock and you're a cheerleader. It's so obvious.

CINDY
Sam, just because you're nervous about the big game, you shouldn't take it out on me and Todd. Excuse me.

Cindy huffs off. Sam is distraught, holding his Viking head and we...

FADE OUT.

END OF ACT THREE

ACT FOUR

FADE IN:

INT. HALLWAY NEAR GYM - LATER

SPECTATORS are arriving, mingling. Nick and Lindsay are among them. A VOICE calls out.

HAROLD'S VOICE
Lindsay!

Lindsay and Nick spin around to see... Harold, standing with a few MIDDLE-AGED MEN. He's waving her over.

HAROLD
Come over here.

LINDSAY
I'll be right back.

We FOLLOW Lindsay over to her father.

(CONTINUED)

CONTINUED:

HAROLD
I want you to meet a few very good friends of mine. Stan Miller, of Miller Motors. <u>Councilman</u> Ritchie. <u>Sheriff</u> MacGruder. This is my daughter, Lindsay.

COUNCILMAN RITCHIE
Pleasure to meet you, Lindsay. Your father's told us all about you.

Harold-gives Lindsay a self-satisfied "I told you so" look.

CUT TO:

INT. LOCKER ROOM - CONTINUOUS

The BASKETBALL PLAYERS suit-up. Sam sits apart from the players, looking dejected, his costume and mask by his side. Neal and Bill enter the locker room and approach.

BILL
Sam. The game's about to start. What are you doing?

Sam looks at them, heavy-hearted.

SAM
Cindy kissed Todd Schellinger.

NEAL
Sam, who cares? You're the school mascot. Now's not the time to get all weepy. You gotta go out there and be funny.

SAM
I don't feel like being funny.

NEAL
Well, you think Steve Martin always feels like being funny? No. But he goes out on that stage every night with his arrow and his banjo and he kills. He's a professional.

SAM
Well, I'm not going out there.

Neal considers this, then he gets a determined look.

(CONTINUED)

CONTINUED:

NEAL
Then give me that head.

BILL
Oh, no. Don't let him, Sam. He doesn't know the cheers.

NEAL
Bill, I've been watching from the bleachers for the last two days. I know every cheer by heart.

BILL
I'm telling you, he's not gonna do the cheers. All he cares about is getting laughs.

NEAL
Hand me the head of that Norsemen.

CUT TO:

INT. HALLWAY NEAR GYM - DAY

Lindsay is standing with Harold and his distinguished pals.

HAROLD
So you really think I should run for the school board, Dale?

COUNCILMAN RITCHIE
Definitely. They could use a man like you.

Harold gives Lindsay another pointed look.

Lindsay sees something over Harold's shoulder that causes her to do a double-take...

It's Ken, Daniel and Kim. They look like they've survived a war - just barely. Daniel has a black eye. Ken's jaw is swollen - cuts all over his arms and face. Kim has a busted lip. Their clothes are bloody and tattered.

They approach Lindsay. Harold and his friends are disturbed by their appearance.

LINDSAY
You guys - what happened?

(CONTINUED)

CONTINUED: (2)

KIM
We got jumped by some boneheads
from Lincoln.

LINDSAY
Why?

KEN
We trashed their car.

DANIEL
They had it coming.

LINDSAY
Dad. You remember Kim and Daniel.

HAROLD
(embarrassed)
No - I don't.

Daniel pats Harold on the shoulder.

DANIEL
Hey, Mr. Weir. How are ya?

HAROLD
Yeah. Hi. Lindsay, why don't you
and your friends run along now?

DANIEL
Uh-oh. I think I got some blood on
your shirt. Sorry, Pops.

HAROLD
(trying to stay cool)
That's okay. You kids go have fun.
Stay out of trouble.

Harold gives his disconcerted friends a feeble smile.

HAROLD (CONT'D)
Teenagers. What are you gonna do?

CUT TO:

INT. ANOTHER PART OF HALLWAY - CONTINUOUS

Nick is standing by himself, when Jean approaches.

JEAN
Hello, Nick. Remember me?
Lindsay's mom.

(CONTINUED)

CONTINUED:

NICK
Yeah. Of course. Hi.

JEAN
(full of compassion)
How are you holding up?

NICK
Okay.

JEAN
I'm sorry about everything.

Nick just stares at her, confused.

JEAN (CONT'D)
Lindsay really does care about you. She told me so last night. She just feels overwhelmed. She needs her space right now.

NICK
(wild-eyed)
Is that what she said?

Jean is suddenly confused.

JEAN
Didn't she talk to you?

NICK
Lindsay wants her space?

JEAN
Oh... umm, gee... I don't know.

Finally, Lindsay approaches them.

LINDSAY
Hey.

Lindsay is struck by their distressed expressions.

LINDSAY (CONT'D)
What's wrong?

Nick doesn't respond. His face flush, he bolts away. Lindsay looks to her mother.

(CONTINUED)

CONTINUED: (2)

LINDSAY (CONT'D)
What's going on?

JEAN
You said you were going to talk to him this morning.

LINDSAY
What did you say to him?

JEAN
I just... I was trying to be nice.

LINDSAY
(realizing)
Mom, did you just break up with my boyfriend?

Jean cringes, mortified.

JEAN
Honey, I thought... oh, goodness.

Lindsay shakes her head in disbelief.

LINDSAY
I knew I shouldn't have told you anything. From now on, just stay out of my life. Please.

Lindsay heads off after Nick. Jean is crestfallen.

CUT TO:

INT. LOCKER ROOM - CONTINUOUS

Sam is alone in the locker room, staring forlornly into the middle distance when he HEARS...

A HORRIBLE RETCHING NOISE coming from the bathroom.

Sam sits up, startled by the noise.

The RETCHING continues, then the sound of a FLUSHING TOILET.

Suddenly, Todd Schellinger walks out of the bathroom. He is in his uniform - his face, ashen. He composes himself, leaning against one of the lockers.

TODD
(seeing Sam)
Oh... hey.

(CONTINUED)

CONTINUED:

SAM
Hey. Are you all right?

TODD
Yeah, I'm fine.

SAM
Are you sick?

TODD
No. It's just nerves.

Todd takes a deep breath.

TODD (CONT'D)
You're the new mascot, right?

SAM
Yeah.

TODD
You're really funny. I saw you doing that 'Funky Chicken.'

SAM
(pleasantly surprised)
Thanks. Good luck in the game.

TODD
Thanks.

Todd musters his strength, then exits the locker room. Sam watches him go. Not sure what to think.

CUT TO:

INT. GYM- DAY

Todd runs out, joining his teammates on the court. He preps for the ball toss. The BUZZER goes off. Todd tips the ball to a teammate.

ON THE BLEACHERS

A despondent Jean tugs at Harold's shoulder.

JEAN
Oh, Harold. I think Lindsay's upset with me.

HAROLD
Jean, shh. The game's started.

(CONTINUED)

CONTINUED:

Nearby sit Ken, Daniel and Kim. Daniel jumps to his feet.

DANIEL
COME ON, MCKINLEY! SHUT'EM DOWN!
LINCOLN, YOU SUCK!

Kim and Ken are surprised.

COURTSIDE

Coach Fredricks nervously paces.

MR. FREDRICKS
Wake up, guys. Now's not the time to be picking your rears.

The Cheerleaders are assembled behind Fredricks. Vicki yells out to Neal, in his Viking costume...

VICKI
Sam. Over here.

Neal stumbles toward them.

NEAL'S POV

He can't see much. The cheerleaders are shadowy figures in a fuzzy landscape. The sound of his own breath is deafening.

ON THE CHEERLEADERS

VICKI (CONT'D)
All right, let's do 'funky chicken'.

The cheerleaders get into position. Neal is in the wrong place, standing directly in front of Cindy Sanders.

CINDY
Sam. Move!

The cheerleaders begin their cheer. As they cheer, Neal is completely out of step.

CHEERLEADERS
How funky is your chicken?! How loose is your goose?!

Neal inadvertently hits Cindy Sanders with his phony dagger.

ON THE BLEACHERS - CONTINUOUS

Bill and an exhausted Herbert are sitting together, watching Neal.

BILL
Oh, no. He's being funny. I knew it.
(looks over at HERBERT)
What's wrong with you?

HERBERT
(groggy)
I haven't slept in forty-eight hours.

BILL
Well, it's better than sleeping for the rest of your life.

BACK ON THE COURT

Neal keeps getting in the way of Cindy and the other irritated cheerleaders.

CHEERLEADERS
So come on everybody! And shake your caboose!

Cindy pushes Neal off of her, sending him to the ground. He falls on his phony dagger.

BACK ON THE BLEACHERS

Bill and Herbert can't help but laugh.

BILL
Neal stabbed himself.

ON CINDY AND NEAL

Cindy angrily pulls Neal aside.

CINDY
Sam, if you're mad at me for some reason, this is a real obnoxious way of showing it.

Neal mumbles something but it is incomprehensible.

(CONTINUED)

CONTINUED:

CINDY (CONT'D)
I can't understand what you're saying!

CUT TO:

INT. BASKETBALL COURT - LATER

Todd dribbles the ball down the court. He shoots and scores.

The CROWD goes wild, particularly Daniel. Even Kim and Ken are getting into the action.

DANIEL
That's right! Nothing but net, baby!

KEN
(standing)
Eat that Lincoln!

KIM
IN YOUR FACE, LOSERS!

Sitting near them, the Pretty Girl from the pep rally takes note of the Freaks' attitude adjustment. She smiles at them.

PRETTY GIRL
That's the spirit.

Vicki looks to Cindy.

VICKI
Where's Sam? It's time to do the spirit cheer.

CINDY
There he is.

NEAL is in the stands, working the crowd. He pretends to stab people with his phony dagger.

Then he pretends to sword-swallow the dagger.

Then he holds the dagger like a guitar and pretends to "rock out." The fans are enjoying his antics, despite the fact that Neal is stumbling and falling into them.

Vicki marches up and grabs Neal brusquely as he's doing the Curly Shuffle. She pulls him back on the court.

He trips and falls.

(CONTINUED)

CONTINUED: (2)

Herbert and Bill find this hilarious.

CUT TO:

INT. SCHOOL HALLWAY - CONTINUOUS

Nick is sitting under the stairs, looking glum, when Lindsay approaches.

LINDSAY
Nick.

NICK
Hey.

LINDSAY
I've been looking all over for you.

Nick composes himself, trying to act strong.

NICK
Listen, Lindsay, I've been thinking... I really like you, but, uh, we've been spending so much time together. And I haven't been hanging with my friends. And I want to spend more time on my drumming. Maybe... you know, maybe we should take a break for a while. What do you think about that?

LINDSAY
(taken by surprise)
Well, yeah... okay.

NICK
Okay. Great.
(then)
No hard feelings, right?

LINDSAY
Right.

NICK
Well, I'm gonna go home and... and, you know, practice. I'll see ya on Monday.

Despite what he says Nick is clearly crushed. He walks away quickly.

(CONTINUED)

CONTINUED:

LINDSAY
(softly)
Nick.

Lindsay watches him walk away, feeling a mixture of emotions.

CUT TO:

INT. GYM - LATER

Todd tries to shoot, but is fouled. The foul is called on Lincoln.

ON THE CLOCK

The score: HOME - 71; VISITORS - 72. Time remaining - THREE SECONDS.

ON THE SIDELINES

Fredricks huddles with Todd and the other players.

MR. FREDRICKS
I don't want to put pressure on you, but our whole season's on the line.

ON THE CHEERLEADERS

We PAN the Cheerleaders as they spell out "SPIRIT" with their arms. Finally, we come to Neal at the end of the row. He is facing the opposite direction, away from the crowd.

NEAL'S POV

He can see almost nothing. The SOUND of his own breath is all he hears.

The cheerleaders get in position to do another cheer. Neal is in their way. He is doing one of his zany dance moves, staggering around like a drunken sailor.

CHEERLEADERS
Hush! Hush! You don't want to mess with us! Do ya? Do ya?

In the middle of the cheer, Vicki walks over to him...

VICKI
What is your deal?!

(CONTINUED)

CONTINUED:

She takes the phony dagger out of his hand and chucks it across the court, then punches him angrily on the side of his mask.

NEAL'S POV: The punch sounds like an explosion. Now there's a huge ringing in Neal's ears.

IN THE STANDS

Not only are Bill and Herbert laughing, but a couple of the people around them are beginning to find this spectacle amusing as well.

ON CHEERLEADERS

VICKI
All right, girls. Pyramid!

The cheerleaders start to form the human pyramid. Vicki pulls Neal over to the human pyramid and puts him in position behind it.

VICKI (CONT'D)
I don't know what your problem is, Sam, but you'd better get up to the top of that pyramid now.

NEAL'S POV: All the cheerleaders' butts form a pyramid in front of him. We hear his breathing increase.

As the cheerleaders chant, Neal moves forward and begins to crawl his way to the top.

CHEERLEADERS
S-P-I-R-I-T. That's spirit! For victory! That's spirit! To win this game!

A few of the cheerleaders SHRIEK in pain as Neal accidentally pulls their hair and sticks his knee in their backs.

CHEERLEADERS (CONT'D)
So come on Norsemen - put Lincoln to shame!

Neal is at the top, but he is wildly off-balance. He sticks his hands in the air to signal victory, when...

Suddenly, the entire pyramid comes toppling down. The cheerleaders SCREAM. It is a dogpile of limbs and hair. CRACK! The Norseman head splits open when Neal hits the ground.

(CONTINUED)

CONTINUED: (2)

ANGLE ON: BILL is laughing so hard, he begins to convulse. Herbert, however, is nodding off.

ANGLE ON:

SAM is standing near the bleachers. He watches the game.

ANGLE ON:

JEAN, in the stands. Lindsay sits down beside her, looking contemplative.

JEAN
Is everything okay?

Lindsay nods. Jean is relieved. She puts her arm around her daughter.

ON THE COURT

Todd's first free throw goes in.

He takes his second shot - it, too, goes in.

The other team takes the ball, but the clock runs out before they can score. The Buzzer goes off.

The NORSEMEN have won. The CROWD ERUPTS IN CHEERS.

IN THE BLEACHERS

Kim, Daniel and Ken are on their feet, screaming.

FREAKS
Yes! Lincoln, you lose! You suck!

ON THE SIDELINES

Vicki and Cindy stand over Neal, furious.

VICKI
You ruined everything!

Vicki pulls open the cracked mask, revealing a sweaty and disoriented Neal. Vicki and Cindy are stunned.

VICKI (CONT'D)
Who the hell are you?

(CONTINUED)

CONTINUED: (3)

NEAL
Neal Schweiber. At your service.

CUT TO:

EXT. PARKING LOT - CONTINUOUS

Nick sits behind the wheel of his car, tears in his eyes, a SAD ROCK SONG on the radio. After a moment, he puts the car into reverse.

CUT TO:

INT. GYM - MOMENTS LATER

Todd is swarmed by his TEAMMATES and Coach Fredricks, who raise Todd over their heads.

ON THE BLEACHERS

Herbert is sprawled across the bleachers, fast asleep. People step over him. We can HEAR his snores.

ON THE SIDELINES

Bill helps Neal to his feet.

BILL
That was incredible. You're the funniest mascot I've ever seen.

NEAL
Thanks, Bill.

BILL
No, I mean it. You're a comic genius.

NEAL
(pleased)
Did you see when she hit me? Wasn't that funny?

BILL
Yeah, you guys should be a comedy team.

But they stop in their tracks when they see...

The angry cheerleaders (except for Cindy) assembled, all glaring at Neal. They want revenge.

(CONTINUED)

CONTINUED:

VICKI
Get him!

CUT TO:

INT. ANOTHER PART OF THE GYM - CONTINUOUS

Cindy Sanders is intercepted by Sam. His disposition is changed. He greets her with a smile.

SAM
Cindy. Hey.

CINDY
Sam, what's going on? Why weren't you out there?

SAM
I'm sorry. I just got really nervous. I didn't mean to take it out on you and Todd.

CINDY
That's okay, Sam.

Suddenly, their attention is captured by...

Neal is being attacked by a mob of unhinged cheerleaders. They chase him across the court.

They grab him, swatting and kicking him. Neal is about to become a comic martyr.

ON HAROLD AND HIS DISTINGUISHED PALS

They look over, concerned.

COUNCILMAN RITCHIE
Is that kid gonna be okay?

HAROLD
It's all part of the act.

And on the tableau of cheerleaders pummeling their mascot, we...

FADE TO BLACK.

THE END

# FREAKS AND GEEKS®
## Scrapbook

- The school Musical - Pirates of Penzance. Lee Shapard is the Pirate King. Sam comes under the wing of the chief lighting designer (played by me) and learns the craft of lighting.

## "FREAKS AND GEEKS"

### The Series Bible

"Dawson's Creek."

"Party of Five."

"Beverly Hills 90210."

Did any of us really know people like that in high sc

Did any of us ever look like that in high school?

Did any of us ever have those problems in high school?

For most of us, high school was about trying to get through each day without getting beaten up or humiliated. It was about constantly being faced with evidence that contradicted the way our parents and churches told us the world was supposed to work. Life *wasn't* fair. People *weren't* that nice. Things *didn't* always work out for the best. And, unlike the kids on TV, we rarely if ever confided in our parents or came to them for help. We never even really bothered to confront them if we were mad at something they'd done. We just tried to get through life as best we could, usually in the face of overwhelming adult, parent and peer pressure.

Band kids selling ca
Drama kids selling
Drama kids walking
Freak couples maki
Kids harassing the j
Janitors sweeping th
Kids trying to step o
Students carrying vo

This isn't a show so much about what teenagers do but about the way they think, perceive and deal with the world around them. It's about confronting the first real obstacles that life throws at you outside the safety of your home and parents. It's about the gradual loss of innocence. For some teenagers, this entails a fight to keep that innocence at all costs and for others, it's about the desperation to get rid of that innocence as quickly and as harshly as possible.

A lot of high school shows deal mainly with dating and the drama that surrounds that. But my experience was that even though dating was something you thought about back then, it was something you rarely had the nerve to do because it entailed actually having to interact with and expose part of your psyche to the opposite sex. And who had the time or nerve to do that? High school was really much simpler than that when you got right down to it.

High school was about survival. And it still is.

It's about avoiding getting beaten up or humiliated or i attention to yourself if you can help it. Because for most of us persecution.

In its simplest form, high school broke down to:

**a)** who you liked,

**b)** who you didn't like,

**c)** who you were attracted to (strictly on a physical leve

**d)** who you were afraid of.

2) a group of seven year olds start terrorizing the geeks, they're really mean and the geeks have no idea what to do but they're flipped.

SAM GETS DE-PANTSED BY A GROUP OF SENIORS IN FRONT OF CINDY SANDERS REVEALING HIS STAR WARS UNDERWEAR.

"F & G"

Homecoming Day - pilot
Sam decides he wants to ask the cheerleader to homecoming the day of the dance - all about the bad lines of communication for those outside of loop (his friend try to get updates on whether she has a date or not - reports say she doesn't even though find when he finally asks her that she does - but he secretly hopes all along she does because he's scared to go to dance). The day puts him in a panic as he's told by others that sex will be involved, he has a crisis with his vow of chastity. basically it leads him into all those goofy wonders things you worry about that the cool kids never seem concerned about.

... to a ...
...rom neigh... ...s.

During the meal I pushed down on my fork and the plat... catapulted the meal onto my lap. Nobody laughed. I ... open my legs and push the food back onto the plate. ... dropped her off we were in the back seat of the car. ... the car stopped I turned to kiss her good-bye and she ... already out of the car and down the street.

10. My best high school date was actually in seventh g... a Bar Mitzvah. For some reason I took an upper. It ...

Lindsay's story – she's a smart girl who decided to go to the druggie's side. Why? Maybe they're the only ones who think about things that she does. They have dark thoughts like her. The popular kids are too surface, the smart kids are too busy studying and thinking about college and the geeks are too goofy and immature. A lot of the freaks are deeper thinkers, many times due to the pot they smoke. But Lindsay defaults to them because they're the closest thing to kindr spirits. In the future, she'll hang out with artis but for now, she doesn' know that community exists because at her mid west highschool, it does

- Lunchroom, eating junk food
- Pep rallies, misspelled signs, bad flo
- Disco classes, going to local disco
- Working at McDonalds, mall
- Debate, yearbook staff, drama, fore
- National Honor Society, geeks not
- Cool kids go on ski trips
- Student government - mysterious a
- Future homemakers, home ec for g
- Sam's a confirmed late bloomer - la
- Business Office Educati

Be careful not to make Linds into Lisa Simpson. She's no disillusioned and dark. Parent don't understand but decid to let it run its cours The drug part makes them cranky, though.

1) Mr. Rosso forces Lindsay to talk to peer counselor since she won't open to him. The peer counselor turns out t

*"Freaks" episode ideas by*

DARKER STORIES

Kim beats up her dad
Alan's brother gets killed in a hunting accide
Kim gets an abortion
The state starts busing in black students and
Ken gets arrested for stealing a car -
Nick gets Lindsay pregnant -
Kim is raped by her father -
A student accuses Mr. Rosso of molesting her
Daniel screws the quarterback's girlfriend and
An Estes rocket explodes and hurts the geeks -
Nick tries to kill himself
Bill wants to prove himself and starts vandaliz
Daniel brings a gun to school to scare a teacher
The freaks get into a huge car accident, are all
Lindsay takes heroin -
Bill stabs one of his mom's boyfriends -
Neal burns down his house
Cindy gets pregnant -

change was prompted
- loss - death of a
grandparent, friend
moves away, losses
spelling bee or academic

Lindsay's journey

How can we keep her off balance. She will always seem too smart to be with the freaks.

Show conflict w/ old friends.

Interest in Franco keeps her with them.

Love w/ Jason. Best friend. Triangle.

Daisy shows her darker view of life.

Must define her lack of a clear goal. What was her job dream before turn.

Show exploration of philosophies. She's a smart rebel, but what does she rebel against.

Can she get carried away w/ sex or drugs or the Grateful Dead. Being a dead head. Believing in love - community - almost a communist. That I can buy. Rebels against materialism.

Could get really into Christ's teachings.

...ld get involved in a cult.

...d have been abused by a family friend.

...ill always seem kind. Needs to ... more of a flower child at ...s. Naive. Hopeful at heart. ...ges against injustice. Can't accept ... harshness of the world.

...gain of reality devastates her. ... feels too much - so ...riodically she shuts off. ... - she becomes ...YPERSENSITIVE.

... a teacher is mean, or ...doesn't care about kids - she'll ... him on it. "Maybe I'd ... if you did. If you're burnt ... - why don't you quit?" ... and he does.

...dsay falls for a jock.

...dsay becomes dangerously close to ...the young guy teacher.

...EED TO DO A WRITE... RETREAT.

**"Freaks and Geeks" Writers' Questionnaire**
(A little something to get you thinking)

1) What was the worst thing that happened to you in high school?
2) What was the best thing that happened to you in high school?
3) Who did you really hate in high school and why?
4) Who did you really like in high school and why?
5) What was the most trouble you ever got in in high school?
6) What's the worst thing you ever saw in high school?
7) What's the nicest thing you ever saw in high school?
8) What was something you were convinced was true in high school that you later found out was completely wrong?
9) What was your worst high school date?
10) What was your best high school date? (if any!)
11) What made you ever want to kill yourself in high school?
12) What did you do that you are most proud of from your high school years?
13) Who among your peers did you wish you were in high school while you were there?
14) What's your biggest regret from your high school years?
15) Who was your favorite teacher and why?
16) Who was your least favorite teacher and why? Flick your head.
17) What's the dumbest thing you ever did in high school?
18) What's the dumbest thing you ever got talked into doing in high school?
19) Who did you make fun of in high school and why?
20) Who did you fight with in high school and why?
21) What ever made you cry in high school?
22) Who were you most attracted to in high school and why?
23) Which one of your friends were you most embarrassed by and why?
24) What were you most scared of in high school and why?
25) Who were you most scared of in high school and why?
26) If you could do anything over again, what would it be?

Maybe a lot of Lindsay's pilot story is about teachers and old friends coping with her new found peak status.

<u>12) What did you do that you are most proud of from your high school years?</u>

I stapled money to my trigonometry final when I handed it in. The final joke towards a passing grade that I got <u>only</u> because the teacher thought I was funny.

8) What was something you were convinced was true in [...] that you later found out was completely wrong?

That my teachers were experts in their fields. I thou[...] had all the answers and must have studied for ye[...] knowledgeable. Later on I found out that one o[...] football player who passed a test and became [...] no experience at all.

9) What was your worst high school date?

There was this girl that my friends thought

# DREAMWORKS
# SKG TV L.L.C.

Interoffice Memorandum

To: David Knoller
From: Joni [redacted]
Subject: Script Clearance/ "Freaks & G[...]
Date: March 11, 1999

Please note the clearance status for the follo[...] names of actual people:

**CLEAR FOR USE:**

CINDY SANDERS
HAROLD SPENCER
KIM KELLY

**NOT CLEAR FOR USE:**

HAROLD WEIR
NICK [redacted]
JEFF ROSSO

Please provide me with alternate names for research. Thanks.

JEFF CRAIG
JEFF JENKINS
JEFF PARKS
JEFF BRETT
JEFF BYRON
JEFF PATTIS
JEFF BRYANT

Lindsay's questioning of God leads Harold to doubt. He starts looking at alter- native religions

Halloween episode?

Tornado

Neal stays over for a week.
Dad loves Scotty Ingrosum

But really, it's a big intervention.

Vacation.

NICK STEPANOS
HOLLINS
ANDOPOLOUS

SANFORD WEIR
&
TOM WEIR
FRED WEIR
BEN WEIR
BUD WEIR

BRETT EDWARDS
COLLINS
WEAVER

# DREAMWORKS
# SKG TV L.L.C.

Interoffice Memorandu[...]

To: David Knoller
From: Charlene [redacted]
Subject: Script Clearance/ "Freaks & G[...]
Date: March 22, 1999

Please note that the name "JEFF ROSSO" is clear for use as a character for the run of the series for "Freaks and Geeks."

– Girl with big bf to concer[t]
she leaves with another guy
– Drama teacher is alcoholic,
typing teacher dies

Maybe Lindsay want to lead an uprising against the homecoming, or more accurately, against the homecoming king and queen contest. Rallied all the freaks who think it's cool to love something

[...]he
[...]er his head
[...]erywhere a
[...]d eventuall
[...]st used Sam
[...]ily after one
[...]e's better of

**Daniel shopl[...]**
complaining [...]

to rebel against

[...]nnel for

OR YOUR EMMY CONSIDERATION

**The Pilot**

Outstanding Writing for a Comedy Series: Paul Feig

Outstanding Directing for a Comedy Series: Jake Kasdan

# FREAKS AND GEEKS

(THIS IS OUR FINAL AD – WE ARE OFFICIALLY OUT OF MONEY.)

Daily Schedule

9 Workout

10 Start Work

11

12

1

2

3

4

5

6

7

8

9

10

11

Freaks + Geeks Emmy

Gruber

Thank you Paul!

8·28·00

F+G Air Schedule

| | | |
|---|---|---|
| Sept. | 18 | Pilot |
| | 25 | #1 |
| October | 2 | #2 |
| Nov | 6 | return |

## The Museum of Television & Radio — Spring 2000

# Freaks and Geeks: The Six Unaired Episodes

*Saturday, May 13, 2000;* ***Tickets on Sale May 5***
*Introduction at 5:00 p.m. by Judd Apatow and Paul Feig; Screenings until 10:30 p.m.*

Forgoing the melodramatics of perfectly complexioned teens and their woe-is-me sex lives, this critically hailed dramedy, set in Michigan circa 1980, zeroes in on the ugly, all-too-real side of the high school social order with dead-on, period-specific humor and a refreshing lack of sentimentality. The Museum will screen the six unaired episodes of the recently canceled show, introduced by Judd Apatow and Paul Feig, who will take audience questions before the screenings.

In Person: **Judd Apatow**, Executive Producer/Creator **Paul Feig**, Executive Producer/Creator; Cast members to be announced.

The twelve previously aired episodes will be screened in chronological order on Wednesday, May 10 to Saturday, May 13 from 12:00 to 5:00 p.m. Tickets are not required for these screenings.

**Tickets: $10 ($8 for individual Museum Members).** Purchase in the Museum lobby during regular hours or order by calling the Museum at (310) 786-1091 from 12:00 to 5:00 p.m. daily. **Sales are final and tickets cannot be refunded.** Programs and participants are subject to change. The seminars, including the question-and-answer period, are videotaped and become part of the Museum's permanent collection.

whenever any Weir is having prob... ...ndsay
crazy.

Lindsay's art teacher takes an interest in her dark, brooding, paintings. Lindsay is excited about it until she finds out the teacher has handed them over to the school psycologist out of concern.

## GENERAL NOTES ABOUT THE SERIES

**- This show must be *real*.** The teens in this series will talk like tea... will never be too clever or grown up sounding. We don't want a bunch of teenage Neil Simons spouting off wittily. These kids generally engage in teenage put-downs, they overextend their language ("Oh, yeah? Well, you're a ... uh ... big idiot, that's what you are") and never talk in that writers' "Now that I'm in my 30's, I know what I'd say in that high school situation, so I'll give this kid a snappy comeback" style of writing. These kids have to deal with each other with whatever is in the lexicon of a teenager and nothing more (and despite the fact that most of us think "if I knew then what I know now, I'd really be cool and in control" the sad truth is that if we knew what we know now when we were in high school, we'd probably get beaten up on a regular basis because teenage bullies don't respond well to clever put-downs at their expense).

**- The students in high schools, as much as we wish they would be, are not at all politically correct** (especially back in the 1970's and early 80's). This means that their language and put-downs are very often harsh. They use words of which they don't understand the full meaning. And for boys, the use of homophobic names and references is just a fact of life. There is nothing more effective when a teenage boy wants to put down a peer or adversary than a homosexual reference. This includes the terms *fag, homo, queer, faggot* and others. Obviously we can only go so... very real fact of life for high schoolers that the... Being as harsh as we can get away w... especi... bullies, will make the sho... ill c... that's what the... day... stu... t...

**Nick gets into horticu... ture** horticulture class but ends u... know he had. He likes deali... him and that don't ever figh... opting inst... spend time...

...army-minded fath... and br... guy who wants to "sell flo... home.)

**Neal gets a calculator -** Ne... becomes his pride and joy. ... it starts to pull his pants do... the school, with all the other... come to view the Holy Grai... do the high school equivale... the cafeteria and help him w... Mathletes. However, Neal'... discover that Neal has no id... They start to use his calcula... just used him to get to his c... going back to the geeks. He... realizes he has no idea how... his name on the back of the... to the Mathletes (and he m... Neal?").

**Ken starts making weapo...** throwing star in metal shop...

Sam - arrested development
Lindsay - over development

Lindsay's too smart to be a teenager - this is the source of her problems she doesn't feel challenged and yet is rejecting higher learning because she's not interested in where higher learning leads to. She'll probably become an artist, although that seems a little shallow. She may end up joining the Peace Corp. But for now, nothing interests her and that's what's throw... her into such a state of depression and misdirect...

FREAKS AND GEEKS
...m Works SKG TV, LLC
...aleigh Studios
...Melrose Av.
...411D
...ngeles, CA 90038
...69-2586 (Off.)
...69-3425 (Fax)
Producer: Judd Apatow
Producer: Paul Feig
...er: Victor Hsu
Andy Stone
...r: Jake Kasdan
...e Title: "Beers And Weirs"

CALL SHEET

7:00 AM REPORT TO LOCATION CREW CALL
Weather: SUNNY AND VERY WARM; HIGH IN MID TO UPPER 90'S; LOW IN MID 60'S.
Sunrise: 6:17 A Sunset: 7:36 P

...ay: Thursday
Date: August 19, 1999
Day 1 out of 8

Crew Call: 7:00 AM
Shooting Call: 8:00 AM
Lunch: 1:00 PM

**SAFETY MEETING TO BE HELD AT CREW CALL**

**No Forced Calls Without Prior Approval Of UPM Or Producer**

| SET/DESCRIPTION | SCENES | CAST | D/N | PGS | LOCATION |
|---|---|---|---|---|---|
| ...moking Patio / ...he Freaks talk Lindsay into hosting a keg party. | 3 | 1,5,6,9,10, Atmos. | D-1 | 2 5/8 | Placerita Junior High School 25015 Newhall Av. Newhall, CA |
| ...moking Patio / ...ll accuses Neal of being in love with Lindsay. | 4 | 1,5,6,7,8,9, Atmos. | D-1 | 1 2/8 | (Please see map for Crew Parking) (You will be shuttled to base camp.) |
| ...Time Permits) / ...aseball Field / ...m tells Neal, "We've gotta do something." (END ACT I) | 8 | 2,7,8,Atmos. | D-1 | 1 4/8 | For emergencies page Tony Schwartz @ 310/917-7029 |
| ...hool Auditorium / ...e Freaks and Geeks react to the ...chool's morality play. | 6 | 1,2,5,6,7,8,9, 11,12,13,15, 34,Atmos. | D-1 | 4 4/8 | |
| | | Total pages: | | 9 7/8 | |

| CAST | PART OF | SW/F | RPT. | MU-HAIR | READY TIME | COMMENTS |
|---|---|---|---|---|---|---|
| ...a Cardellini | Lindsay | | | | | |
| ...n Daley (K) | Sam | SW | 6:30 A | 6:30 A | 8:00 A | Report to Crew Parking |
| ...es Franco | Daniel | SW | 10:45 A | 10:45 A | 11:30 A | Report to Crew Parking |
| ...n Segel | Nick | SW | 6:45 A | 6:45 A | 8:00 A | Report to Crew Parking |
| ...n Starr (K) | Bill | SW | 6:45 A | 6:45 A | 8:00 A | Report to Crew Parking |
| ...n Levine (K) | Neal | SW | 9:00 A | 9:00 A | 10:00 A | Report to Crew Parking |

s and inject them with heroin, …
nd make them freak ou…
f danger in the …
scared …

because she's come to the conclusion that there's no God. She's mad at her parents for telling her there is one, she's scared because she realizes that life may have no meaning and no master plan for her, and she's mad at everyone for believing. This can be the heart of her crisis.

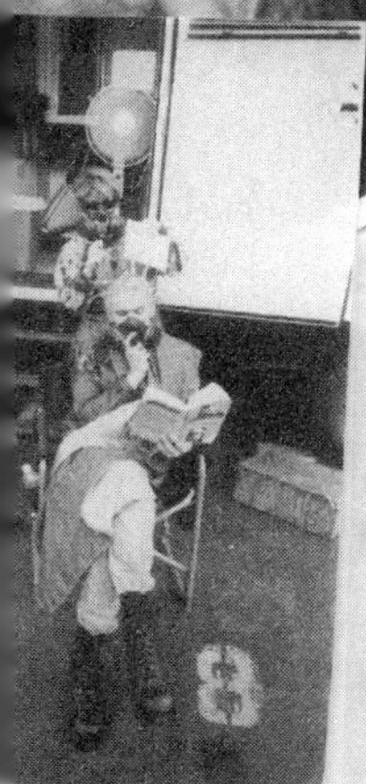

**BROADCAST STANDARDS SCRIPT REPORT**

**SERIES: FREAKS and GEEKS** — **TO: Judd Apatow, Paul Feig**

**EPISODE: Pilot** — **FROM: Ken [redacted]**

**DRAFT: Shooting Script -Blue Revisions 3/11/99** — **DATE: 3/11/99**

**NOTES:**

**Thanks again for addressing our last set of notes. Here are the additional notes we discussed today:**

**p. 4 – Please delete "I think she's on dope."**

**p. 12 – Replace "...nancy boys..." with an alternate (e.g. sissies, wusses, wimps).**

**p. 21 – Please delete Daniel and Ken's dialogue about growing pot.**

**p. 23 – We'll need an alternate for "...on the rag."**

**p. 50 – Again, please replace "...crap your pants..."**

- The sch…
… Sam is …
her slave. …
… Lindsay …
…ends Neal …
…ck has no …
…ervenes …
date. T…
…l's a he…
te -- Neal begs Sam no…
l continues to brag abo…
…indsay. Suddenly, gee…
…t she's the one with a …
…t what Neal told every…
…eal and ends up not …

the same time, we … get a glimpse that some of the freaks a… … their rebellion out of their systems and we'll see the beginnings of yearning for a normal life in them. (This isn't a big thing but it goes toward making the show more realistic.)

**- The show is not about neat resolutions and tidy endings, not about easy solutions and pat answers. There are generally never any big victories at the end of each show -- only small triumphs, bits of headway or realizations that open the door to change and improvement. There should never be a "Gee, you're right, I was wrong" ending. It's a show about people learning about how to get along with other people and unless you're battling the forces of pure evil, which hardly anyone ever is in life, you're simply clashing with people who are looking out for themselves while you're looking out for yourself. And so victories are only based on mutual acknowledgment and the agreement to be tolerant of the other person's quest for self-preservation.**

That is all ...

Have a good semester and here's to year ten of the show!

## THE ONLY OFFICIAL COMPANION BOOKS TO *FREAKS AND GEEKS* AVAILABLE FROM NEWMARKET PRESS